THE
CONTEMPORARY
CONGRESS

SEVENTH EDITION

Burdett A. Loomis

University of Kansas

Wendy J. Schiller

Brown University

ROWMAN & LITTLEFIELD

Lanham • Boulder • New York • London

Executive Editor: Traci Crowell
Assistant Editor: Mary Malley
Senior Marketing Manager: Kim Lyons

Credits and acknowledgments for material borrowed from other sources, and reproduced with permission, appear in the credits section or on the appropriate page within the text.

Published by Rowman & Littlefield
A wholly owned subsidary of The Rowman & Littlefield Publishing Group, Inc.
4501 Forbes Boulevard, Suite 200, Lanham, Maryland 20706
www.rowman.com

Unit A, Whitacre Mews, 26-34 Stannary Street, London SE11 4AB, United Kingdom

Copyright © 2018 by Rowman & Littlefield
Sixth edition 2016

British Library Cataloguing in Publication Information Available

Library of Congress Cataloging-in-Publication Data
Names: Loomis, Burdett A., 1945– author. | Schiller, Wendy J., 1964– author.
Title: The Contemporary Congress / Burdett A. Loomis, University of Kansas,
    Wendy J. Schiller, Brown University.
Description: Seventh Edition. | Lanham, Maryland : Rowman & Littlefield,
    [2018] | Previous edition: 2016. | Includes bibliographical references and
    index.
Identifiers: LCCN 2017038824 (print) | LCCN 2017040827 (ebook) | ISBN
    9781538101575 (electronic) | ISBN 9781538101551 (cloth : alk. paper) |
    ISBN 9781538101568 (paper : alk. paper)
Subjects: LCSH: United States. Congress. | United States. Congress—History.
Classification: LCC JK1021 (ebook) | LCC JK1021 .L66 2018 (print) | DDC
    328.73—dc23
LC record available at https://lccn.loc.gov/2017038824

∞™ The paper used in this publication meets the minimum requirements of American National Standard for Information Sciences—Permanence of Paper for Printed Library Materials, ANSI/ NISO Z39.48-1992.

Printed in the United States of America

Contents

List of Illustrations   ix

Preface   xi

1. **The Drama of Representation**   1

   National Politics Comes Home: The Rise and Fall of Representative Tim Huelskamp (KS-1), 2010–2016   2

   ■ Spotlight on Representative Marjorie Margolies-Mezvinsky: Choosing between a Promise to Her Constituents and Loyalty to Her President   4

   The Centrifugal Congress?   5

   Representation as Collective Choice   7

   ■ Spotlight on Senator Ben Nelson: Party Loyalty with a "Kickback" Assist   8
      Representation as Responsiveness   9
      Deliberation   10
      Making Decisions, Choosing Policies   11

   The Contemporary Congress   13

   Recommended Readings   15

   Useful Resources   15

2. **Congressional Decentralization in Design and Evolution**   18

   The Framers Construct a Congress   19

   The Early Congress: Organization and Tensions   22

   Senate Individualism and House Fragmentation: 1830–1860   23

   The Rise of the Organized Congress: 1860–1920   24
      The House   24
      The Senate   26
      The Drift toward Decentralization   27

   The Development and Decline of the "Textbook" Congress: 1920–1970   28

   Reforming the Congress: The 1970s   29

   The Democratic Postreform Congress: 1980–1994   30

   ■ Spotlight on Senator Elizabeth Warren: The Individual as Agenda Setter   31

   The Republican Majority Era in the House: 1994–2006; 2010 Onward   32

The Rise of Partisanship in the Senate: 1994–2017   34

■ Spotlight on Senator Lindsey Graham: Procedural and Substantive Pressure   36

The Congress over Time   38

Recommended Readings   38

Useful Resources   39

3. The Changing Environment of Congressional Politics   42

Congress: The Permeable Branch   43
The Advocacy Explosion   47
Lobbying: Information, Access, and Influence   48

■ Spotlight on Senator Jim DeMint: DC Right-Wing Insider   49
Complex Lobbying in a Partisan Age: International Trade, 1993–2017   50
The Policy Explosion   53
The Budget: Defining Policy Choices across the Board   56

■ Spotlight on Representative Mick Mulvaney: The Tea Party and the
New Partisan Politics of the Budget   58
Can't Get No Respect: The Unpopular Congress   60

The Inherent Problems of a Powerful, Public, and Professional
Legislature   60

Congress in Context   64

Recommended Readings   65

Useful Resources   65

4. Congressional Elections: All for One and One for All?   70

■ Spotlight on Representative Elise Stefanik: Fresh Energy in Upstate New York   73

Electoral Tensions in the Post-1994 Era   74

Local Elections for a National Office   75
Geographic Constituencies   76
Other Constituencies: Behavior and Perception   79

Elections in a Careerist Congress   82

House Incumbents and the Structure of Competition   83
Increasing Margins and the "Slurge"   83

■ Spotlight on Karen Handel: Georgia's 6th District   85

The Lasting Impact of the Electoral Earthquake of 1994   85

Funding Congressional Campaigns   87
The Rising Costs of Running for the House and Senate   88
The Ups and Downs of Campaign Finance Reform:
From Watergate to the Wild West   90

Local Campaigns for National Office: The Mix of Forces   93

Recommended Readings   94

Useful Resources   94

5. **Parties, Leaders, and Ideology in Congress   98**

The Congressional Party in the Twenty-First Century:
A Return to Centralization   100

The Democratic Majority Party Challenge: Moving from Divisions to
Unity   101

Party Leadership in the Republican Mold: The Dilemma of Minority
Opposition   108

Two Decades of Republican Majority Control in the House:
1994–2006; 2010 Onward   109

■ Spotlight on Representative Nancy Pelosi: The First Female Speaker of the House   112

The Senate: A New Balance between Individual Power and the
Role of the Party   116

■ Spotlight on Senator Catherine Cortez Masto: The First Latina U.S. Senator   119

The Legacy of Exercising Party Leadership in the Senate   120

Party and the Limits of Centralization in the Congress   123

Recommended Readings   124

Useful Resources   125

6. **Presidential-Congressional Relations:
Boundaries of Power   128**

■ Spotlight on Representative Justin Amash: A Republican Opposing Trump in a
Partisan Era   135

The President as Chief Legislator   138

Agenda-Setting and the Prospects for Presidential Influence:
It's All in the Timing   139

■ Spotlight on Representative Darrell Issa: Opposing Obama and Supporting
Trump in an Increasingly Blue District   142

The Contexts of Presidential Influence   143

Legislating: Presidential Tools in a Retail Politics Era   147

The Presidential Record   149

Budgetary Politics: Centralization through Constraint   150

Policy and Power under Divided and Unified Party Government   154

Recommended Readings   155

Useful Resources   156

7. **Policymaking in the House and Senate   159**

■ Spotlight on Senator Rand Paul: Policy Proponent and Policy Critic   161

Rules, Procedures, and the Legislative Process   163

Congressional Lawmaking   164
Committees   165
Subcommittee Reforms   169
Democratic Caucus/Leadership Reforms   169

Differences in the Legislative Process in the House and Senate   177
The House   177

■ Spotlight on Representative Barbara Comstock: The Struggle for Policy Consensus   181
The Senate   184
The Senate Then and Now   185
Obstructionism and the Partisan Impulse in the Contemporary Senate   187

Rules and Policymaking in the Modern Congress   190

Recommended Readings   190

Useful Resources   191

8. **The Individual Enterprise   194**

■ Spotlight on Representative Mark Meadows: Making His Mark   196

The Legislator as Enterprise   197
The Personal Office   198
Committees and Subcommittees   201
Enterprise and Influence: Two Illustrations   203
Congressional Caucuses   205
Congressional Offices and Political Expenditures   207
Additional Enterprise Resources   208

■ Spotlight on Senator Charles Schumer: An Enterprising Leader   210

The Congressional Enterprise: Blessing and Curse   212

Recommended Readings   213

Useful Resources   213

9. **The Competitive Congress: Centrifugal Forces in a Partisan Era   215**

The Oxymoronic Congress: Individualistic Partisanship   217

■ Spotlight on Representative Charlie Dent: The Tuesday Group and the Price of a Narrow House Majority   218

■ Spotlight on Representative Cathy McMorris Rodgers: The View from Party Leadership   222

Congress and the President: What History Can Tell Us   223
   Bill Clinton   223
   George W. Bush   224
   Barack Obama   224
   Donald Trump   227

Prospects for One-Party Domination and Governing in
Congress over the Long Term   228

Recommended Readings   229

Useful Resources   229

Photo Credits   231
Index   233

Illustrations

FIGURES

3.1   Congressional Approval Ratings, 1974–2017   61

4.1   North Carolina Congressional Districts, 1993   77

4.2   Nonparty Independent Expenditures in House and Senate Elections, 1978–2012   93

7.1   Number of Congressional Standing Committees, 1789–2014   168

8.1   The Congressional Enterprise   198

8.2   Email and Postal Mail to Congress, 1995–2011   200

9.1   The 114th House of Representatives   220

TABLES

3.1   Federal Spending, 1940–2020   54

3.2   The Growth of Federal Regulation   55

3.3   High Approval for Members; Low Approval for Congress   62

4.1   Changing Constituencies in a Single Congressional District, the Kansas Second, 1971–2017   81

4.2   Average Campaign Expenditures in the House and Senate   88

5.1   The First and Last Congresses of the Twentieth Century   102

5.2   Average Party Unity Scores by Congress   105

5.3   Percentage of Partisan Roll Calls   106

5.4   Selected Senate and House Party Unity Scores   122

6.1   Electoral, Partisan, and Popularity Context for Newly Elected Presidents, 1960–2016   145

7.1   Congress by the Numbers, 1993–2016   166

7.2   Standing Committees, 103rd, 104th, 109th, and 115th Congresses   172

7.3   Partisan Membership on Sixteen Standing Senate Committees   174

7.4   Seniority of House and Senate Committee Chairs, 115th Congress   175

7.5   Restrictions on Amendments   184

8.1   Growth in Congressional Staff by Number of Employees, 1930–2015   198

8.2 Rep. Justin Amash (R-MI) Staff Salaries, 114th Congress   199

8.3 Congressional Party Leadership Staff Levels, 1981–2015   209

BOX

7.1 Pathway of the Affordable Care Act   178

Preface

In some of the most turbulent times for modern American politics, we are pleased to publish the seventh edition of *The Contemporary Congress*.

Over the past thirty years, polarization and partisanship on Capitol Hill have grown steadily, rising to new levels during the last years of the Obama administration and the first year of the Trump presidency. Congressional caucuses have increased in number and often act as significant players in a tribal era. Presidential-congressional relations have hit both very high and very low points. As president, George W. Bush acted independently of the Congress, which became a significant issue that grew in importance during the Obama years, especially after the Republicans' capture of the House of Representatives in 2010. Although Barack Obama generated fierce personal opposition from the Republican Party in Congress, he and congressional Democrats managed to make major changes in the areas of health care, environmental regulation, and the oversight of the nation's economic recovery. At the same time, the role of money has exploded in the world of campaigns, with outside, difficult-to-trace sources becoming more significant. Party leaders continue their tight control of the legislative process, at the expense of the powers of committees and individual members.

In addition, the election of Donald Trump as president has generated new challenges for all legislators. Democrats have become the opposition party to a unified Republican government, while Grand Old Party (GOP) members must continually struggle with a president who has often acted outside the bounds of executive norms.

We also recognize that the world inside and outside of Congress has changed. With both houses shifting partisan control twice over the past twelve years, we gain a greater capacity to generalize about the Congress in a partisan era. In keeping with changing political times, we have modified the organization and content of this book while maintaining our overall framework of the battle between centrifugal (decentralizing) and centripetal (centralizing) forces on members of Congress. Even in an era of heightened partisanship and increased polarization, these tensions remain as defining elements of the U.S. Congress. Individual senators still can wield substantial power in opposing given legislation; committees continue to shape bills and employ their expertise. Most surprisingly, perhaps, is the fact that the majoritarian House has often proven to be incapable of moving partisan legislation forward, largely because of the party's factionalization within the chamber. Over the past decade, citizens have enjoyed more access to members of Congress than ever before, given the prominence of social media and the increasing incidence of direct action by constituencies at lawmakers' forums and at their district offices.

In chapter 1, we concentrate on representation and the powerful electoral connection between district constituents and Capitol Hill insider politics, focusing on Representative Tim Huelskamp (R-KS), whose iconoclastic behavior as a

Tea Party Republican led to his dismissal from the House Agriculture committee. This in turn opened him up to a successful challenge in the 2016 GOP primary in his rural Kansas district. Chapter 2 takes a sweeping look at the history of Congress, the effects of increased polarization on members' behavior, and the negative impact it has on congressional approval ratings. Chapter 3 examines the enormous increase in advocacy in Congress, primarily from an explosion in lobbying, and it also showcases the evolution of outside interests in trade policy.

Chapter 4 focuses on congressional elections with an eye to the more frequent shifting in party control between the Democrats and the Republicans in the House and Senate. We document the growing importance of the congressional primary as the arena for intraparty conflicts, with a focus on the role of the Tea Party in pushing the Republican Party to the right. At the same time, interparty competition continues to decline, with fewer seats remaining competitive, and outside funding, often party- and ideology-based, has come to play an increasing role in campaigns. This chapter also accounts for the major changes in campaign finance laws that encourage great sums of money to flood into congressional campaigns, as a direct result of U.S. Supreme Court decisions such as *Citizens United v. FEC* and *McCutcheon v. FEC*.

Chapter 5 examines the growing effects of party and ideology in shaping both individual and collective congressional behavior. To reflect the impact of the highly turbulent policy environment over the past decade, including the ending of the wars in Iraq and Afghanistan, the Great Recession, the implementation of Obamacare, and the uncertainties of the Trump presidency, chapter 6 focuses on presidential-congressional relations under both unified and divided government, stretching from the last years of the George W. Bush presidency through the entire the Obama administration, and into the first tumultuous year of the Trump presidency. We chose to put this updated chapter earlier in the book because of the weight these issues have exerted on the federal policy agenda.

In order to reflect greater party control on the entire legislative process and changes in floor procedure, especially in the Senate, chapter 7 presents a comprehensive view of lawmaking, from bill sponsorship to committee hearings and markups to floor consideration to presidential approval (or veto). Chapter 8 emphasizes the growth of the enterprises of members of Congress, especially in terms of their campaigns, their use of social media to communicate, and their relationships to a skyrocketing number of internal caucuses, including one that supports drone aircraft, thus demonstrating the adaptable nature of this form of congressional organization.

We close this book with chapter 9, which now provides a longer view of the changes that have affected Congress and its relationship to the president over the past two decades. It presents a comparative analysis of the relationship between Congress and four presidents—Bill Clinton, George W. Bush, Barack Obama, and Donald Trump—in terms of legislative productivity and partisan cooperation or conflict in presidential-congressional relations. This chapter asks whether increased partisanship has succeeded in centralizing Congress or whether the decentralizing forces in Congress are still powerful enough to push members to go their own way.

As we continue to examine the Congress, we remain impressed by its resilience, even as it increasingly acts in potentially dysfunctional ways. It continues to be a representative body of the nation as a whole, and one that merits our ongoing attention, analysis, and understanding.

We are grateful to Charles S. Bullock, III, University of Georgia; Michael S. Lynch, University of Georgia; Joel Sievert, Texas Tech University; and Ravi K. Perry, Virginia Commonwealth University, for their thoughtful feedback on the sixth edition. We would like to thank Rowman & Littlefield, and especially Traci Crowell and Mary Malley, for their enthusiasm for *The Contemporary Congress*. We would also like to thank Cory Manento for his excellent research assistance. We look forward to future editions as we and the Congress evolve.

Burdett A. Loomis
Lawrence, Kansas

Wendy J. Schiller
Providence, Rhode Island

CHAPTER 1

The Drama of Representation

Members of Congress are expected to interact on a regular basis with their constituents and can pay a political price for not doing so. Here, newly elected House member Roger Marshall (R-KS) is talking to his constituents in the 1st Congressional District in Kansas.

The U.S. Congress is, to be sure, a national political institution. But its roots are planted in 50 states and, especially, in the 435 House constituencies, each of which engages in its own biennial electoral drama. In these congressional districts, candidates conduct locally based campaigns every two years to determine who will make national policy decisions. Portuguese-speaking fishermen from the Massachusetts coast, Chicago suburbanites, upland North Carolinians, and rural Oregonians, among many others, must sort out who can best represent their interests and those of the nation. Incumbent House members must defend their records, often in both primary and general election contests. Most win, but the possibility of losing lurks in every campaign.

NATIONAL POLITICS COMES HOME:
THE RISE AND FALL OF REPRESENTATIVE
TIM HUELSKAMP (KS-1), 2010–2016

In 2010, Republican Rep. Jerry Moran, from the vast western Kansas First Congressional District, made the decision to run for the U.S. Senate, running for the seat vacated by Sam Brownback, who chose to seek the Kansas governorship. After winning a tough primary against fellow Republican Todd Tiahrt (KS-4), Moran easily won the Senate race. Moran's absence paved the way for several Republicans to throw their hats into the ring for the Grand Old Party (GOP) nomination in the "Big First." Obtaining the nomination would be tantamount to winning the congressional seat, given the overwhelmingly Republican nature of the seat. Moreover, the winning primary candidate could hope for a lengthy stay and very likely a good shot at a senate seat at some future date.

The 2010 GOP First District primary attracted a crowded field of candidates, including a moderate state senator who had previously run for Governor, three young moderate-conservatives who attracted substantial media attention, and Huelskamp, a veteran state senator who had consistently taken controversial stands during his fourteen years in the Kansas Legislature. In a fragmented primary, Huelskamp's fund-raising exceeded $1 million, with the Club for Growth adding $120,000. In the end, his less well-funded competitors split the moderate and moderate/conservative vote, allowing him to win with just over a third (34.8 percent) of the primary vote.

Despite this total and Huelskamp's far-right leanings, the solidly Republican district should have constituted a safe seat for virtually any GOP lawmaker. In fact, Huelskamp breezed to victory in the 2010 general election and ran unopposed in 2012; with his traditional Kansas seat on the Agriculture Committee, the Representative appeared ensconced in the heavily rural First District. Nevertheless, on Capitol Hill, he increasingly became a thorn in the side of Republican Speaker John Boehner. Most notably, Huelskamp frequently attacked the Speaker and voted against party leadership positions. In December 2012, after breaking with the GOP majority on various issues and voting against Boehner for Speaker, as well as questioning his leadership repeatedly within the media, the Speaker removed Rep. Huelskamp from his Agriculture

Committee seat. With that move, for the first time in its history, Kansas as a state had no representation on this most important body.[1]

Huelskamp reacted immediately, but without effect: "Someone from Kansas has been on the House Ag Committee for over 100 years—and this because of petty, vindictive politics, you kick a fifth-generation farmer off the Ag Committee."[2]

Over the next two years, as a member of the far-right House Freedom Caucus, Huelskamp continued his attacks on Boehner and the GOP majority; this encouraged a political neophyte, Alan LaPolice, to run against him in the 2014 primary election. Although LaPolice failed to dislodge the incumbent, he received 44 percent of the primary vote and demonstrated Huelskamp's prospective vulnerability. A prominent, conventionally conservative physician, Roger Marshall, almost immediately started to put together a 2016 challenge to Huelskamp. Although he had never held elective office, as a prominent Great Bend doctor who owned a medical center, he had the means to mount a serious campaign. His assessment was that Huelskamp's primary base was simply not strong enough to withstand a challenge from a conservative Republican who had great support from both the local and national agricultural communities.

In the eighteen months leading up to the early August (2016) primary, Marshall crisscrossed the huge district and consistently reported solid fund-raising results (including more than $300,000 in personal loans), which demonstrated his ability to compete in the "wealth primary." Marshall raised more funds than Huelskamp, with each spending around a million dollars on their respective campaigns. While both candidates received substantial outside financial assistance, Marshall's backing amounted to $2 million or so, far more than Huelskamp's. "People regularly overuse the word 'historic'— but this actually is," said Brian Baker, president of ESAFund, a super political action committee (PAC) that spent over $1 million against Huelskamp and for Marshall.[3] Given the 2014 results and Marshall's strength in fund raising and poll results, the press took Marshall seriously, and he gained increasing national support, most notably from the American Farm Bureau Federation and the U.S. Chamber of Commerce.

In essence, the challenger sought to paint the incumbent as out of step with his predominantly rural, agricultural district. Ever ready for a fight, Tim Huelskamp fought back, attacking Marshall and his allies as part of the Washington establishment that he had opposed vigorously and vociferously. Huelskamp lost his seat because he alienated GOP elites, both in Washington and within his district, and his defeat serves as one more cautionary tale for legislators who test the limits of their constituents' support. As for Greg Marshall, newly elected as a U.S. member of the House of Representatives, he won back the Kansas seat on the House Agriculture Committee, and—as a traditional conservative Republican—seems likely to win reelection as easily as have his Republican predecessors, from Bob Dole to current U.S. Senator Jerry Moran.

SPOTLIGHT

Representative Marjorie Margolies-Mezvinsky: Choosing between a Promise to Her Constituents and Loyalty to Her President

If Rep. Tim Huelskamp lost his seat in 2016 because he *confronted* his party leadership too aggressively, Rep. Marjorie Margolies-Mezvinsky lost hers in 1994 largely because she *supported* her party and her president on a crucial, well-publicized vote.

August 5, 1993. The vote was at hand on the most important proposal of President Clinton's initial year in office—a five-year, $492 billion deficit-reduction package. The top House Democratic leaders and the party's extensive whip organization had worked relentlessly to round up every available vote in support of the deficit-reduction proposals that had resulted from endless hours of negotiations in House–Senate conference committee meetings. Almost every representative had come to the floor, eager to witness the concluding scene of this extended struggle. For those who remained undecided, there was no place to run, no place to hide.

As the fifteen minutes formally allowed for voting expired, almost all members had cast their ballots, but the electronic tally board showed that the result was still in doubt. President Clinton's fellow Democrats would have to provide the margin of victory; no Republican had broken party ranks. Unanimously, the 174 minority-party legislators had voted against the Clinton package, with its combination of spending cuts and tax increases. Two Democratic members remained in the well of the House, waiting to cast their votes: Pennsylvania's Rep. Marjorie Margolies-Mezvinsky and

Montana's Rep. Pat Williams, who objected to the 4.3-cent gas tax increase. The president called Williams and pleaded, "I can't win this without you. My presidency is at stake." Williams agreed to support the package, despite his desire to cast a No vote that would please his constituents, who often drove long distances across Big Sky Country.

William's decision left the House's verdict on the Clinton budget proposal in the hands of first-termer Margolies-Mezvinsky, who had previously announced her opposition to the plan and had steadfastly resisted all tax increases. Although Bill Clinton had received 46 percent of the vote—a bit above his average across the nation—in her upscale suburban Philadelphia district, Margolies-Mezvinsky had won her seat, held by Republicans for the previous seventy-six years, by an extremely narrow margin of 1,373 votes out of 254,000 cast. She had triumphed, she argued, because of her stand "on two basic principles: deficit reduction and holding the line on taxes." True to her word, in May, during the initial House consideration of the 1994 budget, she had voted against the Clinton package. But at this point in time, the president and the Democratic leadership turned up the heat.

As she recounted, "The Speaker requested that I come down to the well [of the House chamber] and cast my vote. The scoreboard showed the vote was 216–216. Pat Williams (D-MT) and I stood in the well, surrounded by our Democratic peers. Barbara Kennelly, one of those encircling us, leaned over and said, 'You can't let the president down.' I stood there for a moment, and then I heard someone whisper in my ear, 'We need your vote.' 'You've got it,' I replied." With that, she joined Rep. Williams and signaled her Yes vote in support of the measure. As she walked down the aisle of the House chamber, "one Democrat after another hugged her, patted her on the back and touched her as if she were Joan of Arc. Her Democratic colleagues cheered as the Republicans jeered 'Good-bye, Marjorie.'" Her vote, crucial for her president and her party leadership, had placed her very reelection in jeopardy. Could she explain her actions to her constituents?

On November 9, 1994, voters across the country rose up to defeat thirty-six congressional incumbents—thirty-four in the House, two in the Senate, and every one of them a Democrat. By a margin of

eight thousand votes, Rep. Margolies-Mezvinsky's constituents chose her Republican challenger, Jon Fox, in a rematch of the 1992 election.

In the end, the continuing focus on Margolies-Mezvinsky's budget vote was exceptional—the vote was important, but it was only one of a thousand or so recorded votes she cast before submitting herself to the electorate in November 1994. Rarely does a single vote spell doom for a legislator, but in this instance, the very visibility of her action made it impossible to overcome.

The information in this section is taken from multiple sources as follows: Clifford Krauss, "Whips Use Soft Touch to Succeed," *New York Times*, August 7, 1993, 29; Richard E. Cohen, "Baptism by Fire for House Newcomers," *National Journal*, June 5, 1993, 1366; Marjorie Margolies-Mezvinsky, *A Woman's Place . . .* (New York: Crown, 1994), 202.

THE CENTRIFUGAL CONGRESS?

Every two years, 435 House district electorates and 33 or 34 state electorates (only a third of the Senate seats are contested in any given election) make their separate decisions and create a new Congress. Following the Framers' outline, the Congress brings together a remarkable variety of legislators, especially in an era of increasing representation of minorities and women. Even in the current period of strong congressional parties, party leaders and presidents consistently face difficulties in building coherent majorities that can pass legislation. Why is this so?

For the Congress, at least, the answer seems deceptively simple. In responding to 50 state electorates in the Senate, 435 separate House constituencies, and thousands of distinct interests, the institution has traditionally organized itself in decentralized ways that impede the building of consistent majorities that can legislate on difficult issues. This is not a recent phenomenon. Congress has historically been the "slow institution," emphasizing representation of interests rather than rapid, perhaps overly hasty, responses.[4]

Although members of Congress adopt party labels, express their support or opposition to presidential policies, and seek to solve difficult societal problems, they must ultimately answer to their 435 individual constituencies in the House or 50 state electorates in the Senate. U.S. legislators win their seats as individuals, even when they are tightly wrapped in party ideology; in seeking reelection, they must often survive primary elections within their own party just to claim the Democratic or Republican label that they will carry into the November general election.[5] To mount a campaign takes considerable financial resources, which candidates receive from individuals, groups, PACs, and, after the primary, political party committees. With the rise of outside groups employing multiple campaign techniques, the forces supporting and opposing congressional candidates have grown stronger and more numerous, even as the number of competitive districts has shrunk over the past forty years.

Once on Capitol Hill, legislators seek the help of party leaders and the president, especially if they share a party affiliation; at the same time, they also react to the pressures of interest groups, the pull of the committees to which they have been assigned, the pleas of the bureaucracy that provides seemingly limitless information, and, of course, the often inconsistent communications from their own constituents. They would be, as were Representatives Huelskamp and Margolies-Mezvinsky, pushed and pulled from all directions. This struggle is both mystifying and off-putting to those who seek to understand congressional politics. Indeed, one common criticism of Congress is that its members are constantly "bickering."[6] But Congress is not without order. As we shall see, in the past, Congress depended on committees to provide much of its decentralized (*centrifugal*) structure. Increasingly, however, political parties have served as a more centralized (*centripetal*) organizing force, both as the institution is organized internally and as electoral competition for office is structured.

Although congressional partisanship grew throughout the 1980s and early 1990s, it was the Republicans' success in capturing the Congress in 1994 for the first time in forty years that demonstrated that a reasonably homogeneous party could overcome many of the decentralizing tendencies of Capitol Hill politics. Republican House members accorded substantial authority to their elected party leaders. Most notably, the GOP membership has largely chosen to embrace the order imposed by a centralized party leadership, as opposed to that of a strong committee system. When Democrats held the House majority for four years after the 2006 elections, they generally did the same. In the Senate, both Democrats and Republicans have presided over a closely divided though increasingly partisan body. But the individualism of this chamber has remained resistant to strong party leadership. Still, partisanship in Senate voting patterns has grown to levels almost as high as those found in the House, with the 114th Congress (2015–2017) ranking as the most polarized in more than a century.[7]

Moreover, despite the movement toward party-based centralization,[8] both Republicans and Democrats have discovered some merits within the decentralized framework of the committee system, in which expertise may temper ideology in the policy process. Over the past decade, House Democrats under Speaker Nancy Pelosi (2007–2011) provided the committees with more leeway than have Republicans, whose party leaders sought to impose stringent party loyalty standards on those who became committee chairs.[9] In the Senate, where polarization has also escalated, the smaller, more intimate nature of the chamber has muted some of the most extreme partisanship.[10] Still, as the 115th Congress (2017–2019) proceeds, the *centrifugal* forces that push the institution toward greater decentralization have generally given way to *centripetal* forces that have moved the Congress to become a more highly centralized and partisan place.

REPRESENTATION AS COLLECTIVE CHOICE

The U.S. Congress is a representative institution consisting of two bodies that must make a series of collective, authoritative decisions—laws.[11] Ordinarily, this occurs by majority vote or, more accurately, a series of majority votes. Representatives and senators, although sporting party labels and owing much to their respective leaders within the Congress, are still ultimately beholden to their own district constituents and statewide electorates. Political scientists Roger Davidson and Walter Oleszek distinguished between two different, if overlapping, visions of the U.S. Congress. On one hand, the legislators constitute a *Congress of Ambassadors*, which congregates in Washington to pursue the interests of the individual states and districts. On the other hand, they meet together as a single *deliberative assembly* to address issues and reach accords that roughly serve the broad, collective interest of the nation as a whole.[12]

This sounds straightforward, but since its founding, the United States has embraced an independent, powerful legislature that has often been at odds with the two other branches of government—the executive and the judiciary. Without direct, formal ties to the executive (in contrast to a parliamentary system,[13] whose cabinet ministers are drawn from the legislature), individual lawmakers have prospered by representing their own constituents, districts, states, regions, and specific interests, often at the expense of ill-defined or chimerical national interests. Legislative structures and practices have evolved that facilitate this tendency toward representation of particular interests, thereby making it difficult to construct majorities. The rules of the Senate, for example, have long protected the rights of minorities, most notably by requiring supermajorities (usually sixty votes, but sometimes two-thirds of the members) to shut off debate on legislation. Indeed, extended debate—the filibuster—may be the most distinctive feature of the highly individualistic U.S. Senate, but in recent years partisan pressures have begun to chip away at that feature.[14]

Protecting the rights of individual legislators has forged the nature of the U.S. Senate, but it is the decentralization of the committee system that has historically marked the operation of the House of Representatives. With its large membership, the chamber has used committees to conduct much of its legislative business. Writing in 1885, Woodrow Wilson famously observed that the entire House "sits, not for serious discussion, but to sanction the conclusions of its committees as rapidly as possible."[15] Even in 1885, this statement was hyperbole, but it does convey the House's organizational tendency toward decentralization through subunits, as opposed to a highly centralized party structure (as, for example, in the British Parliament). Although the relative power of committees has varied since 1789 and has certainly declined since the 1970s, the standing committee system, as much as any other characteristic, has defined the operation of the House. The Senate, conversely, with its one hundred individually empowered members representing the fifty states, is by definition highly unrepresentative. This, of course, is by constitutional design. Nevertheless, senators—whether from California or Rhode Island—must act to represent the wishes of the voters who sent them to Washington.

SPOTLIGHT

Senator Ben Nelson: Party Loyalty with a "Kickback" Assist

Sixteen years after Rep. Margolies-Mezvinsky's decisive and consequential vote in favor of President Clinton's budget plan, Senator Ben Nelson of Nebraska found himself in a similarly uncomfortable situation on a key vote: President Obama's health care bill. Following the 2008 elections, Democrats controlled the presidency along with both houses of Congress. When Republican Senator Arlen Specter defected to the Democratic Party in April 2009, the Democrats' new sixty-seat Senate supermajority (including two Independent senators who caucused with the Democrats) was sufficient to invoke cloture and overcome a filibuster without needing any Republican votes, so long as all sixty senators in the majority supported the cloture motion.

At the start of 2009, President Obama made it clear that, along with measures intended to boost the economy in the midst of a recession, enacting significant health care reform was among the top priorities for the new administration. Democratic leadership in Congress worked throughout that year to draft a health care bill and gauge support for various provisions (for a full timeline of the passage of the Affordable Care Act [ACA], see chapter 7). Despite some efforts in the Senate at putting forth a bipartisan bill, it became clear by fall that no Republicans were going to vote to invoke cloture. Thus, Senate Majority Leader Harry Reid and the rest of the party's leadership shifted their focus to trying to convince any remaining Democratic holdouts to support the bill.

Senator Ben Nelson was the final Democratic holdout—the sixtieth vote needed to overcome a Republican filibuster. Much like Rep. Margolies-Mezvinsky, Nelson, a second-term senator and a rare conservative Democrat from the Republican-leaning state of Nebraska, struggled to balance his ideology and his constituents' preferences with his party's and the president's priorities. Democratic Party leaders offered a few concessions in order to try to secure Senator Nelson's vote. First, Nelson viewed the bill as unacceptably pro-choice. To address this concern, the leadership changed the language of the bill to give states the right to prohibit coverage for abortions within their own health insurance exchanges. Second, Nelson disapproved of eliminating federal anti-trust exemptions for health insurers, so the leadership removed that provision from the bill. Finally, Democratic leaders added a provision to the bill that would provide federal funding for Nebraska to expand its Medicaid eligibility. This last provision, unavailable to other states and largely seen as a transparent attempt to secure Nelson's vote, was derisively called the "Cornhusker Kickback" by the bill's critics.

The concessions from party leadership were apparently successful in courting Nelson. On December 23, 2009, the Senate voted 60–39 (one Republican senator did not vote) to invoke cloture and override the Republicans' filibuster of the Senate's version of the health care bill, with Nelson voting with the Democrats. The underlying bill passed the next day with the same margin.

Nelson faced backlash in his home state for his decisive vote to advance the

health care bill, and outside groups immediately began running attack ads against
him for siding with President Obama.
While Rep. Margolies-Mezvinsky faced a
difficult reelection battle the year after her
budget vote, Senator Nelson was not up
for reelection until 2012; a full three years
after his health care vote. But the eventual
final version of the bill—the ACA (which in
the end did not include the "Cornhusker
Kickback")—remained such a prominent
part of the political conversation that
Nelson could not hope to escape the ramifications of his critical vote. Rather than
face an uphill reelection battle in 2012,
Nelson decided at the end of 2011 that he
would retire from the Senate. Republican
Deb Fischer won the open seat race to
replace him. Senator Nelson's example

shows that siding with party leadership
on high-profile votes can be especially
costly for members who are electorally
vulnerable, even when they are able to
secure provisions that are favorable to their
constituents.

The information in this section is taken from
multiple sources as follows: Norman Ornstein,
"The Real Story of Obamacare's Birth," *The
Atlantic*, July 6, 2015, https://www.theatlantic.
com/politics/archive/2015/07/the-real-story-of-
obamacares-birth/397742/; Shailagh Murray
and Lori Montgomery, "Deal on Health Bill is
Reached," *The Washington Post*, December 20,
2009, http://www.washingtonpost.com/wp-dyn/
content/article/2009/12/19/AR2009121900797.
html?sid=ST2009121900844; Adam Sorensen,
"Ben Nelson Retiring, the 'Kickback' Kicks Back,"
Time, December 27, 2011, http://swampland.
time.com/2011/12/27/ben-nelson-retiring-the-
kickback-kicks-back/.

Representation as Responsiveness

Political theorist Hannah Pitkin has argued that political representation means
"acting in the interest of the represented, in a manner responsive to them."[16]
Nevertheless, knowing the wishes of one's constituents across a wide range of
complex issues is difficult at best, given most citizens' low levels of knowledge
and interest in most policy controversies. In recent years, parties have taken
on the task of packaging policies under the umbrella of their label, and individual members rely heavily on that party label to attract support from voters
in congressional elections. At the same time, motivated by their desire to win
reelection as individuals, members of Congress seek to represent their constituents as best they can, often trying to anticipate their desires.[17] In this context,
representation may be best viewed as a set of overlapping attempts to respond
to "a number of targets" within a legislator's environment.[18]

In this vein, Heinz Eulau and Paul Karps advanced our understanding of representation by pushing beyond simple agreement on policy preferences between legislators and their constituents. They outlined four kinds of
responsiveness that, taken together, constitute representation. These are *service*
responsiveness, *allocation* responsiveness, *symbolic* responsiveness, and *policy*
responsiveness.[19] For example, legislators seek to respond to specific constituent
problems, such as a lost social security check (service); they attempt to obtain
funding for district-based programs (allocation); they reassure constituents by
their actions and words (symbolic); and they try to pass programs that will
broadly help the nation as a whole, which by definition includes their constituents (policy).

Put in slightly different terms, representatives act as the *delegates* of their constituents on some issues, especially when their interests and preferences are clear.[20] On other issues, such as the budget, they act more like *trustees*, sorting through complex policy options and deciding what is most "in the interest of the represented," to use Pitkin's language. After making such a policy choice, they then must explain their actions to their constituents. This after-the-fact explanatory behavior is central to representation in that it allows constituents to assess their legislators' broad policy decisions, which are often made with only a vague sense of district opinion. Indeed, it is often the case that constituents do not have opinions on policies that Congress is considering until after they are enacted into law and implemented. Members of Congress must anticipate their constituents' reactions and subsequently educate them in terms of the merits of a vote or policy position. If a legislator has acted responsively on the dimensions of service, allocation, and symbolism, he or she may well have more latitude in convincing district constituents to accept the less popular policy choices made on their behalf.[21]

Deliberation

The focus on individual legislators and their attention to their own districts has often obscured the role of the Congress as a deliberative body capable of engaging in productive debates on policy issues large and small.[22] Such discussions do not always occur. For example, the 1993–1994 and 2009 congressional considerations of the respective Clinton and Obama health-care reform proposals produced little reasoned give-and-take. Rather, deliberation simply disappeared under a deluge of highly publicized claims, counterclaims, and appeals to emotion.[23] More generally, meaningful deliberation has often gone missing in congressional debates, as party leaders try to limit individual members' opportunities to change the content of legislation once it reaches the floor.[24] As David Vogler and Sidney Waldman point out, reaching decisions on difficult issues is more than simply producing a majority that carries the day. They conclude that the democratic legitimacy of Congress rests on both the legislative process and the resulting policies. The value of deliberative democracy, which emphasizes face-to-face discourse, derives not simply from widespread agreement or consensus but also from the creative nature of the process itself.[25]

The potential for creative solutions to difficult problems continues to reside within the Congress, and there is ample opportunity for deliberation, although much more so in committees, during informal meetings, and perhaps in the House gym, than on the floor of either chamber. Only rarely can one tune in to watch floor proceedings and observe substantive deliberation among legislators who are seeking to exercise their creative powers. Rather, the viewer can observe legislative posturing par excellence, in which almost all senators and representatives represent some specific point of view and seek to convey a well-honed message. Effective deliberation, to the extent that it occurs at all, takes place offstage, where legislators need not worry that their constituents and campaign contributors are watching intently.[26] But with the rise of technology and social media, the opportunities for such private discussions are diminishing, even if highly partisan lawmakers might desire to engage in it.

Ironically, when Congress does rise to the occasion and acts either as a decisive policymaking body or as a deliberative assembly, the normally skeptical, even cynical, public often embraces the legislative action. The Congress that worked with Lyndon Johnson to enact his expansive Great Society programs achieved widespread popularity among the public; twenty-five years later, another Congress won accolades for its cogent deliberations over the merits of the 1991 war in the Persian Gulf. Nevertheless, after a major spike in public support after the September 11, 2001, attacks, levels of congressional support have fallen to historic lows as the public has reacted to both the contentiousness and the partisanship on Capitol Hill.[27] To be fair, the public has grown more polarized since then, and voters often view with suspicion anything that the opposing party proposes or enacts. The Affordable Care Act (ACA), otherwise known as Obamacare, is a perfect example of this type of legislation, which, almost eight years after enactment, faces challenges from a new Republican administration, in the U.S. Supreme Court, and from the GOP-controlled Congress. Overall, individual legislators can act in their *own* interests, but Congress as a collective body finds it difficult to act for the *whole*.

Making Decisions, Choosing Policies

The Congress, both as a whole and as a pair of separate chambers, operates as a decision-making machine. That is, the House and Senate continually make decisions that affect major segments of the U.S. public. Both in committee and on the floor of the House or Senate, legislators must choose between policy alternatives day in, day out. Over the course of a full two-year Congress, a legislator will vote more than a thousand times on the floor and at least as many times in committees and subcommittees. In addition, lawmakers must make decisions on what specific legislation they will sponsor or co-sponsor.[28] Just because the Congress makes a great many decisions on an almost routine basis does not mean that congressional decision-making is either efficient or effective. Rather, Congress's choices are frequently constrained—by the president's agenda, by the economy, or increasingly by the requirement of finding a party-based majority of votes to pass a specific proposal. All the while, members of Congress seek to be responsive to their constituents, to their fellow partisans, and, one hopes, to the electorate as a whole.

To put contemporary congressional decision-making into context, examining the 1994–1995 transition to GOP control of the House is worthwhile. The Republicans followed their historic electoral sweep, capturing the chamber for the first time in forty years, with a legislative barrage. Speaker Gingrich and the House GOP set the agenda and brought the fall campaign's ten Contract with America items to a vote.[29] An initial analysis would give them high marks for responsiveness and, perhaps, representation, and low scores for deliberation. By effectively nationalizing the 1994 congressional elections, using the Contract as a legislative agenda, and setting up their individual House offices, Republicans demonstrated all four kinds of responsiveness:

1. By refusing to cut back on office staff, they retained the ability to provide high levels of service to their constituents.
2. By supporting a tax cut, they sought to allocate funds back to their constituents.
3. By passing the balanced budget constitutional amendment, they adopted a policy that the public generally supported.
4. By voting in favor of a term-limits amendment, but by less than the required two-thirds majority, they proved themselves symbolically responsive to a popular public position without endangering their own seats.

More generally, the Contract allowed House Republicans to claim that they were acting in response to an overall mandate from the electorate, even if the Contract played at most a modest role in their triumph.[30]

Contrast the 1994 sweeping victory of both houses to the Republican victory in the 2010 House elections. Both elections were marked by partisan and ideological intensity, but 2010 brought to the House a segment of the GOP—elected from the Tea Party base—that was more conservative in its views than the rest of the caucus. Unlike the Contract with America era, party conflict and disunity made it hard for Speaker John Boehner to run the House in a predictable manner, especially on fiscal matters such as spending and the national debt. Notably, when the majority party in the House is not cohesive in this highly partisan era, congressional business can come to a screeching halt, as has occurred several times since the Tea Party–infused GOP regained control of the House after the 2010 election. More striking, a divided majority party can oust its sitting Speaker, as the Republicans did by forcing Boehner to resign and electing Paul Ryan to take his place in Fall 2015.

The Republican divisions have carried over, into the 115th Congress (2017–2019), but with unified Republican control of Congress and the Presidency, GOP legislators are under great pressure to go along with their leadership. Still, President Trump, with his non-traditional agenda, may seek policy changes that will cause defections within the GOP majorities in both chambers.

As we shall explore in this book, high levels of partisan polarization in Congress and the electorate, the growing influence of money in legislative elections, and the willingness of legislators to grant party leaders substantial, though not unlimited, powers have significantly changed the congressional environment. The idea of a decentralized Congress in the mid-twentieth century remains embedded in how we think about the politics of Capitol Hill, but the contemporary reality is different. So why has the Congress changed from a centrifugal-oriented institution to a more centripetal one? Richard Fenno provides the simplest answer, writing presciently in 1975: "It is the members who run Congress. And we get pretty much the kind of Congress they want. We shall get a different kind of Congress when we elect different kinds of congressmen or when we start applying different standards of judgment to old congressmen."[31]

THE CONTEMPORARY CONGRESS

This book addresses the tension between the constituency-oriented, individualistic Congress that emphasizes the representation of particular interests and a more party-oriented body that has become increasingly less functional—as two partisan teams work relentlessly for political advantage. Still, on occasion, the Congress can act coherently to pursue some broader representative goals, perhaps through creative deliberation. Overall, such instances have become far more the exception than the rule.[32] Much of the congressional tension is expressed in organizational terms, with broad tendencies toward decentralization and individualism being countered by the centralizing forces of party and presidential leadership. Even historically centrifugal forces, such as locally oriented congressional elections, sometimes reflect the unifying pull of national trends, as demonstrated by such elections as those of 1964, 1994, and, more recently, those of 2006, 2008, 2010, 2014, and 2016.

We provide a series of related pictures of the Congress that build on the three aspects of legislative life:

1. The strong element of fragmentation, or decentralization, that reflects centrifugal forces on the Congress. These forces result from the pull of district constituencies, congressional committees, reelection campaigns, individual member offices, and the effects of interests outside the institution.
2. The corresponding centralizing (or centripetal) forces. These include the party leadership, the president, occasional landmark elections, national crises, clear trends in public opinion, and broad coalitions of interests.
3. The continuing tensions between centrifugal and centripetal forces within the Congress. Even in the extremely decentralized, fragmented period of the late 1970s, there were many forces pushing the Congress toward greater centralization. Likewise, in the modern era of strong party leadership, congressional committees and the impact of individual legislators tend to work against the dominant trend. Overall, however, the contemporary Congress has grown increasingly centralized.

It is the interplay between these forces that brings out the most interesting elements of Congress, as was the case when Rep. Margolies-Mezvinsky's wrenching vote choice placed her squarely between her loyalty to Democratic Party leaders and her constituents. In the two decades since that vote, the struggle to balance party allegiance, committee specialization, and responsiveness to constituents continues to define the legislative process, especially in the House.

Chapter 2 traces the evolution of the modern Congress across two centuries of representation, focusing on the development of the internal rules of the two chambers as well as tracing key external events and movements that changed the composition of the membership of the House and Senate. Chapter 3 focuses on the congressional context, especially the growth of organized interests and the explosion of national policy, which create hundreds upon hundreds of new constituencies for members to represent. At the same time, the Congress is increasingly made up of conservative Republicans who express skepticism toward federal spending and many specific programs that they view as wasteful or unnecessary, and they exhibited fierce opposition to former President Obama's priorities.

With a Republican president, albeit an unpredictable one, in Donald Trump, the overarching question is whether the GOP legislators will follow presidential leadership or act to modify his initiatives, based on their own electoral and ideological perspectives. For example, it was far easier to advocate for repealing Obama's ACA than to actually replace it, as Republican lawmakers found in many 2017 town hall meetings.

Chapters 4 and 6 emphasize the internal and external influences on congressional policymaking: elections and parties. In chapter 4, we discuss the nuts and bolts of congressional elections, from fund-raising to messaging to getting out the vote (GOTV), in the larger context of how changes in campaign finance law and technology have changed campaigning in the twenty-first century. In chapter 6, we explain the development of parties over time, and identify periods of weak and strong party leadership in Congress. We also highlight the relationship between a strong party organization in Congress and partisan polarization; the two are not always as much in sync as generally thought.

Chapter 5 offers insights into the channels of coordination and centralization on Capitol Hill, with emphasis on the relationships between congressional party leaders and the president in his role as "Chief Legislator." The 1992 election of Bill Clinton brought with it the promise of single-party control of the executive and legislative branches for the first time in twelve years, yet President Clinton found it difficult to muster party-based majorities, especially in light of the Senate's delaying tactics that often required sixty votes to overcome. President Obama encountered many of the same pressures and obstacles in 2009–2010. And both these Democratic presidents faced a Republican Congress for the final six years of their respective presidencies, whereas George W. Bush governed with Republican majorities in both chambers for more than half of his two-term (2001–2009) administration. The election of Donald Trump as president offers another, if distinct, period of unified party government. Still, given individual senators' powers to delay and stop legislation, as well as the continuing fissures within the GOP House majority, most presidents and party leaders must rely on some level of interparty cooperation on Capitol Hill.

Chapter 7 focuses on the formal and informal elements of congressional decision-making, both in committees and on the floor. The formal rules and procedures of the Congress can determine the outcomes of legislative initiatives and may allow party leaders to dominate the proceedings, especially in the House. At the same time, informal rules of the game, or "folkways," provide an interpersonal context for legislative actions, as lawmakers observe (or do not) norms that encourage civil behavior, even as they disagree. The increase in partisanship on Capitol Hill has challenged the civility of congressional behavior and created chasms between members in the House and Senate that did not exist twenty or thirty years ago.

Chapter 8 focuses on the individual "enterprises" that surround each senator and representative. Individual legislators mount their own campaigns with a party label and ideology, then come to Congress and operate within a party and committee structure, but they still control substantial resources that afford them great flexibility of action in trying to build a reputation as an effective advocate for their constituents.

Chapter 9 seeks to make sense of the contending forces of centralization and decentralization on Capitol Hill. For almost 230 years, members of Congress have come together in a representative body to make decisions affecting the nation. The historically powerful forces in Congress—parties, committees, elections, the individual actions of legislators, and the impact of presidential initiatives—combine to make policies (or not) that serve both the nation and its component parts, that is, states and districts. These contending forces, operating under a blanket of formal rules and informal relationships, produce a continuing tug-of-war between the centrifugal and centripetal forces on Capitol Hill—a struggle well anticipated by the Framers and thoroughly incorporated into our political life by the Constitution and more than two centuries of legislative practice.

Recommended Readings

Bessette, Joseph. *The Mild Voice of Reason*. Chicago: University of Chicago Press, 1982.
Fisher, Louis. *On Appreciating Congress: The People's Branch*. Boulder, CO: Paradigm, 2010.
Mayhew, David. *America's Congress*. New Haven, CT: Yale University Press, 2000.

Useful Resources

American University, School of Public Affairs, Center for Congressional and Presidential Studies: http://www.american.edu/spa/ccps
The Center on Congress at Indiana University: http://centeroncongress.org
Library of Congress: https://www.congress.gov

Notes

[1] Janie Lorber, "Huelskamp Sounds off on Losing Committee Spots," *Roll Call*, December 12, 2012, accessed at http://www.rollcall.com/news/huelskamp_sounds_off_on_losing_committee_spots-219990–1.html.

[2] Todd Beamon and Kathleen Walter, "Rep. Huelskamp: 'Petty, Vindictive Politics' Behind GOP Leadership Changes," *Newsmax*, December 12, 2012, accessed at http://www.newsmax.com/Newsfront/Huelskamp-Boehner-Petty-Politics/2012/12/11/id/467347/.

[3] Elena Schneider, "Huelskamp Loses GOP Primary after Ideological Battle," *Politico* August 2, 2016, http://www.politico.com/story/2016/08/huelskamp-defeated-in-kansas-primary-226603 (accessed March 2, 2016).

[4] Richard F. Fenno, Jr., "Strengthening a Congressional Strength," in *Congress in Change*, ed. Norman J. Ornstein (New York: Praeger, 1975).

[5] Alaska, Washington, and Louisiana hold blanket primaries: If no candidate wins a majority, the top two vote-getters, regardless of party, face each other in a runoff.

[6] John Hibbing and Elizabeth Thiess-Morris, *Congress as Public Enemy* (Lincoln: University of Nebraska, 1995).

[7] See "The Polarization of Congressional Parties," http://voteview.com/political_polarization_2014.htm.

[8] See Barbara Sinclair, *Party Wars* (Norman: University of Oklahoma Press, 2006).

[9] Jim VandeHei and Juliet Eilperin, "GOP Leaders Tighten Hold in the House," *Washington Post*, January 13, 2003, A1. Also see Derek Willis, "Republicans Mix It Up When Assigning House Chairmen for the 108th," *CQ Weekly*, January 11, 2003, 89–94. Also, Mike Allen, "GOP Leaders Tighten Their Grip on House," *Washington Post*, January 9, 2005, A5.

[10] For two differing yet complementary perspectives, see Frances Lee, *Beyond Ideology* (Chicago: University of Chicago Press, 2009) and Ross K. Baker, *Is Bipartisanship Dead? A Report from the Senate* (Boulder, CO: Paradigm, 2014).

[11] David Vogler, *The Politics of Congress*, 6th ed. (Madison, WI: Brown & Benchmark, 1993).

[12] Roger Davidson and Walter Oleszek, *Congress and Its Members*, 6th ed. (Washington, DC: CQ Press, 1998).

[13] In parliamentary systems, the executive (e.g., the prime minister) is often the leader of the majority party (or coalition among parties) within the chamber. The distinction between legislature and executive is thus blurred, especially when compared with the separation of powers as seen in the U.S. government.

[14] Sarah A. Binder and Steven S. Smith, *Politics or Principle?* (Washington, DC: Brookings Institution, 1997) and Gregory Koger, *Filibustering* (Chicago: University of Chicago Press, 2010).

[15] Woodrow Wilson, *Congressional Government* (Boston: Houghton Mifflin, 1885).

[16] Hannah Pitkin, *The Concept of Representation* (Berkeley: University of California Press, 1967), 209.

[17] See Douglas Arnold, *The Logic of Congressional Action* (New Haven, CT: Yale University Press, 1990).

[18] Heinz Eulau and Paul D. Karps, "The Puzzle of Representation: Specifying Components of Responsiveness," *Legislative Studies Quarterly* 2 (August 1977): 241. Much of the following relies on the line of argument in this article.

[19] Ibid.

[20] The trustee/delegate distinction between representative styles has its roots in Edmund Burke's speech to his Bristol parliamentary constituents in the eighteenth century. The modern discussion derives from Warren E. Miller and Donald E. Stokes, "Constituency Influence in Congress," *American Political Science Review* 57 (March 1963): 45–57.

[21] For more extensive development of this theme, see Richard F. Fenno, Jr., *Home Style* (Boston: Little, Brown, 1978) and Arnold, *Logic of Congressional Action*.

[22] Joseph M. Bessette has produced the most cogent examination of congressional deliberation in *The Mild Voice of Reason* (Chicago: University of Chicago Press, 1994).

[23] On Clinton, see James Fallows, "A Triumph of Misinformation," *The Atlantic* 275 (January 1995): 26–37; for the Obama reforms, see Lawrence Jacobs and Theda Skocpol, *Health Care Reform and American Politics* (New York: Oxford, 2012).

[24] See, for example, the arguments put forth by Rep. Gerald Solomon (R-NY) and Donald R. Wolfensberger, "The Decline of Deliberative Democracy in the House and Proposals for Change," *Harvard Journal of Legislation* 31 (1993): 320–70.

[25] David J. Vogler and Sidney R. Waldman, *Congress and Democracy* (Washington, DC: CQ Press, 1984), 166. More generally on deliberation, see Bessette, *Mild Voice of Reason*.

[26] For a fuller examination of Congress as theater, see Herbert F. Weisberg and Samuel C. Patterson, eds., *Great Theater: The American Congress in the 1990s* (New York: Cambridge University Press, 1998).

[27] See Gallup http://www.gallup.com/poll/180113/2014-approval-congress-remains-near-time-low.aspx (accessed January 21, 2015).

[28] For a discussion of bill sponsorship, see Wendy J. Schiller, "Senators as Political Entrepreneurs: Bill Sponsorship in the U.S. Senate," *American Journal of Political Science* 39, no. 1. (1995): 186–203.

[29] Various studies have detailed the work of the new House GOP majority. Among others, see Linda Killian, *The Freshmen* (Boulder, CO: Westview, 1998), Timothy Barnett, *Legislative Learning* (New York: Garland, 1999), and C. Lawrence Evans and Walter J. Oleszek, *Congress under Fire* (Boston: Houghton Mifflin, 1997).

[30] For a discussion of the electoral impact of the Contract with America, see Adam Nagourney, "Gingrich and 1994," *New York Times*, September 24, 2006. http://thecaucus.blogs.nytimes.com/2006/09/24/newt-gingrich-and-1994 (accessed May 25, 2015).

[31] Richard F. Fenno, Jr., "If, as Ralph Nader Says, Congress Is 'The Broken Branch,' How Come We Love Our Congressmen So Much?" in *Congress in Change*, ed. Norman Ornstein (New York: Praeger, 1975).

[32] There is extensive literature here, but a good place to start is with two books by Thomas Mann and Norman Ornstein: *The Broken Branch* (New York: Oxford, 2006) and *It's Even Worse Than It Looks* (New York: Basic Books, 2013).

CHAPTER 2

Congressional Decentralization in Design and Evolution

Congress has come a long way from the white, male-dominated institution it was for most of its history. Here, Democratic House members hold a press conference to denounce President Trump's tweets regarding women.

For heaven's sake, who are Congress? Are they not the creatures
of the people, amenable to them for their conduct and dependent
from day to day on their breath?

—George Washington to William Gordon, July 1783[1]

And to those members of Congress who question my authority
to make our immigration system work better, or question the
wisdom of me acting where Congress has failed,
I have one answer: Pass a bill.

—Barack Obama in an Address to the Nation on Immigration, November 20, 2014[2]

Presidents have been complaining about Congress since before there was a Congress (officially, that is). Even before the adoption of the U.S. Constitution, when there was just a Continental Congress and George Washington was just a military general, he was complaining about the inefficiencies of Congress—his complaints did not decrease when he became president.

To be fair to the Framers of the Constitution, they faced the challenge of how to create a strong national government that would not use its powers in arbitrary or antidemocratic ways. Within the republican construct of federalism and a separation of powers, the powers of the Congress were spelled out in far more detail than were those of the executive and judicial branches. The contradictory concerns of how to concentrate power and simultaneously limit it led the Framers to design a potentially powerful Congress that is capable of acting quickly and decisively but is ordinarily slow and cautious in struggling to represent the disparate interests of its widely varied constituencies. The Framers might well have a difficult time recognizing the size and scope of the modern presidency or the policy reach of the U.S. Supreme Court (e.g., the *Roe v. Wade* abortion decision based on the "right to privacy," which is nowhere detailed in the Constitution). Still, most would have been at home in the 2017 debate over the constitutionality of imposing bans on those immigrants and visitors from countries who are perceived as national security threats.

THE FRAMERS CONSTRUCT A CONGRESS

Although they recognized the need for a strong, effective central government, the Framers worried greatly over the potential for abuse that comes with any concentration of power. After all, they had fought a revolution to rid themselves of the British monarchy. By providing the Congress with large grants of well-defined authority, most notably the powers to tax and spend, they placed the largest share of national power in legislative hands. At the same time, "the Framers regarded [the Congress as likely] to succeed in deceiving and dominating the people."[3] They thus engineered a number of design features into the

Constitution to reduce the possibility of systematic abuse by willful congressional majorities. Its three basic elements were the following:

1. The representation of "a multiplicity of interests" within an "extended republic."[4]
2. The separation of powers at the national level into the legislative, judicial, and executive branches.
3. The creation of a bicameral (two-chamber) legislative body.

These provisions defined a decentralized congressional structure in three distinct ways. First, the representational nature of the legislature would work against the concentration of power. The Framers knew from firsthand experience how difficult it was to build majority positions from the diverse views harbored by legislators with differing state and regional backgrounds. Even so, vigorous representation of various interests and constituencies was scarcely enough to check a determined congressional majority. Curbing the potential for tyranny required permanent structural barriers to legislative dominance. This was accomplished by constructing both external and internal limitations on the congressional majorities—the separation of powers and bicameralism, respectively.

Thus, the separation of powers provides both independence for each of the three branches and the capacity for each branch to retain that independence by checking the actions of the others.[5] This elemental decentralizing feature of the U.S. government has produced legendary intragovernmental confrontations, ranging from the congressional censure of President Jackson in 1834 to the Supreme Court's unanimous 1974 decision requiring President Nixon to hand over the Watergate tapes to the Congress.[6] The 1998–1999 impeachment and acquittal of President Clinton appeared at the time to be the height of destructive confrontation, but more recently that memory has been replaced by the intense partisan warfare between Republicans and Democrats in both the House and the Senate.

At the same time, interbranch cooperation is crucial to address important issues, such as the economy, infrastructure, and the federal deficit. Presidents continually act to promote their legislative agendas, while the Congress presses its own oversight of the executive branch and government bureaucracy. In addition, the judicial branch imposes serious constraints on congressional actions, given its powers to rule laws unconstitutional and to interpret their applications. For example, in early 2017, the federal courts issued struck down parts of President's Trump's Executive Order 13769, which was the first attempt of his at banning individuals from predominantly Muslim countries from entering the United States. A second version of the ban, more narrowly defined, was issued by the Trump administration, and it was allowed to remain in effect pending full consideration by the Supreme Court in its 2017–2018 session. Just as the Trump administration had to adjust its policy to a court decision, Congress also responds to judicial decisions, as with bills to reverse the effects of *Citizens United v. Federal Election Commission*, which removed limits on campaign contributions by corporations and unions.

Finally, not content to rely on external checks on the Congress, the Framers also created formidable internal restraints. Most of these derive from the adoption of a bicameral structure, with distinctive bases of power for each legislative chamber. Given the tendency of legislative authority to dominate in a representative government, James Madison concluded that "the remedy for this inconvenience is, to divide the legislature into different branches; and to render them, by different modes of election, and different principles of action, as little connected with each other, as the nature of their common functions and their common dependence on society, will admit."[7]

The Constitutional Convention's fundamental compromise created a two-chamber structure in which only members of the lower body, the House of Representatives, would be elected directly by the people. State legislatures would elect senators, with each state represented by two senators, regardless of its population. The Seventeenth Amendment to the Constitution, ratified in 1913, changed the mode of election for senators from indirect election by state legislatures to direct election by the people.[8] The Framers set Senate terms at six years, as opposed to the two years given to representatives in the House. The Senate was empowered to ratify treaties and confirm executive-branch appointments, while the House was granted the sole authority to originate revenue bills.

Among their myriad accomplishments, the Framers succeeded in laying the groundwork for a strong national government. This potential for centralized power—realized in fits and starts over the past two hundred years—was simultaneously checked by representation of diverse interests, the separation of powers, and a bicameralism that roughly balanced the strengths of the two chambers. Even before the first Congress met or before George Washington assumed the presidency, the stage had been set for the tensions between *centrifugal (decentralizing)* and *centripetal (centralizing)* forces that have characterized U.S. legislative politics since 1789.

What follows is in no way a complete history, even in outline form, of the U.S. Congress. Rather, laying out a succession of congressional eras offers a series of sketches on how the national legislature has developed since its inception and how the initial tensions over representation and structural experiments, such as bicameralism, have shaped the nature of the institution. From the ascent of Republicans in Congress in 1994 when they won control of both houses of Congress for the first time in forty years to the Democratic wins of both houses in 2006 to the emergence of the Tea Party in 2010, and the return to Republican control of both houses in 2014 to the emergence of the Freedom Caucus in 2017, some clear trends remain. The House is a majority-party institution, the Senate is individually focused—but far less so now than in the past—and the Congress as a whole has to deal with a president who can exercise his constitutional powers by issuing executive orders and by vetoing legislation. Overall, as the president has continually gained power in recent decades, Congress has seen its influence wane in certain areas of government. However, with unified Republican control of the Congress and the executive branch for the first time in a decade, the 115th Congress may regain some or much of that influence.

THE EARLY CONGRESS: ORGANIZATION AND TENSIONS

Despite defining congressional powers more clearly, and at much greater length, than the powers of the other national branches of government, the Constitution did little to dictate how the two houses would be organized.[9] No mention is ever made of committees or political parties; only the offices of Speaker, president of the Senate (the vice president of the United States), and the Senate's president pro tempore are noted, but there is no delineation of their duties. The larger size of the House (65 members in 1789, and 181 by 1813, in contrast to 26 and 36 senators for the same years, respectively) led to the development of a more complex structure to conduct its business. To take advantage of its numbers, the House soon developed the decentralized standing committee system that remains an organizational hallmark of the body. Concurrently, however, the House's size also fostered the growth of political parties that served to pull together the diverse interests of their members, who had begun to feel the centrifugal pull of their committees and that of their constituencies.

For the first ten Congresses, most committees operated as ad hoc bodies to "perfect" the work done by the Committee of the Whole House,[10] but gradually—especially after 1825—standing committees, which continued from one Congress to the next, took on the major tasks of writing and revising legislation.[11] Reliance on growing numbers of committees illustrates the increased decentralization of the House. This organizational style benefited the average representative by allowing each committee to become an expert in its own policy area and to share that knowledge with the rest of the members.[12] Moreover, by facilitating a division of labor, the House could take advantage of the very condition—its large number of members—that rendered it most unwieldy.

As committees were beginning to develop the specialized expertise essential to address particular issues, the House also needed some way to build consistent majorities. As with committees, congressional leaders turned to a structural answer. U.S. politicians of the 1790s to the 1830s gradually invented a new organization designed for a republican form of government—the political party.[13] Although scholars disagree about the extent of partisanship and party organization in the first two decades of constitutional government, there were distinct factions that opposed each other in elections and within the legislature. As early as the 2nd Congress (1791–1793), even though parties had not become formalized, "common ideas and concerns were fast binding men together, and when Congress met, many individuals in both houses became more or less firmly aligned into two voting groups—Federalists on one side and Republican-minded [a Madison–Jefferson faction] on the other."[14]

The central figure in establishing strong parties and leadership in the House was Rep. Henry Clay of Kentucky, who energized the speakership during his three periods of service in that chamber. By 1814, Clay and his colleagues "had succeeded in erecting a new system, based on the party caucus, in which legislative leadership was now the prerogative of a group of prominent men in the House of Representatives."[15]

Party divisions and organizational strength would vary over the next four decades, but by 1825, the beginnings of a stable party system with regular leaders and consistent voting patterns had taken firm hold as a centralizing force within the House. Indeed, by this time, both committees and parties were developed to the point that a scholar could write in 1917, "So far as its organization was concerned, the House of Representatives had assumed its present form."[16] This is a significant observation for contemporary legislative politics because the House of the 1825 and 1917 eras contained both strong committee systems and powerful party leadership.

Through the early 1820s, the House, with its emerging structure and growing numbers, was accorded more weight than the Senate, largely because of the direct election of its members.[17] The Senate, however, was also changing, if more through evolution than through the impatient leadership of Clay. By 1830, the Senate had moved from being an elitist imitation of the British House of Lords to a strongly American institution. As political parties started to grow more powerful in state legislatures, which elected U.S. senators, they became more responsive to local party elites and economic interests, and were thus a less reliable source of support for the president.[18]

SENATE INDIVIDUALISM AND HOUSE FRAGMENTATION: 1830–1860

By the beginning of the Jackson administration in 1829, the Senate had begun to attract the most formidable leaders of the day, such as Kentucky's Henry Clay. Clay had instituted vigorous party leadership in the House before serving as secretary of state; he continued his illustrious, meandering career by returning to Congress in 1831 as a Whig senator. There he would join such notables as Daniel Webster (Whig-MA), John Calhoun (D-SC), and Thomas Hart Benton (D-MO) in a chamber composed of the most notable men of the era. The French observer Alexis de Tocqueville contrasted the "vulgarity" he found in the House with the Senate, which he described as being filled with "eloquent advocates, distinguished generals, wise magistrates, and statesmen of note."[19] Although many senators operated skillfully behind the scenes, this was a time of great individual oratory and sweeping attempts to hold the union together. Setting the stage for the era's politics was the legendary Webster–Hayne debate of 1829, which defined the slavery issue in terms of the survival of the union as a whole. Several other subthemes also ran through the Senate of the 1830s, most of them revolving around the roles of the states and the national government, slavery, the populist aims of Jackson and the Democratic Party, and the sectional split within the Democrats' ranks between New York's Martin Van Buren and South Carolina's John Calhoun.[20] The freedom of individual action within the still small Senate (forty-eight members in 1831) meant that coalitions could form and re-form as these able legislators jockeyed for advantage over a wide range of issues. All the while, they understood that their fundamental division over slavery might destroy the very system of government in which they operated so freely.

In contrast, the House found it difficult to organize itself coherently in the 1830–1860 period. With a larger, less stable membership than the Senate, the

House could neither rely as easily on the leadership of strong individual legis-lators nor could it count on its party factions and sectional interests to provide the organizational coherence demanded by the fractious body. As Jeffrey Jenkins and Charles Stewart demonstrate in their work, extended, bitter contests for the speakership became commonplace.[21] In 1849, for example, five major group-ings vied for control, and a Speaker was finally elected on the sixty-third ballot after the members agreed that the office could go to the candidate who won a plurality, not a majority, of the votes. In 1855, a mix of Whigs, Republicans (a newly formed party), Democrats, and various minor parties went to 133 ballots before selecting (again by plurality) antislavery Rep. Nathaniel Banks (MA) of the nativist American (Know-Nothing) Party.

Finally, in the 36th Congress (1859–1861), which again harbored no clear party majority, forty-four ballots over three months were required to elect the most unlikely of Speakers: William Pennington (R-NJ), who was serving his first (and last) term in the House. His election to this post matched Henry Clay's 1811 victory as a first-term representative, but Clay had won the speakership because of his strong personality and forceful leadership qualities; conversely, Pennington was the lowest common denominator in a highly fragmented cham-ber of a nation that was about to burst apart.

THE RISE OF THE ORGANIZED CONGRESS: 1860–1920

Between the Civil War years and the end of World War I, the U.S. Congress underwent a series of organizational restructurings; these culminated in the organization that serves as its foundation today. The combination of a growing national industrial base and an increasing U.S. role in world affairs required the legislative branch to adapt to a very different environment than that of the pre-1860 United States, in which an agrarian nation had wrestled with the fun-damental, highly divisive slavery issue.

Over the 1860–1920 period, the Congress experimented with strong party leadership in both chambers, created and then limited a separate committee for appropriations, first dominated a series of weak presidents and later looked to the president for coherent leadership initiatives, and eventually moved toward the mixture of standing committee decentralization and oligarchy that would characterize the institution until the mid-1960s. Why such a flurry of activity? As a representative body, the Congress adapts to its environment. New mem-bers enter the body, new issues come before it, and new party alignments arise. In the course of adapting to broad societal changes, such as industrialization in the late 1800s and early 1900s, the Congress has often restructured itself inter-nally to consolidate power and regularize procedure.[22]

The House

For more than a quarter century after the Civil War, Congress stood astride national politics and policymaking, but battles raged over the control of both chambers. Standing committees dominated the legislative process, especially after the House stripped the upstart Appropriations Committee (established in

1865) of much of its authority. At the same time, a number of strong Speakers increased the power of their office; in particular, the Speaker could appoint all committee members and aggressively employ his power to recognize members who wished to speak. Still, Roger Davidson and Walter Oleszek conclude that in the 1880s, "despite growth in the Speaker's prerogatives, centrifugal forces in the House remained strong, even dominant."[23] Although committees contributed to this dominance, even more significant was the almost total inability of House majorities to work their will, largely because of delaying tactics that allowed any member to slow actions of the chamber to a crawl.

Enter Speaker Thomas Brackett Reed (R-ME), elected to lead the House in 1889. In his first three months as Speaker, he rewrote the House rules from his position as chair of the Rules Committee, and as presiding officer revised the rules for recognition of a quorum (a majority of all members). Since the 1830s, the House had operated under the odd but powerful precedent of not recognizing the presence of those who sat mute in the chamber and refused to answer a quorum call.[24] As Rep. Benjamin Butterworth (R-OH) put it, a member may "while present, arise in his place and assert that he is absent, and we must take his word for it. What an absurdity on the face of it. . . . It is the weapon of anarchy."[25] A unanimous, if slender, Republican majority upheld Reed's decision that all members physically present would be counted as present in constituting a quorum. This ruling was reconfirmed by the Democrats when they took control of the House in the early 1890s.

Reed's quorum ruling and other rules that consolidated organizational power opened the way for twenty years of great centralization in the House.[26] Speakers Reed, Charles Crisp (D-GA), and, most notably, Joseph Cannon (R-IL) increasingly employed the formidable weapons that the position had accumulated. From 1903 to 1909, "Uncle Joe" Cannon steadily became more dictatorial (the word is not too strong) in his command of the House.[27] Finally, in 1910, a coalition of minority Democrats and Republican reformers (many from the Midwest) broke the Speaker's hold over the combination of power levers that permitted him to dominate the process and outcomes of House decision making. As we shall see later in more detail, Cannon had lost control of the majority that allowed him to function as an autocrat. The support of his fellow Republicans, which was crucial to his dominance, had crumbled. Cannon remained as Speaker for the rest of the term, but both his personal power and that of the office were greatly diminished.

For a few years, the Democratic Party caucus and the presidential leadership of Woodrow Wilson combined to retain some relatively strong centripetal momentum in the House, but this dissipated with increasing disagreement over international policies surrounding World War I.[28] By 1920, strong party leadership had given way to a decentralized committee system as the principal means of organizing the House—a condition that was not to change for more than fifty years. Although the decline in the party system within the House was dramatic, it did not flow just from the internal dynamics of the chamber. Rather, as Joseph Cooper points out, during the 1903–1910 period, Republican Party machines came under increasing attack from Progressives, and the weakening of local organizations gave members of Congress more leeway in constraining Speaker Cannon and seriously weakening the congressional party organization.[29]

The Senate

In his classic account of the nineteenth-century Senate, historian David Rothman concludes that the Senate of 1869 was very much like its predecessors; by 1901, all this had changed. The party caucus and its chieftains determined who would sit on which committees and looked after the business calendar in detail. Members were forced to seek their favors or remain without influence in the chamber. At the same time, both organizations imposed unprecedented discipline on roll calls.[30]

Though the House could consolidate power around the constitutional office of the Speaker, the Senate had no similar touchstone. Ironically, strong political parties at the state and local levels formed the context from which centripetal forces flowed into the Senate, where party ties rose in importance through the 1880s and 1890s. Most members of this sizable body (ninety lawmakers in 1901) functioned as party loyalists, who provided the votes for the policy positions endorsed by the leadership-dominated party caucus.[31]

Iowa's William Allison and Rhode Island's Nelson Aldrich occupied the central positions within the Republican caucus of the 1890s and were perhaps the most talented and influential members of the chamber. They dominated Senate policymaking through a combination of formal and informal linkages. The Allison/Aldrich faction gained control of overlapping party committees and standing committee positions to dominate the chamber's agenda and its policy outcomes. For example, controlling the Republican Steering Committee "confirmed the power of the Allison/Aldrich faction over the Senate business. Arranging the legislative schedule in detail, week by week, the committee extended the party leaders' authority unimpaired from the caucus to the chamber. Senators knew they had to consult the Steering Committee before attempting to raise even minor matters."[32]

Remnants of traditional Senate individualism remained, but those Republicans who refused to cooperate with the Allison/Aldrich group found themselves without influence. As Rothman notes, "Anyone could use the chamber as a forum and address the nation. Senators willing to abandon the opportunity to increase their own authority could act freely, following their own inclinations. . . . But barring a takeover of the party offices, they could hardly affect the exercise of power. The country might honor their names, but the Senate barely felt their presence."[33]

Given the underlying differences among senators, based on region, party, interests, and ideology, the Senate's centralization could not hold for long, and the Republican caucus's domination eroded over the 1901–1912 period. The individualistic, centrifugal forces of the chamber came to the fore in caucus challenges to Aldrich, the growing strength of the Progressive movement in states (which translated into electing senators who were more willing to buck the party leadership), and the election of a Democratic Senate to complement the presidential victory of Democrat Woodrow Wilson in 1912. In addition to the partisan turnover of 1912 came the 1913 adoption of the Seventeenth Amendment to the Constitution, which provided for the direct election of senators by the voters. The supporters of the Seventeenth Amendment hoped that it would limit the influence of state party machines and wealthy elites on the selection of senators by freeing up senators to appeal directly to voters. We will delve more deeply into whether the Seventeenth Amendment accomplished its goals in a subsequent chapter.

Finally, the Senate did change one further fundamental element of its procedure. From its inception, the Senate had allowed unlimited debate on any subject. The *filibuster*—or its threat—had proved a powerful tool for many Senate giants of the past. This was one of the strongest decentralizing elements within the entire legislative process. An individual senator (or, more likely, a band of legislators with similar, intense feelings) could indefinitely delay consideration of a crucial bill. This occurred in 1917, when, in President Wilson's words, "a little group of willful men" blocked his armed neutrality bill, which had the public support of seventy-five of ninety-six senators.[34]

In the aftermath of this inability to act, the Senate adopted *cloture*, the first measure that provided a mechanism to shut off debate; cloture could be imposed by a two-thirds vote of those present and voting. Although this procedure was employed in 1919 to end a filibuster on ratification of the Treaty of Versailles, until the late 1970s, the Senate rarely approved cloture, save in extraordinary cases, such as the 1964 civil rights bill. The filibuster remained a potent weapon, both in its occasional implementation and in its frequent use as a threat.[35] Later in this chapter, and again in chapter 7, we will address the relatively recent changes to the filibuster, notably as a result of more intensified partisanship, that lowered the threshold for invoking cloture to end debate on executive and judicial nominations.

The Drift toward Decentralization

Because they were allied with the Republican presidencies of William McKinley (1897–1901) and Theodore Roosevelt (1901–1909), the House's strong speakership and the Senate's dominant Allison/Aldrich faction served to concentrate legislative power in the congressional parties at the turn of the twentieth century. The ability of legislative party leaders to set the nation's policy agenda became increasingly important in that the industrializing U.S. society was demanding more of the federal government.[36] In the 40th Congress (1867–1869), lawmakers introduced a total of 3,003 bills; by the 52nd Congress (1891–1893), that number had grown to 14,518, and the 60th Congress (1907–1909) witnessed the introduction of almost 38,000 bills, more than a twelvefold increase in forty years.[37] This volume of legislation eventually benefited those restive representatives and senators who desired to reduce the power of their party leaders because it gave them an opportunity to build individual reputations around their attempt to address issues through bill sponsorship.

Some mechanism was needed to handle this immense flow of prospective legislation. The committee system offered the most obvious organizational response for the Congress. In fact, the number of standing committees had proliferated in both chambers to the point that in 1918, the House had sixty such units and the Senate a staggering seventy-four. The sheer number of committees might imply the development of a highly decentralized Congress, but through 1910 party leaders combined their leadership roles with those of key committees to produce strongly centralized operations in both chambers.[38] With Speaker Cannon's defeat, the subsequent waning of Democratic caucus unity in the House after 1914, and the Senate's growing fragmentation during the period 1901–1919, congressional party organizations could no longer move bills through the legislative process in a predictable, timely manner. Relying on committees would be essential for the sake of coherence. Such reliance dictated that both chambers reform their committee systems, which they did in 1919 and again, more meaningfully, in 1946.

THE DEVELOPMENT AND DECLINE OF THE "TEXTBOOK" CONGRESS: 1920–1970

Gradually, over the 1920s, 1930s, and 1940s, the committee strength grew, and members almost universally advanced on the basis of their seniority—the length of their consecutive tenure on a given committee. The 1946 Legislative Reorganization Act sharply reduced the number of committees in both chambers and thus increased the value of the remaining standing committee chairmanships—today there are twenty in the House, sixteen in the Senate.

The committee-dominated Congress of the 1950s coincided with the first systematic analysis of the Congress by political scientists trained in behavioral methods.[39] With his term *textbook Congress*, political scientist Kenneth Shepsle has captured the extent to which the studies created a conventional wisdom that still shapes many perceptions of legislative politics.[40] In representing their constituencies and making national policy, legislators confront tensions that "derive from three competing imperatives—geographical, jurisdictional, and partisan. . . . Congress is [thus] an arena for constituencies, committees, and [party-based] coalitions. The textbook Congress of the 1950s represented an equilibrium among these imperatives involving an institutional bargain that gave prominence to committees."[41] Although legendary party leaders such as Speaker Sam Rayburn (D-TX) and Senate Majority Leader Lyndon Johnson (D-TX) wielded substantial personal power in the 1950s, the Congress of these years emphasized the work of autonomous committees as directed by a set of senior chairmen.[42] The textbook Congress was both decentralized and oligarchic: decentralized in that committee chairs dominated their own policy domains; oligarchic in that top party leaders, committee chairs, and chairs of the thirteen Appropriations Committee subcommittees in each chamber all benefited from their joint control of the domestic policy agenda. Although the House relied more heavily on committee work than did the Senate, the same general committee-based equilibrium existed in both chambers.

The organizationally stable Congress of the 1950s did not bend easily to the winds of change. Popular pressure for more educational spending fell victim to procedural wrangling. In the face of filibusters and a hostile bloc of southern senators, civil rights legislation proceeded slowly in the aftermath of the Supreme Court's 1954 *Brown v. Board of Education* school desegregation ruling. The committee-dominated system proved superb at slowing the pace of policy change in a narrowly Democratic Congress that faced the moderate-to-conservative Republican presidency of Dwight Eisenhower.[43]

The congressional equilibrium began to change with the Democratic landslide in the 1958 congressional elections, which greatly increased the size of the party's majorities in both chambers. More important, many of the newly elected legislators were relatively liberal and committed to policy changes. Six years later, another surge of Democratic legislators ascended Capitol Hill, brought there in part by Lyndon Johnson's sweeping presidential victory over Senator Barry Goldwater (R-AZ). Despite coming in disproportionate numbers from Republican districts, these rank-and-file Democratic legislators proved crucial to the passage of several of Johnson's ambitious domestic programs.[44] Liberal voting records denied many first-termers a chance for reelection; those who survived, however, felt entitled to a real voice within the legislative process. The major outlet for this voice came in positions taken by the Democratic Study Group, a body of House Democrats that formed after the 1958 elections.[45] This unofficial but well-organized group consistently pressed for a reform agenda, which included reducing the power of committee chairmen. The standing committee oligarchy was thus ripe for challenge by the late 1960s. Party leaders had begun to chip away at the chairs' powers, while reformist junior members hungered for responsibility within the committee structure. Both leaders and backbenchers stood to gain from reining in the chairs; change was inevitable, but with it came great disruption that lasted a decade.

REFORMING THE CONGRESS: THE 1970s

In the end, the thing the House needs most is legislators. What's important is getting things through—then you've done everything. . . . Running the House is the only thing that makes a difference.

—Rep. Richard Bolling[46]

When voters in the 1970s began choosing different representation in congressional elections, they indirectly caused change in the institution itself, without even knowing how or why it happened. In general, the newly elected legislators were impatient, eager to use their expertise, and unconcerned if they ruffled some senior members' feathers.[47] In the House, subcommittees gained a measure of independent authority; members sought and received many more resources for their offices; most votes on the floor were recorded and thus open to public scrutiny; and the Democratic caucus provided enhanced powers for the Speaker and the top party leaders. Shepsle summarizes:

> The revolt of the 1970s thus strengthened four power centers. It liberated *members and subcommittees*, restored to the *Speakership* an authority it had not known since the days of Joe Cannon, and invigorated the *party caucus*. Some of the reforms had a decentralizing effect, some a recentralizing effect. Standing

committees and their chairs were caught in the middle. Geography and party benefited; the division-of-labor jurisdictions were its victims.[48]

These reforms produced a highly unstable political environment on Capitol Hill, especially in the House, because they distributed power more widely across more members and reduced committee chairs' power. There was also an ideological divide between more senior southern conservative Democrats and the newly elected junior members who were more liberal. Under these conditions, Democrats could not generate consistent congressional majorities to pass major policy initiatives, despite their large majorities in both chambers and a sitting Democratic president, Jimmy Carter.[49]

THE DEMOCRATIC POSTREFORM CONGRESS: 1980–1994

In 1980, Republicans ran a national campaign for the presidency and Congress that emphasized the dysfunction of the Democratic Party then in power. The Republican candidate, Ronald Reagan, won the presidency and the Republicans won control of the Senate, but the Democrats maintained control of the House and were led by Speaker Tip O'Neill (D-MA), an old-time pol from Boston. O'Neill famously coined the phrase "all politics is local," meaning that members of Congress had to worry about their constituents back home and their colleagues in the party who surrounded them in Congress.

Speaker O'Neill was a popular leader in and outside of the House because he had found common ground to bring together the different strands of the legislative Democratic Party and he managed to work across the aisle with an opposite-party president on major tax and immigration legislation. Under his watch, the Democratic Party in the House grew more unified, partly because of greater participation among the rank-and-file members, and partly because of the election of new members who shared the more liberal wing's policy goals.[50] Tip O'Neill built a party leadership organization that encouraged party unity through a combination of carrots, such as including many members within the leadership, and sticks, such as controlling the process of appointing members to committee seats.

By the 1980s, majority-party members, most of whom had been elected in 1974 or later, decided that they wanted, in Fenno's words, a "different kind of Congress." When these members judged, finally, that the "legislative process was no longer producing the legislation they needed, the costs of maintaining the legislative status quo [embodied in the committee-dominated textbook Congress] became very high."[51] At the same time, continued congressional scholar Barbara Sinclair, "the costs of change in the direction of stronger party leadership declined" as House Democrats grew more similar in their ideology.[52]

Over the same time period, the Senate underwent a less striking, more evolutionary transformation.[53] The Democrats won back control of the Senate 1986, picking up eight seats, and Senator Robert Byrd (D-WV) resumed his role as Senate majority leader, with Senator Dole (R-KS) assuming the role of Republican minority leader for the first time. Byrd stepped down in 1989, and

SPOTLIGHT

Senator Elizabeth Warren: The Individual as Agenda Setter

Senator Elizabeth Warren (D-MA) was elected to the U.S. Senate in November, 2012 defeating incumbent Scott Brown (R) in a closely contested election. Prior to running for the Senate, Warren was a professor at Harvard Law School where she focused her work on consumer protection laws. President Obama used her model of consumer protection as the basis for the provisions in the 2010 Dodd-Frank Wall Street Reform and Consumer Protection Act, which created the Consumer Financial Protection Bureau (CFPB). The CFPB had the power to issue federal regulations to ensure that banks and credit card companies inform consumers about interest rates and late payment fees among other things. One problem remained: the CFPB could not function unless a director was appointed to run it. Warren was rumored to be the leading candidate to become the CFPB's first director, but Senate Republicans announced their intention to block any appointee to that position to prevent the bureau from issuing any regulations. Ultimately, President Obama made a recess appointment (made when Congress was out of session), but Warren was shut out.

Blocked from serving as director of the CFPB, Elizabeth Warren took her passion for consumer protection to the next level by deciding to run for U.S. Senate. When she won, the very colleagues who had previously blocked her from serving in the Obama Administration ended up having her as a colleague. Since entering the Senate, Warren has built a reputation as a progressive politician who advocates for consumer protection, workers' rights, and policies that help the middle class. Some activists in the Democratic Party wanted her to run for the party's nomination in 2016, but she chose to endorse Hillary Clinton instead. After Clinton lost the presidential election, Warren again picked up the mantle as an advocate for progressive causes.

It took very little time after the beginning of the 115th Congress for a showdown to ensue between Warren and the Majority Leader Mitch McConnell. During the floor debate on the nomination of then-Senator Jeff Sessions (R-AL) to be Attorney General, Warren went to the Senate floor and read a nine-page letter from Coretta Scott King, widow of Dr. Martin Luther King, to her then senator Strom Thurmond (R-SC) in 1986 objecting to the appointment of Sessions as a federal judge. In that letter, Mrs. King wrote that when Sessions was a U.S. attorney, he had worked to block elderly blacks from voting. Warren also read from a statement at the time made by one of her predecessors from Massachusetts, Senator Ted Kennedy, which called Sessions a "disgrace." Senator McConnell asked the presiding officer of the Senate to rule that Senator Warren had violated Rule XIX of the Senate, which prevents one senator from "directly or indirectly, by any form of words impute to another Senator or to other Senators any conduct or motive unworthy or unbecoming a Senator." The Senate voted 49–43, divided by partisan lines, to uphold the ruling of the presiding officer. Warren was required to relinquish the floor and was prevented from speaking for the remainder of the debate over the Sessions nomination.

In explaining his decision to seek that ruling, McConnell said that "she was warned. She was given an explanation. Nevertheless, she persisted." Almost immediately, the hashtag #LetHerSpeak and #ShePersisted began trending on Twitter and other social media platforms; Senator Warren left the Senate floor and read the entire King letter livestreaming on Facebook. She likely received more publicity and campaign contributions for her 2018 reelection campaign, after being silenced than if she had been allowed to continue talking on the Senate floor. The debate over Sessions' cabinet nomination highlights the extent to which partisanship can cause deep conflict in the Senate, while demonstrating how important the individual right to speak remains in the Senate.

—————

The information in this paragraph comes from a compilation of *Washington Post* articles: Amy Wang, "'Nevertheless, she persisted' becomes new battle cry after McConnell silences Elizabeth Warren." *Washington Post*, February 8, 2017, accessed online at https://www.washingtonpost.com/news/the-fix/wp/2017/02/08/nevertheless-she-persisted-becomes-new-battle-cry-after-mcconnell-silences-elizabeth-warren/?tid=sm_tw&utm_term=.455d9bf1f2e1 and Wesley Lowery, "Read the letter Coretta Scott King wrote opposing Sessions's 1986 federal nomination." *Washington Post*, January 10, 2017, accessed at https://www.washingtonpost.com/news/powerpost/wp/2017/01/10/read-the-letter-coretta-scott-king-wrote-opposing-sessionss-1986-federal-nomination/?utm_term=.2920c05b670e.

George Mitchell (D-ME) took over as majority leader. These Senate leaders were strongly loyal to their party, but they also understood the importance of individual power in the Senate and, therefore, balanced those competing interests. A lone senator could often tie the institution in knots as the whole deferred to the "rights" of a single willful legislator. In those days, it was Jesse Helms (R-NC) or Howard Metzenbaum (D-OH), but today we see Rand Paul (R-KY), and Elizabeth Warren (D-MA) engaging in the same sort of "objection" tactics that their predecessors did. These types of senators have shown time and again that they can and will bring Senate business to a halt if their desires are not accommodated, or they will force the Senate to shut down their speech as Majority Leader McConnell (R-KY) did to Senator Warren in February 2017.[54]

THE REPUBLICAN MAJORITY ERA IN THE HOUSE: 1994–2006; 2010 ONWARD

At the same time that the Democratic Party was becoming more liberal, it was increasingly dominated by members elected from the Midwest and Northeast. In the South, which had been the source of major Democratic dominance, white conservative voters were increasingly turning to Republican candidates. One such candidate was Newt Gingrich (R-GA), who was elected to the House in 1978. Gingrich was more conservative than the average Republican in the House at that time, and he fought to rise up the ranks in party leadership, culminating in his election as majority party whip. In that position, he recruited a number of candidates to run for office and raised money for their campaigns. From that position, he engineered one of the greatest party sweeps of the House in history when in 1994 he led the Republicans to majority control of the House, after forty years of Democratic control. That same year, Republicans also won the Senate back, giving Republicans control of both houses of Congress, which—with a brief exception in the Senate from May 2001 to December 2002 when Senator Jeffords (R-VT) switched his party allegiance from Republican to Independent and caucused with the Democrats—they retained until 2006.

As Speaker, Gingrich took steps to consolidate party power over committee assignments and chairmanships, and he imposed six-year term limits on committee chairs. The Republicans even imposed an eight-year limit on serving as Speaker. However, Gingrich would not serve long enough to test that limit. In 1998, at the prodding of then majority whip Tom DeLay (R-TX), Republicans pushed through impeachment of President Clinton, which stemmed from charges that he lied about his involvement with a White House intern, Monica Lewinsky, and charges of obstruction of justice. But in the Senate, where moderation sometimes prevails, some Republicans refused to toe the party line and voted to acquit the president. Voters responded negatively to the impeachment proceedings, and the Republican Party lost seats in the midterm elections that year. Ironically, the first victim of the Republicans' reduced majority was Gingrich, who was pushed out of the speakership when six Republican representatives announced in December 1998 that they would not vote for him as Speaker when the House organized itself in January 1999.

To replace Gingrich, Republicans sought a less flamboyant and controversial leader and decided on the little-known Rep. Dennis Hastert (R-IL), a conservative who had maintained cordial relations with all wings of his own party and also with many Democrats. Although he was lower key than Gingrich, Hastert firmly believed in party caucus power; indeed, under his speakership, Republicans adopted the *Hastert Rule*, which requires that no bill can go to the floor without the support of a majority of Republican Party members.

From 1995 to 2001, Republicans as the majority faced a Democratic president (Bill Clinton), but the election of George W. Bush in 2000 and the recapture of the Senate in 2002 gave them unified party government for four years. But by 2005, cracks in the Republican Party started to emerge over the Iraq War, federal spending, immigration, and Social Security reform; Speaker Hastert decided to retire from Congress. By 2006, the issue of the Iraq War overwhelmed all other issues, and the Democrats, led by the then minority leader Nancy Pelosi (D-CA), strategically focused their campaigns for the House and Senate that year on opposition to the war. Democrats won control of both the House and Senate in the 2006 midterm elections, and Nancy Pelosi was elected the first female Speaker of the House. John Boehner (R-OH), who had been House majority leader under Hastert, served as Republican minority leader during this time.

In 2008, the Democrats held the House and Senate and won the White House with the election of Barack Obama to his first presidential term. At the same time, the nation was facing a major economic downturn, under which millions of workers were unemployed, banks were in crisis, and large auto manufacturers were facing bankruptcy. Democrats passed legislation to address these issues, with little to no Republican Party support, and they faced criticism for increasing the federal deficit as a result. Democrats also enacted the Affordable Care Act, otherwise known as Obamacare, which required individuals to purchase health insurance, prohibited discrimination for preexisting conditions, and allowed people under the age of twenty-six to stay on their parents' health insurance plan. Republicans fiercely opposed Obamacare because they claimed the voters did not want a mandate and it was too expensive. They used it as a major issue in the 2010 midterm elections, and with the rise of the Tea Party movement among conservative voters, Republicans rode this wave of opposition to victory in the House elections, even as the Senate remained under Democratic control.

Although Republicans did not have to wait long to recapture control of the House, the electoral victory for the House Republicans came at a price in terms of party cohesion. The new Tea Party members who were elected were considerably more conservative than their colleagues, and as their ranks grew in the 2012 elections, they became a major force within the Republican caucus. For example, the Tea Party members opposed increasing the federal government's borrowing authority, known as the debt limit, and opposed authorizing spending in certain areas. They were powerful enough in 2013 to shut down parts of the government until Speaker Boehner decided to violate the Hastert Rule and work with the Democrats to approve spending measures that were essential to the operation of the federal government.

Despite historically low negative approval ratings for Congress (hovering around 20 percent) and public opposition to the partial government shutdown in 2013, Republicans held control of the House in 2014 and won eight seats in the Senate to win control of that chamber as well. In 2016, the Republicans lost a net of six seats but still held a 241–194 majority over the Democrats. In the Senate, two incumbent Republicans, from New Hampshire and Illinois, lost their seats, but the Republicans retained their majority, 52–48. Even though the Republicans retained control of Congress, many of those in office have only experienced divided party government, which enabled them to consistently oppose President Obama.[55] In the 115th Congress, they are working with a president from their own party, whom many of them opposed during the primary process, under what is typically referred to as a unified party government. However, because of the unconventional nature of the Trump campaign and subsequent presidency, it is not clear that there will be total agreement on policy priorities or partisan strategy between the two branches of government.

THE RISE OF PARTISANSHIP IN THE SENATE: 1994–2017

Less dramatically, but at least equally important, the Senate has also grown more partisan since 1994, under either Republican or Democratic control. Historically, the Senate tends to change majority control more than the House; party control has switched four times in the last twenty years. Over that same time, party unity has grown stronger on both sides of the aisle, and the parties now engage in "message politics," in which each party tries to frame every policy and major vote as a partisan campaign issue. As a result, party leaders put more pressure on senators to vote with the party.[56] As political scientists Sean Theriault and Frances Lee have each demonstrated, the pressure to vote with your party in the Senate extends to all votes, procedural and substantive, and the culture in the Senate has shifted considerably to be much more like the House than ever before.[57] One of the hallmarks of the Senate is that each individual senator has the right to be recognized to speak, and from that comes the right to filibuster or delay legislation. However, when Democrats used that power to block a number of President George W. Bush's judicial nominations, the Republican majority leader at the time, Bill Frist (R-TN) broached the possibility of altering Senate rules to eliminate or restrict the use of filibusters on judicial nominations. Then Democratic minority leader, Senator Harry Reid (D-Nev.), warned against trying to limit individual power, and both Republican and Democratic rank-and-file senators expressed opposition to the move; Senator Frist decided against trying to limit the filibuster.[58]

When the Democrats won control of the Senate in 2006, Harry Reid became majority leader and used his position to consolidate majority-party power over floor proceedings by limiting opportunities to amend bills. By late 2013, Republican opposition to President Obama's nominations had been so forceful that Senator Reid put in place the exact restriction on filibustering executive and judicial nominations (lower than the Supreme Court) that he had earlier opposed; the threshold of votes to invoke cloture was reduced from sixty to fifty-one votes, thus making it significantly more difficult to sustain a filibuster. Reid explained that this limitation was in direct response to the Republican use of delaying tactics to block President Obama's nominations. Reid also benefited from turnover in the Senate; in 2013, there were enough new Democratic senators who were not as invested in the traditional power of the filibuster when it came to presidential appointments and judicial nominees to support the rules change.

By 2014, the Senate was for all intents and purposes as polarized along party lines as the House, and its ability to moderate the House had diminished. In the November 2014 midterms, the Republicans won back majority control of the Senate and elected Mitch McConnell (R-KY) the majority leader; the Democrats retained Harry Reid as their minority leader. McConnell kept in place the limits on the filibuster put in place by his predecessor. With the presidential election of 2016 looming large over the 114th Congress, not much was accomplished in either rule changes or policy. Perhaps the greatest Senate casualty of the electoral politics of 2016 was the confirmation process for the Supreme Court. Justice Antonin Scalia died in early 2016, and President Obama named Merrick Garland, a Circuit Court of Appeals Justice, as his nominee to the Supreme Court to replace Scalia. Majority Leader McConnell refused to allow the Senate Judiciary Committee to hold hearings on that nomination or to have the Senate as a whole consider it. By failing to act either to confirm or reject President Obama's nominee, the Senate left the Supreme Court with eight members; several important rulings were left standing because the court voted 4–4 on these cases. At the time, McConnell reasoned that the nomination was so close to an election for a new president, it was best to wait for the new president to make this lifetime appointment. Never in the history of the Senate had it left a Supreme Court nomination unaddressed for this length of time.

SPOTLIGHT

Senator Lindsey Graham: Procedural and Substantive Pressure

Senator Lindsey Graham (R-SC), a Republican who has cultivated a reputation for working across the aisle, embodies the increasing pressure on senators to vote with their party. Graham first entered politics in 1992 when he was elected to the South Carolina House of Representatives. Prior to entering politics, Graham served as a prosecutor and defense attorney in the U.S. Air Force. Defending an Air Force pilot accused of marijuana use in 1984, Graham garnered national attention when he was featured in a *60 Minutes* segment that exposed faulty military drug-testing procedures. After serving a two-year term as a state representative, Graham set his sights on South Carolina's second congressional district for the 1994 midterm elections after a long-serving Democratic representative decided to retire. Aided by an endorsement from incumbent U.S. Senator Strom Thurmond in the Republican primary and boosted in the general election by a successful Republican showing across the nation in 1994, Graham won the House seat and marked the first time Republicans were able to capture that seat since 1877.

While in the House, Graham frequently opposed the prevailing party position; for example, he was the only Republican on the House Judiciary Committee to vote against the articles of impeachment for President Clinton in 1998. Graham was elected to the Senate in 2002, filling the open seat left by the retiring eight-term senator Strom Thurmond. Senator Graham continued in many ways to try to work across the aisle on both procedural and substantive issues. In 2010, Graham devoted a significant amount of time toward trying to garner conservative support for a Democratic climate-change bill sponsored by Senators Kerry (D-MA) and Lieberman (I-CT). Graham called it an "energy independence" bill in order to shift the focus toward jobs and attract hesitant Republicans. In 2013, Graham was one of four Republicans—and the only Republican from a state without a significant immigrant population—to join onto the bipartisan "Gang of Eight" senators who were tasked with crafting a comprehensive immigration reform bill. Neither the climate-change nor the immigration initiatives were able to draw enough support in the Senate to be sufficient for passage.

Senator Graham's desire for bipartisan consensus extended to procedural issues as well, but recent events show how the pressure to go along with party leadership has increased significantly. In the 2005 battle over whether to eliminate the filibuster for presidential appointees, Graham was among the senators who opposed Majority Leader Frist's (R-TN) potential deployment of the nuclear option. As part of another bipartisan "gang" of senators, this time called the "Gang of Fourteen," Graham (and other Republicans) helped to derail that limitation on minority party procedural rights despite the preferences of party leadership.

Lindsey Graham threw his hat into the presidential ring for the 2016 elections. He announced his candidacy on June 1, 2015, but ultimately did not gain enough traction to stay in the race and suspended his campaign on December 21, 2015. He did not endorse any other Republican candidates at the time and spent most of 2016 criticizing Donald Trump. Since Trump's election, Graham has both supported and opposed actions taken by the president.

One of those instances of support was on eliminating the filibuster on the Gorsuch nomination. After twelve years of trying to defend the filibuster, Senator Graham, seemed somewhat reluctant to vote to eliminate it this time around, "I'm sorry we got here, but we are where we are and I'm going to vote to change the rules because I'm not going to be part of a Senate where Democrats get their judges and Republicans can never get theirs." In the contemporary Senate, especially when the majority party's hold on the Senate is so narrow, even the more moderate and consensus-building senators like Senator Graham are expected to vote with their party.

———————

The information in this section is taken from multiple sources as follows: Lloyd Grove, "Lindsey Graham, a Twang of Moderation," *The Washington Post*, October 7, 1998, Page D01; Robert Draper, "Lindsey Graham, This Year's Maverick," *The New York Times*, July 1, 2010, http://www.nytimes.com/2010/07/04/magazine/04graham-t.html?pagewanted=all&_r=0; Molly Ball, "How Lindsey Graham Stomped the Tea Party," *The Atlantic*, June 10, 2014, https://www.theatlantic.com/politics/archive/2014/06/how-lindsey-graham-stomped-the-tea-party/372521/?single_page=true; John Nolen, "Neil Gorsuch Confirmation Vote: The 'Nuclear Option,'" *CBS News*, April 5, 2017, http://www.cbsnews.com/news/neil-gorsuch-confirmation-vote-the-nuclear-option/; Senator Lindsey Graham (@LindseyGrahamSC) on Twitter, https://twitter.com/LindseyGrahamSC/status/605393927152103425.

Within three weeks of his inauguration, President Trump nominated Neil Gorsuch, also a Circuit Court of Appeals judge, and Republicans went to great lengths to claim that this Supreme Court nominee, unlike Garland, ought to be given hearings and a speedy confirmation. At that time, individual senators still retained the right to filibuster Supreme Court nominees but McConnell made it clear that he would consider lowering the threshold for cloture on these nominations to fifty-one just as Reid had done for cabinet and lower court nominations. Indeed, the Reid rules change had already come back to haunt Democrats in the Senate in 2017 when the Trump administration nominated a number of cabinet secretaries that could be confirmed with fifty-one votes rather than the traditional sixty votes necessary to shut down a filibuster.

Ultimately, Gorsuch was subsequently confirmed by the Senate on April 7, 2017, by a vote of 54–4; three Democratic senators from North Dakota, West Virginia, and Indiana crossed the aisle to vote for him and one Republican senator was absent due to illness. But the victory for Republicans came at procedural cost in terms of the erosion of the individual power of the filibuster. With Democrats intent on filibustering Gorsuch, and without the sixty votes needed to invoke cloture to shut down debate and proceed to a final vote, McConnell finished what Reid had started. He invoked the nuclear option and with the support of his fellow Republicans in the Senate eliminated the filibuster for Supreme Court nominations.

THE CONGRESS OVER TIME

Regardless of which party holds the House and Senate majorities on Capitol Hill, the postreform Congress has evolved from its constitutional roots and institution forms from previous eras. Individual legislators remain responsive to constituency interests even when they address national issues, such as health care, homeland security, and education. But the twenty-first-century Congress, in an era of delay and obstructionism, that responsiveness is often overwhelmed by partisanship. As we saw in the above discussion of the Gorsuch nomination, the lure of growing party power even overtook staunch supporters of individual rights in the Senate when time came to do away with the right to filibuster Supreme Court nominees. Doing so creates the potential for smoother nomination and confirmation processes in the Senate, but there are always unintended consequences to any rules change. The Democrats were on the winning end of that change in 2013, but four years later, the tables turned and they lost more of their power to effectively counter the majority party in the Senate.

Although the separation of powers continues to affect the bounds of Congressional action, and committees and party leaders remain central to congressional organization, Capitol Hill has witnessed great changes, both within the Congress and in its relations with its environment. In addition, the relative size and scope of the federal government is much larger than Henry Clay and John Calhoun would have dared to imagine it could be, which changes the nature of congressional lawmaking considerably. Clay and Calhoun may have faced the slavery question, the single most divisive issue in the American experience, but they did not have to parcel out a $4 trillion annual budget and respond to tens of thousands of special interests and lobbyists seeking to influence thousands of separate federal programs.

In many ways, the seeds of fragmentation and individualism on Capitol Hill are sown by interests from across the country (and beyond) whose lobbyists congregate in committee rooms and whose email messages and phone calls clog the communication lines of 535 legislators and their staffs. The explosion of participatory media outlets, such as Facebook and Twitter, has also expanded the set of voices that make their preferences known to Congress. The politics of Congress remains a politics of representation, ideologies, and interests, even as partisan electoral lines harden in individual constituencies and strong party leadership flourishes on Capitol Hill.

Recommended Readings

Mayhew, David R. *The Imprint of Congress*. New Haven: Yale University Press, 2017.

Draper, Robert. *When the Tea Party Came to Town: Inside the U.S. House of Representatives' Most Combative, Dysfunctional, and Infuriating Term in Modern History*. New York: Simon & Schuster, 2013.

Jenkins, Jeffrey A., and Charles Stewart, III. *Fighting for the Speakership: The House and the Rise of Party Government*. Princeton, NJ: Princeton University Press, 2012.

Lee, Frances E. *Beyond Ideology: Politics, Principles, and Partisanship in the U.S. Senate.* Chicago: University of Chicago Press, 2009.

Theriault, Sean. *Party Polarization in Congress.* New York: Cambridge University Press, 2008.

Useful Resources

United States House of Representatives: http://www.house.gov
United States Senate: http://www.senate.gov
Voteview: http://www.voteview.com

Notes

[1] Buckner F. Melton, Jr., ed., *The Quotable Founding Fathers: A Treasury of 2,500 Wise and Witty Quotations* (Washington, DC: Potomac, 2004), 34.

[2] "Remarks by the President in Address to the Nation on Immigration," White House Office of the Press Secretary, November 20, 2014.

[3] For an extended discussion, see Martin Diamond, Winston M. Fish, and Herbert Garfinkle, *The Democratic Republic* (Chicago: Rand McNally, 1966), 75ff.

[4] Ibid.

[5] See Louis Fisher, *The Politics of Shared Power,* 2nd ed. (Washington, DC: CQ Press, 1987), 4ff.

[6] On the Jackson episode, see Sen. Robert C. Byrd, "The Senate Censures Andrew Jackson," in his *The Senate, 1789–1989: Addresses on the History of the United States Senate* (Washington, DC: Government Printing Office, 1988), 127–41. Among many sources on Nixon and the White House tapes, see Louis Fisher, *Constitutional Conflicts between Congress and the President* (Princeton, NJ: Princeton University Press, 1985), 213ff.

[7] From James Madison, "Federalist 51," in *The Federalist Papers,* U.S. Constitution Online, http://www.constitution.org/fed/federa51.htm.

[8] For more on the way that elections were conducted in state legislatures and the impact of this change, see Wendy J. Schiller and Charles Stewart, III, *Electing the Senate: Indirect Democracy before the Seventeenth Amendment* (Princeton, NJ: Princeton University Press, 2015).

[9] See Elaine Swift, *The Making of an American Senate* (Ann Arbor: University of Michigan Press, 1997).

[10] George Galloway, *History of the House of Representatives* (New York: Thomas Crowell, 1961), 70. The Committee of the Whole House is the organizational format in which the House conducts almost all of its business. Rules are somewhat more permissive in this circumstance, and the legislative process is expedited. See Walter Oleszek, *Congressional Procedures and the Policy Process*, 8th ed. (Washington, DC: CQ Press, 2011), 180–82, 386.

[11] Joseph Cooper concludes that a standing committee system was established by the time of Jackson's presidency. See his *Origins of the Standing Committees and the Development of the Modern House* (Houston, TX: Rice University Press, 1970). Galloway, *History of the House*, puts the date at 1816, but he notes that "by 1825, with the appointment of their chairmen by the Speaker . . . so far as its organization was concerned the House of Representatives had assumed its present form" (99).

[12] The contribution of committees to both particularism and the beneficial sharing of expertise is explored at some length in chapter 7.

[13] The scholarship here is extensive. In relation to Congress, see, for example, James S. Young, *The Washington Community: 1800–1828* (New York: Columbia University Press, 1966); Allan G. Bogue and Mark Marlaire, "Of Mess and Men: The Boardinghouse and Congressional Voting, 1821–1842," *American Journal of Political Science* 19 (May 1975): 207–30; and John F. Hoadley, *Origins of American Political Parties* (Lexington: University of Kentucky Press, 1986).

[14] Alvin M. Josephy, Jr., *On the Hill* (New York: Touchstone, 1979), 79.

[15] Galloway, *History of the House*, 99.

[16] Ralph V. Harlow, *The History of Legislative Methods in the Period before 1825* (New Haven, CT: Yale University Press, 1917), 176–77.

[17] Ross K. Baker, *House and Senate*, 3rd ed. (New York: Norton, 2001), 37–39.

[18] Swift, *Making of an American Senate*, 140.

[19] From *Democracy in America*, quoted in *Origins and Development of Congress*, 2nd ed. (Washington, DC: Congressional Quarterly, 1982), 215.

[20] Byrd, *The Senate, 1789–1989*, 107.

[21] Jenkins and Stewart, *Fighting for the Speakership*.

[22] See Roger Davidson and Walter Oleszek, "Adaptation and Consolidation: Structured Innovation in the U.S. House of Representatives," *Legislature Studies Quarterly* 1 (1977): 37ff.

[23] Ibid., 23.

[24] Davidson and Oleszek note that the "disappearing quorum appears to have originated with [former President] John Quincy Adams, . . . who served with distinction in the House after leaving the White House." Adams refused to vote on a proslavery measure in 1832, and enough fellow members joined him so that a quorum was not present. The House could not conduct business absent a quorum (a majority of its members). "Armed with this precedent, obstructionist minorities for more than fifty years could bring the work of the House to a halt" (Roger Davidson and Walter Oleszek, *Congress against Itself* [Bloomington: University of Indiana Press, 1977], 23).

[25] Quoted in Samuel W. McCall, *The Life of Thomas Brackett Reed* (Boston: Houghton Mifflin, 1914), 170.

[26] Randall Strahan, "Thomas Brackett Reed and the Rise of Party Government," in *Masters of the House*, ed. Roger H. Davidson, Susan Webb Hammond, and Raymond W. Smock (Boulder, CO: Westview, 1998), 33–62; Randall Strahan, *Leading Representatives: The Agency of Leaders in the Politics of the U.S. House* (Baltimore: Johns Hopkins University Press, 2007).

[27] A compact summary of Cannon's actions can be found in Davidson and Oleszek, *Congress against Itself*, 25ff. See also Ronald Peters, *The American Speakership* (Washington, DC: CQ Press, 1990).

[28] James S. Fleming, "Oscar W. Underwood: The First Modern House Leader, 1911–1915," in Davidson, Hammond, and Smock, *Masters of the House*, 91–118.

[29] Joseph Cooper, "From Congressional to Presidential Preeminence: Power and Politics in Late Nineteenth-Century America and Today," in Lawrence C. Dodd and Bruce I. Oppenheimer, *Congress Reconsidered*, 8th ed. (Washington, DC: CQ Press, 2005), 363–93.

[30] David J. Rothman, *Politics and Power* (New York: Athenaeum, 1969), 4. Some of the arguments in the following paragraphs are drawn from Rothman's work.

[31] Over the years, Republicans have often called their caucus the Republican Conference. The term "caucus" is used here as a generic description of all the members of one party in one legislative chamber.

[32] Rothman, *Politics and Power*, 58–59.

[33] Ibid., 60.

[34] Congressional Quarterly's *Origins and Development of Congress*, 2nd ed., cites congressional scholar George Galloway on page 244.

[35] Sarah A. Binder and Steven S. Smith, *Politics or Principle?* (Washington, DC: Brookings Institution, 1997), 114–15.

[36] See Stephen Skowronek, *Building the New American State* (New York: Cambridge University Press, 1982).

[37] Roger Davidson and Walter Oleszek, *Congress and Its Members*, 3rd ed. (Washington, DC: CQ Press, 1990), 30.

[38] Steven S. Smith and Christopher J. Deering, *Committees in Congress*, 2nd ed. (Washington, DC: CQ Press, 1990), 34.

[39] Although many careful scholars had described and analyzed the Congress prior to the 1950s, never before was there such a systematic examination of the institution. The American Political Science Association's Study of Congress project sponsored much of the work by such scholars as Richard F. Fenno, Jr., Robert Peabody, John Manley, and Charles Jones.

40 Kenneth A. Shepsle, "The Changing Textbook Congress," in *Can the Government Govern?* ed. John E. Chubb and Paul E. Peterson (Washington, DC: Brookings Institution, 1989), 238–66.

41 Ibid., 239.

42 In the 1950s, with the exception of Rep. Leonore Sullivan (D-MO), chair of the Merchant Marine and Fisheries Committee, committee chairs were men, and Congress was a bastion of white, middle-aged (and older) men. On Johnson, among many others, see Ralph Huitt, "Democratic Party Leadership in the Senate," *American Political Science Review* 60 (1961): 331–44; on Rayburn, see D. B. Hardeman and Donald C. Bacon, *Ray-burn* (Lanham, MD: Madison, 1987).

43 James Sundquist's *Politics and Policy* (Washington, DC: Brookings Institution, 1968) provides an excellent guide to the obstructionism of the 1950s and the policy changes of the 1960s.

44 See, in particular, Jeff Fishel, *Party and Opposition* (New York: David McKay, 1973), 161ff.

45 Arthur G. Stevens, Jr., Arthur H. Miller, and Thomas E. Mann, "Mobilization of Liberal Strength in the House, 1955–1970: The Democratic Study Group," *American Political Science Review* 68 (1974): 667–81.

46 Rep. Richard Bolling (D-MO), quoted in Burdett A. Loomis, *The New American Politician* (New York: Basic Books, 1988), 131.

47 See Burdett Loomis, *The New American Politician* (New York: Basic Books, 1988), chap. 1.

48 Shepsle, "Changing Textbook Congress," 256.

49 A good collection of articles by leading scholars that captures the difficulties of the reform era can be found in Frank Mackaman, ed., *Understanding Congressional Leadership* (Washington, DC: CQ Press, 1981).

50 These issues will be considered at greater length later in this book (in chapter 4, especially). A minimal list of key sources includes David Rohde, *Parties and Leaders in the Postreform House* (Chicago: University of Chicago Press, 1991); Barbara Sinclair, *Leg, Leaders, and Lawmaking* (Baltimore: Johns Hopkins University Press, 1995); and Roger H. Davidson, ed., *The Postreform Congress* (New York: St. Martin's, 1992).

51 Fenno, "If, as Ralph Nader Says, Congress Is the 'Broken Branch,' " 287.

52 Sinclair, *Legislators, Leaders, and Lawmaking*, 301. See also Sinclair, "Tip O'Neill and Contemporary House Leadership," in *Masters of the House*, ed. Davidson, Hammond, and Smock, 289–318.

53 See Barbara Sinclair, *The Transformation of the U.S. Senate* (Baltimore: Johns Hopkins University Press, 1989).

54 Why this is so requires some detailed untangling; see chapters 7 and 8.

55 Matthew Glassman and Amber Wilhelm, "Congressional Careers: Service Tenure and Patterns of Member Service: 1789–2015," *Congressional Research Service*, January 3, 2015. https://www.fas.org/sgp/crs/misc/R41545.pdf.

56 C. Lawrence Evans, "Committees, Leaders, and Message Politics," in *Congress Reconsidered*, 7th ed., ed. Lawrence C. Dodd and Bruce Oppenheimer (Washington, DC: CQ Press, 2001); also see Patrick Sellers, "Strategy and Background in Congressional Campaigns," *American Political Science Review* 92 (1998): 159–71; Patrick Sellers, *Cycles of Spin: Strategic Communication in the U.S. Congress* (New York: Cambridge University Press, 2009); Humberto Sanchez, "2012 Vote Studies: Party Unity," *CQ Weekly*, January 21, 2013, 132; Staff, "Party Unity Background," *CQ Annual Report*, January 21, 2013, 137.

57 Sean Theriault, *Party Polarization in Congress* (New York: Cambridge University Press, 2008); Frances E. Lee, *Beyond Ideology: Politics, Principles, and Partisanship in the U.S. Senate* (Chicago: University of Chicago Press, 2009).

58 Charles Babington, "GOP Moderates Wary of Filibuster Curb," *Washington Post*, January 16, 2005, A5.

CHAPTER 3

The Changing Environment of Congressional Politics

Reflecting a timeless preoccupation for all legislators, this cartoon depicts a congressman racing home to explain his legislative record to his constituents.

June 22, 2009. Setauket, NY

Representative Tom Bishop (D-NY) headed for a town hall meeting in his eastern Long Island congressional district. He knew that President Obama's proposed health care legislation was certain to stir controversy, but he was unprepared for the rancor that he encountered. The meeting hall was packed with angry opponents of President Obama's proposed health care reforms as well as his positions on energy policy and his support of bailout legislation. Bishop has held more than one hundred such meetings, but this one was different, to the point that he required police help in leaving the venue. He noted, "I have no problem with someone disagreeing with positions I hold. But I also believe no one is served if you can't talk through differences." Representative Bishop's experience was mirrored in dozens of other Democratic seats in 2009 and 2010, as legislators confronted Tea Party activists who energetically protested Obama's policies.

February 22, 2017. Branchburg, NJ

Representative Leonard Lance (R-NJ) thought he knew what he was getting into, as he addressed a "passionate anti-Trump crowd" of more than one thousand constituents at an overflowing town hall meeting. He sought to diffuse the audience's hostility by stating that he simply wanted to reform the Affordable Care Act (ACA), not repeal it; likewise, he expressed his suspicion of Russia and Vladimir Putin. In the end, however, he could not overcome the crowd's hostility toward President Trump. Lance excused Trump's "misstatements," but the crowd would have none of it, labeling them "lies, lies, lies" and later chanting, "Push back! Push back! Push back! Push back!" While the local police did keep a close watch, they did not have to extract the congressman from the meeting. Unlike his New Jersey GOP colleagues, not only did Rep. Lance hold this meeting, but he also scheduled another one for the next week, certain that he would face another contentious crowd.

Historically, such meetings have rarely produced confrontation. Rather, legislators seek out audiences to present themselves, discuss issues, and discover what is on their constituents' minds. Indeed, Members of Congress are highly accessible—to constituents, journalists, and lobbyists, among others.

CONGRESS: THE PERMEABLE BRANCH

Many of the *centrifugal* forces affecting Congress originate outside the institution. As a representative body, Congress was designed to offer easy access to those interests and individuals who sought influence over policy. To a greater or lesser extent, it has always fulfilled this goal. Until the mid-twentieth century, save in extraordinary circumstances (war, the Great Depression), Congress met for about half the year. From July through January, members would remain at home, living among their constituents. With the New Deal, World War II, and the growth of government, to say nothing of the widespread installation of air-conditioning in Washington, congressional sessions have come to run virtually year-round. At the same time, air travel has afforded almost all members the opportunity to live in their districts and join the "Tuesday through Thursday" club of those who spend three days a week in Washington. Although many recently elected legislators have made this choice, the sight of California lawmakers stumbling into committee hearings after returning on the Tuesday-morning red-eye flight scarcely offers the promise of serious legislating. In addition, large increases in staff allotments, the growth of district offices, and advances in communication mean that almost all members know a great deal about their districts, regardless of whether they live in Washington or back in their home states. For all the talk of legislators being out of touch with their constituents, a strong case exists that they know altogether too much about the preferences of their most vocal and visible local district interests, as Representatives Bishop and Lane discovered in 2009 and 2017, respectively.

In Washington, members of Congress can almost always carve out a few minutes from their busy schedules to chat with visitors from their districts. Moreover, responding to constituent communications (increasingly electronic) receives priority attention from legislative offices. After all, it is the home folks who have sent the representatives to Capitol Hill, but access to Congress is scarcely limited to members' constituents. Traditionally, interest groups have found lawmakers hospitable to their requests for time and attention.

The ease of obtaining a legislative audience contrasts markedly with the lengthy process of winning a hearing in the Supreme Court or the difficulty of gaining an audience with top-level executive-branch officials, to say nothing of the president. In recent years, for example, the Supreme Court has agreed to hear only about eighty cases from the more than ten thousand appeals filed every year. Likewise, the office of the president and the top rungs of the bureaucracy are highly insulated from most citizens, electronic mail and town hall–style meetings notwithstanding. This trend has, if anything, escalated in the wake of the September 11, 2001, terrorist attacks and their aftermath. In contrast, despite enhanced security measures, the Congress remains hospitable to receiving complaints and requests from citizens and organized interests.[1]

Over the years, as the national government has grown larger and made increasingly important decisions, the demands on Congress have risen in number and intensity. Even before the policy explosions of the New Deal and the Great Society, there were many instances of intense, sophisticated, and frequently successful lobbying efforts by organized interests. As far back as 1870, organized interests, such as the National Association of Wool Manufacturers, had a regular and powerful presence in Washington. As industries expanded and flourished over time, interests swarmed around Congress, often exerting both legitimate and illegitimate influence over individual legislators. For example, in the years following World War I, the farm lobby, led by the American Farm Bureau Federation (AFBF), demonstrated its worth—in terms of information and support—for dozens of legislators, who repaid the agriculture interests with increasing access to the process of lawmaking.[2] More subtle than most interests, the farm lobby often worked through farmers back in the legislators' home districts, and the political and policy information that they provided gave members of Congress good reason to listen to these organizations. Legislators have always faced great uncertainties in understanding both the policy and political effects of their actions; well-informed groups such as the AFBF could offer information that would make members a bit less uncertain, especially in terms of their constituents' opinions and the positions of the farm community. Providing regular access to the Farm Bureau thus benefited both the lawmakers and the interest group.

The "textbook Congress" that emerged by the 1950s offered committees as venues for interests in search of access. Many committees served as one corner of close-knit triangular relationships, variously labeled "cozy" or "iron" triangles, that linked them to key outside interests and, as the third corner, to particular agencies within the federal bureaucracy.[3] For example, sugar interests worked with the appropriate Agriculture Committee subcommittees in the House and Senate and the relevant U.S. Department of Agriculture officials to maintain domestic sugar prices that were consistently several times higher than those in world markets. By the 1960s, various interests began to challenge the tidy, profitable sugar subsystem. Consumer and environmental groups, among others, began to influence agriculture policies. In 1974, the sugar triangle broke apart, as the subcommittee could not maintain control over the price-support policies.[4] Subsequently, however, sugar interests succeeded in lobbying a broad mix of legislators to reconstruct a similar marketing system that continues to fix U.S. prices at a considerably higher level than elsewhere in the world.

More generally, while the Congress changed greatly from 1960 into the 1980s, so, too, did its environment. In parallel, related developments, more interest groups became politically active as more governmental policies prompted them to action.[5] Environmental groups, for example, possessed almost no political clout in the 1950s; in fact, there were very few such organizations, which limited their efforts to promoting land conservation, largely in low-key ways. By 1970, both traditional and newly formed environmental organizations had become major players in policymaking on issues that ranged from pesticide levels to air quality standards to toxic waste disposal. In short, there were many "new kids on the block" in the interest group community, and they were more vocal, more public, and far more assertive than the old guard. Policies that benefited one industry over another were no longer simply accepted, but readily challenged. In reaction, business interests, which had historically held structural advantages in Washington politics, increased their activity through lobbying within this more competitive environment.[6]

Not only did interest groups serve as effective advocates for existing programs, but with the growth of the country and new federal programs, new agencies and even whole new departments, such as Energy and Education, were established, each creating its own array of programs and related interest groups. As the federal budget rose from $100 billion in 1969 to about $4 trillion in 2017, large numbers of interests have become entrenched within government and outside it. Legislative consideration of issues thus has proceeded within a complicated, dense environment of complex policies and myriad organized interests.[7]

Equally important, in the 1960s, presidents John F. Kennedy, Lyndon Johnson, and Richard Nixon could promise new programs for particular constituencies, such as the poor and the elderly, which would largely distribute new benefits.[8] Indeed, the impulse to distribute benefits to specific constituents and interests has historically operated as a key centrifugal force within the Congress.[9] Lawmakers seek to deliver concentrated benefits (such as a dam or farm support payments) that are supported by widely dispersed costs (a cent or two from every tax dollar). But as both federal programs and budget deficits have grown, distributive politics has proved an increasingly difficult game to play.

The first truly sizable budget deficits not related to wars developed in the early 1980s because of major tax cuts and vastly increased defense spending. Congress tried several different mechanisms to cut the budget, but the forces of constituency politics overwhelmed their efforts; almost every member of Congress wanted to reduce spending, but no legislator wanted to cut funds directed at her district or state. The inability of Congress to rein in spending in the 1980s and early 1990s did little to increase its standing within the public, largely because individual legislators continued to funnel benefits to their constituencies and their favored interests. It was not until President George H. W. Bush raised taxes and President Clinton did likewise (see chapter 1, re Rep. Margolies-Mezvinsky) that deficits were brought under control in the late 1990s. Since the 1990s, budget rules have generally decreed that for every policy winner, there must be a policy loser; in various forms, this practice is labeled PAYGO.[10] In times of large budget deficits, new programs have to compete against established policies. Moreover, so-called entitlement programs, such as Medicaid or crop support payments, often require more funds, and the expenditures must increase the deficit or come from some other program. The restrictions on spending that Congress has put in place for itself pose difficulties in responding to new priorities, such as increased defense allocations, even when there is a federal budget surplus. The post-9/11 expansion of costs for homeland security and national defense demonstrates one way to increase spending. Few senators or representatives wanted to be seen as unsupportive of measures designed to enhance our security. Indeed, the budget surpluses of 1999–2001 quickly disappeared by 2002–2005, as the effects of the Bush tax cut interacted with the costs of fighting terrorism at home and abroad; this was followed by the dramatic slowdown in the economy starting in late 2008 and the mounting costs of Iraqi and Afghan wars. In recent years, the Republican Congress and the Obama administration clashed repeatedly on spending levels, the national debt, and priorities, which led to sequestration policies that produced wholesale cuts in both domestic and military spending, while not touching entitlements like Social Security and Medicare.

This chapter explores four major changes in the congressional environment: the advocacy explosion, as the number and specialization of interests have grown steadily since the 1960s; the impact of sixty years of an activist federal government and greatly expanded policy programs; the overwhelming attention given to budgetary considerations since the early 1980s—the so-called *fiscalization* of policymaking; and the lack of respect for Congress, whose approval ratings have sunk to all-time lows in recent years. The growing numbers of interests and policies have exerted significant decentralizing pressures on the Congress, whereas the fiscalization of policy has operated to centralize congressional actions as budgetary concerns dominate decision making. Finally, the low public standing of Congress may make it all the more difficult for its members to address divisive, and potentially unpopular, policies.

Related to these developments, several other external changes also have occurred, which range from the gradual weakening (and then substantial strengthening) of political parties to the growing political sophistication of business interests to major transformations in the media and in information technology. In short, the Congress of the 1950s did its work in a very different context than does the Congress of the twenty-first century. Overall, the contemporary Congress has grown both highly responsive to particular interests yet remarkably insular within the highly competitive, highly partisan environment of Washington policymaking and politics.

The Advocacy Explosion

Although organized interests have a long and storied history of making their case on Capitol Hill, and many contemporary lobbying techniques have their origins near the turn of the twentieth century, current patterns of legislative advocacy derive from the growth of interest groups since the 1960s. In the early 1960s, political scientists, if not journalists, often discounted the impact of interest groups on most policymaking. Lobbyists plied their trade, of course, but many interests lacked the resources and sophistication to wield much influence.[11] Between 1960 and 1990, the number of active organized interests and their use of a wide range of techniques for influencing policymakers rose sharply. Simply put, more lobbyists have been working for more interests and have been employing more tactics to affect policy outcomes. Although much popular attention has been directed toward the tremendous post-1974 growth of political action committees (PACs), from 608 in 1974 to 4,009 in 1984, with the number fluctuating a bit above 4,000 since then, House candidates only receive about a third of their funding from PACs, compared with 15 percent for Senate candidates.[12] At the same time, PACs have spent rapidly increasing amounts of money directly on behalf of congressional candidates, to the point that for every dollar contributed to campaigns, three more are spent directly on the campaigns' behalf.[13] More generally, organized interests have expanded their actions across the board. Although the number of registered lobbyists in DC stands at about twelve thousand circa 2017, the actual number of lobbyists and those within the influence industry is much larger, perhaps totaling as many as 100,000.[14] Moreover, the amounts of money spent on lobbying have soared over the past two decades. Although official reports place annual lobbying spending at about $3.2 billion, academic experts such as Lee Drutman and James Thurber argue that it may well total $6.7 to $9 billion annually, far surpassing electoral expenditures.[15]

The advocacy explosion has not affected all sectors of the Washington community with equal force. Most notable, perhaps, have been the declining role of labor unions, the growing presence of corporate and professional interests, and the increasing importance of large-scale citizens' groups, ranging from Common Cause to the Sierra Club to AARP (formerly the American Association of Retired Persons) with its 37 million members.[16] Many of these membership groups have become less tied to dues collected from their members, as patrons, such as the Koch brothers with Americans for Prosperity, have underwritten many organizations.[17] States, cities, and other governmental units came to Washington in droves during the 1970s era of revenue sharing, stayed to press their cases during the leaner years of the Reagan administration, and have remained to lobby against unfunded federal mandates.[18] In addition, foreign governments and private interests, often acting through sophisticated Washington lobbying and public relations firms, have become important players in the complex politics of trade, foreign aid, and international business.[19]

Equally important have been the many strategies and tactics that organized interests have employed in their efforts to gain advantage. By the end of the 1980s, a majority of Washington-based organizations reported using more than twenty different techniques for exercising influence—these ranged from testifying at legislative hearings to joining coalitions to mounting grassroots lobbying efforts.[20] For example, two-thirds of the organizations noted that they paid increased attention to press relations, worked harder at building coalitions, and spent more time contacting government officials.[21] In the Internet and digital age, these groups have expanded the methods they use to wage their battles, and they have worked hard to maintain their relevance as sources of information to both their own members and Congress. Over the past twenty years, organized interest groups have found ways to use the Internet for building support, identifying contributors, organizing grassroots operations, and constructing issue-specific coalitions.[22] With the intensive use of social media, the distinction between DC lobbying and grassroots lobbying has shrunk, as individuals across the country can have real-time conversations with members of Congress and their staffs.[23]

In the end, the advocacy explosion encompasses at least three distinct elements. First, there are more groups and interests in the fray. Second, many new techniques, often quite inexpensive, are available to all interests. Third, both well-established groups and new entrants are employing this more extensive range of techniques to influence policy decisions. As a result, more messages from more interests are aimed at legislators at faster speeds than ever before. Whether they hear those messages remains an open question.

Lobbying: Information, Access, and Influence

Members of Congress employ thousands of staffers in their personal offices and through committees, and they can call on major support agencies, such as the Congressional Research Service and the General Accounting Office, to provide them with legislative assistance. Even so, lawmakers have trouble staying informed on a wide range of policies. There is a great deal to know, and time pressures can be intense. This does not mean that information is in short supply. Quite the contrary. Capitol Hill is awash in information: from congressional staff (see chapter 8), think tanks, the media, and, of course, organized interests and lobbyists. But truly useful information can be difficult to come by. Legislators operate under highly uncertain conditions much of the time, and they must frequently act with less than perfect information on a given subject.

Useful information comes in three general types: (1) political intelligence that lays out the reelection consequences of members' actions; (2) process-oriented

SPOTLIGHT

Senator Jim DeMint: DC Right-Wing Insider

Although many Members of Congress pass through the so-called revolving door between Capitol Hill and the Washington world of advocacy, most move into lobbying firms (former Democratic leader Tom Daschle) or win lucrative positions at trade associations (former House member Billy Tauzin). South Carolina Republican Jim DeMint, who served in the House (1999–2005) and the Senate (2005–2012), took a different path. A far-right iconoclast, DeMint spent his time in the Senate using his individual power to push his conservative agenda even when it clashed with his fellow Republicans, who also had conservative leanings but recognized when compromise was necessary to pass legislation.

As a result, DeMint never felt completely at home in the Congress, especially in the small and still-clubby Senate or what he viewed to be the establishment wing of the GOP. For example, Senator DeMint often publicly opposed Senate leaders and President George W. Bush, consistently arguing for conservative social policies, including opposition to abortion and, most notably, a complete rejection of same-sex marriage. He also worked tirelessly in supporting and fund-raising for conservative candidates, some of whom challenged GOP incumbents.

As something of an outcast on Capitol Hill, with little wealth, DeMint decided in December 2012 to leave the Senate and become the President of the Heritage Foundation, the powerful right-wing DC think tank. By 2015, he earned $1.1 million, or six times his congressional salary. DeMint escalated Heritage's move from a policy operation, albeit a politicized one, to an advocacy organization.

Under DeMint, the Heritage Foundation became overtly political and he directed its policy analysts to put forward policies that supported his political views, rather than the other way around which would be to suggest policies and build political support for them afterwards. DeMint also wanted to coordinate more heavily with the Heritage Foundation's political PAC and a number of staff members resisted that push. One Heritage staff member was quoted as saying, "DeMint changed how it functioned. It's not expert-heavy anymore. His vision was different [from its previous policy focus]." The shift from policy to politics—which had become highly contentious within the foundation—led to DeMint's ouster in May 2017, as the Heritage board sought to return to a more policy-oriented approach as its mission.

The information in this section is taken from multiple sources as follows: Elania Johnson and Nancy Cook, "The Real Reason Jim DeMint Got the Boot." *Politico*, May 2, 2017. http://www.politico.com/story/2017/05/02/why-jim-demint-was-ousted-from-heritage-237876 (accessed May 4, 2017).

details that allow for assessing the chances that a bill will make it through the legislative process; and (3) policy data and analyses that spell out the impact of a proposal.[24] As one insider account puts it:

> Lobbyists see it as their job to persuade legislators that voters are on the lobbyists' side. . . . [They] know that the best way to guarantee that their point of view will be heard is to take the constituents with them when they go to speak to members of Congress. Lobbyists also function as unpaid staff to the decision-makers . . . [and] provide information about both policy and process that [legislators] cannot get.[25]

Thus, from an informational perspective, lobbyists are providing a kind of subsidy to lawmakers. The lingering question remains: What do they expect from such subsidies?[26]

Although lobbyists are important sources of information, they must first gather bits and pieces of relevant data that will be of use to legislators, and then, they must have access to those they desire to influence. Thus, much of lobbying resides in accumulating useful (i.e., not widely known) information and finding ways to get the material to relevant legislators.[27] Lobbyists gain access in various ways, including socializing (subject to some restrictions in the wake of 1995 and 2007 reforms),[28] making campaign contributions, and developing reputations for providing accurate and useful information.

Since the 1990s, one steady growth of access-based lobbying has come from the growing numbers of former legislators and congressional staff members who have moved from Capitol Hill to "K Street," the literal and symbolic locus of much DC lobbying. LaPira and Thomas conclude that these migrants offer both expertise and access to their new employers, with their singular connections providing much of their value to their new, private-sector employers.[29]

Once access has been obtained, however, two questions remain: Whom does one seek to lobby? And under what conditions does access allow for influence? Despite the intriguing first steps of some congressional scholars, there is no clear answer concerning who becomes the target of lobbying.[30] Although hard-boiled foes are rarely sought out, both allies and the undecided (and even non-dogmatic opponents) are frequently the objects of attention. As for influence, lobbying most often succeeds when it focuses on low-profile issues and legislation, as opposed to matters that stir the public's interest. It is no accident that highly complex issues, such as telecommunications reform and tax law, generate tremendous amounts of lobbying. The complexities of both policies and procedures offer great opportunities for advocates to turn access into influence as they shape arguments that favor their causes, often on an obscure procedural point or some dense wording buried deep inside a comprehensive piece of legislation.[31]

Complex Lobbying in a Partisan Age: International Trade, 1993–2017

Even in a congressional era defined by intense partisanship, organized interests can and do affect decisions on Capitol Hill. The continuing struggles over U.S. trade policy illustrate how the interest group environment can shape congressional actions. In the early 1990s, the Congress was faced with implementing the North American Free Trade Agreement (NAFTA) and ratifying the General Agreement on Tariffs and Trade (GATT). More than twenty years later, the Congress is embroiled in a new round of trade decisions, addressing a host of issues, ranging from the scuttling of President Obama's proposed Trans-Pacific Partnership (TPP) to reforming the NAFTA agreement to general addressing the terms of trade between the United States and the world under the Trump Administration.

Trade initiatives in different eras have enjoyed the strong support of presidents Reagan, Bush (41), Clinton, and Obama, respectively, although the Trump Presidency has moved away from the previous consensus. The Congress represents the logical venue for opponents to mount their attacks, which emphasized the loss of American jobs (with NAFTA/TPP) and national sovereignty (with GATT/TPP), in that international tribunals could rule against some practices of U.S. businesses.

In the Clinton era, opponents of NAFTA included an unlikely coalition of organized labor, including textile and apparel workers, consumer advocates (particularly Ralph Nader), some environmental groups, and, perhaps most importantly, the 1992 Reform Party presidential candidate Ross Perot. Nader, the environmentalists, and Perot combined to produce an effective outside attack on the trade accord; they could direct their own supporters to lobby hundreds of members of Congress, while they simultaneously advertised extensively against the pact. Only late in the day did NAFTA backers, many prompted by President Clinton, counter these public arguments.

NAFTA opponents did not have to rely solely on sophisticated grassroots lobbying techniques, clever public relations, and considerable paid advertising to gain ground in the House; they enjoyed the support of key Democratic legislators near the core of the party leadership. House Democratic whip David Bonior (D-MI) proved inexhaustible in his coordination of opposing forces within the House. Less public, to reduce the embarrassment for his own party's president, was the firm opposition of House Majority Leader Richard Gephardt (D-MO). As a highly representative body (both Bonior's and Gephardt's districts included large numbers of union members), the House encourages interests to seek out powerful champions to provide inside leadership on key issues.[32] NAFTA foes could scarcely have done better than to enlist two of the three top leaders in the House. Only after the Clinton White House made some last-minute pleas, accepted a few modest concessions, and issued several specific policy clarifications did NAFTA win House approval.

Many of the same interests came together to oppose GATT's approval in late 1994. Obscured by the debate over health-care reform, GATT provides a different illustration of the ways in which organized groups and the Congress can serve each other's needs. Although some business interests opposed NAFTA, virtually all major corporate bodies expressed strong support for the lower tariffs promised by GATT.[33] GATT induced less public opposition than did NAFTA. Nonetheless, congressional consideration of the treaty offered an attractive opportunity for foes of the trade pact. In the Senate, which usually supported free trade, opponents had a champion in Senator Ernest Hollings (D-SC), whose state's textile industry desired protection from the competition of cheap foreign labor. Using his individual power as a senator, Hollings succeeded in holding up a vote on GATT for forty-five days—from early October until after the 1994 congressional elections. Opponents hoped that this delay would allow them to mount a vigorous and public challenge to GATT. Helped by generally supportive Republican leaders, the Clinton administration won approval for the treaty, but only after vigorous debate. Given its institutional design, which ordinarily discourages speedy or efficient decision making, Congress offered organized interests, with their increased numbers and capacities to mobilize key constituents, an inviting opportunity to take advantage of the very openness that defines the institution.[34]

In 1998, the protectionist coalition forces prevailed when the House decisively defeated (243–180) a bill that would have granted President Clinton the same "fast-track" authority enjoyed by every president since Gerald Ford.[35] Such authority is crucial to passing a trade bill through the Congress in that it allows a single up or down vote on the legislation. By denying Clinton fast-track power, the House essentially killed trade legislation by opening it up to dozens, even hundreds, of interest-group provisions. Members of the House and Senate were reacting to the negative effects of NAFTA and GATT on local industries in their districts and states, and some members who had previously supported free trade changed their votes.[36]

In 2000, Bill Clinton waged a rugged battle against the same set of forces to extend "permanent normalized trading relations" with China, and, in 2002, George W. Bush narrowly regained the right to negotiate on a fast-track basis, overcoming the opposition of labor unions and environmentalists to win a House vote, 215–212. To obtain this bargaining authority and the guarantee of an up or down vote on the package, Bush agreed to a Senate compromise put forward by then Majority Leader Tom Daschle (D-SD), which expanded by $12 billion the Trade Adjustment Assistance Program, which provides both direct payments and training for workers whose jobs are lost because of enhanced trade. In short, even when opponents lose sequential battles against free trade, they can win significant concessions.

Although the Obama administration supported the TPP, other priorities kept it from pressing for the pact's passage, to say nothing of the opposition of many Democrats in the House and Senate. With Republicans controlling both chambers as of 2015, TPP supporters inside the Congress and out, including President Obama, saw a chance to move the legislation forward. In the end, President Obama did not win congressional approval for fast-track authority to get the TPP enacted quickly, given the opposition he faced both from some Republicans and from members of his own party.[37] Since the debates over NAFTA, trade policies have been fought *across* party lines, with presidents building eclectic bipartisan congressional coalitions, aided by organized interests who have much to gain by the passage of new trade rules.

Donald Trump as president opens this formula up to questions, if not substantial revision. In the end, as presidents have discovered, the Congress has the power to circumscribe and delay trade policy, or even kill it. President Trump, despite ending U.S. participation in the TPP, has moved slowly to renegotiate NAFTA and to possibly reset American trade policy with the rest of the world.[38] As with many complex issues, such as health care and immigration, Members of Congress must respond to diverse, well-represented (by lobbyists) interests who will seek to protect the status quo of policies—policies that will often benefit their constituents.

The Policy Explosion

In 1930, the reach of the federal government did not extend very far in terms of expenditures, taxation, or regulation. Congressional committee chairs may have been gaining independent power at this time, but they had very little to control. Political analyst Michael Barone writes that "macroeconomic fiscal policy, redistribution of wealth, and government spending programs were not major issues [because] the federal government neither raised nor spent . . . much money in the late 1920s."[39] Most federal spending went to pay for the military, either in the form of current expenses, interest on the national debt incurred by borrowing to pay for past wars, or veterans' benefits. Of the $3.3 billion budget for 1930, less than $1 billion went to fund all other governmental activities.[40]

Even after the increased spending commitments of the New Deal, domestic expenditures stood at just $7.8 billion in 1940 and $12.6 billion in 1946, the first post–World War II year. As late as 1954, domestic spending amounted to only $21.6 billion, a figure that almost doubled by 1960, the last year of the Eisenhower administration. Defense costs averaged $47 billion between 1952 and 1960; when John F. Kennedy was elected in 1960, total annual federal spending totaled $92 billion—a substantial increase since 1930, to be sure, but a figure that provided little in the way of ambitious social programs.

The pent-up demand for more federal domestic intervention, such as Medicare, and more regulation, like the Environmental Protection Agency, along with continued requirements for high levels of Cold War defense spending (including Vietnam), produced great increases in both domestic and military spending during the 1960s (see table 3.1).[41] Still, the major story told in table 3.1 is that of the great escalation in governmental expenditures during the 1970s and 1980s, when Republicans controlled the presidency for all but Jimmy Carter's 1977–1981 term.

No single explanation adequately accounts for burgeoning federal budgets, but the very existence of new programs in the 1960s and 1970s helped to create great pressures, both inside and outside the government, to increase spending levels. For example, the 1965 adoption of Medicare, the federal health insurance program for people 65 and over, produced a continuing rise in federal health-related costs over the next decade—from $9.9 billion in 1965 to $41.5 billion in 1975. More important than the mere cost, however, was the fundamental redefinition of health care as an issue in U.S. politics. As one scholar notes, "By nationalizing a large portion of the bill, Medicare made health care inflation a public-sector problem and placed it on the policy agenda."[42] Indeed, health-care costs—most notably Medicare, Medicaid (for low-income recipients), and veterans' care—have risen steadily since the 1960s, as have overall

Table 3.1 Federal Spending, 1940–2020

Year	National Defense ($)	Nondefense ($)	Total, Including Interest on Debt ($)
1940	1.66	7.81	9.47
1950	13.15	29.41	42.56
1960	48.13	44.06	92.19
1970	81.69	113.96	195.65
1980	134.0	456.94	590.94
1990	299.32	953.67	1,252.99
2000	294.36	1,494.59	1,788.95
2010	683.59	2,772.62	3,456.21
2015	589.56	3,098.73	3,688.29
2020 (est.)	605.95	4,273.87	4,879.82

Source: *The Budget for Fiscal Year 2017: Historical Tables*, https://www.gpo.gov/fdsys/pkg/BUDGET-2017-TAB/pdf/BUDGET-2017-TAB.pdf.

Note: In billions of dollars, not adjusted for inflation.

medical expenses, which have also received substantial congressional attention. In 2003, Congress passed a major expansion of the Medicare program, the Medicare Prescription Drug and Modernization Act, to offer prescription drug benefit coverage to retirees. Ironically, it won approval from a Republican party that has repeatedly called for the reduction in the size of the federal government. In 2014, the Medicare budget stood at $522 billion, and as a single federal program, it now has a budget more than ten times the total costs for all federal health care programs that existed in 1975.

The most intense and long-lasting battle over the growing reach of federal policy came with the ACA, proposed by President Obama and passed by a Democratic-controlled Congress in 2010.[43] The ACA expanded coverage to millions of Americans and sought to reduce health-care costs in a host of ways. Despite attempts to bring some Republicans into the legislative coalition, especially by the then Senate Finance Committee chair Max Baucus (D-MT), the ACA won approval with just Democratic votes.

Indeed, congressional Republicans never accepted the existence of the ACA, even seven years after its passage and with more than 20 million Americans added to the rolls of the insured. Between 2011 and 2016, the Republican-controlled House voted to repeal or alter Obamacare at least sixty times, even though there was no chance that any such legislation could survive a presidential veto.[44] With unified Republican control of the executive and legislative branches, in 2017, the Congress sought to unwind the ACA but failed, given its inability to produce a clearly acceptable, politically palatable alternative.

Along with any new policy commitment come new regulatory responsibilities. With the growth of new federal policies in such areas as health, education, and nutrition (in the form of food stamps), the reach of federal regulatory programs has been at least as extensive. Indeed, much of the ACA was fleshed out not by the Congress, but by the Department of Health and Human Services, which legislators tasked with writing many of the specific rules and regulations. As shown in table 3.2, from 1940 to 1980, the length of one year's body of regulations, printed in the *Federal Register*, grew almost twentyfold; the Reagan administration cut back substantially on regulations but still managed to average fifty-four thousand pages of *Federal Register* material per year. More importantly, most regulations stayed on the books, thus producing an overwhelmingly dense policy environment by the 1980s. Nor has the *Register*'s publication rate slowed down in the post-Reagan era (see table 3.2). As with the repeal of the ACA, the Trump Administration, in concert with the GOP-controlled Congress, appears dedicated to rolling back substantial numbers of regulations. Still, it is unlikely that the Congress will legislate in such detailed ways, as with health care reform, that new regulations will not be essential, based either on politics (vagueness allows for interpretation by the bureaucracy) or technical reasons.

By the 1970s, Theodore Lowi described a national government that had fundamentally changed the nature of American political life. He saw the results as a "two-part model" of highly institutionalized politics, in which:

- "The national government by some formal action monopolizes a given area of private activity." This may be accomplished through spending, regulation, or other means.
- "Following that, a program is authorized and an administrative agency is put into operation to work without legal guidelines through an elaborate, sponsored bargaining process [between governmental agencies and specific interests]."[45]

Table 3.2 The Growth of Federal Regulation

Year	Number of Pages in the Federal Register
1940	5,307
1950	9,562
1960	14,479
1970	20,032
1980	87,012
1990	53,618
2000	83,293
2010	81,405
2015	80,035

Source: Law Librarians' Society of Washington, DC, http://www.llsdc.org/assets/sourcebook/fed-reg-pages.pdf.

In the end, tens of thousands of governmental units and interests have large stakes in countless discretionary decisions made within the bureaucracy, inside the presidency, by the judiciary, and on Capitol Hill. Lowi argued that there is virtually no accountability for most decisions—instead of clear policy and well-defined procedure, there is only process.[46]

This "process" has become the heart and soul of relations between organized interests, the bureaucracy, and the Congress. Robert Salisbury observes that much activity by groups and other interests emphasizes the monitoring of information sources: "Washington is, after all, the main source of what governmental officials are doing or planning to do. To get that information in a timely way, a continuous and alert presence . . . is vital."[47] Moreover, it is accurate information on political contingencies, not on policy alternatives, that is often most at a premium. Given its size and diversity, the Congress is ideally suited to provide such knowledge. Individual members and their staffs are well positioned to convey valuable political information to particular interests; in turn, these interests will have good reason to support their reelection bids. Through the 1980s, ideology played little role in the game. Rather, majority House Democrats became the vehicles for many business interests that wanted to "invest" in careerist legislators who would, it seemed, control the Congress, and especially the House, for the foreseeable future.[48] Of course, once Republicans won a majority of the House seats in 1994, such an arrangement lost much of its luster for many corporate and professional interests, whose support for the GOP increased dramatically.

In fact, the entire lobbying environment changed markedly during the post-1994 GOP era, and especially with the George W. Bush and Obama presidencies, along with the creation of the Department of Homeland Security. To be sure, the Lowi–Salisbury version of Washington awash with lobbyists and overrun with process has not changed fundamentally, but it has been overlaid with the increased partisanship of this congressional era. Not only do some lobbyists increasingly identify with one party or the other, but they also participate actively in raising immense sums for the respective parties and their candidates.[49] This has continued in the Trump administration, as a new wave of well-connected lobbyists has joined the ranks of Washington veterans.[50]

The Budget: Defining Policy Choices across the Board

The growth of organized interests and the extended reach of national policies are developments that have reinforced each other. For the most part, both trends reflect an increased fragmentation of the decision-making context. Historically, the way the Congress appropriated funds also contributed to this decentralization. After the president proposed a unified budget, the House and Senate would break up the spending proposals into thirteen separate pieces, each initially considered by one House appropriations subcommittee. Only at the end of the legislative process, with the passage of thirteen distinct bills, would the Congress and the president know the actual levels of appropriations. This decentralized format worked reasonably well into the 1960s,[51] but by the early 1970s, pressures began to mount for a more coherent congressional approach to the entire budget.

Legislators began to face major budgetary problems as a result of enacting numerous policies and having many groups capable of competing to influence them—policies cost money (obtained from taxes) in addition to conferring benefits. During the 1950s and 1960s, the appropriations committees could maintain a check on overall spending by the Congress, but by the early 1970s, this informal constraint had weakened substantially.[52] In the 1970s, the Congress provided itself with the staff and committee structure to increase its role in constructing annual budgets, which had been almost totally the province of the president and the well-staffed Office of Management and Budget (OMB).[53] After 1974, when the Budget Reform Act established Senate and House budget committees and the Congressional Budget Office, members of Congress could fight their "budget wars" with the executive branch on roughly equal footing.[54] Over the 1980s, a centralizing change, implicit in the new budget arrangements, modified the nature of congressional actions: the *fiscalization* of the policy process. In short, fiscalization simply means that the question of paying for services and programs has become the focusing lens of much legislative action. Within the contemporary Congress, this focus drives policy debates in almost every committee room and leadership meeting. Controlling spending levels and the funding (or killing) of continuing programs have become central within the postreform Congress. In sum, the budget has ceased to be an "empowering process," at least for federal initiatives. Rather, the contemporary budget "often appears to be a limiting process . . . [and it] crowds out genuine choice; it forces tomorrow's programs to give way to yesterday's decisions."[55]

With little ability to fund new programs, legislators have sought to control those spending commitments already enacted into law. Congress has gained more well-informed control of the budget as a whole, but it has failed—in conjunction with the president—to control the growth of spending and the growth of the federal debt. As budget scholar James Thurber concludes, "The budget process rules have not prevented the growth of deficits. The reforms have not forced members of Congress to make hard decisions about taxing and spending in order to control the deficit."[56] This party-based, centralized process is what crashed down on first-term Democratic representative Marjorie Margolies-Mezvinsky (see chapter 1) as she came under intense pressures from the party leadership and the Clinton administration to vote in favor of the 1993 budget agreement, whose taxation provisions she had consistently opposed. The context for such pressures is a budget process that regularly produces high-visibility votes on the entire set of spending and taxing commitments for an entire year. Every increase in funding for one program requires a similar reduction for some other governmental activity. Debate over policies thus turns more and more on fiscal considerations. Put bluntly, how much will each program cost? In such an environment, those who can survey the entire budget—members of the budget and appropriations committees and the party leadership—have the most leverage in determining outcomes. The very nature of redistributive, or zero-sum, decision-making is to empower those whose reach facilitates negotiations and whose power can enforce agreements, as long as they can convince even a bare majority of members to agree. Short of voting against the entire budget

SPOTLIGHT

Representative Mick Mulvaney: The Tea Party and the New Partisan Politics of the Budget

Mulvaney and his electoral and congressional career are emblematic of the Tea Party as a whole. Like many Tea Party Republicans across the country, Mulvaney launched his first congressional bid in 2010. With some experience as a member of the South Carolina House of Representatives and State Senate, Mulvaney was not a total political outsider when he launched his congressional bid in 2010. Running in South Carolina's third congressional district against powerful fourteen-term Democratic incumbent and House Budget Committee chairman John Spratt, Mulvaney campaigned on a promise to bring fiscal responsibility to Washington. He successfully characterized Spratt as a big-spending liberal, despite Spratt's reputation in DC circles as a deficit hawk. Mulvaney's impressive ten-point victory over Spratt placed his among the sixty-five House districts that flipped from Democratic to Republican in the 2010 elections. After joining Congress, Mulvaney consistently rejected short-term continuing resolutions and scoffed at the prospect of raising the debt limit in order to avoid default.

Many of the incoming Tea Party legislators in the 112th Congress made deficit and debt reduction through spending cuts a prominent part of their campaigns. As we have seen above, these members of Congress, especially Mulvaney, viewed both budget and debt ceiling negotiations as prime opportunities to deliver on those campaign promises. In July 2011, the White House and the Treasury

Department warned that the borrowing authority of the United States would be exhausted by August 2 if Congress did not act to raise the debt limit. Republicans controlled the House but were the minority in the Senate. To appease Tea Party House members, Speaker Boehner demanded that a debt ceiling increase be accompanied by both spending cuts and a vote on a balanced-budget amendment to the Constitution (a demand that even Senate Republicans denounced). On July 31, three days before default would have occurred, the House and Senate passed a bill that raised the debt ceiling and included significant spending cuts; a political victory for the Tea Party. A similar episode played out in 2013, with Speaker Boehner struggling to unify the Republican caucus on a measure to keep the government funded into the new fiscal year, as the Tea Party refused to allow a continuing resolution without language that delayed or defunded the ACA. Congress failed to reach a funding agreement and the government was partially shut down from October 1 to October 16. For the full account of the partial government shutdown of 2013, see chapter 5.

In sum, Tea Party members such as Rep. Mick Mulvaney have been the most overt and perhaps most powerful proponents of the decades-long fiscalization of the policy process in recent years. The latest iteration of the Tea Party Caucus, the House Freedom Caucus, was formed in 2015 and has continued to be an organized force that puts budget politics at the center of its agenda. For Mulvaney's part, his reputation for relentless budget tactics apparently paid off when President Trump appointed him to direct the OMB at the start of his term. To be sure, Mulvaney has brought his brand of budget brinksmanship to the executive branch; when asked about the prospect of a government shutdown at the start of the new fiscal year in October 2017, he replied that if there is a shutdown, "so be it . . . I think a good shutdown would be one that could help fix that [appropriations process]." The fact that a former member of Congress and current OMB Director needs a government shutdown as a lever to fix the budget and appropriation process is just one clear indication of the extent to which Congress has become less than functional.

_____

The information in this section is taken from multiple sources as follows: Jennifer Steinhauer and Michael D. Shear, "In Mick Mulvaney, Trump Finds Anti-Establishment Leader for Budget Office," *The New York Times*, December 17, 2016, https://www.nytimes.com/2016/12/17/us/politics/trump-mick-mulvaney-budget-office.html; Jason M. Breslow, "In Their Own Words: The GOP's 2010 Freshmen and the Politics of Debt," *PBS Frontline*, Stephanie Condon, "McCain Blasts 'Bizarro' Tea Party Debt Limit Demands," *CBS News*, July 28, 2011, http://www.cbsnews.com/news/mccain-blasts-bizarro-tea-party-debt-limit-demands/; Emily Tillett, "Mick Mulvaney: If Fixing Budget Requires a Shutdown, 'So be it,'" *CBS News*, May 7, 2017, http://www.cbsnews.com/news/mick-mulvaney-if-fixing-budget-requires-a-shutdown-so-be-it/.

agreement, rank-and-file members of both parties can exercise little influence over the budgets that their leaders construct.[57] And such negative votes have become increasingly common, ushering in a new era of fiscal politics.

In the period after the 2010 elections, when Republicans have controlled the House (and the Senate since 2015), many rank-and-file legislators have indeed upped the ante, moving from partisan votes on budgets to those on continuing resolutions, which keep the government functioning.[58] Especially in the House, Speaker Boehner had a difficult time in finding GOP majorities on budget votes, and he often needed to turn to Democrats to maintain funding without interruption.

At the center of the contentious votes over raising the debt limit and maintaining continuous government funding have been members of Congress who are associated with the conservative Tea Party movement. These Tea Party legislators viewed essential budget votes as a means of extracting concessions from the president as well as from more moderate members of their own party in order to further their conservative agenda by threatening to withhold their votes from measures that would keep the government functioning. In essence, Tea Party legislators knew that the president and party leadership had a stake in avoiding the perception that they were incapable of governing—which is the perception that a government shutdown or failure to raise the debt limit would undoubtedly exude—and used that to deliver on promises to cut spending and limit the federal debt and deficit.

Former congressman and now Director of the OMB, Mick Mulvaney (R-SC), used this strategy to actively cultivate a reputation as a fiscal hawk while he was a member of the Tea Party and House Freedom Caucuses.

Similar issues have dogged Speaker Ryan. More seriously, votes on raising the debt limit, which have historically won majority support, have proved
contentious. The very idea that the Congress would fail to raise the debt limit,
and thus open up the possibility of default on the federal debt, illustrates how
partisan fiscal politics have grown in the twenty-first century.[59] Moreover, the
politics of budgets, deficits, and debt has deepened the public's distrust of the
Congress. As routine issues, such as approving increases in the debt limit to
keep the government functioning, have become highly contentious on a regular
basis, the public has reacted by consistently reducing its already tenuous support for the institution of the Congress.

Can't Get No Respect: The Unpopular Congress

> The very openness of the legislative process, which might otherwise
> be thought to endear Congress to the people, is much more likely to
> have the opposite effect. . . . Thus, while Congress is sometimes viewed
> by the public as an enemy, we wish to call attention to the fact that
> it is often viewed as an enemy because it is so public.
>
> —John Hibbing and Elizabeth Thiess-Morse, *Congress as Public Enemy*

Let there be no mistake about congressional popularity: the legislative branch,
despite its putative ties to "the people," has never won great adulation from
the public at large or from editorial pages. Historically, the Congress has been
savaged by editorialists, much as it has been in more recent times. Most individual legislators do not help the situation, as they often engage in the practice of
seeking reelection by running vigorously against the institution.[60] The percentage of the population viewing the Congress in favorable terms has remained a
minority since the mid-1960s—since then, on average, only one in three adults
has had a favorable image of the Congress.[61] The approval rating for Congress
reached a high point just after 9/11, but in recent years, it has plummeted to
new lows, often standing at less than 20 percent (see figure 3.1).[62] Adding insult
to injury, evaluations of the president and the Supreme Court have been consistently more positive than those of the legislative branch. Why is this so, we may
well ask, especially since most incumbent members of Congress regularly win
reelection? The evidence points to two complementary culprits: first, the Congress itself, and second, the media.

THE INHERENT PROBLEMS OF A POWERFUL, PUBLIC, AND PROFESSIONAL LEGISLATURE

Various scholars have concluded that the modern Congress is its own worst
enemy. One study observes, "When Congress acts as it was constitutionally
designed to act—passing major legislation and debating the issues of the day—it
is rewarded by the public with lower levels of approval."[63] In effect, congressional

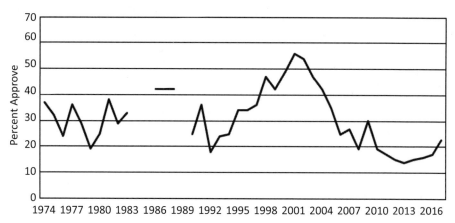

Figure 3.1 Congressional Approval Ratings, 1974–2017.

Source: Adapted from Gallup.com, "Congress and the Public," http://www.gallup.com/poll/1600/congress-public.aspx.

Note: Gallup did not measure congressional approval in 1984–1985, 1989.

disapproval is built into our constitutional structure of decision-making; to the extent that Congress does its prescribed job, it will remain unpopular. Hibbing and Thiess-Morris argue that not only does the constitutional role of the Congress expose it to public criticism, but the Congress has also changed in various ways since the 1950s:

> The elaborate institutional infrastructure, the committees, the subcommittees, the staffers, the partisanship, the nature of debate, the puffery, the boundaries, the sense of insularity, the lengthy careers, the perquisites, the salary, the maldistributed pork, and the special-interest representatives attracted to Congress like bees to honey all serve as tremendous turn-offs for large portions of the citizenry.[64]

Indeed, the very professionalism of the modern Congress, which we will examine in some detail over the remainder of the book, stands at the core of the public's contempt for the legislature. Both professional legislators and professional interest-group representatives win the scorn of the public, but more generally, "a surprising number of people . . . dislike being exposed to processes endemic to democratic government." Citizens desire a sanitized politics, without disagreement, without procedural wrangling—"in short . . ., a patently unrealistic form of democracy."[65]

The denigration of Congress as an institution has contrasted sharply with the generally positive evaluations given individual legislators by their constituencies, as witnessed both by polling data (see table 3.3) and the overwhelming proportion of incumbents who win reelection. In 2016, for example, 97 percent of House incumbents and 93 percent of Senate incumbents won reelection, results that outpaced the overall post–World War II figures of 93 percent (House) and 80 percent (Senate), respectively. Individual legislators can usually

Table 3.3 High Approval for Members; Low Approval for Congress

Individual Members	Congress as an Institution
Serve constituents (usually done effectively)	Resolves national issues only with difficulty or not at all
Run against Congress	Has few defenders
Emphasize personal style and outreach to constituents	Operates as collegial body, difficult to understand
Are reported on by local media in generally positive terms	Is often reported upon negatively by national media (scandals, etc.)
Respond quickly to most constituent needs/inquiries	Moves slowly; cumbersome procedures limit rapid responses
Are able to highlight personal goals and accomplishments	Has many voices, but none can speak clearly for the Congress as a whole

Source: Adapted from Roger Davidson and Walter Oleszek, *Congress and Its Members*, 4th ed. (Washington, DC: CQ Press, 1995), 444.

present themselves in positive terms, whereas the Congress as whole depends on the characterizations of others, especially those of the president and the media. Although there are always interbranch tensions, the prevalence of divided government during much of the 1969–2017 period encouraged presidents to issue regular attacks on an allegedly obstructionist and partisan Congress. One upshot of this sustained criticism of the Congress from inside the chamber, the executive branch, organized interests, and the media (see below) is that by 2014, the public's distaste for the legislators spilled over to individual lawmakers. For the first time, more than half the public expressed a negative view of *their own member of Congress*, even though incumbents won reelection at traditionally high levels in the 2014 elections.[66]

As much as interbranch bickering and congressional structure may contribute to disapproval, declining support for Congress may result from the nature of congressional press coverage in the post-Watergate era. "Over the years," concludes one study, "press coverage has moved from healthy skepticism to outright cynicism. . . . To believe the modern reporter or editor, legislators are egregiously overpaid, indulged, and indifferent to the problems of constituents, who lack six-figure incomes and fantastic job perquisites."[67]

The press's relationship with Congress has become more complex over the years. In sheer numbers, the Washington press corps has grown steadily since about 1960, when it had fewer than one thousand reporters, who predominantly represented newspapers and periodicals. By 2000, more than five thousand reporters were at work in the capital, with a slightly growing edge to those from television and radio.[68]

However significant the growth of the press corps and the rising importance of the electronic media, other developments have been equally telling. First, the nature of political reporting has changed since Watergate (ca. 1973); the historically cozy relationships between Washington politicians and reporters, although not disappearing, became more contentious, even adversarial. Second, technical advances, such as satellite linkages, allow many members of Congress to communicate directly with their constituents, often through local television outlets that are far less critical than the national media. Finally, and perhaps most importantly, the explosion of social media has heightened both criticism from myriad sources and the ability of legislators to communicate directly with their constituents and especially their core supporters.

At the same time, the steady growth of cable television, which carries C-SPAN and its intense, unfiltered coverage of the Congress, and FOX, MSNBC, and CNN, along with Facebook, Twitter, and talk radio, has dramatically increased the amount of intense immediate pressure on members of Congress. Media sources are simply more varied and less subject to the control of any one voice, be it the president's or a legislative leader's. And many of the voices take a relentlessly negative approach to what they see as the needlessly complex and insular context of Capitol Hill politics.

The capacity of talk shows to affect the Congress became clear as early as 1993. Then Rep. James Inhofe (R-OK), an obscure minority-party congressman, relentlessly traveled the talk show circuit, pushing his proposal to open up the process of prying a bill out of committee through the use of a discharge petition, which, to succeed, requires a majority of members' signatures. His campaign turned on the highly technical point that House members who signed the petition should have their names made public. The House leadership wanted to retain the cloak of anonymity on signees; such a practice allowed them privately to urge members not to sign, whereas public disclosure would increase pressures from outside interests to discharge a bill (and thus upset the leadership's control of legislative business). In a clever move, Inhofe constructed his own discharge petition to bring to the floor a bill that would open up the discharge process. Despite intense leadership opposition, this tactic succeeded, and the bill moved to floor debate and eventual approval. Representative Inhofe subsequently won a Senate seat in 1994 and has won reelection three times since.[69]

On a broader scale, as noted, Republicans used the unpopularity of Congress against the Democratic majority in 1994, essentially stating that the institution failed to work because the Democrats had been in power for too long (forty years). Reporters were happy to present this narrative, which was both reasonably accurate and guaranteed to highlight an additional dimension of conflict beyond the ordinary partisan battle. Two decades later, the allegedly dysfunctional nature of Congress remains fodder for many journalists, especially with the prominence of filibusters and delay in the Senate and hyperpartisan conflict, and sometimes interparty division, in the House. Representatives and senators have created a highly partisan and contentious Congress. The post-1994 Congress, in which both parties in both chambers think they have a chance to win a majority in the next election, encourages lawmakers to focus on partisan messaging rather than productive policy-making.[70] It can come as no surprise that both mainstream journalists and their more partisan colleagues can easily continue the narrative of an unresponsive, dysfunctional institution.

CONGRESS IN CONTEXT

As a representative body, Congress necessarily responds to changes in its context, and we can best understand it within its contemporaneous environment. On occasion, the electorate has modified its partisan preferences and thus changed the nature of Congress.[71] In such circumstances, national forces overwhelm local forces in determining the outcome of congressional elections, as in 1994, 2006, and 2010. Still, the 1994 Republican victory was bound to occur at some point—the forty-year period of Republican minorities in the House was historically unprecedented. The post-2010 census period indicates a systematic GOP advantage in House elections, in that Republican voters are spread throughout the country more efficiently than are Democrats; to an extent, the Republicans' capture of seven hundred-plus state legislative seats across the country in the 2010 elections also put them in a position to draw favorable House districts in many states.

For the most part, tendencies toward centralization and decentralization *within* the Congress flow from *outside* forces that continually affect the legislature and its members. For example, local economies place tremendous constituency-based pressures on legislators who seek emergency aid for drought-plagued farmers, extended assistance for unemployed high-tech workers, or subsidized loans for a global firm like Boeing, which must compete against the European Airbus consortium. As public policies and organized interests have grown in number and scope, lawmakers face increased lobbying pressures that can pit constituency against constituency.

As we shall see in chapter 4, congressional reapportionment and redistricting in 1992, 2002, and 2012 have created a partisan alignment in which House members represent increasingly distinct constituencies—the Democrats' relatively concentrated core liberal-to-moderate base and the more broadly distributed conservative, both fiscally and socially, base of the Republicans. Enhanced partisanship in House districts has meant that both parties' legislators have been willing to grant their leaders substantial powers, which has centralized the decision-making process.

Despite the increased partisan control of the congressional agenda, it is still true that members of Congress know best how to serve constituents and groups with particular interests, even though they may desire to make large-scale changes to address broad societal problems. The very responsiveness of individual members to specific constituencies can render the Congress as an institution unresponsive to major long-term societal concerns. Given the continuing budgetary restraints in shaping new programs or an institutional reluctance to eliminate old ones, legislators have contributed to a context that often breeds distrust and invites cynicism, a combination that makes coherent policymaking all the more difficult. Into this breach has ridden an aggressive, ideological Republican Party in the House and, increasingly, in the Senate.[72] The continuing question is whether this centralizing element in national politics and on Capitol Hill can constrain the centrifugal forces that remain ingrained in our governmental structure. So far, the answer has generally been a qualified yes, as it pertains to the Republican and Democratic majorities that have controlled the Congress during the Clinton, Bush (43), and Obama presidencies.

As political scientist John Bader concluded after examining the agenda-setting powers of Congress: "A balance, however precarious and in need of adjustment, between heavy-handed leadership and fragmenting anarchy, should be maintained. . . . The ability to set priorities [by the Congress] fits into a larger set of factors that keep the system separated and in check."[73] Both parties on Capitol Hill, while achieving record-setting levels of partisanship in voting, must confront forces of fragmentation, whether these come from geographical concerns, such as climate-change implications for agriculture and coastal areas, or ideological issues, as with Tea Party pressures on Republican Speaker Boehner. At the same time, for all of its increased partisanship, the U.S. Senate remains a body in which individual legislators and partisan minorities can exert disproportionate influence. The tension between centrifugal and centripetal forces remains, even as Donald Trump, a Republican president, seeks to push his agenda through a Congress with relatively narrow GOP majorities in both chambers.

Recommended Readings

Baumgartner, Frank, Jeffrey M. Berry, Marie Hojnacki, David C. Kimball, and Beth L. Leech. *Lobbying and Policy Change: Who Wins, Who Loses, and Why.* Chicago: University of Chicago Press, 2009.

Brill, Stephen. *America's Bitter Pill.* New York: Random House, 2015.

LaPira, Timothy, and Herschel Thomas, *Revolving Door Lobbying: Public Service, Private Influence, and the Unequal Representation of Interests* (Lawrence, KS: University Press of Kansas, 2017).

Skocpol, Theda, and Vanessa Williams. *The Tea Party and the Remaking of Republican Conservatism.* Revised edition. New York: Oxford University Press, 2016.

Useful Resources

Gallup, Inc.: http://www.gallup.com

Office of the United States Trade Representative: http://www.ustr.gov

U.S. Government Publishing Office: http://www.gpo.gov

Notes

[1] For examples of the earliest lobbying of the House and Senate, see Kenneth R. Bowling and Donald R. Kennon, eds., *The House and Senate in the 1790s: Petitioning, Lobbying, and Institutional Development* (Athens: Ohio University Press, 2002).

[2] See John Mark Hansen, *Gaining Access* (Chicago: University of Chicago Press, 1991), 57–58.

[3] There is a very large body of literature here. For a contemporary summary, see James A. Thurber, "Dynamics of Policy Subsystems in American Politics," in *Interest Group Politics*, 3rd ed., ed. Allan Cigler and Burdett Loomis (Washington, DC: CQ Press, 1991), 319–44.

[4] The "three pillars" of the sugar program are loans for the sugar industry, import restrictions, and regulations, at times, of domestic sugar allotments for planting. See David Hosansley, "Florida Sugar Growers Edgy as Farm Bill Nears," *Congressional Quarterly Weekly Report*, May 13, 1995, 1311–15.

[5] Kay Lehman Schlozman and John T. Tierney, *Organized Interests and American Democracy* (New York: Harper & Row, 1986).

[6] David Vogel, *Fluctuating Fortunes* (New York: Basic Books, 1989).

[7] Lawrence Brown, *New Policies, New Politics* (Washington, DC: Brookings Institution, 1983); see also Paul Light, *Thickening Government* (Washington, DC: Brookings Institution, 1995).

[8] James Sundquist, *Politics and Policies* (Washington, DC: Brookings Institution, 1968).

[9] Congressional scholars differ as to how effective legislators are in distributing their largesse to their geographic constituencies. In *Congress and the Bureaucracy* (New Haven, CT: Yale University Press, 1979), Douglas Arnold, summarizing several works, sees as too simplistic the approach of looking at only the variations in programs and policies as they affect members' districts (15–16). See also Robert M. Stein and Kenneth M. Bickers, *Perpetuating the Pork Barrel* (New York: Cambridge University Press, 1995).

[10] "The Budget Process: What Is PAYGO?" Tax Policy Center. See http://www.taxpolicycenter.org/briefing-book/background/budget-process/paygo.cfm (accessed February 2, 2015).

[11] See, for example, Daniel J. Tichenor and Richard A. Harris, "Organized Interests and American Political Development," *Political Science Quarterly* 117 (Winter 2002/2003): 587–612 and Burdett A. Loomis, "Interests, Lobbying, and the U.S. Congress: Past as Prologue," in *Interest Group Politics*, 6th ed., ed. Allan J. Cigler and Burdett A. Loomis (Washington, DC: CQ Press, 2002), 184–92.

[12] Indeed, the number of active PACs has always been less than the total. As of 1992, there were 1,677 inactive PACs that made no contributions, of which 910 were defunct as organizations. See Paul Herrnson, *Congressional Elections* (Washington, DC: CQ Press, 1994), 109.

[13] "Political Action Committees," Center for Responsive Politics, https://www.opensecrets.org/pacs/ (accessed March 3, 2017).

[14] Thomas Mann, Norman Ornstein, Michael Malbin, Andrew Rugg, and Raffaela Wakeman, eds., *Vital Statistics on Congress 2014* (Washington, DC: Brookings Institution), table 3.8.

[15] See Tim LaPira, "Shadow Lobbyists and the Revolving Door," *The Monkey Cage*, May 6, 2013, http://themonkeycage.org/2013/05/06/shadow-lobbyists-and-the-revolving-door-or-what-anthony-weiner-and-newt-gingrich-have-in-common (accessed February 6, 2015). See also Lee Fang, "Where Have All the Lobbyists Gone?" *The Nation*, March 10–17, 2014, http://www.thenation.com/article/178460/shadow-lobbying-complex (accessed February 6, 2015).

[16] Schlozman and Tierney present data that demonstrate the rise of individual corporate representation, the decline of trade groups (as a percentage of all groups), and the decline of the percentage of citizens' groups. At the same time, the overall number of groups with Washington representation had shot up, so that even labor unions, whose presence had decreased from 11 percent of all interests in 1960 to around 2–3 percent in 1980, still increased in absolute numbers, from about fifty-five groups in 1960 to more than one hundred in 1980. Individual corporate representation, in contrast, rose from about eighty firms in 1960 to approximately three thousand in 1980. Given differences among data, these comparisons may be a little loose, but the overall trends are clear. See Schlozman and Tierney, *Organized Interests and American Democracy*, 77.

17 Christopher J. Bosso, "Competition among Interest Organizations: The State of the Literature and an Application to Environmental Advocacy," paper presented at the Midwest Political Science Association meeting, Chicago, April 25–27, 2002.

18 See, in particular, Donald Haider, *When Governments Come to Washington: Governors, Mayors, and Intergovernmental Lobbying* (New York: Free Press, 1974) for the 1970s era, and Beverly Cigler, "Not Just Another Special Interest: The Intergovernmental Lobby Revisited," in *Interest Group Politics*, 8th ed., ed. Allan Cigler and Burdett Loomis (Washington, DC: CQ/Sage, 1995), 1264–96. See also Eric Uslaner, "All Politics Is Global," in *Interest Group Politics*, 4th ed., ed. Allan Cigler and Burdett Loomis (Washington, DC: CQ Press, 1995).

19 Kishore Gawande, Pravin Krishna, and Michael J. Robbins, "Foreign Lobbies and U.S. Trade Policy," *Review of Economics and Statistics* 88, no. 3. (2006): 563–71.

20 Schlozman and Tierney, *Organized Interests and American Democracy*, 180.

21 Ibid., 155.

22 Almost all publications on Internet use for lobbying become obsolete quickly. Two good starting points are James A. Thurber and Colton Campbell, eds., *Congress and the Internet* (Upper Saddle River, NJ: Prentice-Hall, 2003) and Christopher J. Bosso and Michael Thomas Collins, "Just Another Tool? How Interest Groups Use the Internet," in *Interest Group Politics*, 6th ed., ed. Allan J. Cigler and Burdett A. Loomis (Washington: CQ Press, 2002), 95–116.

23 See Catherine Ho, "The New Landscape of Lobbying," *Washington Post*, June 1, 2014, http://www.washingtonpost.com/business/capitalbusiness/the-new-landscape-of-lobbying/2014/06/01/0c3d35b8-e67a-11e3-afc6-a1dd9407abcf_story.html (accessed February 2, 2015).

24 Various scholars note these different forms of education. John Wright provides a good summary in his *Interest Groups and Congress* (Boston: Allyn & Bacon, 1996), 88ff.

25 Jeffrey H. Birnbaum, *The Lobbyists* (New York: Times Books, 1993), 6.

26 Richard L. Hall and Allen V. Deardorff, "Lobbying as Legislative Subsidy," *American Political Science Review* 100, no. 1. (2006): 69–84.

27 Ibid.

28 For a battlefield report, see Karen De Witt, "In Washington, Giving Is Now Art of Making Gifts Pass through the Eye of the Needle," *New York Times*, January 5, 1997, 10.

29 Tim LaPira and Herschel F. Thomas, III, "Revolving-door lobbyists and Interest Representation," *Interest Groups & Advocacy*, 3, no. 1. (February 2014): 4–29. See also, LaPira and Thomas, *Revolving Door Lobbying: Public Service, Private Influence, and the Unequal Representation of Interests* (Lawrence, KS: University Press of Kansas, 2017).

30 There is burgeoning literature here that is both useful and oversimplified. See, for example, Frank R. Baumgartner and Beth L. Leech, "The Multiple Ambiguities of Counteractive Lobbying," and David Austen-Smith and John R. Wright, "Theory and Evidence of Counteractive Lobbying," both in *American Journal of Political Science* 40 (May 1996): 521–42 and 543–65, respectively. Also, Marie Hojnacki and David C. Kimball, "Organized Interests and the Decision of Whom to Lobby in Congress," *American Political Science Review* 92 (December 1998): 775–90.

31 For the best contemporary analysis, see Frank Baumgartner, Jeffery M. Berry, Marie Hojnacki, David C. Kimball, and Beth L. Leech, *Lobbying and Policy Change: Who Wins, Who Loses, and Why* (Chicago: University of Chicago Press, 2009).

32 Christine A. DeGregorio, *Networks of Champions* (Ann Arbor: University of Michigan Press, 1999).

33 Keith Bradsher, "Foes Set for Battle on GATT," *New York Times*, October 3, 1994.

34 In *Home Style* (Boston: Little, Brown, 1978), Richard F. Fenno, Jr., concludes that the representativeness of the Congress makes it, at least most of the time, "the slow institution" (245)—a description that should not be taken as criticism.

35 David Hosansky, "How Two Fervent Free-Traders Helped Set Back 'Fast Track,'" *Congressional Quarterly Weekly*, October 3, 1998, 2675.

36 For a comprehensive discussion of the coalitions on each side of the trade debate during the 1990s, see Wendy J. Schiller, "Has Free Trade Won the War in Congress, or Is the Battle Still Raging: A Study of the Influence of Industry Coalition Building on Congressional Trade Policy," *NAFTA: Law and Business Review of the Americas* 6 (2000): 363–87.

[37] Siri Srinivas, "Trans Pacific Partnership: Obama Ready to Defy Democrats to Push Secretive Trade Deal," *The Guardian*, January 20, 2015, http://www.theguardian.com/business/2015/jan/20/barack-obama-trans-pacific-partnership-republicans; see also "Trans-Pacific Partnership (TPP): Job Loss, Lower Wages and Higher Drug Prices," Public-Citizen, http://www.citizen.org/TPP (both accessed February 4, 2015).

[38] Binyamin Applebaum, "Trump Is Off to a Slow Start on Trade Promises," *New York Times*, February 24, 2017, https://www.nytimes.com/2017/02/24/business/economy/trump-trade-policy.html?_r=0 (accessed March 5, 2017).

[39] Michael Barone, *Our Country* (New York: Free Press, 1990), 31.

[40] Ibid.

[41] See James Sundquist, *Politics and Policy: The Eisenhower, Kennedy, and Johnson Years* (Washington, DC: Brookings, 1968); Julian Zelizer, *The Fierce Urgency of Now* (New York: Penguin, 2015).

[42] James A. Morone, *The Democratic Wish* (New York: Basic Books, 1990), 266.

[43] See Lawrence Jacobs and Theda Skocpol, *Health Care Reform and American Politics* (New York: Oxford University Press, 2012) and Steven Brill, *America's Bitter Pill* (New York: Random House, 2015).

[44] Richard Cowan and Susan Cornwell, "House Votes to Begin Repealing Obamacare," *Reuters*, January 14, 2017, http://www.reuters.com/article/us-usa-obamacare-idUSKBN14X1SK (accessed March 5, 2017).

[45] Theodore Lowi, *The End of Liberalism*, 2nd ed. (New York: Norton, 1979), 278.

[46] Ibid., 63.

[47] Robert H. Salisbury, "The Paradox of Interest Groups in Washington—More Groups, Less Clout," in *The New American Political System*, rev. ed., ed. Anthony King (Washington, DC: American Enterprise Institute, 1990), 203.

[48] The key figure for congressional Democrats was Rep. Tony Coelho, first in his role as chair of the Democratic Congressional Campaign Committee and then as Democratic whip. Coelho brought Democratic House members and various business interests together to their mutual benefit. In 1989, Coelho resigned from the House after reports surfaced of his favored treatment in the purchase of bonds, but no charges were ever brought against him. In the 1990s, Coelho, as a managing partner of a New York investment firm, maintained contacts with the Democrats and emerged as a key adviser to President Clinton. See Brooks Jackson, *Honest Graft*, rev. ed. (Washington, DC: Farragut, 1990), and Ruth Shalit, "The Undertaker," *New Republic*, January 2, 1995, 17–25.

[49] See, among others, Robert Draper, *When the Tea Party Came to Town* (New York: Simon & Schuster, 2012); Burdett Loomis, "Does K Street Run through Capitol Hill?" in *Interest Group Politics*, 7th ed., ed. Allan Cigler and Burdett Loomis (Washington, DC: CQ Press, 2007), 412–32.

[50] Nicolas Confessore, "How to Get Rich in Trump's Washington," *New York Times Magazine*, September 5, 2017, https://www.nytimes.com/2017/08/30/magazine/ (accessed September 5, 2017).

[51] In his 1966 book, *The Power of the Purse* (Boston: Little, Brown), Richard F. Fenno, Jr., could characterize the appropriations process in the Congress as a system. Within a few years, that system had broken down in terms of controlling expenditures and priorities, and Congress was unable to limit presidential intervention, as Richard Nixon aggressively used his informal powers to withhold or "impound" funds as a means of altering congressional spending priorities. See James Pfiffner, *The President, the Budget, and Congress* (Boulder, CO: Westview Press, 1979).

[52] See various works by Allen Schick and later editions of Aaron Wildavsky, *The Politics of the Budgetary Process* (Boston: Little, Brown, 1964).

[53] There is a vast literature here. A good starting place is Allen Schick, *Congress and Money* (Washington, DC: Urban Institute, 1980).

[54] Allen Schick introduces the term "budget war" in reference to the 1966–1974 period, but there has scarcely been a peace after the adoption of the Budget Reform Act. See Schick, *Congress and Money.*

[55] Allen Schick, *The Federal Budget* (Washington, DC: Brookings Institution, 1995), 2.

[56] James Thurber, "The Dynamics and Dysfunction of the Congressional Budget Process," in *Congress Reconsidered*, 10th ed., ed. Lawrence Dodd and Bruce I. Oppenheimer (Washington, DC: CQ/Sage, 2013), 336.

[57] One notable exception lies in the Senate's post-1985 use of the Byrd Rule, named after Senator Robert Byrd (D-WV), who served as Appropriations Committee chair from 1987 through 1994. This rule subjects reconciliation bills (those that address total income and spending) to objections if language in the bill goes beyond the overall balancing of revenues and spending. Individual items can be challenged as extraneous, and a three-fifths vote is required to sustain an item.

[58] See Frances Lee, *Insecure Majorities: Congress and the Perpetual Campaign* (Chicago: University of Chicago Press, 2016).

[59] Jonathan Wiseman and Ashley Parker, "House Approves Higher Debt Limit without Condition," *New York Times*, February 11, 2014, http://www.nytimes.com/2014/02/12/us/politics/boehner-to-bring-debt-ceiling-to-vote-without-policy-attachments.html (accessed February 6, 2015).

[60] Of the many key findings in Fenno's *Home Style*, none was more important or more surprising than his conclusion that campaigning against the Congress was a ubiquitous strategy (168). This contradicted the notion that members of Congress felt a strong sense of "institutional loyalty" to their body. Although this norm of loyalty may have had some continuing impact in Washington, it had virtually no impact on members' behavior back in their home districts.

[61] Among others, see Glenn Parker, *Characteristics of Congress* (Englewood Cliffs, NJ: Prentice-Hall, 1989), chap. 3 and Roger H. Davidson and Walter J. Oleszek, *Congress and Its Members*, 4th ed. (Washington, DC: CQ Press, 1994). See also John Hibbing and Elizabeth Thiess-Morse, *Congress as Public Enemy* (New York: Cambridge University Press, 1995), chaps. 2 and 3.

[62] See Gallup Poll results, Feburary 7, 2017, http://www.gallup.com/poll/203606/congress-job-approval-jumps-highest-2009.aspx?g_source=Politics&g_medium=newsfeed&g_campaign=tiles (accessed March 6, 2017).Early in the Trump Administration, congressional approval rose to 28 percent, propelled by Republicans' increased support. A similar spike, to 39 percent, occurred in 2009, with President Obama, but support levels steadily declined after this early increase.

[63] Robert H. Durr, John B. Gilmour, and Christina Wolbrecht, "Explaining Congressional Approval," *American Journal of Political Science* 41 (January 1997): 199.

[64] Hibbing and Thiess-Morse, *Congress as Public Enemy*, 161.

[65] Ibid., 147.

[66] Peyton Craighill and Scott Clement, "A Majority of People Don't Like Their Own Congressman. For the First Time Ever," *Washington Post*, August 5, 2014, http://www.washingtonpost.com/blogs/the-fix/wp/2014/08/05/a-majority-of-people-dont-like-their-own-congressman-for-the-first-time-ever (accessed February 5, 2015).

[67] Mark J. Rozell, "Press Coverage of Congress," in *Congress, the Press, and the Public*, ed. Mann and Ornstein, 109–110.

[68] Harold W. Stanley and Richard G. Niemi, *Vital Statistics on American Politics*, 2nd ed. (Washington, DC: CQ Press, 1990), 52 and Kevin Phillips, *Arrogant Capitol* (Boston: Back Bay Books, 1995), 45.

[69] In something of an upset, Rep. Inhofe won a Senate seat in 1994, but the Republican sweep was probably more responsible than any credit that he could claim from his discharge petition triumph.

[70] Lee, *Insecure Majorities*, 198ff.

[71] David Brady, *Critical Elections and Congressional Policy Making* (Stanford, CA: Stanford University Press, 1988).

[72] See Thomas Mann and Norman Ornstein, *It's Even Worse Than It Looks* (New York: Basic Books, 2013).

[73] John Bader, *Taking the Initiative* (Washington, DC: Georgetown University Press, 1997), 223.

CHAPTER 4

Congressional Elections
All for One and One for All?

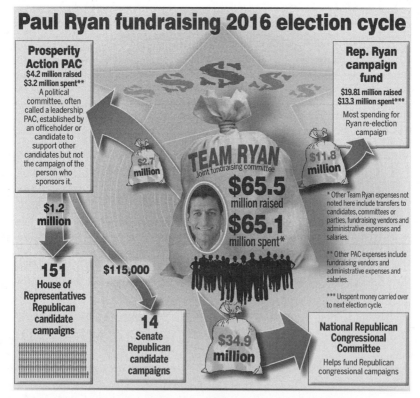

Paul Ryan fundraising 2016 election cycle

Prosperity Action PAC
$4.2 million raised
$3.2 million spent**
A political committee, often called a leadership PAC, established by an officeholder or candidate to support other candidates but not the campaign of the person who sponsors it.

$1.2 million

151 House of Representatives Republican candidate campaigns

$115,000

14 Senate Republican candidate campaigns

$2.7 million

TEAM RYAN
Joint fundraising committee
$65.5 million raised
$65.1 million spent*

$11.8 million

$34.9 million

Rep. Ryan campaign fund
$19.81 million raised
$13.3 million spent***
Most spending for Ryan re-election campaign

* Other Team Ryan expenses not noted here include transfers to candidates, committees or parties, fundraising vendors and administrative expenses and salaries.

** Other PAC expenses include fundraising vendors and administrative expenses and salaries.

*** Unspent money carried over to next election cycle.

National Republican Congressional Committee
Helps fund Republican congressional campaigns

As the Speaker of the House and its top Republican, Representative Paul Ryan and his associated groups generated more than $65 million to support Republican candidates, through various channels. Ryan's fund-raising benefits both his fellow partisans and his own standing as a party leader, whose primary job is to retain his Republican majority.

Republican congresswoman Elise Stefanik (R-NY), age thirty-two, was only ten years old when her party gained control of the U.S. House of Representatives in the 1994 congressional elections. She may have been interested in politics at that age, but there is little chance she understood how significant that victory was, or how important it would be to setting the stage for Congress ever since. Indeed, it is hard to imagine that the 1994 elections would pave the way for her to serve as a member of the majority party in the House in 2014. Stefanik became active in politics in high school, went to Harvard University, and then worked for President George W. Bush before leaving to join an advocacy group on behalf of defense spending. She was active in the GOP presidential campaign in 2012 and decided to run for Congress after returning home to upstate New York to work in her family's lumber business.[1]

Elise Stefanik's platform of low taxes and less regulation, repealing Obamacare, supporting national defense, and gun rights reflects the lasting legacy of the 1994 campaign that returned the GOP to power in Congress, after forty years of minority status. Several factors contributed to the Republicans' unexpected victory that year, including major redistricting after the 1990 census and a number of primary defeats and retirements within the Democratic ranks that opened up opportunities for a successful Republican challenge. As we will see in chapter 5, the leadership of Rep. Newt Gingrich (R-GA) played a huge role in producing a body of GOP candidates who were ready to take advantage of the favorable circumstances of the 1994 election. Republicans picked up fifty-two additional seats in the House and eight seats in the Senate to gain control of both bodies.[2] All Republican incumbents in both the House and the Senate won their bids for reelection, while thirty-four Democratic representatives and two Democratic senators lost.[3]

In sum, the 1994 elections shook up much of the conventional wisdom about congressional elections, a conventional wisdom that emphasized stability, incumbency, and the insularity of sitting legislators to effective challenges. Moreover, few scholars or political professionals had viewed the Democratic House as vulnerable to a Republican takeover. Nonetheless, on January 3, 1995, Republican Gingrich, widely viewed as the architect of the Republican takeover, was sworn in as Speaker of the House—a House in which more than half the members had served for four or fewer years. The post-1994 decade represented something of a return to the incumbency-dominated electoral politics that had been the norm for the U.S. Congress. Although there were some ups and downs for the GOP majorities in both chambers, including a brief span of Democratic control in the Senate in 2001–2002, the local politics of congressional districts and individual states came to the fore, despite vast spending by independent groups and national political parties to influence results across the country.

Incumbents generally won reelection in these years, with Republicans maintaining an edge, but the post-1994 decade also produced highly competitive elections between the congressional parties. For example, in 2000, Republicans retained the majority in the House with a precarious six-seat margin, and Senate elections produced a 50–50 tie in party control. The Republicans controlled the Senate as the majority in 2001 because Vice President Cheney, a Republican, counted as the fifty-first vote when the Senate was organized into a majority- and minority-party structure. With such a slim margin, Senate Republicans had to negotiate with the Democrats to agree on committee ratios that favored the majority by only a single vote (see chapter 7). In June 2001, Vermont Senator James Jeffords left the Republican Party and effectively gave the Democrats a 51–49 governing majority. With his switch, the Democrats also assumed majority control of the committees.

The 2002 elections reflected the results of congressional redistricting in which district boundaries were redrawn in ways that often protected incumbents and left relatively few (thirty or so) House seats in actual competitive play. Given the parity between the two parties, even modest changes in either chamber could have shifted majority control. Ultimately, the Republicans in the House picked up six seats and held the 229–205–1 margin; in the Senate, the Republicans regained the majority with a margin of 51–48–1 (effectively 51–49). The 2004 elections shifted the balance between Republicans and Democrats in Congress a bit more in the Republicans' favor, but overall, the 1996–2004 period witnessed few significant changes in a Congress where most seats were safe, and the GOP governed with modest majorities.

Although parties had gained substantial strength in the Congress since 1994, the new electoral alignments did not produce much in the way of large-scale party swings; rather, as congressional elections became more expensive, the basic strength of incumbency remained intact.

If politicians, pundits, and academics had begun to grow accustomed to a new era of marginal electoral shifts, the elections of 2006, 2008, and 2010 demonstrated how partisan forces within the electorate could change the political landscape quickly and profoundly. To summarize briefly, in the 2006 congressional elections and the 2008 presidential year, Democrats first won control of both chambers, and then expanded their majorities, to the point that initially the Senate of the 110th Congress (2009–2011) included sixty Democrats, a crucial number, given that sixty votes are often needed to move important legislation in that body.[4] The series of partisan wave elections continued in 2010, when Republicans gained sixty-four seats to win control of the House; the Democrats' margin in the Senate was cut to 53–47 (with two independents). The presidential-year election of 2012 did not produce much change in partisan balances, but the midterm 2014 elections, in which the smaller turnout favored Republicans, saw a mini-wave result, in which Republicans gained control of the Senate (54–46, with 2 independents caucusing with Democrats) and increased their House margin to 247–188, its largest majority since the 1920s. In 2016, despite losing a few seats, Republicans retained their majorities in both chambers within a unified GOP control of the national government, given Donald Trump's presidential victory.

SPOTLIGHT

Representative Elise Stefanik: Fresh Energy in Upstate New York

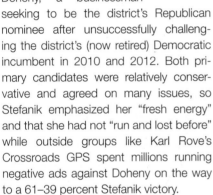

Elected in the 2014 midterm elections at the age of thirty, Elise Stefanik (R-NY) is the youngest woman ever elected to Congress. In the 2014 Republican primary, Stefanik's candidacy represented an alternative to perennial-candidate Matt Doheny, a businessman seeking to be the district's Republican nominee after unsuccessfully challenging the district's (now retired) Democratic incumbent in 2010 and 2012. Both primary candidates were relatively conservative and agreed on many issues, so Stefanik emphasized her "fresh energy" and that she had not "run and lost before" while outside groups like Karl Rove's Crossroads GPS spent millions running negative ads against Doheny on the way to a 61–39 percent Stefanik victory.

Stefanik's previous experience working in the Bush administration certainly helped her gain powerful allies like Rove, a former Bush adviser. She also received key endorsements from national party leaders such as the then Speaker Boehner and Majority Leader Kevin McCarthy (R-CA), both of whom actively campaigned for her. The national Republican Party's support of Stefanik is not necessarily surprising, as the party attempts to reach out to two demographic groups that they have struggled to connect with recently: women and younger voters.

New York's 21st Congressional District had been represented by a Democrat since 1993, but after the state's post-2010 census redistricting, the district's boundaries were changed to exclude Albany and include a wider array of rural upstate areas. The newly drawn district, now the state's largest in terms of land area, borders Vermont, Canada, and Lake Ontario and includes Lake Placid, the Adirondack Mountains, and parts of Saratoga Springs. When incumbent Bill Owens retired before the 2014 elections, the open seat became a prime candidate for a Republican pickup: a rural district with no incumbency advantage to contend with. Stefanik won the general election with 55 percent of the vote to Democrat Aaron Woolf's 33 percent, while third-party candidates obtained 12 percent. In 2016, now-incumbent Rep. Stefanik cruised to reelection, increasing her vote share to 63 percent.

In Congress, Rep. Stefanik serves on the Committee on Armed Services and the Committee on Education and the Workforce. Though she has opposed President Trump on some issues during the 115th Congress, such as the president's immigration ban executive order, Stefanik has supported the administration on key issues including voting for the American Health Care Act on May 4, 2017. While that vote may come back to haunt some more electorally vulnerable Republicans, especially considering that the out-party historically picks up congressional seats in midterm elections, Rep. Stefanik's reelection chances in 2018 may be buoyed by her strong institutional support from party leadership and the rural composition of her district.

___

The information in this section is taken from multiple sources as follows: Jimmy Vielkind, "Stefanik Cruises to a Win, as Doheny Blames Rove," *Politico*, June 24, 2014, http://www.politico.com/states/new-york/albany/story/2014/06/stefanik-cruises-to-a-win-as-doheny-blames-rove-013933; Noah Weiland and John Parkinson, "Meet Elise Stefanik, the Youngest Woman Ever Elected to Congress," *ABC News*, November 4, 2014, http://abcnews.go.com/Politics/elise-stefanik-youngest-woman-elected-congress/story?id=26694806.

All in all, recent elections have illustrated an electorate that has become increasingly partisan, reflecting the divisions in national politics. This chapter explores a fundamental building block of the *centrifugal* Congress—the politics of congressional elections—but it also examines circumstances in which large-scale partisan swings illustrate the importance of centralized parties, especially in the House. In the past fifty years, the politics of congressional elections has meant the politics of *reelection*, because more than 90 percent of successful candidates have been sitting representatives and senators. In that partisan majorities have remained generally slim since 1994, party leaders have placed a great deal of pressure on members of Congress to consider the partisan control implications of every vote they cast. Combined with post-2010 census districts, which through overall sorting (the distribution of partisans) and redistricting that has favored one party (GOP) more than the other, the institutional needs of each party increasingly coincide with the electoral needs of individual members.

ELECTORAL TENSIONS IN THE POST-1994 ERA

Partisan tendencies run headlong into political realities, at least for many legislators. Because members harbor the goal of reelection, they rarely put the collective policy good ahead of their own electoral future. Indeed, the very success of this strategy represents part of a perplexing problem. Writing before the 1992 and 1994 elections, scholar Gary Jacobson observed, "political incapacity and stalemate are encouraged by a peculiar shortcoming of contemporary congressional election processes. They give us representatives and senators who are individually responsive but collectively irresponsible."[5]

Ironically, the voters as a whole—the electorate—can succeed where individual voters may fail. As Robert Erickson and Gerald Wright conclude:

> The average voter knows little about his or her representative and only a bit more about his or her senators. House challengers are almost invisible, and only a portion of the electorate has even a modest amount of information about senatorial challengers. Nevertheless, the electorates that candidates and parties face are smart and discerning, and they reward faithful representation. [In listening to and anticipating the electorate's wishes,] candidates . . . work to give them what they want. Elections bring about much higher levels of policy representation than most observers would expect based on the low levels of citizen awareness.[6]

In one way, therefore, congressional elections present a continuing set of puzzles because every two years, a new Congress is forged from local decisions that may or may not converge with national policy trends. Historically, local forces have dominated congressional decision-making, but over the past twenty years, national issues have sometimes displaced these local, centrifugal forces. The legislative and executive branches, on occasion, respond to partisan waves in the electorate by moving significant policy initiatives, such as health care, through the complex and slow lawmaking process. This occurred dramatically after the 1994 and 2008 elections, as partisan initiatives dominated the Congress's agenda. Moreover, not only did Republicans win majorities in 1994, they also proved themselves capable—at least in the House—of passing an impressive array of legislation, much of it drawn from a single campaign document, the Contract with America. Despite subsequent failures to push much of this program into law, House Republicans did succeed in shaping the terms of many national policy debates (e.g., welfare reform in 1996). This chapter first examines the interaction of the forces of fragmentation—localism, incumbency, and campaign finance—with national party pressures that have grown increasingly important in congressional elections since the 1970s. Then, more general forces are explored to see how much a Congress might reflect a "national verdict"[7] on hotly contested issues. Under periods of unified party control of Congress and the presidency, congressional leaders and the president may well overcome, or at least balance, the tendencies of members to look homeward in developing their policy positions. Alternatively, strong legislative parties within a divided government may dictate policy deadlock, even on important national issues.

LOCAL ELECTIONS FOR A NATIONAL OFFICE

All politics is local.

—Former Speaker Thomas P. (Tip) O'Neill (D-MA)

Congressional elections are, at heart, local events, especially for representatives whose districts remain relatively homogeneous. To be sure, a few constituencies cover immense areas, such as the whole of Alaska, Montana, or Wyoming, each with a single representative. Other districts reflect highly diverse populations, such as those metropolitan seats that include substantial numbers of the urban poor, various racial and ethnic groups, small-business owners, and wealthy suburbanites. Nonetheless, when compared to a presidential campaign or a Senate race in a large state, most congressional races take place within a narrow, well-defined local context. Indeed, homogeneity may well be rising, as people "sort" themselves geographically, producing congressional districts (and states) that are increasingly "red" or "blue";[8] such sorting also reduces the number of truly competitive House districts.

Members of Congress often speak of their constituents as if they know exactly who they are. In fact, all legislators relate to several different, overlapping constituencies. Richard Fenno finds that "each member of Congress perceives four concentric constituencies: geographic, reelection, primary, and personal."[9] Roughly speaking, the geographic constituency reflects the physical boundaries of the district; the reelection constituency consists of the number of voters that have provided (and will provide) general electoral success; the primary constituency is that group which "each congressman believes would provide his last line of electoral defense in a primary";[10] and the personal constituency consists of those longtime intimates whom the legislator can trust to offer unvarnished advice and useful political information.

Geographic Constituencies

In the wake of a series of key Supreme Court decisions and voting rights legislation in the 1960s, all congressional districts have had roughly equal populations.[11] Post-2010 districts average about 711,000 people, based on the regular decennial apportionment, which allocated seats to states in accord with their populations. Thus, California's House delegation grew from forty-five in the 1980s to fifty-three in 2002, while New York, which had thirty-nine seats in 1970, was allocated just twenty-seven after the 2010 census.[12] Because congressional seats are awarded to states through a mathematical formula and districts cannot cross state lines, population variations from state to state can be substantial. For example, in 1991, the state of Montana filed an unsuccessful suit over the loss of one of its two congressional districts in the 1992 reapportionment process, which left the state with a single constituency of almost 800,000. In 2002, Montana had 902,195 constituents but still had only one at-large congressional district. In contrast, Iowa's congressional districts consisted of 585,000 residents, about 10 percent less than the national average.[13] After the 2010 census, Montana, with almost a million residents, still had just one representative, but Iowa's delegation shrank from five to four, and the average district there rose to more than 750,000.

Still, members of the House all represent roughly the same number of constituents and receive roughly the same resources (see chapter 8 on congressional enterprises). This ensures that the inherent fragmentation embedded in the House stems not from differences in the population size of constituencies but from the great differences in culture, race, ethnicity, age, wealth, and so forth across the nation. Since the early 1980s, the issue of racial representation has become a major element of redistricting, both through the 1965 Voting Rights Act (extended in 1982) and in a series of court cases. The 1982 legislation required that redistricting—the actual redrawing of congressional districts, usually by state legislatures after reapportionment—could not dilute minority voting strength. Minorities were explicitly defined as African Americans and Latinos. Congressional redistricting in 1991–1992 thus produced a slew of "minority-majority" districts that elected fifty-eight minority representatives in 1992, up from thirty-eight in 1990.[14] Minority populations were concentrated in districts by legal gerrymandering; that is, many odd-shaped districts were created specifically so that minority legislators would be elected. These expectations came to fruition in that "sixteen new black elected officials joined the 1992 Congress, each from a majority black district."[15]

Perversely, the emphasis on districts' racial composition has turned the notion of gerrymandering on its head. Although gerrymandering—drawing political boundaries to benefit one candidate, party, or population grouping— has a long history in the United States, it has always been considered unethical.[16] The Voting Rights Act of 1965 and a series of important Supreme Court decisions in the mid-1960s established a "one-person, one-vote" rule that opened up the electoral system to minorities, but the impact of minority voters often appeared diluted. For example, in North Carolina, African Americans made up 22 percent of the population in 1990, but the state had elected no minority member to Congress in the twentieth century. The state's 1992 redistricting produced two districts designed to send an African American to Washington. In the American context of single-member districts, gerrymandering to concentrate minority voting strength had become an officially sanctioned policy.[17]

In fact, the most remarkable example of racial gerrymandering came in North Carolina's "I-85 district," so labeled "because it consists of a series of urban black areas, many of them poor, partially connected by a line sometimes no wider than I-85, splitting adjacent districts in two"[18] (see figure 4.1). The government-sanctioned gerrymander worked; African American candidates, both Democrats, won the seats that had been carved out for them.

In the 1990s, the Supreme Court began to closely examine oddly drawn geographic districts designed to give minority populations majority power within a congressional district. In 1995, the Supreme Court reaffirmed its 1993 ruling (*Reno v. Shaw*) that cast doubt on any district lines drawn to consider as "the predominant factor."[19] Although the legal gerrymandering of North Carolina's First District survived judicial scrutiny, in 1996, the Supreme Court struck down the Twelfth District's lines and mandated the alteration of the racially based "majority-minority" seats in other southern states (Georgia, Louisiana, and Texas), where boundaries had increased the emphasis on their racial composition.[20]

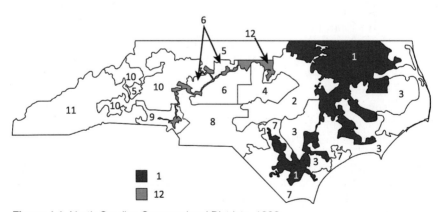

Figure 4.1 North Carolina Congressional Districts, 1993.

Source: Based on Digital Boundary Definitions of United States Congressional Districts, 1789–2012, "United States Congressional District Shapefiles" (http://cdmaps.polisci.ucla.edu), by Jeffrey B. Lewis, Brandon DeVine, and Lincoln Pritcher, with Kenneth C. Martis.

Protecting and preserving minority representation continues to be a crucial element of U.S. politics, but the old routes to accomplishing full minority representation have attracted increased scrutiny. In recent years, some scholars have challenged the effectiveness of majority-minority districts in terms of both producing policies that are favorable to minorities and sending more minority representatives to the House.[21] If the purpose of majority-minority districts is to elect more minority members to Congress, the current system can be counterproductive by marginalizing the electoral prospects of minority candidates. Thus, after a series of recent court decisions, the 2002 election season witnessed two instances of African American candidates competing against each other for their party's nomination in majority-minority districts. In Alabama's Seventh District, Rep. Earl Hilliard, elected in 1992 as the first African American elected from the state in more than a century, lost to another African American, Earl Davis, who went on to win election in the predominantly black district. Denise Majette defeated Georgia representative Cynthia McKinney in a hotly contested party primary. Rather than being viable candidates across four different districts, these four African American candidates were forced to compete with each other for two seats. In each instance, the candidate perceived as the more moderate emerged victorious. Ironically, McKinney returned to the House in the 2004 elections, when she won the seat held by Rep. Majette, who unsuccessfully ran for the U.S. Senate.

More generally, one impact of bringing race into the redistricting calculus has been to concentrate African Americans (and other minority voters) in particular districts. Given historic voting patterns, these districts become reliably Democratic seats, but this concentration means that white voters, disproportionately Republican, are spread more evenly across the remaining districts. Especially in the South, this has meant that Democrats have been placed at a net disadvantage, to the point that, in the wake of 2010 redistricting, "minority influence has been packed into a greater number of heavily nonwhite districts, and the number of more heavily white House districts has also grown."[22] Ironically, in the wake of the 2014 elections, record numbers of African American (46) and Hispanic (32) legislators sit in the House, with most coming from heavily Democratic, largely nonwhite districts. The very existence of these districts, many in densely populated urban areas, means that across the country, Democratic votes remain less efficiently distributed than Republican votes.

In recent years, more traditional gerrymandering—that is, drawing district lines to favor one party over another—has reemerged as a powerful political tool. The most blatant case of partisan gerrymandering occurred in Texas in 2003, when the state legislature redrew districts to the distinct disadvantage of Democratic House members. After the 2000 census, Texas redrew its Congressional lines, as it was required to, to reflect population shifts. But in 2003, after Republicans took control of the state government, they redistricted again, drawing new lines that broke up safe Democratic seats and swooping around the state to scoop up Republican voters, all to increase the Republican share of the Texas congressional delegation.

The redistricting fight became so bitter that Democratic legislators fled the state, hiding out in neighboring Oklahoma, and the Republicans sent state troopers after them. Subsequently, the House Ethics Committee admonished the House Majority Leader, Tom DeLay, for telling Federal Aviation Administration officials to look for the missing Democrats.[23]

As it turns out, the Republicans in Texas picked up eight congressional seats in the 2004 elections; four Democratic incumbents, including the minority whip, Martin Frost (D-TX), lost their seats as a direct result of redistricting that moved them into majority Republican areas.

Less egregious, but more systematic, were advantages that accrued to Republicans across the country in the wake of the 2010 GOP landslide, which led to their net gain of more than seven hundred state legislative seats. This increase allowed Republicans to dominate the redistricting process in many states—given the ready availability of sophisticated map software, state legislatures could draw districts to benefit, at least marginally, their respective majority parties.

In some instances, such as in California's 2002 redistricting, the parties agreed not to rock the boat and thus created fifty-three essentially noncompetitive districts, which protected the sitting incumbents of both parties. The public was not amused, and in two referenda, California voters created an independent redistricting commission. It is unclear whether this body devised more competitive districts, but 2012 did produce a large turnover within the California House delegation. As of the last redistricting in 2010, thirteen states had commissions that possessed some level of responsibility for recommending congressional district boundaries, with two other states using a backup commission in the event the legislature deadlocked. The vast majority of state redistricting processes remain governed by the political parties within state legislatures. Iowa is the only state that does not have any role for the state legislature; its congressional district boundaries are completely drawn by a nonpartisan staff.[24]

In recent years, various court cases have begun to address the issue of partisan gerrymandering, mostly at the state legislative level, with direct implications for congressional redistricting. Most notably, a panel of three federal judges has ordered the Wisconsin Assembly to redraw its districts to reduce partisan bias; the state has appealed to the U.S. Supreme Court, which in June 2017 agreed to hear the case.[25]

Other Constituencies: Behavior and Perception

If the geographic constituency is unambiguous (if irregular) in its boundaries, the other constituencies identified by Fenno are subjectively defined. Even in the same district or state, no two incumbents, even from the same party, would put together the same reelection constituency. Nor would we expect their primary supporters or their personal backers to be the same. In particular, personal constituencies are unique. Fenno recalls sitting in the living room of one member's top district staffer and best friend, watching an NFL game with the congressman, the district aide, the state assemblyman from the congressman's home county, and the district attorney of the same county. The last three were among the five people with whom the congressman had held his first strategy meeting four years earlier. . . . Between plays and at halftime, over beer and pretzels, the four discussed every aspect of the congressman's campaign. . . . Ostensibly they were watching the football game. Actually, the congressman was exchanging political advice, information, and perspectives with three of his oldest and closest political associates.[26]

Examining the evolution of constituencies within a single congressional district demonstrates both how the geographic boundaries can change through redistricting and how a series of incumbents construct their own unique bases of support. From 1971 through 2019, for example, Kansas's Second District has changed its representative stripes about as much as any seat in the country as eight different individuals held the seat during that period. Not only was the district redrawn every ten years between 1972 and 2012, but also each of the incumbents developed his or her own set of personal, primary, and reelection constituencies (see table 4.1).

Over this 47-year period, the population of the Second District grew dramatically—from a low of 454,000 in the 1970s to 715,000 after the 2010 census (Kansas lost one of its five House seats after the 1990 census)—and its geographic configuration changed as much. Historically, the district had encompassed a relatively compact area of northeast Kansas; since 1992, however, its reach has extended from the Nebraska border on the north to the Oklahoma line on the south.

Even more significant have been the changes in the reelection, primary, and personal constituencies represented by the eight incumbents, including five men and three women. A district with roughly the same geographic boundaries elected two fairly liberal Democrats, two moderate-to-conservative Democrats, two traditionally conservative Republicans, and two extremely conservative Republicans—each with his or her own set of personal supporters and winning election coalitions.

Incumbents also develop their own funding constituencies, often bringing in hundreds of thousands of dollars from outside the confines of their physical districts. With a seat on the powerful Energy and Commerce Committee, in the late 1980s, Rep. Jim Slattery proved especially adept at obtaining substantial PAC funding from groups with little direct interest in Kansas's Second District. Former Republican Rep. Jim Ryun served for ten years after his 1996 election, and he had to raise increasingly large amounts of money during his tenure, often from socially conservative sources. In 2004, he raised $977,032 ($549,497 from PACs) and spent it all to win by a margin of 56–41 percent.[27]

After defeating Ryun in an upset in 2006, Democrat Nancy Boyda lost the Second District seat to Republican Lynn Jenkins in the next election, and since 2008 Jenkins has won reelection handily, if not overwhelmingly. But even in this

Table 4.1 Changing Constituencies in a Single Congressional District, the Kansas Second, 1971–2017

Member/Term	Geographic	Constituency Type		
		Reelection	Primary	Personal
Bill Roy (D)/ 1971–1975	479K, NE 1/4 of KS, rural/urban	Democrats/Independents/ Moderate Republicans	Kansas City, KS, Democrats; federal/state employees	State legislators' support, medical doctors
Martha Keys (D)/ 1975–1979	454K, NE 1/4 of KS, rural/urban	Democrats/Independents/ Moderate Republicans	McGovern Democrats	Antiwar Democrats, 1972 campaign
Jim Jefferies (R)/ 1979–1983	454K, NE 1/4 of KS, rural/urban	Republicans/Conservatives	Conservative Republicans	Reagan backers in 1976
Jim Slattery (D)/ 1983–1995	472K, NE 1/4 of KS, rural/urban	Democrats/Independents/ Moderate Republicans	Topeka and Moderate Democrats	Loyalists from state legislature days
Sam Brownback* (R)/ 1995–1996	619K, east 1/3 of KS, except suburban Kansas City	Republicans/Perot supporters/Reagan Democrats	Traditional Republicans	Agricultural community, Kansas State University, family media base
Jim Ryun (R)/ 1997–2007	672K, east 1/3 of KS, except suburban Kansas City	Most Republicans/ Christian Right	Christian Right	Personal friends with religious and athletic ties
Nancy Boyda (D)/ 2007–2009	672K, east 1/3 of KS, except suburban Kansas City	Democrats/Independents/ Moderate Republicans	Moderate Democrats	Personal network of friends
Lynn Jenkins (R)/2009–	715K, east 1/3 of KS, except suburban Kansas City	Republicans	Traditional Republicans	Republican Establishment

Source: Almanac of American Politics, various editions.

*Won the Senate seat vacated by Senator Dole in 1996.

now relatively uncompetitive district, Jenkins spent almost $3.5 million in 2014 to retain her seat, and her need to attend to a funding constituency had become central to her congressional career.[28] As of 2017, Jenkins announced her retirement, opening up her district to a highly competitive 2018 campaign.

Careful cultivation of Fenno's four concentric constituencies (geographic, reelection, primary, personal) and maintenance of a strong funding base allow incumbents considerable latitude in deciding how to represent their districts, especially if they are skilled at explaining their positions. Nevertheless, there are real limits to this flexibility because incumbents can face problems because of unpopular votes, well-funded opponents, strong national trends, scandals of their own making, or some combination of the above. Even the most successful members are risk averse, and most incumbents run as if the next election could be their last. Incumbents can lose, even those in leadership positions—just ask former Speaker of the House Tom Foley (D-WA), who lost his seat in 1994 after thirty years in the House, or former Senate minority leader Tom Daschle (D-SD), who lost his bid for reelection in 2004 after serving in Congress for twenty-six years. In 2014, House Majority Leader Eric Cantor (R-VA) was upset in a primary election by a Tea Party challenger who appeared to have little chance of success. As recently as thirty years ago, there were distinctions between governing and campaigning, even in the House with its two-year terms. Those days are gone in the current age of permanent campaigning.

ELECTIONS IN A CAREERIST CONGRESS

If a group of planners sat down and tried to design a pair of American electoral assemblies with the goal of serving members' electoral needs year in and year out, they would be hard pressed to improve on what exists.

—David Mayhew, *Congress: The Electoral Connection*

Over the past one hundred years, the Congress has developed into an institution that fosters long careers. Between 1911 and 1971, the number of "careerists" (legislators serving ten or more terms) rose steadily, from 2.8 percent to 20 percent. After substantial turnover in the 1970s, the percentage of careerists stabilized at about 15 percent of the House for almost twenty years. Then the post-1990 elections witnessed enough turnover (often through Democratic retirements and defeats) to reduce the careerist numbers to fifty-five, or 13 percent, in the 105th Congress, but since then the number of careerists has risen to an average of 17 percent, shooting up to a historic high of 22 percent in the House for the 112th Congress (2011–2013).[29] Careerist legislators want to remain in office; thus, every two (or six) years, they must win reelection. Unsurprisingly, with the careerist, professional Congress have come both increased incentives to run for reelection and enhanced capacities for incumbents to emerge victorious. Since 1950, 90 percent of House incumbents ordinarily have run for reelection, and well over 90 percent of them have won.[30] Sitting senators are more vulnerable than are House incumbents, but their post-1952 reelection rate still exceeds 80 percent. At the same time, the average tenure of House members, as of 2017 is a bit less than ten years; for senators, a bit more than ten years. Legislators do lose and do retire, and with occasional "wave" elections (1974, 1994, 2006, 2010), there is considerable infusion of new blood, usually coming disproportionately from one party or the other.

Still, incumbents are difficult to unseat. What difference does it make that they remain relatively safe? The answers to both these questions are central to understanding the extent of fragmentation in the U.S. Congress. Most of our attention will focus on House elections, given the greater safety of Representatives and the extensive research that has focused on these contests. At the same time, since 2010, a number of Republican senators have faced surprisingly strong opposition in primary elections, almost all from right-leaning Tea Party candidates, who see the incumbents as too attached to Washington's status quo. Incumbent senators have generally warded off such challenges, but they must work to win both their party's nomination (primary elections) and the general election.

HOUSE INCUMBENTS AND THE STRUCTURE OF COMPETITION

Although House members have consistently won reelection at high rates, major changes have occurred in the past fifty years. First, incumbents' margins rose substantially over this period; second, freshman members, who were historically more vulnerable than their more experienced colleagues, improved their success rates to match those of the chamber as a whole.

Increasing Margins and the "Slurge"

In the 1960s and 1970s, scholars and political observers began to take note of the fact that fewer congressional races were decided by narrow margins. By historical standards, the "marginals," or closely contested seats in which the winning candidate receives no more than 55–60 percent of the vote, were vanishing. Political scientist Morris Fiorina concluded in 1977 that "the bureaucracy did it," as legislators created a series of programs to which they could subsequently control access (thus winning credit for their assistance in providing benefits).[31] The entrenched nature of incumbency really became evident during the 1980s. By this time, only the occasional scandal provided a likely avenue for challenger success. Over the next decade, numerous scholars weighed in with their own assessments of the growing margins of victory as they looked at congressional redistricting, the growth of the congressional enterprise and its resources (such as staff, franking, and trips home), levels of casework, and patterns of campaign funding (see chapter 8). Basically, they sought to identify shared advantages that all incumbents had over their challengers. This cottage industry of research found no single cause for the increasing margins of victory, but a rough consensus formed about what did and did not explain the reduced levels of congressional competition in the 1970–2016 era.[32] Findings include the following:

- *Redistricting has had little, if any, systematic effect on margins of victory.* The conventional wisdom through 1990 was that although some incumbents may have been protected, redrawing district lines after decennial censuses did not cause increasing margins.[33] The 1992 redistricting produced both heavily Democratic majority-minority districts and many new seats in which Republicans could and did compete effectively. Subsequently, in 2002, a somewhat different kind of gerrymandering occurred, which served to protect incumbents of both parties in state after state. In 2012, partisan attempts at gerrymandering did return, but much of the post-2010 GOP advantage in House elections derives from sorting—in which Republican votes are spread across the country more efficiently than are Democratic votes, which often are bunched in urban areas.[34]

- *Constituency service is important, but it will not ensure large-scale victory.* In reviewing research on constituency service, various studies have found no relationship between electoral results and casework, federal spending in the district, travel back to the district, or size of staff. The fact that there are 435 districts and 435 different ways to serve those districts can dilute the impact of constituency service on an aggregate level. It may very well be that the most vulnerable incumbents, in potentially marginal districts, engage in the most constituency service, so even when they win, they do not win by very large margins. In contrast, the incumbents from the safest districts engage in the least constituency service, but they continue to win with large margins. Therefore, any large-scale study of incumbency advantage would not be able to uncover a systematic benefit to constituency service.

- *Campaign spending is important, but mainly for challengers.*[35] If a challenger can spend enough money to gain substantial recognition, the chances of a close race rise sharply. But the amount of money required merely to stage a legitimate challenge has become increasingly daunting. Indeed, in 2016 the top ten House races raised an average of $11.7 million. Overall, the average incumbent (most of them in safe seats) raised $1.6 million, in contrast to $238,000 for the average challenger, including those in primary elections.[36]

- *The incumbent's most effective electoral strategy is to discourage serious opposition.*[37] So-called high-quality challengers—state senators, mayors, previous losers who did reasonably well—start out with substantial name recognition and may well be able to raise funds more easily than neophytes. Incumbents thus seek to maximize their victory margins, raise substantial sums of campaign funds, and provide excellent service at home in hopes of discouraging strong potential candidates from making what could prove to be a serious challenge. After a series of Senate elections in 2010 and 2012 where upstarts knocked off incumbents in primaries but lost the general election, Republicans joined forces with business groups to squeeze out upstarts by denying them enough money to mount a strong campaign and, at the same time, providing abundant campaign funds to incumbents.

SPOTLIGHT

Karen Handel: Georgia's 6th District

In the wake of his election as president, Donald Trump selected Georgia congressman Tom Price to be Secretary of the Health and Human Services Department, leaving vacant Georgia's 6th Congressional District. Price easily won this consistently Republican seat for several elections, and the initial assumption was that a Republican candidate would easily win the April 2107 special election. Indeed, GOP candidates filed for the office along with Democrat Jon Ossoff, an unknown thirty-year-old documentary filmmaker. As the campaign progressed, however, more than $8 million, most from out of state, flowed into the race in support of Ossoff. As the April 18 election grew near, it became apparent that Ossoff might be able to win the seat outright by receiving more than 50 percent of the total vote. He faced multiple opponents from the Republican side of the aisle and he came close, winning more than 48 percent, but failed to cross that winning

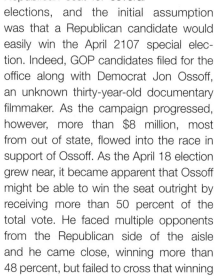

threshold. Because of that, he had a run-off election against Karen Handel, the top Republican vote-getter in June 2017, and she emerged victorious with 51.8 percent of the vote to 48.2 percent for Ossoff.[38] This election became a national focal point for both parties, as national fund-raising produced record expenditures in a single House race. Ossoff raised $24.5 million, complemented by an additional $8 million in outside funds; Handel raised just $4.5 million, but supporting groups provided $18 million.* Altogether the election cost more than $55 million, as Handel eked out a narrow but decisive victory in this GOP district.

---

*Figures from Center for Responsive politics, cited in Philip Wegman, "Jon Ossoff spent six times more than Karen Handel but complains about 'money in politics,' " *Washington Examiner*, June 21, 2017, http://www.washingtonexaminer.com/jon-ossoff-spent-six-times-more-than-karen-handel-but-complains-about-money-in-politics/article/2626628 (accessed June 22, 2017).

THE LASTING IMPACT OF THE ELECTORAL EARTHQUAKE OF 1994

In 1994, the unthinkable happened; Democrats lost control of the House of Representatives for the first time in forty years. All observers had predicted some gains for House Republicans, but almost none foresaw the Democrats losing their majority, save for the GOP partisans.[39] The House Republicans needed to win forty seats to gain control; their fifty-two-seat swing represented the largest shift since 1946, when Democrats suffered a fifty-five-seat loss. The Republicans' 1994 triumph was all the more significant because it came in an era of enhanced incumbent safety (despite some decline in 1990 and 1992) and swept Democrats out of office all across the country. In 1994, at least, all politics was not local.

The nationalization of the 1994 election was no random event. Rather, congressional Republicans infused traditionally local congressional elections with national themes and national issues. Rep. Newt Gingrich (R-GA), the minority whip at the time, worked with the National Republican Congressional Committee (NRCC) and Republican-affiliated PACs on behalf of Republican candidates on a district-by-district basis. Indeed, Gingrich helped recruit many members of the Republican majority, instructed them on key issues, campaigned for most of them, and raised money for their campaigns. Through GOPAC, a Gingrich-directed group, funds and campaign assistance flowed to Republican candidates, and the NRCC could guarantee the maximum allowable contribution of $25,000 to any seriously competitive candidate. Overall, Republicans spent more than half their funds (51 percent) on challengers in competitive races, a tactic that allowed them to counter the PAC receipts of Democratic incumbents.[40] Gingrich thus followed the Democratic representative Tony Coelho's strategy in using leadership PAC money to consolidate political power in his own party.

The efforts at nationalizing the 1994 elections culminated in the Contract with America, a campaign pledge document that all but three Republican candidates signed. In conjunction with political consultant and pollster Frank Luntz, Gingrich announced early in the year that on September 27, 1994, Republican House candidates would gather on the steps of the Capitol to offer their support for a ten-item Contract with America, which would explicitly lay out the changes they would propose in the first one hundred days of the new Congress (see chapter 5 for more on the Contract with America). Although most voters neither knew nor cared about what was in the Contract, it provided a succinct and clear message that the Republicans would govern the House as a unified majority party. The Republican capture of the House came one district at a time, with each new member owing a great deal to Gingrich for the assistance he provided. For Gingrich, the Contract nationalized the voting decision and offered him, as incoming Speaker, a useful vehicle to push a series of reforms. In the end, the national themes and the leader's expertise, funding, and energy all contributed to a great unity among first-term members, in particular, and the entire Republican majority, in general. Moreover, the electoral victory became thoroughly linked to the House Republicans' aggressive policy proposals that followed.

Republican Senate candidates, whether incumbents or challengers, did not join in the Contract with America, nor did they actively campaign with their House colleagues. Although the Republicans' 1994 Senate triumph, which produced a 53–47 margin (gaining eight seats in the election and adding the partisan defection of Alabama Democrat Richard Shelby to the Republican Party), was noteworthy, it was not a great surprise in that Senate elections have proved much more competitive than House contests. Still, Republicans who ran for the Senate in 1994 benefited from the general campaign theme that they would govern as a more unified and more effective majority party, especially given the electorate's rejection of the long-term Democratic control of the Congress, which had rendered the entire institution highly suspect.[41]

The electoral earthquake of 1994 ushered in a new era of congressional electoral politics. First, control of both the House and the Senate has been up for grabs in almost every election since 1994. Second, congressional elections have grown increasingly nationalized, especially when it comes to fund-raising. Third, House Republicans have come to enjoy a structural advantage in the allocation of seats, to the extent that they can win control of the chamber while receiving fewer votes than Democrats. In the twelve congressional elections from 1994 to 2016, the GOP has won a House majority ten times. The Senate has proven far more competitive, with Democrats regaining control of the Senate in 2001 (because of Jeffords's defection), relinquishing it in the 2002 elections, winning majorities from 2006 through the 2012 elections, and losing control in 2014. Given the relatively even divisions in each chamber, since 1994, both parties in the House and Senate can generally anticipate the possibility of prevailing in the next election. This has given electoral politics greater importance than policymaking, in many instances, contributing to the lack of policy deliberation and compromise in the contemporary Congress.[42]

Finally, since 1994, congressional elections have grown more ideological in various related ways. As elections scholar Gary Jacobson summarizes, "The congressional parties did not polarize [see chapter 5] in a vacuum. . . . Ordinary Democrats and Republicans have grown increasingly distant from one another in ideology and policy preferences. The links between partisanship and voting have strengthened. The president has become a more compelling— and more partisan—focal point for congressional elections."[43] In addition, especially among Republicans, primary election challenges from the Tea Party right have either elected far more conservative legislators or have pressured sitting lawmakers to embrace increasingly conservative positions, thus widening the gap between the parties in Congress and producing some problems for GOP leaders.[44]

FUNDING CONGRESSIONAL CAMPAIGNS

In 2014, incumbent senator Kay Hagan (D-NC) faced a vigorous challenge from Republican Thom Tillis, the speaker of the North Carolina House. In the end, Tillis won a narrow victory of fewer than 50,000 votes out of more than 2.9 million cast. Most notable, however, was that this single Senate race cost more than $110 million, including all spending by candidates, parties, and outside groups.[45] Compare that to the $1.1 million spent forty years earlier in the 1974 North Carolina open-seat Senate race. To be sure, the 2014 contest stands as the most expensive Senate race in U.S. history, and the huge growth in spending in North Carolina is part of a much wider trend in the remarkable escalation of money in congressional politics in the past forty years.

Since the early 1970s, congressional campaign finance has experienced continual changes, in two related ways. First, campaigns have consistently grown more expensive. Second, the campaign finance rules, such as they are, have changed frequently, and informal means of circumventing those rules have often proved as significant as the formal regulations. As of the 2016 election, despite hundreds of rules and regulations that govern many specifics of campaign finance, *in practical terms, there are no real limits to raising and spending money in congressional campaigns,* largely because of major Supreme Court rulings and the impact of large sums of difficult-to-track outside money.

The Rising Costs of Running for the House and Senate

Although inflation has affected campaign expenses in the post-1974 period, the overall growth in campaign expenditures remains striking. In 1974, the average House candidate spent $55,000 on his or her campaign; by 1984, that figure had more than quadrupled, to $241,000, a sum that almost doubled in the next ten years, to $440,000 in 1994.[46] In 2004, the average House general candidate spent $773,000, and by 2012, that figure reached $1.2 million. As can be seen in table 4.2, Senate expenditures have risen at comparable levels, to the point that the average Senate candidate spent more than $12 million in 2016, compared to $596,000 in 1976. Looking at average expenditures is misleading, however, in that spending by incumbents has increased much more sharply than has that by challengers. Between 1974 and 1982, House challengers' total

Table 4.2 **Average Campaign Expenditures in the House and Senate (Selected Off-Years)**

	1982	1994	2002*	2010	2014
House					
All	228,000	409,000	624,000	1,263,000	1,093,000
Incumbents	265,000	595,000	831,000	1,686,000	1,446,000
Challengers	152,000	168,000	256,000	755,000	499,000
Open Seats	284,000	436,000	1,044,000	1,249,000	1,358,000
Senate					
All	1,782,000	2,877,000	4,061,000	8,689,000	7,827,000
Incumbents	1,858,000	3,852,000	4,072,000	10,335,000	10,898,000
Challengers	1,217,000	1,825,000	2,401,000	5,711,000	5,024,000
Open Seats	4,143,000	2,939,000	7,445,000	9,462,000	7,184,000

Source: Norman J. Ornstein, Thomas E. Mann, Michael J. Malbin, Andrew Rugg, and Raffaela Wakeman, eds., *Vital Statistics on Congress, 2017 Edition* (Washington, DC: Brookings Institution), tables 3.2 and 3.5. Based on Campaign Finance Institute analysis of Federal Election Commission data.

Note: Numbers are rounded to nearest 1,000.

*In 2002, Republican candidates running for open seats spent almost twice as much as their Democratic opponents, $9,201,000 to $5,690,000. But in 2004, Democrats achieved near parity in competition for open seats, spending an average of $7,636,368 to $7,718,386 for Republicans.

spending amounted to about 65 percent of what incumbents spent; in the five elections from 2004 to 2012, this proportion has decreased to 38 percent. In 2016, House incumbents spent an average of $1.6 million challengers $232,000, or just 14.5 percent of incumbent expenditures.

In the Senate, there is less of a difference between challenger and incumbent general election campaign spending, in part because the longer, six-year period to raise money allows challengers to plan in advance. In addition, Senate challengers often have more visibility, as when Hillary Clinton (D-NY) won the election to the U.S. Senate in 2000, or have previously won local or statewide office, as with former governor Lamar Alexander (R-TN). More generally, as the battle to control the Senate has intensified and national fundraising has grown, the high stakes of individual races, such as the 2014 North Carolina election, have led to increased funding of Senate races, especially in competitive seats.

As the role of money became much more pronounced in winning a congressional seat, incumbents learned to use the powers of their office to raise campaign funds, and contributors learned that campaign contributions could frequently buy access to specific legislators. While candidates have come to rely more heavily on PACs and individual contributions, much greater roles have opened up for national interest groups, parties, and wealthy individuals as rules on outside funding have loosened over the past decade. Certainly, members themselves acknowledge the pressure to raise funds for reelection and how this facilitates access for those who contribute. Former Senator Ernest "Fritz" Hollings (D-SC) observed in 2004:

> At my last campaign six years ago, it was $8.5 million. That factors out to about $30,000 a week, each week, every week for six years. . . . So if I miss a week this time, Christmas week, or New Year's week, I'm $60,000 in the hole . . . we can't see everybody. . . . So you're bound to see those who are the big givers.[47]

The pressures on incumbents have only grown in the years since Hollings made his comments. Traditionally, senators could spend the first four years of their term emphasizing legislation and then turn to reelection concerns in the two years before the next election. Those days are long gone—senators constantly raise money, either to fight the next electoral battle or to ward off potential challengers. Even relatively "safe" legislators often raise huge sums, either for their own campaign coffers or for "their individual legislator PACs," which serve as a source of funding for congressional colleagues. These PACs exist to enhance the personal power of individual members, as they make substantial contributions to their peers; each party now requires members who wish to be subcommittee or full committee chairs to raise money solely to donate it to colleagues who might be more vulnerable in their reelection campaigns.

Overall, individuals and groups who contribute to congressional campaigns and leadership PACs compose another constituency for a candidate, beyond those within his or her district. Much funding reinforces the local forces that shape representation (such as a tobacco PAC's funding of a North Carolina legislator), but many contributions come from interests far beyond the district's confines. On balance, this trend increases congressional fragmentation by creating a new set of influential constituents whose interests must be taken into account. At best, such constituencies of contributors compete for a legislator's attention with their district's voters. At worst, notes former Senator Russ Feingold (D-WI), "the very notion of representative democracy [is lost]. Money cuts the link between the representative and the represented."[48]

The Ups and Downs of Campaign Finance Reform: From Watergate to the Wild West

Along with the increasing official resources available to sitting members and the rising number of federal programs to which members could provide access and ombudsman services, the structure of campaign financing helped increase the margins and safety of House incumbents in the wake of post-Watergate 1974 campaign reform legislation. The 1974 amendments to the Federal Election Campaign Act, which had limited individual donations to $1,000 per campaign, and a 1976 Supreme Court decision (*Buckley v. Valeo*) that struck down limits on campaign spending combined to encourage the proliferation of PACs, which could give candidates up to $5,000 for each separate election (e.g., a primary in August followed by the general election in November). Although labor unions and a few other groups had long given money to candidates through PACs, the 1974 legislation opened the door to businesses (such as oil companies), trade associations (e.g., Realtors), and ideological groups (like the National Rifle Association) to raise funds and make congressional campaign contributions at the individual level and through affiliated PACs.

In 1972, PACs contributed a bit more than $8.5 million to congressional candidates, about 17 percent of all House campaign spending in that year. Twenty years later, PACs gave more than $127 million to House candidates, a fifteen-fold increase; PAC funds amounted to 38 percent of all campaign spending.[49] By 2012, PACs contributed $335 million to House candidates (35 percent), with incumbents relying on PACs for 43 percent of their donations.[50] As significant as PAC funding may have become by then, by the elections of 2014 and 2016, it was surpassed by the huge waves of outside money that have washed over U.S. electoral politics in the wake of the 2010 Supreme Court ruling in the case of *Citizens United v. Federal Election Commission*, which we discuss below (see figure 4.2).

The story of outside funding from large, often difficult-to-trace, donors begins, ironically, with the passage of the Bipartisan Campaign Finance Reform Act (BCRA), otherwise known as the McCain-Feingold bill, named after its two primary sponsors in the Senate, John McCain (R-AZ) and Russ Feingold (D-WI); it was the first major campaign finance overhaul in thirty years. The Congress had seriously considered campaign finance reform several times during that time, but the two parties could never agree on contribution limits from specific sources. Democrats had traditionally received more money from PACs, and Republicans had more success among independent contributors. But after the 1994 elections, the two parties reached more parity in the distribution of funds from these sources.

The role of money in campaigns had intensified in the mid-1990s for several reasons. First, a 1996 Supreme Court ruling largely freed political parties at the state and national levels from restrictions of spending so-called party-based (or soft) money directly on behalf of federal candidates' campaigns. In addition, many congressional leaders and other legislators funneled money from their own campaigns or from their personal PACs into tight races. Second, organized interests spent enormous amounts of "independent expenditures" on behalf of individual candidates. In 1996, the AFL-CIO embarked on the most visible campaign—at least $35 million spread across fewer than fifty districts. Other soft-money expenses were equally substantial, if not so focused; at least thirty-four businesses, unions, and trade associations each contributed more than $1 million in 1996, led by Philip Morris's $2.7 million-plus.[51] In 1998, party-based soft-money funding rose sharply. With a maximum of about thirty House seats in play, parties could concentrate their resources on a small number of races. In 1994, the previous midterm election, Democrats and Republicans raised $49 million and $53 million, respectively, in soft money; four years later, the totals roughly doubled, to $89 million and $111 million.

The electoral politics of the late 1990s demonstrated that even when competition levels are low and incumbents dominate, national funds from groups and parties can still play a great role in determining the balance of power in a closely divided Congress. Indeed, this relatively even division has proven a hallmark of the post-1994 Congress. Although the origins of the 2002 BCRA legislation date back to 1995, when McCain and Feingold introduced a bill that banned PAC contributions and provided free advertising time to candidates who agreed to spending limits, it was only after 2000 that momentum was sufficient to get a bill passed in both chambers. In 2001, the Senate passed a version of campaign finance reform that banned soft-money contributions to national political parties but allowed smaller amounts to be given to state and local parties, limited issue advertising by interest groups in the period up to sixty days before election day, required full disclosure of sponsorship of issue ads, and raised individual contribution limits. Sponsors in the House and Senate negotiated a modified version of that Senate bill, and bipartisan majorities in each chamber passed the BCRA in 2002. Opponents of the bill, led by Senator Mitch McConnell, filed suit against the bill and argued that the provisions limiting contributions violated the free-speech clause of the First Amendment to the Constitution. By a 5–4 vote, the Supreme Court, in *McConnell v. Federal Election Commission,* decided in favor of upholding the key provisions of the law in December 2003.[52] This ruling might have appeared to settle the fate of campaign reform and rules for campaigns, but the maneuvering, in and out of the courtroom, had just begun.

Prior to the passage of campaign finance reform, parties could raise unlimited amounts of money from individual contributors and distribute them to any number of candidates in the party. In this way, soft money became an alternative gateway of access to legislators via the party organizations and strengthened the influence of the party over individual legislators as a result. With the

closing of that gateway after the 2002 elections, national parties sought alternative resources to forge strong ties with House and Senate members.

The 2004 elections illustrated some of the unintended consequences of
the law. Prior to McCain-Feingold, political parties could spend money running issue ads against opposite-party candidates without clearly identifying
themselves. Subsequently, "527s," which are tax-exempt independent organizations, such as MoveOn.org and Club for Growth, rose up to take their place
in campaign politics. In the 2004 elections, 527s raised and spent more than
$523 million, most of which went to campaign ads.[53] Contributors could fun-
nel money to these independent groups, which can promote voter registration
and run issue ads in favor of or against candidates. In other words, 527s could
do the very same things that political parties used to do but in a much wider
and more varied ways. Over the 2006–2010 period, outside groups continued
to spend through 527 organizations while challenges to parts of BCRA made
their way through the courts. In 2010, under Chief Justice Roberts's direction,
the Supreme Court decided in *Citizens United v. Federal Election Commission*
to declare unconstitutional BCRA's restrictions on outside spending, based on
free speech concerns.[54] This decision opened the door for a host of interests to
spend directly on campaigns through various forms of organization (such as
SuperPACs and 501(c) groups), which are established by corporations, labor
unions, candidates, and wealthy individuals. The impact on congressional
campaigns has been substantial, but the total that all candidates raise remains
greater than the amount of money raised and spent by outside groups.[55] Still, the
recent growth of these funds has been dramatic (see figure 4.2), and spending
from these difficult-to-track sources rose to more than $500 million in 2014.[56]

How does the impact of outside funding, often referred to as "dark money"
because it is so hard to trace back to the donors, affect congressional campaigning? In the 2014 North Carolina Senate race, noted at the start of this chapter,
more than $60 million of the campaigns' total spending of $110 million came
from outside groups.[57] In other words, well over half the record funding for
this race came from beyond the candidates and the parties. On a lesser scale, in
Kansas, three-term incumbent Senator Pat Roberts, faced with a formidable and
unexpected general election challenge, won reelection in large part with outside
spending of $17 million in the last two months of his race, which far surpassed
his campaign's fund-raising efforts. Outside or "dark" money tends to be concentrated in highly publicized competitive races where the groups believe that
their money will make a real difference in the outcomes, so it is possible to have
outside groups outspend individual candidates in specific campaigns while still
spending less overall than all candidates combined.

In 2016, combined candidate and outside funding of the top ten Senate
races amounted to an average of $38.3 million, while the figures for the top ten
House races stood at $12.6 million, far in excess of the candidate-only fund-
raising. Overall, the total cost of all congressional races in 1998 amounted to
$1.62 billion; in 2016, this figure came to $4.06 billion. Far more than any legislative body in the world, elections for Congress are awash in money, much of
it difficult, if not impossible, to trace (figure 4.2).

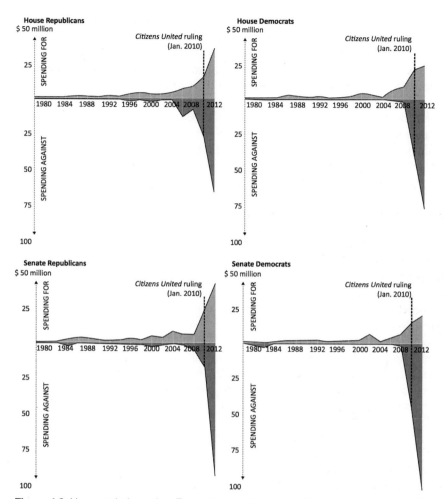

Figure 4.2 Nonparty Independent Expenditures in House and Senate Elections, 1978–2012.

Source: Norman J. Ornstein, Thomas E. Mann, Michael J. Malbin, Andrew Rugg, and Raffaela Wakeman, eds., *Vital Statistics on Congress, 2014 Edition* (Washington, DC: Brookings Institution). Based on Campaign Finance Institute analysis of Federal Election Commission data.

Note: All values in millions, U.S. dollars.

LOCAL CAMPAIGNS FOR NATIONAL OFFICE: THE MIX OF FORCES

Former Speaker O'Neill's homey advice that "all politics is local" has long held up as the defining principle of congressional elections. Increasingly, the caveat must be added: "Except when it's not." What has changed is the way in which local forces interact with national forces to create or diminish competition in congressional districts. Beginning in the late 1970s and early 1980s, incumbents began winning by larger margins, and the number of competitive seats diminished, mostly because of the power of incumbents to raise campaign funds. By

2002, the cumulative effects of redistricting by state legislatures and the rising costs of campaigns combined to make districts more homogeneous and less accessible to challengers. This trend has continued in the wake of the 2012 redistricting cycle—population movements and some redistricting activity have produced smaller numbers of competitive seats and more intense competition in those districts that are competitive.

Increasingly, outside funding, often in the form of untraceable dark money from networks of groups and wealthy individuals, has exerted great influence on congressional election outcomes. Indeed, by one accounting, outside funding accounted for almost $800 million (20 percent) of the total $4 billion cost of the 2014 elections.[58] Parties have also upped their participation in the post–*Citizens United* world, as have highly partisan activists and groups, who often influence primary elections, especially within the Republican Party.

Congress is more partisan at present than at any time in the past century, and by some measures more so. The partisan wave elections of 2006, 2008, and 2010 (with a smaller surge in 2014) have produced a polarized and arguably dysfunctional Congress. Unified party control can be a blessing when the party stays unified and enacts a set of policies that wins approval among voters. Conversely, it can become a curse when those policies do not pass because of intra-party squabbling, or they do pass but they are not successful; either way voters can clearly assign blame to a single majority party. With the divided, yet partisan, government of 2011–2016, the Congress has demonstrated that partisan, electorally oriented scuffling—in both the House and Senate—may well be associated with the historically low levels in the public's trust for its legislature. At some point, such lack of trust may well call into question the Congress's very legitimacy.

Recommended Readings

Heberling, Eric, and Bruce Larson. *Congressional Parties, Institutional Ambition, and the Financing of Majority Control*. Ann Arbor: University of Michigan Press, 2012.

Herrnson, Paul. *Congressional Elections: Campaigning at Home and in Washington*, 6th ed. Washington: CQ/Sage, 2011.

Jacobson, Gary. *The Politics of Congressional Elections*, 9th ed. Lanham, MD: Rowman & Littlefield, 2015.

Lublin, David. *The Paradox of Representation*. Princeton, NJ: Princeton University Press, 1999.

Useful Resources

Center for Responsive Politics: http://www.opensecrets.org
Democratic Senatorial Campaign Committees: http://www.dscc.org
National Republican Congressional Committee: http://www.nrcc.org
Campaign Finance Institute: http://www.cfinst.org/

Notes

[1] According to her campaign site at http://eliseforcongress.com/about.

[2] A ninth Senate seat came to the Republicans through the November 1994 party switch of Alabama Democrat Richard Shelby. They added a tenth seat with Colorado senator Ben Nighthorse Campbell's switch in March 1995.

[3] Beyond the thirty-four Democratic incumbents who lost in the general election, two more lost in Democratic primary contests.

[4] The Democrats' advantage, though central to passing the Affordable Care Act in 2010, was short-lived. In the wake of Senator Edward Kennedy's death in early 2009 (and his temporary replacement by an appointed Democrat), Republican Scott Brown won an upset victory in a 2010 special election, thus leaving the Democratic majority at 59 for the remainder of the Congress.

[5] Gary Jacobson, *The Politics of Congressional Elections*, 3rd ed. (New York: HarperCollins, 1992), 2.

[6] Robert S. Erickson and Gerald C. Wright, "Voters, Candidates, and Issues in Congressional Elections," in *Congress Reconsidered*, 6th ed., ed. Lawrence C. Dodd and Bruce I. Oppenheimer (Washington, DC: CQ Press, 1997), 156.

[7] Ibid., 91.

[8] Bill Bishop, *The Big Sort* (New York: Mariner, 2008).

[9] Richard F. Fenno, Jr., *Home Style* (Boston: Little, Brown, 1978), 27.

[10] Ibid., 18.

[11] The Constitution mandates the reapportionment of House seats among the states every ten years, after the decennial census. Each state must then redraw its district lines to comply with equal representation requirements. For a good contemporary overview of the redistricting and reapportionment, see David Butler and Bruce Cain, *Congressional Redistricting* (New York: Macmillan, 1992).

[12] National Committee for an Effective Congress, Redistricting Resource Center, November 2002, http://www.ncec.org.

[13] Ibid. See also U.S. Census, 2010, http://www.census.gov/prod/cen2010/briefs/c2010br-08.pdf (accessed February 12, 2015).

[14] See Jon Meacham, "Voting Wrongs," *Washington Monthly*, March 1993, 28. Of the fifty-eight minority House members, fifty-two came from minority-majority districts.

[15] Lani Guinier, "Don't Scapegoat the Gerrymander," *New York Times*, January 8, 1995, 36–37.

[16] See Butler and Cain, *Congressional Redistricting*, 1ff.

[17] Several legal cases challenged this policy; in its 1997 session, the U.S. Supreme Court had approved maps in Louisiana and Georgia that reduced the role of race in redistricting.

[18] Michael Barone and Grant Ujifusa, *The Almanac of American Politics, 1994* (Washington, DC: National Journal, 1993), 969.

[19] Linda Greenhouse, "High Court Voids Race-Based Plans for Redistricting," *New York Times*, June 14, 1996, A1.

[20] Holly Idelson, "Court Takes a Harder Line on Minority Voting Blocs," *Congressional Quarterly Weekly Report*, July 1, 1995, 1944.

[21] For two excellent studies of majority-minority districting, see David I. Lublin, *The Paradox of Representation: Racial Gerrymandering and Minority Interests in Congress* (Princeton, NJ: Princeton University Press, 1997) and David T. Canon, *Race, Redistricting, and Representation: The Unintended Consequences of Black-Majority Districts* (Chicago: University of Chicago Press, 1999).

[22] Scott Bland, "More Minorities, Less Clout?" *National Journal*, April 19, 2012.

[23] Staff Editorial, "Rethinking Texas' Redistricting," *New York Times*, October 22, 2004, A22.

[24] Fair Vote: The Center for Voting and Democracy, http://www.fairvote.org/research-and-analysis/blog/did-the-california-citizens-redistricting-commission-really-create-more-competitive-districts (accessed February 12, 2015); see National Conference of State Legislatures, "Redistricting Commissions: Legislative Plans," http://www.ncsl.org/research/redistricting/2009-redistricting-commissions-table.aspx (accessed February 23, 2015).

[25] Michael Li, Thomas Wolf, and Alexis Farmer, "The State of Redistricting Litigation (March 2017 Edition)" https://www.brennancenter.org/blog/state-redistricting-litigation-march-2017-edition.

[26] Fenno, *Home Style*, 25.

[27] FEC, http://www.fec.gov (Candidate Summary Reports as of November 22, 2004).

[28] Center for Responsive Politics, *Open Secrets*, https://www.opensecrets.org/politicians/summary.php?type=C&cid=N00029077&newMem=N&cycle=2014 (accessed February 13, 2015).

[29] Norman J. Ornstein, Thomas E. Mann, Michael J. Malbin, Andrew Rugg, and Raffaela Wakeman, *Vital Statistics on Congress* (Washington, DC: Brookings Institution, 2014), http://www.brookings.edu/research/reports/2013/07/vital-statistics-congress-mann-ornstein (accessed February 13, 2015); https://www.opensecrets.org/politicians/summary.php?type=C&cid=N00029077&newMem=N&cycle=2014 (accessed February 13, 2015).

[30] Ibid., table 1.6.

[31] Morris P. Fiorina, "The Case of the Vanishing Marginals: The Bureaucracy Did It," *American Political Science Review* 71 (1977): 177–81.

[32] Among an avalanche of studies, see the summary presented in Bruce Cain, John Ferejohn, and Morris Fiorina, *The Personal Vote* (Cambridge, MA: Harvard University Press, 1987), 121ff.

[33] Among others, see John Ferejohn, "On the Decline of Competition in Congressional Elections," *American Political Science Review* 71 (March 1977): 166–76. More generally, see the discussion in Gary Jacobson, *Politics of Congressional Elections*, 4th ed. (New York: Longman, 1997), 19ff.

[34] For the best recent academic consideration of the occurrence and impacts of gerrymandering, see Nolan McCarthy, Keith T. Poole, and Howard Rosenthal, "Does Gerrymandering Cause Polarization?" *American Journal of Political Science* 53, no. 3. (2009): 666–80. See also, Seth Masket, "The Convenient Scapegoat of Gerrymandering," *Vox*, March 29, 2017, http://www.vox.com/mischiefs-of-faction/2017/3/29/15109082/gerrymandering-convenient-scapegoat (accessed April 21, 2017).

[35] Gary Jacobson, *Politics of Congressional Elections*, 8th ed. (Boston: Pearson, 2012), 52–56. For a differing view, see Donald P. Green and Jonathan S. Krasno, "Salvation for the Spendthrift Incumbents," *American Journal of Political Science* 32 (1988): 844–907.

[36] Open Secrets, https://www.opensecrets.org/overview/incumbs.php (accessed April 25, 2017).

[37] Gary Jacobson, *Politics of Congressional Elections*, 3rd ed. (New York: HarperCollins, 1992),

[38] Eric Bradner, "Republican Karen Handel wins Georgia House special election." *CNN Politics*, http://www.cnn.com/2017/06/20/politics/georgia-house-results-ossoff-handel/index.html (accessed September 6, 2017).

[39] Two weeks before the 1994 election, then minority leader Gingrich put the odds at 2-to-1 that Republicans would win the House. Katharine Q. Seelye, "With Fiery Words, Gingrich Builds His Kingdom," *New York Times*, October 27, 1994, A1.

[40] Paul Herrnson, "Money and Motives: Spending in House Elections," *Congress Reconsidered*, 6th ed., ed. Lawrence C. Dodd and Bruce I. Oppenheimer (Washington, DC: CQ Press, 1997), 101.

[41] For detailed discussions of Republican Party governance in the 104th Congress, see James G. Gimpel, *Legislating the Revolution: The Contract with America in Its First 100 Days* (Boston: Allyn & Bacon, 1996) and Richard F Fenno, Jr., *Learning to Govern: An Institutional View of the 104th Congress* (Washington, DC: Brookings Institution Press, 1997). A good analysis of the fates of the freshman Republican class of 1995 can be found in Linda Killian's book, *The Freshmen: What Happened to the Republican Revolution?* (Boulder, CO: Westview, 1998).

[42] For a book-length treatment of the implications of this relative electoral parity, see Frances Lee, *Insecure Majorities* (Chicago: University of Chicago Press, 2016).

[43] Gary Jacobson, "Partisanship, Money and Competition," in *Congress Reconsidered*, 10th ed., ed. Lawrence Dodd and Bruce Oppenheimer (Washington, DC: CQ/Sage, 2013), 140.

[44] Sean Theriault, *The Gingrich Senators* (New York: Oxford University Press, 2013).

[45] Grace Wallack and John Hudak, "How Much Did Your Vote Cost?" Brookings Institution, http://www.brookings.edu/blogs/fixgov/posts/2014/11/07-spending-per-voter-2014-midterm-senate-wallack-hudak (accessed May 26, 2015).

[46] All figures from the Campaign Finance Institute, http://www.cfinst.org (accessed February 15, 2015).

[47] Senator Fritz Hollings (D-SC), quoted in a 60 Minutes interview with Mike Wallace, aired on December 10, 2004, http://www.cbsnews.com/news/parting-shots-from-fritz-hollings.

[48] Quoted in Brigid Shulte and Jodi Enda, "Fund Raising Is Always on Political Agenda," *Lawrence Journal-World*, January 13, 1997, 6b. Feingold tested this notion in 1998 when he limited his spending to $3.8 million and actively discouraged outside funding from the national Democratic Party. His opponent, Rep. Mark Neumann, spent $4,316,928. Feingold won reelection, with just over 50 percent of the vote. He subsequently lost in 2010.

[49] These figures include general election candidates' spending in both the primary and the general elections. Defeated primary candidates are not included. These figures and others in this section are from Ornstein et al., *Vital Statistics on Congress*, table 3.10, http://www.brookings.edu/research/reports/2013/07/vital-statistics-congress-mann-ornstein (accessed February 15, 2015).

[50] Campaign Finance Institute, "House Receipts from Individuals, PACs, and Other, All General Election Candidates, 1999–2012," http://www.cfinst.org/pdf/historical/Donors_HouseCand_2000-2012.pdf (accessed February 15, 2015).

[51] David E. Rosenbaum, "In Political Money Game, the Year of Big Loopholes," *New York Times*, December 26, 1996, A11. Soft money represents funds meant ostensibly for so-called party-building activities.

[52] John Cochran, "Supreme Court Narrowly Upholds Core Campaign Finance Provisions," *CQ Weekly*, December 13, 2003, 3076–77.

[53] "527s: Advocacy Group Spending," *Opensecrets.org*, https://www.opensecrets.org/527s (accessed February 15, 2015).

[54] *Citizens United v. Federal Election Commission*, Justia, https://supreme.justia.com/cases/federal/us/558/08-205.

[55] "Whose Voices Were Loudest?" Campaign Finance Institute, http://www.cfinst.org/Press/PReleases/14-11-07/Parties_and_Candidates_Outspent_Non-Party_Groups_in_Almost_Every_Close_House_Race_in_2014_Non-Party_Groups_Were_More_Important_in_the_Senate.aspx (accessed February 16, 2015).

[56] "Outside Spending," *Opensecrets.org*, https://www.opensecrets.org/outsidespending (accessed March 6, 2015); see also Lee Drutman, "The Rise of Dark Money," in *Interest Group Politics*, 9th ed., ed. Allan J. Cigler, Burdett Loomis, and Anthony Nownes (Washington, DC: CQ/Sage, 2015), 139–58.

[57] Paul Blumenthal, "Here's Your First $100 Million Senate Race," *Huffington Post*, http://www.huffingtonpost.com/2014/11/04/2014-citizens-united-elec_n_6100330.html (accessed February 15, 2015).

[58] "Outside Spending," *Opensecrets.org*, https://www.opensecrets.org/outsidespending/fes_summ.php (accessed February 16, 2015).

CHAPTER 5

Parties, Leaders, and Ideology in Congress

Each political party in both the House and Senate has a group of members who comprise the leadership team. Here, we see the Senate Republican Party leadership team, led by Senator Mitch McConnell (R-KY) as Senate Majority Leader.

On November 9, 2016, Paul Ryan, the Republican Speaker of the House, and Mitch McConnell, Republican Majority Leader of the U.S. Senate, woke up knowing that they would be leading a united GOP government that controlled the executive branch and both Houses of Congress. This was new territory for both Ryan and McConnell because neither of them had ever served as chamber leaders under their party's president. Up until the early morning hours of that day, most political observers believed Hillary Clinton would be elected president of the United States, the Senate would return to Democratic control, and the Republicans would hold on to the House but lose seats. Only one of three of those predictions was confirmed. For Paul Ryan, the moment was yet another step in a relatively fast rise to power in American politics.

Paul Ryan was elected to the House of Representatives in 1998 representing the 1st congressional district in Wisconsin. Before that, he spent time working on Capitol Hill for Senator Bob Kasten (R-WI) from Wisconsin and Senator Sam Brownback (R-KS) before returning home to Wisconsin to work for his family's business. When the Republican member of Congress representing his hometown retired, Ryan ran in the primary, won the nomination, and went on to win the general election at the age of twenty-eight.

Within Congress, he built a reputation as a policy-oriented conservative who chaired the House Budget Committee and then the House Ways and Means Committee. Mitt Romney chose him as his 2012 vice presidential running mate, and he was elected Speaker of the House in the wake of John Boehner's October 2015 resignation (for more, see chapter discussion below). He spent a year leading the House GOP against President Obama but also showed a willingness to compromise in order to pass crucial legislation in areas including budget and spending bills, infrastructure reauthorization, and education.

Ryan now stood poised to be able to propose and pass legislation, not just obstruct Democratic presidential proposals. The first one hundred days of a new presidential administration is often viewed as crucial to laying the foundation for policy success, especially under unified party government. But there was a complication. Ryan had not supported Donald Trump for most of the Republican Party presidential nomination process; only after Trump received the requisite number of delegates did Ryan formally endorse him at the GOP convention in July 2016. More to the point for Ryan, his House GOP membership was also divided on the Trump candidacy and although Republican voters ended up rallying around their nominee and propelling him to victory, there was lingering doubt about his agenda in the GOP-controlled Congress.

Formally, the ingredients for united party governance were in place, but some of them were combustible and would present both partisan and ideological challenges in the 115th Congress. Indeed, congressional party leaders must bring together their members and bridge policy differences as they carry out their leadership responsibilities.

This chapter focuses on the history of party leadership in the House and Senate and how that leadership has evolved over time. In the House, majority-party leaders are granted substantial agenda-setting and committee-appointment powers by their rank-and-file members, and the extent of those powers can often depend on the ideological agreement within the party. In contrast, Senate party leaders hold less power over the Senate floor agenda and committee appointments. The House, under Democrats and Republicans alike, encourages strong party leadership, but the Senate, despite increased partisanship over the past decade and stronger use of floor powers by party leaders, continues to preserve significant individual powers.

THE CONGRESSIONAL PARTY IN THE TWENTY-FIRST CENTURY: A RETURN TO CENTRALIZATION

Legislatures, like all institutions, must function with some overall coherence. Political parties provide much of the glue that holds together the disparate ambitions of 535 legislators, buttressed by their own enterprises, and the fragmented collection of committees, subcommittees, and special-interest caucuses. Assessing the role of parties in the early 1960s, a strong committee era, Richard F. Fenno, Jr., concluded that parties "organize decision making across committees and across stages [of the legislative process], thereby functioning as a centralizing force in the making of House decisions." Although most members shared emotional attachments to their party and regarded it as one means to exercise power, Fenno noted that the "party label masks a pluralism of geographic, social, ideological, and organizational sources of identification, support, and loyalty. The roots of this pluralism lie outside the chamber, in the disparity of conditions under which the members are elected and in the decentralized organization of the parties nationally."[1] Congressional parties thus grow stronger when partisanship among voters grows stronger, and divisions between the parties in the electorate solidify.

Ultimately, the best opportunities to exercise effective party leadership on Capitol Hill have depended on forces largely beyond the control of the leaders, forces that emanate from the society and the electorate. Periods of strong, centralized leadership and high levels of partisan voting on Capitol Hill reflect polarization between the parties in the electorate.[2] Circa 1900, Republican Speakers Thomas Reed and Joseph Cannon benefited from electoral results built on clear philosophical differences between two legislative parties that shouldered responsibility for ruling and accountability for their actions. In that era, individual representatives, having won their seats "on the basis of a party's platform," were expected to "support party positions, even against personal convictions or desires."[3] Internal allegiances to a party leader fit neatly into a world in which party machines controlled the candidate selection process.[4] Opposing the party might well mean that a legislator would be denied renomination, and thus reelection, especially in an era before the widespread adoption of primary elections as the means of choosing nominees. Today, parties still use the nomination process to enforce party loyalty among their members, but the candidate-oriented nature of primary elections can open doors to activist wings of the party from the right and the left.

If party machines and a polarized electorate provided the external context for strong direction, the Speaker could act forcefully on party issues within the House.[5] Reed (1889–1891, 1895–1899) and Cannon (1903–1911) each combined their extensive formal prerogatives under the rules with their status as Speaker to carry out their legislative agendas. Speaker Cannon, for example, chaired the Rules Committee, and his majority leader headed Ways and Means—at the time, the two most powerful committees in the chamber. He appointed all committee members and all chairs and could delay making these appointments until well after the Congress had convened. He controlled the legislative schedule with an iron hand and used his power of recognition to reduce opponents' capacity to participate meaningfully in floor debate. Moreover, the Speaker was also a party leader who could define those issues appropriate for partisan position taking. Straying from the party might well mean that a dissident would be disciplined by the Speaker through removal from a powerful committee or the rejection of his preferences in fashioning a key piece of legislation. At worst, the Speaker could encourage the dissident's local party organization to reject him as a candidate in the next election.

Why should we care much about century-old congressional party politics and voting alignments? Because studying these topics allows us to explain periods of strong *and* weak party leadership in Congress. Table 5.1 presents a set of descriptive characteristics about the first and last Congress of the twentieth century. After the fall of Speaker Cannon, it took almost seventy years for strong party leadership in the House to reemerge, first among Democrats and then within the Republican Party under Newt Gingrich. As the majority party, Democrats organized both the House and Senate for all but two Congresses between 1933 and the 1990s.[6] This means they named the Speaker, the Senate majority leader, various other majority-party offices, and all the committee chairs, all the while holding a majority of seats on all legislative committees. But this "procedural majority," which ensured Democratic control in formal terms, often vanished when important, substantive issues came to a vote.[7] Not only was the Congress fragmented among constituencies in ordinary pluralistic ways, but it also frequently split sharply along the related lines of region and ideology, as southern Democrats joined with Republicans to form a "Conservative Coalition" that opposed the liberal initiatives of Democratic presidents and their northern Democratic allies in the Congress, especially on civil rights and social welfare policies.[8]

The Democratic Majority Party Challenge: Moving from Divisions to Unity

Although parties weakened in the mid-twentieth-century Congress, party leadership remained essential, as Democratic Speaker Sam Rayburn demonstrated during his seventeen years in the office between 1940 and 1961. Rayburn controlled his party members through informal persuasion rather than formal party powers because he possessed few of the leadership tools that Cannon had wielded so effectively to dominate the agenda and steer the legislative results of the House.[9] The seniority principle had become so firmly entrenched within the Congress that advancement on committees was virtually automatic, regardless of one's loyalty to the party. Nor did Rayburn control the initial assignments of Democrats to committees.[10]

Table 5.1 The First and Last Congresses of the Twentieth Century

	57th Congress	106th Congress
Party Identification		
House	199 R	222 R
	151 D	211 D
	8 Other	1 Other
Senate	55 R	55 R
	31 D	45 D
	4 Other	0 Other
Average Age		
House	49	53
Senate	58	58
Average Number of Previous Terms		
House	2	4
Senate	1	1
African Americans	0	38
Women	0	65
Most Common First Name	William (45)	John (40)
Most Common Last Name	Smith (7)	Smith (6)
Members Named Elijah	1	1
Members Named Nehemiah	1	0
Members with Military Experience	28%	33%
Most Common Former Profession	Lawyer (90%)	Lawyer (40%)
Former Blacksmiths	1	0
Former Plastic Surgeons	0	1
Members from Alaska, Arizona, Hawaii, New Mexico, or Oklahoma	0	28

Source: *Roll Call*, January 18, 1999.

Yet legislators almost universally viewed him as a powerful Speaker. How could this be so? Rayburn did retain significant, if limited, formal powers and the discretion to recognize whom he wanted on the House floor. He also determined the final scheduling of legislation, and he often used his position to trade favors with other members—both Republicans and Democrats.[11] Favors such as campaigning for a fellow Democrat, postponing a vote to accommodate a freshman Republican, and supporting a new constituent project for a marginal-seat member allowed the Speaker to build up positive "balances" in his exchanges with legions of representatives (including those in the minority). These favors allowed Rayburn to request assistance on specific issues from various legislators who would be hard-pressed to rebuff him.[12] In addition, Rayburn's work ethic, his absolute integrity, and his total dedication to the House provided strong foundations for his politicking on specific legislative items.

From the 1960s through the 1970s, the Democratic Party grew in numbers, but became more and more fractured on issues ranging from voting rights to the Vietnam War. The influx of northern liberal Democrats to both the House and the Senate presented a challenge to conservative dominance, and over time the conflict between the liberal and conservative wings of the party weakened party leadership. It was simply too difficult to craft a set of party policies that would command the loyalty of a majority of the Democratic Party over and over again. Neither of the two Speakers who followed Rayburn—John McCormack (D-MA, 1961–1969) and Carl Albert (D-OK, 1969–1977)—proved forceful or effective in countering these decentralizing forces. The old "informal persuasion" that Sam Rayburn had used so effectively was not suited to the changing nature of the party.

To reduce the stranglehold that the senior conservative southerners had over party policy, the more liberal members of the House Democratic caucus began a concerted effort to empower party leaders who shared their policy ideas. Liberals continually prodded the Democratic caucus to reduce the autonomy of full committee chairs and increase the authority of the leadership and the full caucus, which the northern Democrats increasingly dominated.[13] Over time, the number of liberal and moderate members of the Democratic Party grew sufficiently large to make changes in the way the party ran the House. In particular, the party gave the Speaker the power to appoint members of the Rules Committee, thus making the committee a loyal "arm of the Leadership."[14] Next, the party moved the committee-assignment responsibility to the Steering and Policy Committee (dominated by the party leadership) and thus greatly enhanced the leaders' roles in this process. Finally, to coordinate policymaking within the fragmented committee system, the Speaker was granted broad powers to refer bills to multiple committees, often in a well-defined sequence that imposed deadlines on committee action.[15]

In 1974, the Democratic Party enacted a series of major reforms that expanded the number of subcommittees and gave subcommittee chairs separate authority over legislation from the chairmen of the full committee. These provisions actually increased decentralization within the House for a few years, even as the leadership was gaining centralized power. At the same time, the committee reforms diminished the role of seniority in determining who would head committees by requiring that the party members approve all full-committee chairs and each of the thirteen appropriations subcommittee chairs. At the outset of each new Congress, members of the party would not only select their Speaker, but they would also vote on a number of other top leadership posts that previously were solely under the Speaker's purview. In short, the Democratic reforms gave the party rank and file a biennial opportunity to defeat any top party or committee leader who had lost their confidence.[16]

When Rep. Thomas P. (Tip) O'Neill (D-MA) took the reins as Speaker in 1977, he and his lieutenants created a new leadership style within a House that encouraged more individual participation from virtually all members, but especially those of the majority party.[17] O'Neill had to walk a fine line to balance the increased structural powers given to individual members through subcommittee participation and his attempts to craft unified party majorities. In this democratized context, leaders became service providers to their colleagues by offering meaningful support to incumbents, by keeping all the Democratic legislators well informed and by granting a number of particular favors. The leaders consciously adopted an inclusive strategy, bringing large numbers of members into the leadership, both in permanent positions (e.g., as whips) and in ad hoc capacities (such as task force heads and members). At the same time, the Democratic leaders used their formal powers to schedule bills and dominate the Rules Committee to increase their ability to structure the decision-making process. Collectively, congressional Democrats were willing to allow their leadership considerable leeway here, as long as its actions did not conflict with clear membership preferences.

In 1986, Tip O'Neill retired from the House, and Democrats accepted a strengthened leadership that allowed Jim Wright (D-TX) to become, in 1987–1989, one of the House's most powerful Speakers in history. By this time, the composition of the Democratic Party had changed considerably in the House. The traditional conservative southern Democrats had all but disappeared, replaced in large measure by legislators from urban areas and districts with high percentages of African American voters. As the Democratic Party overall moved to the left, conservative southern ("Yellow Dog") Democratic voters gradually switched parties and elected Republicans in rising numbers.[18] The result produced more uniformity within both the Democratic and Republican parties and a more stark division between them, culminating in the 1994 Republican takeover of the House (and with it the Senate) after forty years of Democratic control. This Republican revolution, led by the eventual new Speaker, Newt Gingrich (R-GA), laid the foundation for the intense partisan polarization we see today.

Such polarization is reflected in their roll call voting behavior on the House floor. In assessing the strength of political parties within the Congress, political scientists frequently analyze changes in two different but related measures of partisanship on roll call votes: the proportion of votes on which a majority of one party opposes a majority of the other, and the extent to which party members vote with their party on a given roll call vote.[19] There is no question that both the proportion of party-based votes and the level of party loyalty on these votes increased considerably during the 1980s; tables 5.2 and 5.3 show trends in party unity and the proportion of roll calls that divided along party lines. With the departure of southern conservatives from the Democratic Party, party unity scores for Democrats from the South rose steadily, from an average 53 percent party unity score in the 94th Congress (1975–1977) to an average of 79 percent in the 100th Congress (1987–1989).[20] At the same time, the Republicans grew increasingly united and vocal in their protests against both

Table 5.2 Average Party Unity Scores by Congress

Congress	Democrats	Republicans	Congress	Democrats	Republicans
87th (1961–1962)	80.8	80.6	100th (1987–1988)	87.7	78.8
88th (1963–1964)	83.2	82.0	101st (1989–1990)	86.3	76.9
89th (1965–1966)	78.1	80.4	102nd (1991–1992)	86.2	82.2
90th (1967–1968)	74.8	79.1	103rd (1993–1994)	88.6	87.2
91st (1969–1970)	70.9	72.1	104th (1995–1996)	83.1	91.8
92nd (1971–1972)	70.2	76.0	105th (1997–1998)	85.7	89.6
93rd (1973–1974)	73.8	72.5	106th (1999–2000)	86.5	89.3
94th (1975–1976)	74.7	76.4	107th (2001–2002)	87.7	93.5
95th (1977–1978)	72.7	76.4	108th (2003–2004)	90.6	93.8
96th (1979–1980)	76.3	78.8	109th (2005–2006)	90.5	92.4
97th (1981–1982)	77.6	77.5	110th (2007–2008)	95.6	90.4
98th (1983–1984)	81.5	78.4	111th (2009–2010)	93.9	90.9
99th (1985–1986)	86.1	77.7	112th (2011–2012)	91.0	93.5

Source: Adapted from Christopher Ingraham, "Historical House Ideology and Party Unity, 35th–113th Congress (1857–2014)," Brookings Institution, November 25, 2013, http://www.brookings.edu/research/interactives/2013/historical-house-ideology-and-party-unity.

Table 5.3 Percentage of Partisan Roll Calls

How Often a Majority of Democrats Voted against a Majority of Republicans

Year	House	Senate	Year	House	Senate	Year	House	Senate	Year	House	Senate
1954	38	47	1969	31	36	1984	47	40	1999	47	63
1955	41	30	1970	27	35	1985	61	50	2000	43	49
1956	44	53	1971	38	42	1986	57	52	2001	40	55
1957	59	36	1972	27	36	1987	64	41	2002	43	45
1958	40	44	1973	42	40	1988	47	42	2003	52	67
1959	55	48	1974	29	44	1989	55	35	2004	47	52
1960	53	37	1975	48	48	1990	49	54	2005	49	63
1961	50	62	1976	36	37	1991	55	49	2006	57	57
1962	46	41	1977	42	42	1992	64	53	2007	60	62
1963	49	47	1978	33	45	1993	65	67	2008	52	53
1964	55	36	1979	47	47	1994	62	52	2009	51	72
1965	52	42	1980	38	46	1995	73	69	2010	40	79
1966	41	50	1981	37	48	1996	56	62	2011	76	51
1967	36	35	1982	36	43	1997	50	50	2012	73	60
1968	35	32	1983	56	44	1998	56	56	2013	69	70

Source: "CQ Roll Call's Vote Studies—2013 in Review," February 3, 2014, http://media.cq.com/votestudies (accessed February 9, 2015).

the Democrats' policy positions and their use of procedures to limit meaningful minority participation within the House.[21]

As Speaker Wright consolidated his power, those protests grew more vocal and even began to include disgruntled Democrats. Speaker Wright was eventually forced to resign his post as Speaker in 1988, ostensibly over charges of ethics violation (filed by none other than Newt Gingrich), but it was widely accepted that Democratic Party members believed that the Speaker had overstepped his authority in the name of party unity.

Jim Wright was replaced by his polar opposite in terms of leadership style: Tom Foley (D-WA), a mild-mannered leader who relied on persuasion and coalition building rather than top-down party control. When Tom Foley assumed the speakership there was a fairly large group of leaders in place as the day-to-day directors of House business. The traditional leaders—the Speaker, the House majority leader, and the whip—were joined by three chief deputy whips, along with the caucus chair and vice chair. "As the leadership has become more central to the legislative process," political scientist Barbara Sinclair noted, "members' desires for representation in the leadership . . . intensified."[22]

The active Democratic caucus both empowered and restrained the party's leaders. The core leadership, aided by a formidable staff, served as information source, sounding board, strategic and tactical decision maker, and, under divided government, interbranch negotiator. Nevertheless, given its highly inclusive style of operation, even an expanded core leadership could not maintain adequate communication lines with more than 250 House Democrats, so the Democrats established a much more extended leadership apparatus, which included almost half the party's 256 legislators in the 103rd Congress (1993–1995). Of special note was the systematic expansion of the whip system, which acted as a conduit for information between members and leaders and as an organization for mobilizing votes on the House floor. The whip system included the majority whip, four chief deputy whips, a floor whip, an "ex officio whip," eleven deputy whips, two "whip task force" chairs, fifty-six leadership-appointed at-large whips, and eighteen assistant whips elected by members of regional zones. All in all, the whip system included ninety-two Democratic members, well over a third of the party's ranks in the House. And the expansion in the ranks of Democratic leaders did not stop with the whip system. Rules Committee members clearly occupied leadership slots, as did the chair of the Budget Committee and a host of ad hoc task force heads appointed by the majority leader to organize party efforts on specific legislative initiatives.[23] In addition, the chairmanship of the Democratic Congressional Campaign Committee (DCCC) represented an important leadership position.

At first with great hesitancy, and later with vigor and conviction, the Democratic majority came to structure the context of decision-making in the House, which meant that the minority Republicans became even less able to influence outcomes.[24] The movement toward strong party leadership during this time reflected increasing ideological cohesiveness within both parties in the House. Members calculated that since they were united in policy preferences, they should grant their leaders more latitude in using the rules to structure outcomes on the House floor.[25] Strong party leadership remained contingent on these calculations by the members and on the ideological divisions between the two parties. This combination of two coherent, but distinct, ideological sets of partisans was labeled "conditional party government" by congressional scholars David Rohde and John Aldrich.[26] In the end, Democratic leaders became heavily dependent on manipulating the agenda and structuring floor votes through the aggressive use of the Rules Committee.[27] Many, if not most, Republicans found themselves holding no stake in the institution of the House; thus, it was with little remorse that they would seek to tear down the House that the Democratic majority had constructed.

Party Leadership in the Republican Mold: The Dilemma of Minority Opposition

After forty years as the minority, Republicans gained control of the House in 1994 in the one of the greatest "upset" congressional elections in history. Before we explore the strong, centralized leadership adopted by the GOP when it assumed majority control, let us briefly examine how the Republican Party operated as a minority within the contemporary House.

For the forty years that they were in the minority, the Republicans were relatively unified, voting as a party block about 70 percent of the time (see table 5.2). As members of a long-standing minority in the House, Republicans found themselves holding little authority, which freed them to pursue a variety of strategies in seeking to affect policy outcomes.[28] Simple hard-boiled opposition was one alternative, of course, but historically many Republicans opted to cooperate with the Democratic majority, hoping to affect policies in committee or by providing key votes on the floor. The Rayburn-era House presented frequent opportunities for committees' ranking minority members to become important forces in shaping congressional policies. It may seem almost impossible to imagine that, in today's era of high partisan polarization, members of the opposition minority party would "cross the aisle" to work with their majority party colleagues but it happened on a fairly regular basis.

During the 1970s and 1980s, House Republicans found themselves in increasingly difficult straits. First, they were often expected to support the policies of a Republican president, even though their minority status denied them any effective means to implement the executive agendas articulated by presidents Nixon, Reagan, and Bush. Second, House Democratic majorities, especially after 1982, acted in highly partisan ways within committees and on the floor. Republicans could do little in the face of Rules Committee decisions to structure floor debates and votes, and the Speaker's control of scheduling allowed them little voice in decision-making on either policies or procedures. A strong Democratic leadership and an increasingly unified set of Democratic members meant that House Republicans enjoyed few opportunities to influence outcomes. This system of overwhelming majority dominance over the House agenda has remained in place ever since.

In step with its generally conservative membership and often in reaction to the strengthened, sometimes arrogant Democratic leadership, the House Republicans frequently chose confrontational strategies through the 1980s and into the 1990s. Newt Gingrich enlisted other young, activist representatives to join him in the Conservative Opportunity Society, an informal group that functioned simultaneously as an in-House think tank and a launching pad to challenge the established powers of both parties.[29] The turning point for Gingrich's ascendance to party power came in 1989, when he ran for the position of minority whip of the Republican Party.

The sitting minority whip at the time, Dick Cheney (R-WY), was appointed secretary of defense in March 1989. The ensuing leadership contest pitted Gingrich against veteran representative Edward Madigan (R-IL). Buoyed by early support from some frustrated moderates, Gingrich won the whip post with an 89–87 count. By this narrowest of margins, the Republican caucus decided to move in a more confrontational direction.

It was at this moment that the Republican Party in the House opted to end any cooperation with the Democratic majority and aggressively seek to unseat them using partisan-message politics. If this sounds familiar, it should, as subsequent minority party leaders have adopted similar strategies since then in the Republican and Democratic Party. Such a strategy only works when there is no cooperation between the parties, so that voters can clearly distinguish between the proponents and opponents of particular policies. By refusing to work with the Democrats, Republicans could credibly disavow any policies coming out of the Congress that the public might not favor. This strategy should sound familiar as it is the exact strategy that Republicans have employed during the Obama presidency. In both cases, the opposition-at-all-costs strategy proved to be very successful electorally, with the Republicans taking over of the House (and Senate) in 1994 and regaining control of the House in 2010 and the Senate in 2014. Over the longer haul, however, the single-minded focus on partisan politics, at the expense of cooperation to produce public policy, may well have hurt the House as a legislative institution, as noted in chapter 3's consideration of Congress's very low approval ratings.

TWO DECADES OF REPUBLICAN MAJORITY CONTROL IN THE HOUSE: 1994–2006; 2010 ONWARD

Newt Gingrich built an electoral strategy around consistent opposition to the Democrats in the House (and Democratic president Bill Clinton) and crafted a campaign platform called the *Contract with America* in 1994, which almost every House Republican candidate signed. The Contract had ten items, ranging from limiting federal spending to reducing crime to setting term limits on federal office. When the Republicans gained fifty-two seats and a 230–204–1 margin in the House,[30] Gingrich moved from minority whip to Speaker of the House because sitting minority leader Robert Michel (R-IL) retired in 1994. Subsequently, the Republican caucus approved rules for the party and the chamber that centralized leadership authority more completely than at any time since the 1910 overthrow of Speaker Cannon, all in an effort to show that the GOP would stay true to their campaign party platform now that they controlled the legislative agenda. Building on the examples and structures provided by congressional Democrats in the postreform era, the Republican membership empowered Speaker Gingrich to dominate the reconfiguration of many House practices and procedures, and gave him great power in selecting committee chairs and making committee appointments. Notably, the Republican Party imposed limits of six years (three terms) on committee chairs, which meant that no committee chair would likely develop the kind of seniority-based power that conservative Democratic chairmen had held for so long.

Beyond the Contract and a policy vision of a smaller national government, Gingrich's 1995 backing in the caucus derived in large part from two perceptions: (1) many junior members concluded that they owed their elections to him because of financial support, a nationalized election, and, for many of them, personal campaign visits; and (2) almost all House Republicans understood that they would not have won control in 1994 save for Gingrich's persistence and majority-building activities over the previous decade. As we see in the current House Republican Party, however, the new members who helped propel the GOP to victory in 1994 were more conservative and ideologically rigid than the incumbent members of the caucus at the time. As with Speaker Ryan today (and Speaker Boehner before him), this more conservative wing of the party ultimately caused enough conflict to undermine Gingrich's legislative ambitions.

The first few months of the 104th Congress gave the impression that the Congress, at least in the House of Representatives, had become a parliamentary body; that is, the majority party could move its agenda through the legislature on its own schedule, essentially ignoring the minority Democrats. But the U.S. House is not a parliamentary body, nor was Speaker Gingrich a prime minister. The Republican majority had to contend with the constitutional constraints embodied in a Democratic president and a Senate that often requires a supermajority (sixty votes to break a filibuster) to work its will (see below in this chapter and in chapter 6).[31] As 1995 wore on, the euphoria of the first one hundred days gradually changed to exhaustion brought on by endless negotiations over the unresolved budget issues and a series of continuing resolutions to fund the government for short periods of time (from a few days to a few weeks, during the fall of 1995).[32] Moderates and hard-line conservatives in the Republican Party disagreed about how much compromise was necessary to successfully deal with President Clinton. Gingrich and the hardliners in the party tried to stare down President Clinton over the budget and ultimately lost, which in turn hurt the Republican's ability to negotiate with the president for the remainder of his first term. As with the strengthened Democratic leadership of the 1980s, the Republican version of enhanced party leadership remained constrained by the preferences of the party's membership. For Democratic and Republican leaders alike, power depended on the relative unity of their rank and file on any given issue, and this remains the case.

The narrow Republican majorities of the Gingrich speakership (230–204 in the 104th Congress, 228–206 in the 105th [1997–1998], both with one independent) allowed the Republican leader little leeway. Even as party voting reached historically high levels, Republicans found themselves at a great disadvantage in dealing with a generally united Democratic Party in the House, a politically astute Democrat in the White House, and a Senate Republican majority that could not overcome Democratic filibusters. Although moderate Republicans could and did hold the majority hostage to their demands on occasion, it was the die-hard conservatives, who had provided the margin of the GOP's, and Gingrich's, initial 1994 victory, who caused the lion's share of trouble for the leadership. Indeed, as congressional scholar Dan Palazzalo concluded, Gingrich's military allusions did not fit the partisan situation in that "political parties aren't armies. They're fractious organizations."[33]

Ultimately, the conflict within the Republican Party came to a head when Gingrich sided with conservatives who pushed hard to impeach President Clinton, despite public polling that showed opposition to that effort. In the 1998 congressional elections, the GOP lost seats and Gingrich was ousted as Speaker; Dennis Hastert (R-IL) assumed the post of Speaker, with Richard Armey (R-TX) as his majority leader and Tom DeLay (R-TX) as his minority whip. At that point, congressional Republicans were barely holding on to their slim majority. The 106th Congress began in 1999 and was essentially a standoff between the Republicans and an embattled President Clinton. In 2000, presidential candidate George W. Bush distanced himself from House Republicans, which was an additional signal that the congressional Republican Party was in some disarray.

But in the Bush years, up until 2006, the leadership of Speaker Hastert and Rep. DeLay (House majority leader) succeeded in maintaining a Republican House majority that dictated most major policy decisions within the House. Having a Republican president in office helped immensely, but the Republican success at holding the majority also depended on the leadership's tactics. Both Hastert and DeLay were party loyalists, but they differed in their approaches. Hastert was viewed as a Speaker willing to use the rules to his utmost advantage, but also willing to negotiate in order to pass legislation.[34] DeLay was a hard-line conservative who demanded complete party loyalty, but he also used his leadership position to raise millions of dollars for his colleagues' reelection campaigns. The Republicans continued to maintain consistently high party unity—they voted together close to 90 percent of the time, in contrast to 70 percent unity when they were in the minority (see table 5.2).

As discussed in chapter 2, the Iraq War and President George W. Bush's unpopularity took its toll on the Republican majority in the 2006 midterm congressional elections, when the Democrats won control of the House and Senate. The Democrats elected the first female Speaker, Nancy Pelosi (D-CA), who continued the trend of consolidating party support among the rank and file, although she rejected the term limits on committee chairs and the speakership that the Republicans had instituted twelve years earlier.

SPOTLIGHT

Representative Nancy Pelosi: The First Female Speaker of the House

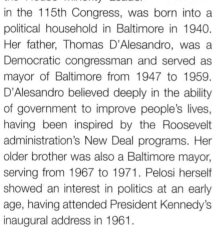

Democratic House leader Nancy Pelosi's (D-CA) political rise was incremental, but her patience and persistence were rewarded when she became the nation's first female Speaker of the House in 2007. Pelosi, the House Minority Leader in the 115th Congress, was born into a political household in Baltimore in 1940. Her father, Thomas D'Alesandro, was a Democratic congressman and served as mayor of Baltimore from 1947 to 1959. D'Alesandro believed deeply in the ability of government to improve people's lives, having been inspired by the Roosevelt administration's New Deal programs. Her older brother was also a Baltimore mayor, serving from 1967 to 1971. Pelosi herself showed an interest in politics at an early age, having attended President Kennedy's inaugural address in 1961.

After moving to San Francisco with her husband Paul in the late 1960s, Pelosi became involved in California politics. She made her inroads with the state Democratic Party, becoming a delegate to the Democratic National Committee in 1976, working her way up to being the chair of the California State Democratic Party in 1981, and then serving as finance chair of the Democratic Senatorial Campaign Committee for the 1986 election cycle. Upon the death of California's fifth district representative Sala Burton, Pelosi made her first foray into electoral politics and won the special election to fill Burton's U.S. House seat in 1987. Representative Pelosi has been subsequently reelected fifteen times without a competitive challenge, as her district—which has been changed due to redistricting from California's fifth congressional district to the eighth in 1992, and then from the eighth to the twelfth in 2012—is heavily Democratic. Pelosi's district is a diverse, densely populated, and relatively affluent urban district that is entirely within the boundaries of the city of San Francisco.

In Congress, Pelosi served on the House Appropriations Committee and as the Ranking Democrat on the House Intelligence Committee. In 2001, fourteen years after joining Congress, she was elected to party leadership, becoming the House Democratic Whip. The next year, she was elected the House Minority Leader, becoming the first woman to ever lead a major party in Congress. When Democrats regained the House majority in the 2006 midterm elections for the first time since 1994, Pelosi was elected Speaker for the start of the 110th Congress. She has remained the Democratic House leader through the 115th Congress, serving as minority leader after the Republicans took over the majority in the 2010 elections.

Representative Pelosi used her time as Speaker to continue the trend of consolidating rank-and-file party support. Both Congresses during the period of 2007 to 2010—one under President Bush and one under President Obama—achieved passage of significant legislation while Pelosi was Speaker. During the 110th Congress (2007–2008), the Democratic majority passed (and President Bush signed) bills including raising the federal minimum wage from $5.15 per hour to $7.25 per hour, a $152 billion economic stimulus bill, and a bill designed to address the subprime mortgage crisis. With President Obama in office during the 111th Congress (2009–2010), the Democratic majority passed a $787 billion economic stimulus bill, Dodd-Frank Wall Street Reform, a repeal of the "Don't Ask, Don't Tell" military policy, and the ACA. By all accounts, Pelosi was particularly instrumental in gathering the necessary votes during 2009 and 2010 to pass the ACA through the House. Although aided by the relatively large Democratic majorities during her tenure as Speaker, Pelosi's ability to consolidate party support for her

agenda makes her notable not only for being the first female House Speaker, but also for being one of the most productive party leaders in recent memory.

The information in this section is taken from multiple sources as follows: Andrea Stone, "Pelosi to be First Woman to Lead Congress," *USA Today*, November 9, 2006, https://usatoday30.usatoday.com/news/washington/2006-11-08-pelosi-congress_x.htm; Chris McGreal, "Nancy Pelosi: Is this the Most Powerful Woman in US History?" *The Guardian,* March 26, 2010, https://www.theguardian.com/world/2010/mar/26/nancy-pelosi-politician-speaker; Office of Congresswoman Nancy Pelosi, "Pelosi Statement on President Trump's Inaugural Address," January 20, 2017, https://pelosi.house.gov/news/press-releases/pelosi-statement-on-president-trump-s-inaugural-address.

However, Democratic control of the House of Representatives only lasted four years. On November 3, 2010, John Boehner's party won sixty-five seats and recaptured majority control of the House of Representatives. Typically, the opposition party (to the president) wins seats in a midterm election but not so many as to take majority control away from the president's party. But the victory came with a price tag in terms of party unity, because it was driven in large part by a new and more conservative movement known as the Tea Party. The Tea Party was not actually a single political party but instead a collection of disparate groups that decided to run candidates for congressional office in the Republican primaries that year. They were driven by intense opposition to President Obama, whose policies they saw as expanding federal power and uncontrollable budget deficits. Their grassroots organizing brought GOP voters to the polls and gave enough lift to the party that they wrested control of the House from the Democrats.

Structurally, the Republicans reinstituted term limits on committee chairs and the Speaker, and tried to adhere to the Hastert Rule. Politically, things were far more complicated. The problem for Speaker Boehner was that the very same zeal that boosted the GOP's electoral fortunes was hard to control once the task of governing began. Over the next four years, the GOP faced the continuing tension between the conservative establishment rank and file and even more conservative Tea Party members. Tea Party Republicans were determined to not only block President Obama, but also to stop the exercise of federal power more generally, even if it meant causing a partial shutdown of the government and slowing the economic recovery. Cooperation with the president was out of the question. Even when Boehner tried to broker a deal to rein in federal spending, the Tea Party members in his caucus opposed it. The conflict made it hard for Boehner to enforce and rely on party unity, even when simply considering whether to bring a bill to the House floor, much less passing it.

Still, legislation needed to be passed, including annual appropriations bills to fund the government; Boehner had to find a way to unify his party enough to accomplish that basic congressional responsibility. He also knew that every time there was a public intraparty fight, it undermined the majority party's power in the House. Conflict within his party prevented him from maximizing the powers of the House majority and as Speaker; in the end, he simply could not move many preferred GOP policies through the legislative process. Even as President Obama was reelected (in 2012) and the GOP held onto the House, majority cohesion remained elusive for Boehner. With fifty or more members refusing to cooperate with Obama on anything and a requirement that the majority party approve any measure before it goes to the House floor, Boehner found himself all too frequently in a situation where he could not move legislation through the House.

The most extreme example of the force of the far-right wing of the GOP in Congress was the partial government shutdown in October 2013. In order to fund federal government operations, Congress must pass separate appropriations bills or one large bill, known as the Continuing Resolution (CR), by October 1, which is the start of the official federal budget year. The House GOP, with the urging of some conservative members of the Senate GOP, sent two versions of the CR to the Democratic-controlled Senate, each of which contained measures to repeal or water down provisions of Obamacare. The Democratic Senate rejected each bill, in order to both protect Obamacare and save the president the political costs of vetoing the CR, which would have made him look as if he was responsible for the partial government shutdown. To make matters worse, the Congress also had to approve an increase in the federal debt ceiling, which is the cap on the amount of money that can be borrowed to pay government obligations.

The standoff on both key bills lasted sixteen days, and by some accounts cost the U.S. economy nearly $2 billion in lost productivity.[35] Ultimately, Speaker Boehner succumbed to enormous public pressure, and he violated the Hastert Rule by bringing the CR and debt-ceiling increase to the House floor with the support of House Democrats. The final tally was 285–144, with all the No votes coming from Republicans.[36]

Party unity remained high on the bills that did make it to the House floor (see table 5.2), but the overall number of bills voted on, passed, and enacted into law dropped considerably in comparison to past Congresses. This demonstrated the intense polarization between the parties and limited effectiveness of the GOP majority in the House.

Obstruction may have made lawmaking difficult, but it was an effective electoral strategy. The 112th and 113th Congresses were described by observers as the least productive in fifty years, and at the end of 2014, approval of Congress stood at among the lowest in history, at 14 percent.[37] But it has long been known by Congressional observers that voters judge the Congress collectively much more harshly than they judge their own individual member of Congress and the midterm elections of 2014 were no different. The GOP not only held on to control of the House, but it also won back majority control of the U.S. Senate. So, at the beginning of 2015, the GOP was optimistic that it could make progress on its agenda, not in actual bills passed but in solidifying their unified message against the policies of President Obama and the Democrats.[38]

That optimism quickly dissolved into the same party in-fighting that had existed in the previous Congress. The conservative wing of the House GOP lost faith in Boehner to the point where he believed he could no longer serve effectively as Speaker, and he resigned from his position in October 2015. Paul Ryan (R-WI) was persuaded by various House GOP factions to put his name forward for the Speaker position. The Speaker is technically voted on by the entire House of Representatives, and the candidate with the majority of votes wins; each party puts forth a candidate for the job. Because it is a majority vote election, almost always it means that the majority party candidate wins; Ryan won the Speakership with the promise of unifying the House GOP.

As noted in the beginning of this chapter, however, the presidential election of 2016 put strains on the GOP in Congress and beyond, as Republicans were intensely divided over whom to support (or not) as their party's nominee. As the Trump presidential candidacy gained momentum, Ryan found himself torn between the passionate base who wanted Trump, the conservative members of Congress who were highly skeptical that Trump was a true conservative, and the more establishment GOP members who were concerned about Trump's rhetoric on immigrants, Latinos, and Muslims, as well as his protectionist positions on trade policy. Up until election night, the conventional wisdom was that the congressional GOP would lose seats in a Trump defeat; while the House GOP did lose six seats, it held the majority overall in the House (241–194) and retained the Senate majority (52–48) with Trump's surprise victory.

January 2017 marked the first time the GOP had control of both the executive and congressional branches since 2006. With President Trump in office, the GOP was set to embark on an ambitious legislative agenda which included repealing the Affordable Care Act (ACA) (Obamacare) and revamping the federal tax code among other things. However, the politics surrounding the repeal of the ACA, under which nearly 20 million Americans received their health insurance, proved far more turbulent within the GOP than expected. Speaker Ryan found himself in territory that was familiar to his predecessor John Boehner—a clash between the most conservative wing of his party, which wanted a full repeal with no replacement, and the more establishment wing of his party, which wanted to fix the issues with the ACA while not leaving those millions of Americans without health insurance. We discuss the legislation to repeal the ACA and the politics surrounding it in greater detail in chapter 6.

In this age of clear party divisions, party labels have to represent cohesive policy agreement or voters find it difficult to reward or punish their House members. Paul Ryan's job as Speaker is to maintain the cohesion and clarity of the Republican Party brand in the House of Representatives. How well Ryan will do that will be demonstrated in part by the results of the 2018 midterm congressional elections.

THE SENATE: A NEW BALANCE BETWEEN INDIVIDUAL POWER AND THE ROLE OF THE PARTY

He's got a tough job over there. I've got a tough job over here.

God bless him and good luck.

—John Boehner, Former Speaker of the House, concerning Senator Mitch
McConnell's challenges as majority leader of the Senate[39]

As in the House, Senate party leaders face the formidable task of trying to get their party's preferred policies passed on the chamber floor. Their challenge is twofold in that they have to first unite their own party and then overcome minority opposition. Unlike the House, however, the Senate is not a majoritarian body. As an institution, the Senate is designed to preserve the powers of individual senators at the expense of party leaders. And unlike the House, where the majority party can use the Rules Committee to dictate which bills get to the floor and which amendments can be offered to them, the Senate has no such gatekeeper. The Senate majority leader is selected by fellow partisans and heads the majority party, in contrast to the Speaker, who serves as a constitutional officer of the House.

The powers of the Senate majority leader are limited at best. The majority leader has the right of first recognition by the presiding officer (ordinarily a party colleague) and typically brings bills up for consideration on the floor. In that sense, the majority leader can ask to bring certain bills to the Senate floor, but any individual senator, whether of the majority or minority party, can block a bill by simply objecting to its consideration. This power stems from the right of senators to speak on the Senate floor.[40] It is from this right of speech that the power to filibuster (delay indefinitely) originates, and senators use it as a threat and in full force when it serves their political purposes. A determined minority of forty-one senators can stop the body in its tracks through the filibuster, and a single member can often hold the Senate hostage by rejecting a request for a unanimous consent agreement that governs the conduct of floor debate on a given issue. It is only when sixty senators vote in favor of cloture, which effectively ends discussion on a measure, that debate can be limited and the Senate can move ahead to resolve difficult issues. Filibusters have changed and grown more common over the years, but their central import for the modern Senate is that sixty votes are required to move along many key pieces of legislation.

Moreover, senators use this same right of speech to offer amendments to any bill, and they can do so (with a few exceptions) at any time, in any order. Senate leaders operate under rules that do not allow them to dictate the pace of floor debate or the content of amendments offered by individual senators.[41] Because senators can filibuster or offer amendments at most any time in the legislative process, Senate leaders cannot easily structure votes or schedules, nor can they routinely set time limits for debate. Rather, leaders must cajole their colleagues, privately and publicly, compromise with them, and provide consideration for a hundred different schedules, preferences, and egos. This is strikingly different from the way the House organizes itself, where the majority-party leadership strictly controls access to the floor.

Undeniably, Senate party leaders possess many fewer weapons than do their House counterparts. Each Senate party caucus elects a floor leader, a whip, and chairs of committees on policy, committee assignments, and campaigns.[42] Although Republicans have traditionally distributed these jobs more widely than have Democrats, the fact is that aside from the majority and minority leader positions, no one slot is especially important. The majority leader walks a fine line in trying to control the chamber's schedule, all the while having to endlessly negotiate and renegotiate with senators to allow bills to proceed to the Senate floor and to define the conditions under which they will be considered. The Senate minority leader serves as the chief sparring partner and negotiator in these sessions,[43] and each leader must represent the interests of their own party's members. Nor do Senate party caucuses provide broad grants of authority to their respective leaders; rather, the fundamental expectation of party leaders is to serve "the personal political needs of party colleagues."[44] This means that the party leaders must continually communicate with each other as they reflect their members' preferences.

Historically, the Senate as an institution has discouraged strong collective partisanship in favor of preserving individual senators' political flexibility. Although partisanship has increased in recent years, senators still remain less rigidly partisan than House members because they represent more constituents and enjoy six-year terms of office. These fundamental differences in electoral environments translate into different incentives within the Senate. Senators have more individual power than House members and are therefore judged on a more comprehensive basis than simple party-line voting. Because they represent states with populations ranging from 585,501 (Wyoming) to 39 million (California), senators have to appeal to wide ranges of constituent opinions and ideologies, which means that they cannot always toe the party line.[45] Their longer terms also insulate them from pleas and threats from party leaders; party control can shift every two years, but a senator's term is triple that. In addition, senators have to deal with another colleague from the same state, who may or may not share his or her party affiliation. These senators sometimes have to work together, even if they come from opposite parties; the range of cooperation depends on the partisanship of their states and their own individual personalities. It is therefore in a senator's interest to maintain working relationships with many colleagues in both parties.

During the past decade, however, the dominant trend has emphasized stronger party leadership and diminished individual power in the Senate, especially under former majority leader Harry Reid's (D-NV) tenure (2006–2015). For example, Reid employed a previously little-used procedure known as "filling the amendment tree" forty-four times from 2007 to 2011.[46] Using his power of first recognition, Reid essentially offered all the possible amendments to a bill under Senate rules and thereby denied every other senator the opportunity to offer an amendment until votes had taken place on each of his amendments. He typically used the same language of the bill that was being considered and forced senators who opposed the legislation to vote against it numerous times in a row. Republican minority-party members in the Senate complained fiercely about this practice, but Reid countered that he would not have used that power if they had not insisted on offering amendments of their own that were designed to make the bill so unpalatable that it could not pass, or which were designed to put Democrats in a bad political position in casting a vote on them.

In 2011, Reid and then Senate minority leader Mitch McConnell (R-KY) came to an agreement that they would try to work on making the Senate floor more open to amendments, but in reality, the years from 2011 to 2016 (the last two under a GOP majority) did not see a such to openness. In fact, some Democratic senators complained that their inability to offer amendments tailored to their specific states left them open to attack in their home states because they had no way of carving out distinctions between their views and the Senate Democrats as a whole.[47] One reform that did take place after 2011 was the elimination of the "secret hold," whereby a senator could simply inform the party leaders of his intention to filibuster a bill and the leaders would prevent the bill from coming to the floor for twenty-four hours. Today, the hold exists, but it is no longer secret—party leaders reveal the name of the senator who is delaying the bill.

Although the Democratic caucus tacitly allowed their majority leader to use his powers to deny them amending opportunities to avoid controversial votes, they did not grant the leadership expanded powers to control committee and subcommittee chairmanships, which are still primarily determined by seniority. Senators make their requests for committee assignments to the party leadership, and when they accrue more seniority, they can request shifts to more prestigious and powerful committees. Typically, these requests are honored based on seniority within the party and the Senate. Seniority remains a very strong guiding principle—even when a senator does not seem to be in lock-step with every party policy, the general rule in the Senate has been to allow that senator to ascend to, or keep, his or her chairmanship (see chapter 8). Republican senators have also preserved seniority in the committee system, both in the minority and now again in the 115th Congress as the Senate majority.

In 2015, the Republicans again assumed majority control of the Senate, and Mitch McConnell moved from being minority leader to majority leader. He pledged to his own party caucus, and the Democratic minority, that he would open up the Senate floor process more than his predecessor and allow senators to offer amendments. McConnell, recognizing how Reid's strategy hampered Democrats from Republican-leaning states, sought to give Republicans in Democratic-leaning states the chance to strike out on their own when necessary to establish their individual reputations.[48] It may be this very willingness to let Republicans favor their home state in their Senate speeches and amendments that allowed the GOP to keep control of the Senate, with endangered incumbents like Ron Johnson (R-WI) and Pat Toomey (R-PA) coming from behind to win their reelection campaigns in 2016.

In 2016, Harry Reid retired from the Senate, to be replaced by Catherine Cortez Masto (D-NV), the first Latina ever elected to the U.S. Senate.

SPOTLIGHT

Senator Catherine Cortez Masto: The First Latina U.S. Senator

On March 27, 2015, Senator Harry Reid (D-NV) announced that he would not seek reelection in 2016 after serving for thirty years in the Senate and twelve years as the leader of the Senate Democrats. In response, U.S. Representative Joe Heck (R-NV) jumped into the fray to run for the open seat. Nevada Democrats were eager to find a strong opponent to run against Heck and a potential replacement for Harry Reid that would be supported by the retiring senator but not overshadowed by him. Catherine Cortez Masto (D-NV) fit that bill.

Born and raised in Las Vegas, Cortez Masto worked as a prosecutor in the U.S. Attorney's Office and as former Nevada Governor Bob Miller's Chief of Staff before entering electoral politics in her own right. She successfully ran to become Nevada's 32nd Attorney General in 2006, and was reelected to a second four-year term in 2010. Cortez Masto's family is well known in Nevada; her father, Manny Cortez, is widely credited with transforming the Las Vegas strip into a prominent tourism destination while he was the head of the Las Vegas Convention and Visitors Authority. As Attorney General, Cortez Masto worked to combat the use of methamphetamines in the state, and worked to strengthen laws preventing sex trafficking and violence against women. Between her experience in statewide elected office, her family pedigree in the state's largest population center, and receiving a wholehearted endorsement from Senator Reid, Cortez Masto was a formidable Senate candidate.

The campaign for Reid's old seat was a contentious one as both candidates sought to equate their opponent with an established national party figure. Representative Heck tried to cast Catherine Cortez Masto in a negative light as the second coming of Harry Reid. But Harry Reid's record of serving Nevada for three decades and effectively balancing his role as partisan leader of the Democrats with strong advocacy for the state of Nevada made this line of attack less effective than it might have been to audiences outside of the state. Cortez Masto drew associations of her own between Heck and Donald Trump: "Joe Heck has been Donald Trump's strongest supporter in Nevada as Trump has demeaned and disrespected women, made racist comments towards Latinos and showed himself completely unfit to be president," she said in an October Facebook post. In a state with a surging Latino population, and with Republican presidential nominee Donald Trump highly unpopular with that voting demographic, Cortez Masto's strategy was particularly effective.

In the end, Catherine Cortez Masto defeated Joe Heck with 47 percent of the vote to Heck's 45, and Cortez Masto became the nation's first Latina U.S. Senator. The vote totals tracked very closely to the presidential race—Hillary Clinton received 48 percent of the statewide vote while Donald Trump received 45 percent—suggesting that the voters may indeed have associated the Senate candidates with national party leaders.

As U.S. Senator, Cortez Masto serves on the Banking, Housing, and Urban Affairs Committee, the Committee on Commerce, Science, and Transportation, the Committee on Energy and Natural Resources, the Indian Affairs Committee, the Special Committee on Aging, and the Committee on Rules and Administration. Thus far, Senator Cortez Masto has translated her opposition to candidate Trump during her campaign into opposing President Trump as senator; for example, she voted against ten of Trump's cabinet nominations and his nomination of Neil Gorsuch to the Supreme Court. With her impressive resume, winning electoral strategy, and being the nation's first Latina senator, it is safe to say that Senator Cortez Masto need not worry about being overshadowed by Senator Reid.

The information in this section is taken from multiple sources as follows: Andrea Drusch, "Meet the Woman Harry Reid Wants to Replace Him in the Senate," *The Atlantic*, March 27, 2015, http://www.theatlantic.com/politics/archive/2015/03/meet-the-woman-harry-reid-wants-to-replace-him-in-the-senate/435099/; Catherine Cortez Masto, Facebook, October 8, 2016, https://www.facebook.com/catherinecortezmasto/posts/1280141472037784?comment_id=1280218345363430&comment_tracking=%7B%22tn%22%3A%22R0%22%7D; FiveThirtyEight.com, "Congress Tracker: Catherine Cortez Masto," https://projects.fivethirtyeight.com/congress-trump-score/catherine-cortez-masto/.

Reid was replaced as Democratic leader by Charles (Chuck) Schumer (D-NY), who was first elected to the Senate, as a House member, in 1998 and is known to be press savvy and as deeply partisan as Reid. In the early months of the Trump administration, it appeared that Schumer would be a feisty opponent to the newly elected president, despite the fact that the two of them shared a home state connection.

The Legacy of Exercising Party Leadership in the Senate

How Senate party leaders run the upper chamber without the type of formal power that House leaders possess has varied across time and depended on the unity of the parties, external pressures, and the personal leadership style of the leaders. Even the strongest majority leaders, such as Lyndon Johnson, relied more heavily on persuasion than outright control to win votes on the Senate floor.[49] As Senate majority leader, Lyndon Johnson forcefully asserted himself in forming a cohesive Democratic coalition among liberals and southern conservatives, but it was a fragile coalition at best.[50] When Lyndon Johnson became vice president in 1961, Senator Mike Mansfield (D-MT) assumed the leadership post, serving from 1961 to 1977. He practiced a restrained leadership style that failed to unify his Democratic colleagues, though he retained great personal popularity and respect from them. From 1977 to 1981, the Democrats ran the Senate under the leadership of Robert Byrd (D-WV), who invoked his limited formal powers to try to bring together the disparate members of his party.

In 1981, the Republicans took control of the Senate, first under the leadership of Howard Baker (R-TN) and then, in 1985, under Robert Dole (R-KS). Both Baker and Dole sought to shepherd President Reagan's policies through the Senate and to lead negotiations with the Democratic House. In 1986, the Democrats recaptured control of the Senate, with Senator Byrd again serving as majority leader. Despite the fact that Democrats in the House had moved over this period of time to consolidate and strengthen the powers of their party leaders, Senate leaders' powers remained modest at best. Senators were still more interested in preserving their individual power than giving their leaders the tools to pass a set of unified party-based initiatives.

The Senate resisted strong partisan division until the early 1990s when Majority Leader George Mitchell began to run the body in a more partisan fashion. He did so by structuring committee bills and floor debates to emphasize partisan policy differences between the Senate Democrats and President George H. W. Bush. In 1994, when the Republicans took back control of the chamber and Senator Dole once again became majority leader, the environment in the Senate changed in two important ways. First, the Republicans assumed control of both chambers at the same time, which had not happened in forty years. Second, the Republicans reached parity with the Democrats in most southern states, which changed the composition of the Senate. The division within the Democratic Party between North and South subsided because conservative Republicans replaced southern conservative Democrats. In the North, moderate Democrats often won seats previously held by liberal Republicans. Consequently, the differences between the two parties in the Senate surpassed the differences within each party, giving rise to more opportunities for stronger partisan leadership than had previously existed in the Senate.[51]

As Senator Dole began his second tenure as Senate majority leader in 1995, his Republican majority was different than it had been ten years earlier. Southern conservative Republicans, many of whom had come from the House,[52] agitated for more aggressive party leadership and majority rule in the Senate. They signaled this by electing Senator Trent Lott as assistant majority leader rather than Senator Alan Simpson (R-WY), who was generally considered more moderate.

Ultimately, Senator Dole, preoccupied by his campaign for president, resigned his post as majority leader and his Senate seat in June 1996, clearing the way for Senator Lott to become the majority leader. Although Lott quickly proved himself a skillful deal maker, he also reflected a style of leadership that was honed in the House. As majority leader, Lott structured the Senate leadership in a more collegial, participatory way than did Dole, who tended to keep his own counsel as floor leader.[53] Thus, Republican senators, while defending their individual rights within the institution, moved to mute some of the intense individualism that had characterized the Senate of the previous twenty years. At the same time, in 1996, twelve moderate Republican and Democratic senators announced their retirements from the Senate, and their replacements in both parties were more partisan. Subsequently, the character of the Senate changed markedly to become more rigidly ideological and more intensely partisan.

This trend is illustrated in the patterns of partisan voting, which culminated in historically high levels during the 104th Congress (1995–1996) and have remained very high since then. Most notably, during the second session of the 104th Congress, Senate Republicans compiled a higher party unity score (89 percent loyalty on all party votes) than did their House colleagues (87 percent), and the 89 percent figure represented the highest level of partisan voting by either party in the Senate for more than forty years.[54] Thus, even in a year that produced substantial legislative compromises between the Congress and President Clinton, Senate voting patterns reached a historic level of partisanship. Since then, both parties have maintained these historic highs in unity on roll call voting—table 5.4 breaks down party unity scores by chamber (see table 5.4). Moreover, there are so few remaining southern Democratic senators that the subcategory for them no longer exists.

For the next six years, both Senator Lott and Senator Tom Daschle (D-SD), the Democratic minority leader, used their powers over committee appointments and floor schedules to structure debate in the Senate along clearer party lines. When Senator Lott was forced to resign his position because of controversial remarks he made about civil rights, Senator Bill Frist (D-TN) took over as majority leader for the 108th Congress (2003–2005). He had little previous leadership experience, and he had pledged to serve only two terms in the Senate, so senators already knew that he would leave the Senate in 2007. Senator Frist employed

Table 5.4 Selected Senate and House Party Unity Scores

Chamber and Party	1969–1972 Unity* (%)	1995–1998 Unity* (%)	2003–2004 Unity* (%)	2009–2010 Unity* (%)	2011–2012 Unity* (%)
House Democrats (all)	71	81	87	90	87
House Southern Democrats	48	74	n/a	n/a	n/a
House Republicans	74	88	90	88	91
Senate Democrats (all)	73	76	84	91	92
Senate Southern Democrats	51	90	n/a	n/a	n/a
Senate Republicans	73	81	87	87	92

Source: Norman J. Ornstein, Thomas E. Mann, and Michael J. Malbin, eds., "Chapter 8: Political Polarization in Congress and Changing Voting Alignments," *Vital Statistics on Congress*, http://www.brookings.edu/research/reports/2013/07/vital-statistics-congress-mann-ornstein (accessed February 9, 2015).

*Averages. Scores reflect the percentage of occasions that members vote with a majority of their fellow partisans on votes in which most (>50 percent) Democrats vote against most (>50 percent) Republicans.

a softer leadership style than either Senator Dole or Senator Lott, but, as noted in chapter 2, he came close to restricting minority rights in response to Senate Democratic obstruction of President Bush's judicial nominations.[55] By 2007, Bill Frist left the Senate, the Democrats regained the majority, and Mitch McConnell (R-KY), who served as Republican whip, became the minority leader.

Perhaps the most important change in Senate party leadership over the past twenty years is the emphasis that leaders place on representing the party and the Senate to the media and in negotiations with the president. Both parties now have significant media operations to coordinate messages of the day, and senators in both parties are assigned the task of making speeches and framing the party's position to traditional and social media. Senators have also become more willing to let their party leader negotiate on behalf of the party with the president on major policy initiatives. Individual senators are more strongly discouraged from publicly disagreeing with the party leaders because it dilutes the clarity of policy differences between the parties. However, in recent years, with limited opportunities to express their opinions through amendments on the Senate floor, senators have taken their individual opinions directly to the media, which can greatly complicate the leaders' jobs. The bottom line for Senate party leaders is that their main job is to sell their party's position to their members and to the public at large—their power derives largely from winning the public relations battle rather than from any internal structure that allows them to control outcomes on the Senate floor.[56]

Despite the shifts in party control of the Senate over time, the power of the individual senator relative to the party has remained consistently strong when compared to the individual House member. The Senate as an institution requires a great deal of consultation and collegiality in order to function; when those components are absent, Senate business can come to a complete stop. A functioning Senate, no matter how slow and inefficient, requires that its leaders act more as facilitators than as aggressive commanders. In the final analysis, the notion of strong party leadership in the Senate remains largely a contradiction in terms within an institution that is, at its core, designed to empower its individual members.

PARTY AND THE LIMITS OF CENTRALIZATION IN THE CONGRESS

Given the high levels of partisan voting in the contemporary Congress, it is tempting to see the congressional party, especially the House majority, as dominating the legislative process—at least on many of the most salient issues. When legislative parties consist of homogeneous groups of partisans (e.g., mostly conservative Republicans and liberal Democrats), and the gap between them is wide, it makes sense that individual legislators, at least in the House, are willing to give up some individual power to give the larger group—the legislative party—more power. But when party divisions arise, or the leaders fail to secure legislative and electoral victories, Democratic and Republican rank-and-file members have voted to restrain, and even replace, their leaders. At the same time, leaders have strong incentives to hold party majorities together to the extent that those majorities reflect their members' policy preferences.[57]

In the House, party leadership has grown extremely strong, as evidenced by partisan voting levels, the extended whip system, and the formidable powers that leaders possess to control appointments, schedules, and legislative procedures. The Senate remains individualistic (although it too has become much more partisan in recent years), and that individualism limits the potential for strong, centralized party leadership that can span across both chambers. Ironically, the apparently majoritarian House has suffered some of the most serious challenges to strong party leadership, as the members of the Republican House Freedom Caucus have not always agreed to abide by the wishes of their party leadership, thus demonstrating how centrifugal forces can emerge in unlikely settings.

Moreover, both the House and Senate remain national institutions consisting of individuals who are elected locally. There have been a number of issues over recent years that have generated division within parties in Congress, including the debt ceiling, immigration, homeland security, the attempted repeal of Obamacare, and infrastructure spending. However, partisan divisions on a single issue rarely lead to irreconcilable splits. Party leaders in both the House and the Senate spend a great deal of energy building cohesion on a wide range of issues, and in an era of close parity between the parties, neither majority nor minority leaders can afford to shut out any members because of their opposition on a single issue.

Party leadership, in the contemporary U.S. Congress, is surely at its strongest since the days of Speaker Cannon, but such leadership remains based on power willingly, but not unreservedly, granted by the individual representatives.[58] Members of the House and Senate must constantly balance their partisan affiliation and ideology with the national party's objectives, and the best interests of their local constituents. There will always be examples of national party leaders asking their rank and file to support a policy that is not beneficial to members' constituents. However, they try to set agendas to avoid such choices, because on those occasions where a member is asked to choose between constituency and party policy, constituency often prevails. Constituency pressures, campaign contributors' concerns, and the entreaties of outside groups demonstrate the continuing power of local forces on House and Senate members, both as individuals and as a bloc within their caucus.

Recommended Readings

Baker, Ross. *House and Senate.* 4th ed. New York: W. W. Norton, 2008.

Lee, Frances. *Insecure Majorities: Congress and the Perpetual Campaign.* Chicago: University of Chicago Press, 2016.

Rohde, David W. *Parties and Leaders in the House of Representatives.* Chicago: University of Chicago Press, 1991.

Theriault, Sean. *The Gingrich Senators: The Roots of Partisan Warfare in Congress.* New York: Oxford University Press 2013.

Useful Resources

Paul Ryan, Speaker of the House: http://www.speaker.gov

Mitch McConnell, Majority Leader, U.S. Senator for Kentucky: http://www.mcconnell.senate.gov

Nancy Pelosi, Democratic Leader: http://www.democraticleader.gov

United States Senate Democrats: http://democrats.senate.gov

Notes

[1] Richard F. Fenno, Jr., "The Internal Distribution of Influence: The House," in *Congress and America's Future*, ed. David B. Truman (Englewood Cliffs, NJ: Prentice-Hall, 1965), 61.

[2] Joseph Cooper and David W. Brady, "Institutional Context and Leadership Style: The House from Cannon to Rayburn," *American Political Science Review* 75 (June 1981): 411–25.

[3] Ibid., 413.

[4] Peter Swenson, "The Influence of Recruitment on the Structure of Power in the U.S. House, 1870–1940," *Legislative Studies Quarterly* 7 (February 1982): 7–36.

[5] The following discussion relies in part on Cooper and Brady, "Institutional Context and Leadership Style," 412ff. See also relevant chapters in Roger H. Davidson, Susan Webb Hammond, and Raymond W. Smock, eds., *Masters of the House* (Boulder, CO: Westview, 1998).

[6] The exceptions were narrow Republican majorities in both houses for the 80th and 83rd Congresses (1947–1949 and 1953–1955, respectively).

[7] David S. Cloud, "Speaker Wants His Platform to Rival the Presidency," *Congressional Quarterly Weekly Report*, February 4, 1995, 331.

[8] See John Manley, "The Conservative Coalition in Congress," *American Behavioral Scientist* 17 (1973): 223–47; Mack C. Shelley, *The Permanent Majority: The Conservative Coalition in the United States Congress* (Tuscaloosa: University of Alabama Press, 1983).

[9] For a brief summary of the tools of powerful leadership, see Robert L. Peabody, *Leadership in Congress* (Boston: Little, Brown, 1976), 41–47. See also Ronald M. Peters, Jr., *The American Speakership* (Baltimore: Johns Hopkins University Press, 1990).

[10] Traditionally, Democratic members of the House Ways and Means Committee had served as the party's "committee on committees." In 1975, this power was transferred to the Steering and Policy Committee, where party leaders possessed much more influence on appointments.

[11] Peters, *American Speakership*, 42–46; see also Lewis L. Gould and Nancy Beck Young, "The Speaker and the Presidents: Sam Rayburn, the White House, and the Legislative Process, 1941–1961," in *Masters of the House*, ed. Davidson, Hammond, and Smock, 181–221.

[12] These tactics were similar to those used by former Ways and Means chair Rep. Wilbur Mills (D-AR), as detailed by John Manley, "Wilbur Mills: A Study in Congressional Influence," *American Political Science Review* 63 (June 1969): 442–64. Mills served as Ways and Means chair from 1958 through 1974.

[13] Arthur G. Stevens, Arthur H. Miller, and Thomas E. Mann, "Mobilization of Liberal Strength in the House: 1955–1970: The Democratic Study Group," *American Political Science Review* 68 (1974): 667–81.

[14] Bruce I. Oppenheimer, "The Rules Committee: New Arm of Leadership in a Decentralized House," in *Congress Reconsidered*, 5th ed., ed. Lawrence C. Dodd and Bruce I. Oppenheimer (Washington, DC: CQ Press, 1995), 1977.

[15] See Gary Young and Joseph Cooper, "Multiple Referral and the Transformation of House Decision Making," in *Congress Reconsidered*, ed. Dodd and Oppenheimer, 211–36.

[16] The whip was appointed until a 1985 rules change mandated election by the caucus.

[17] The following discussion draws on Barbara Sinclair, *Majority Leadership in the U.S. House* (Baltimore: Johns Hopkins University Press, 1983), 28–29 and Sinclair, "Tip O'Neill and Contemporary House Leadership," in *Masters of the House*, ed. Davidson, Hammond, and Smock, 289–318.

18 "Yellow Dog" Democrats were so named because they would sooner vote for a cur than a Republican.

19 Most, though not all, important votes are recorded. If twenty-five House members or one-fifth of the senators present request a roll call vote, the chamber goes on the record. This was not always the case; through the 1960s, many key issues were decided on "unrecorded teller" votes, in which representatives would signify their vote by lining up and walking past vote counters on the Aye or Nay side of a given proposal. In the early 1970s, the House ceased this practice and installed an electronic voting system. The number of roll call votes rose from an average of 175 annually in the 1960s to more than 600 per year in the 1970s. Subsequently, the average declined to about 450 in the 1980s. Virtually all major decisions are still on the record, however. In the Senate, the patterns have been similar, but the rise has been more gradual and the number of roll call votes has averaged 100–200 fewer per year since the late 1970s.

20 Figures from Norman Ornstein, Thomas Mann, and Michael Malbin, *Vital Statistics on Congress, 1993–1994* (Washington, DC: CQ Press, 1993), 201–2 and *Congressional Quarterly Weekly Report*, December 31, 1994, 3659. See also David W. Rohde, *Parties and Leaders in the Post-Reform House* (Chicago: University of Chicago Press, 1991), 57.

21 The Republican position was thoroughly articulated in a paper issued by representatives Richard T. Armey (R-TX), Jennifer Dunn (R-WA), and Christopher Shays (R-CT), "It's Long Enough: The Decline of Popular Government under Forty Years of Single-Party Control of the U.S. House of Representatives" (Washington, DC: House Republican Conference, 1994).

22 Barbara Sinclair, "House Majority Leadership in an Era of Divided Control," in Dodd and Oppenheimer, *Congress Reconsidered*, 243 (emphasis added).

23 On task forces, see Sinclair, *Majority Leadership in the U.S. House*.

24 On the theory of partisan control, see Gary W. Cox and Mathew McCubbins, *Legislative Leviathan* (Berkeley: University of California Press, 1993); for a Republican analysis of Democratic control of the House, see Armey, Dunn, and Shays, "It's Long Enough."

25 Barbara Sinclair, "The Emergence of Strong Leadership in the 1980s House of Representatives," *Journal of Politics* 54 (August 1992): 657–84.

26 Rohde, *Parties and Leaders*.

27 Ibid., 174.

28 See Charles O. Jones, "Somebody Must Be Trusted: An Essay on Leadership of the U.S. Congress," in *Congress in Change*, ed. Norman J. Ornstein (New York: Praeger, 1975), 266.

29 For a pre-Republican majority view of the party as minority, see William F. Connelly, Jr., and John F. Pitney, Jr., *Congress' Permanent Minority?* (Lanham, MD: Little-field, Adams, 1994).

30 Democrats actually won 204 seats, but Bernie Sanders (I-VT) caucused with them. By late 1995, the defections of Democratic representatives raised the Republicans' ranks to 234.

31 On the limitations imposed by constitutional constraints and Senate rules, see Keith Krehbiel, *Pivotal Politics* (Chicago: University of Chicago Press, 1998).

32 This is a complex and difficult story, best told, perhaps, in Elizabeth Drew's dense insider account, *Showdown: The Struggle between the Gingrich Congress and the Clinton White House* (New York: Touchstone, 1996).

33 Dan Palazzalo, quoted in Katherine Q. Seelye, "Gingrich Draws Fire from the Right," *New York Times*, October 25, 1998, A22.

34 For a view on Speaker Hastert, see Sheryl Gay Stolberg, "Quietly but Firmly, Hastert Asserts His Power," *New York Times*, January 3, 2005, http://www.nytimes.com/2005/01/03/politics/03hastert.html.

35 Office of Management and Budget, "Impacts and Costs of the October 2013 Federal Government Shutdown," November 2013, http://www.whitehouse.gov/sites/default/files/omb/reports/impacts-and-costs-of-october-2013-federal-government-shutdown-report.pdf (accessed February 12, 2015).

36 Darla Cameron and Wilson Andrews, "Votes to End the Government Shutdown," *Washington Post*, October 16, 2013, http://www.washingtonpost.com/wp-srv/special/politics/congress-votes-to-end-shutdown/house.html (accessed February 12, 2015).

37 "Bills by Final Status," https://www.govtrack.us/congress/bills/statistics (accessed February 9, 2015); Jonathan Topaz, "Worst Congress Ever—By the Number," *Politico.com*, http://www.politico.com/story/2014/12/congress-numbers-113658.html (accessed February 9, 2015).

[38] See Frances Lee, *Insecure Majorities* (Chicago: University of Chicago Press, 2016) for a more complete discussion of how obstruction and messaging have often become more important than legislating for congressional parties.

[39] J.M. Rieger. "Boehner on McConnell's DHS Strategy: 'God Bless Him and Good Luck.'" *Rollcall.com*, http://www.rollcall.com/news/-239883-1.html.

[40] Floyd M. Riddick and Alan S. Frumin, *Riddick's Senate Procedure* (Washington, DC: Government Printing Office, 1992), 1092–97.

[41] See Steven Smith, *The American Congress* (Boston: Houghton Mifflin, 1995), 232ff, for an excellent extended example of the problems inherent in making the Senate move with even moderate speed on a major issue.

[42] Roger Davidson and Walter Oleszek, *Congress and Its Members*, 4th ed. (Washington, DC: CQ Press, 1994), 192.

[43] A brief period of viewing the Senate will flesh out this description. Majority Leader Mitch McConnell (R-KY) and Minority Leader Charles Schumer (D-NY) along with a handful of other interested senators, often converse at length about how the schedule will proceed. Nothing is resolved until all actors are satisfied with the arrangements or, in more recent times, both sides acquiesce to a stalemate and turn to other business.

[44] Steven S. Smith, "Forces of Change in Senate Party Leadership and Organization," in Dodd and Oppenheimer, *Congress Reconsidered*, 262 (emphasis added).

[45] United States Census Bureau, "U.S. and World Population Clock," https://www.census.gov/popclock/.

[46] Wendy J. Schiller, "Howard Baker's Leadership in the Senate: Lessons in Civility, Persuasion, and Success," *Baker Center Journal of Applied Public Policy* 4, no. 2. (2012): 28–48.

[47] Mark Strand and Tim Lang, "Cracks in the Senatorial Saucer: Filling the Tree, Cloture, and Curtailing Senate Debate," Congressional Institute, April 1, 2014, http://conginst.org/2014/04/01/cracks-in-the-senatorial-saucer-filling-the-tree-cloture-and-curtailing-senate-debate.

[48] David M. Drucker, "Mitch McConnell's Trick Play in the Senate," *Washington Examiner*, February 6, 2015, http://www.washingtonexaminer.com/mitch-mcconnells-trick-play-in-the-senate/article/2559961 (accessed February 9, 2015).

[49] Ralph K. Huitt, "Democratic Party Leadership in the Senate," *American Political Science Review* 55 (June 1961): 333–44.

[50] Robert A. Caro, *Master of the Senate: The Years of Lyndon Johnson* (New York: Knopf, 2002). Also see Huitt, "Democratic Party Leadership in the Senate."

[51] Barbara Sinclair, "The Senate Leadership Dilemma: Passing Bills and Pursuing Partisan Advantage in a Nonmajoritarian Chamber," in *The Contentious Senate*, ed. Colton C. Campbell and Nicol C. Rae (Lanham, MD: Rowman & Littlefield, 2001).

[52] See Sean Theirault, *The Gingrich Senators: The Roots of Partisan Warfare in Congress* (New York: Oxford University Press, 2013).

[53] Donna Cassatta, "Lott's Task: Balance the Demands of His Chamber and His Party," *Congressional Quarterly Weekly Report*, March 8, 1997, 567–71.

[54] Figures drawn from *Vital Statistics on Congress, 1995–1996*, ed. Norman J. Ornstein, Thomas E. Mann, and Michael J. Malbin (Washington, DC: CQ Press/AEI, 1995), 213–14; and from *Congressional Quarterly Weekly Report*, December 21, 1996, 3461.

[55] Staff, "Senators Compromise on Filibusters," *CNN.com*, May 24, 2005, http://www.cnn.com/2005/POLITICS/05/23/filibuster.fight/index.html.

[56] Lee, *Insecure Majorities*.

[57] There is extensive theoretical literature about the importance of parties, their capacity to organize the legislative chamber, and their ultimate impact on policy outcomes. See, among others, John H. Aldrich and David W. Rohde, "The Transition to Republican Rule in the House: Implications for Theories of Congressional Politics," *Political Science Quarterly* 112 (Winter 1997–1998): 541–67, and Aldrich and Rohde, "The Consequences of Party Organization in the House," paper presented at the Congress and the President in a Partisan Era conference held at Texas A&M University, February 5–6, 1999.

[58] Rohde, *Parties and Leaders*.

CHAPTER 6

Presidential-Congressional Relations

Boundaries of Power

Newly elected Presidents always address Congress early in their first year in office. Here, President Donald Trump addresses Congress with Vice President Mike Pence and Speaker of the House Paul Ryan (R-WI) standing behind him.

Donald Trump entered the White House in 2017 after having pulled one of the biggest upsets in modern political history. Faced with strong opposition within the Republican Party during the nomination process, he was not the typical party nominee for president. His communication style relied heavily on his use of social media, especially Twitter, to communicate his ideas to the voters directly and indirectly through press coverage of his tweets, a tactic he continues to use as president. In the general election, he trailed his Democratic opponent, Hillary Rodham Clinton, by double digits just a few weeks before the election, and lagged in the polls on Election Day. But with slim victories in three key Midwestern states—Michigan, Wisconsin, and Pennsylvania—that were widely expected to go into Clinton's victory column, he won the Presidency with an Electoral College victory of 306–232. However, he lost the popular vote by over 2.5 million votes. On the one hand, President Trump had great political latitude because he had not relied on the Republican Party for his victory and he had communicated directly with his voters. On the other hand, he did not have the strong personal or public support of many Republicans in Congress whose votes he would need to follow through on his campaign promises.

As with all presidential candidates, Trump made a lot of promises, including a pledges to repeal and replace the Affordable Care Act (ACA; known as Obamacare), to renegotiate trade agreements, and to restore jobs in the coal and manufacturing sectors. He also promised to make the country safer both at home and abroad through measures such as increasing deportations of undocumented residents and instituting a travel ban on individuals from countries alleged to support or export terrorism. At the outset of his administration, some of his proposals were viewed as extreme by Democrats and many Republicans in Congress. In addition, once he became president and set out to fulfill some of these promises, he quickly discovered the limits faced by all presidents in a separation of powers system that empowers both the Congress and the judiciary.

His predecessor, Barack Obama, could have saved him some time and trouble with all he had encountered after serving as president for eight years, 2009–2017. Obama entered the White House in 2009, making history from the start as the first African American president of the United States even as he faced an economic recession of historic proportions, with many observers saying at the time that the United States was one step away from another Great Depression.

From a political perspective, Obama had the luxury of working with a unified party government as the Democrats controlled both chambers of Congress and the White House. Moreover, presidents typically accomplish more of their legislative agenda in the first two years of their presidency, and Barack Obama was no different. He took full advantage of his presidential powers, buttressed by his own party's control of the House and Senate, to address the economic crisis and move his own policy priorities forward. By the end of 2009, his first year in office, Obama had expanded the fiscal stimulus (TARP) program begun by his predecessor, George W. Bush, provided a financial bailout for the auto industry, and passed a nearly an additional $800 billion stimulus bill to provide funds and tax credits to encourage job growth. At the same time, however, tax revenues flowing into the U.S. treasury declined, and the cumulative cost of the wars in Iraq and Afghanistan reached far into the billions. The combined pressure of these events greatly increased the federal deficit—the difference between what the federal government takes in and what it spends every year—to more than $1 trillion for several years, which put pressure on Obama and Congress to drastically reduce federal spending.

In 2010, the economy was still perceived to be in a downturn, but President Obama turned his attention to fulfilling his campaign promise of enacting health-care reform, specifically, passing a bill that would provide the opportunity to purchase health insurance on an open market, rather than through an employer. The number of uninsured Americans was very high before the recession, but when millions of people lost their jobs during that time, the pressure grew on the Democrats to pass some form of Obama's bill. In March 2010, with support from only Democrats in both chambers, and using a procedure known as Reconciliation to protect the bill from a filibuster in the Senate, the ACA was passed and signed into law by President Obama.

The bill, commonly known as Obamacare, mandated that every individual had to purchase health-care insurance or face a fine for not doing so. It established state and federal health-care exchanges, where individuals could go to buy health insurance directly and lower-income people could receive federal or state subsidies to help defray the costs. The ACA also prohibited insurance discrimination against people with preexisting conditions, allowed individuals up to age twenty-six to stay on their parents' health insurance plans, and provided federal funds to states willing to expand Medicaid eligibility to 138 percent of poverty.

Republicans in and outside of Congress challenged Obamacare in the public and judicial arenas; twenty-six Republican state attorneys general signed onto a lawsuit against the bill that made its way to the Supreme Court. In June 2012, the Supreme Court ruled the key premise of Obamacare—the individual mandate to purchase health insurance—constitutional. After that, the Obama administration set to work to fully implement all parts of the law. Still, in 2015, another lawsuit made its way to the Supreme Court that challenged the constitutionality of the federal government paying subsidies to individuals to purchase health insurance on federally run exchanges. Without these subsidies, it was unclear how many people could still afford to purchase health insurance, which put the entire program under a cloud of uncertainty. However, on June 25, 2015, the Supreme Court upheld this part of Obamacare by a 6–3 ruling in *King v. Burwell* that these subsidies are constitutional.

Although Obama won the health care fight, he and his Democratic allies in Congress absorbed devastating political costs. Republicans in the House and Senate used Obamacare as a rallying cry in the 2010 midterm elections, and, at the same time, the rising conservative movement known as the Tea Party helped fuel the fervor among Republican voters against the Act. As we discussed in chapter 4, the Republicans took control of the House of Representatives in 2011 (the Democrats held the Senate), and in 2015, they took control of the Senate. Thus, for the majority of President Obama's time in office, he worked with a divided government.

Similar to Obama's first two years in office, the elections of 2016 produced a unified party government scenario for President Trump, with the Republicans holding control of the Senate and the House of Representatives; Mitch McConnell (R-KY) remained as Senate majority leader and Paul Ryan (R-WI) remained as Speaker of the House.

In his systematic study of presidential leadership of Congress, political scientist George Edwards concludes, "the president is not the ruler of the American state but a vital centralizing force, providing direction and energy for the nation's policy making."[1] Setting the agenda is only one aspect of the president's ability to direct the actions of an often-fragmented Congress. With the growth of programs, regulations, and spending since the New Deal, the institution of the presidency has held the responsibility for making sure that prospective legislation, specific appropriations, and budget decisions compose a roughly coherent whole.

Yet, even as the presidency has consistently grown in size and power, Congress has remained—both constitutionally and politically—central to national policymaking. Political scientist Mark Peterson points out that "both presidents and the public must learn to recognize Congress as the executive's legislative partner."[2] As in any partnership, the actors play distinct roles; Peterson argues that presidents

> should exploit the vantage point of their lofty position to bring coherence to policy making by functioning as agenda focusers ... Ideas for the nation's agenda will have originated in Congress and elsewhere in the nation.... Rather than attempting to be the government and the repository of all solutions for all problems, presidents would identify the problems, challenge others to respond, and work with other participants in the process to craft possible policy solutions.[3]

President Trump's first one hundred days illustrate the challenges of working with Congress, even under unified government. What should have been very smooth sailing turned rockier than expected with the first big item on the agenda: repeal and replace the ACA. Ever since the midterm elections of 2010 when the GOP regained majority control of the House, Republicans have been advocating for the repeal of the ACA but because Obama remained president and the Senate was under Democratic control until 2015, they knew they would not be able to pass a repeal through both houses of Congress. In 2015 and 2016, Republicans in the House and Senate did manage to pass bills to repeal the ACA but without enough votes to override President Obama's veto power.

By 2017, nearly 20 million people were getting health insurance through the ACA, either by expanded Medicaid, the social insurance program for low-income people, or by federal subsidies of health insurance premiums for individuals who were not poor enough for Medicaid but could not afford to cover the entire costs of health insurance premiums. Therefore, any "repeal and replace" bill would have to address ways to offer coverage to those people. Moreover, since states are constitutionally mandated to balance their budget and typically bear some of the cost of Medicaid, any contraction of Medicaid would negatively affect state budgets. In 2017, about two-thirds of states were under unified Republican control, so taking away health care became both a financial and a political issue for the Republican Party in Congress and at the state level.

President Trump was anxious to make good on his promise to repeal the ACA, but when he turned to Congress for a bill, there were several key problems. First, because the GOP members of Congress knew they would not actually have to deal with the consequences of actually repealing the ACA, they did not spend time or energy crafting a bill that would be effective once enacted. Consequently, they had to scramble to write legislation that would appease the most conservative wing of their party—known as the Freedom Caucus—but also keep the moderates in their party. Led by Speaker Ryan, members of the committees with jurisdiction over the bill, notably the Energy and Commerce Committee and the Ways and Means Committee, produced a bill by literally pulling all-night sessions.[4] The bill would have repealed the mandate to purchase health insurance, eliminated subsidies to buy premiums, and rolled back federal support for expanded coverage under Medicaid. It did, however, maintain two popular provisions: allowing parents to keep children up to age twenty-six on their health insurance and barring discrimination in coverage based on pre-existing health conditions.

As expected, the bill was met with swift and loud opposition from the Democrats, as well as from major interest groups representing insurance companies, doctors, hospitals, and a number of Republican governors. The opposition not only mobilized quickly in Washington DC, but at home, where Republicans were met with intense criticisms at town meetings in their districts from both Democratic and Republican constituents. At the same time, the Freedom Caucus, led by Rep. Mark Meadows (R-NC) (see chapter 8), viewed the bill as too generous and not a true "repeal" of the ACA. The debate within the Republican caucus in the House reflected the same divisions between moderate and conservative GOP members that Speaker Ryan's predecessor, John Boehner, faced and that caused him to resign from the House. As with Boehner over budget policy, Ryan faced a difficult choice; if he made the ACA repeal bill more conservative, he risked losing enough moderate Republicans, but if he did nothing, the bill could not pass the House without Democratic support. Unlike the issue of keeping the government open, Democrats were never going to vote for the repeal of the ACA.

With the Freedom Caucus Republicans remaining opposed, President Trump met with them in the House and warned that opposing the bill would hurt them in the November 2018 midterm elections. But Trump himself was having issues with his own approval ratings, which were hovering at less than 40 percent, which limited his ability to exert political pressure on members of his own party in Congress. Even as Ryan and Trump worked to make changes to the bill to appease conservatives, they were steadily losing support from Republican moderates who took to social media outlets to announce their opposition to the bill. One poll found the level of public support for the bill at only 17 percent; with those numbers, Republicans in the Senate signaled that they would be reluctant to pass the House bill in its current form.

Ultimately, faced with deep divisions within the House GOP, popular opposition, and a Senate that would not pass the repeal and replace bill, Speaker

Ryan decided not to put the bill on the House floor for an up or down vote, even going so far as to say that Obamacare would remain intact for the near future.[5] Trump agreed and expressed his frustration with Republicans in Congress by saying he would not entertain any new proposals to repeal Obamacare and wanted to move on to other issues such as tax reform.

However, President Trump did not give up so easily and returned to the issue a few weeks later by putting new pressure on Speaker Ryan to bring a repeal bill to the floor and pass it. Ryan went back to the Freedom Caucus and agreed to eliminate the federal guarantee of protections for individuals with preexisting conditions. Instead, the bill provided an opportunity for states to apply for a waiver from that requirement. Even with this change, there were still enough Republican holdouts that the bill was in limbo until President Trump and Speaker Ryan agreed to add $8 billion to the bill to subsidize the cost of insurance for high risk individuals at the state level. With that, Trump and Ryan swung enough votes to seal the deal and the American Health Care Act passed the House of Representatives by four votes (217–213) on May 4, 2017; but a warning sign for the bill came from the approximately twenty moderate GOP members of Congress who voted against the bill. With that kind of opposition, the House majority could not afford to lose any supporters, yet they would have little control over the content of the bill that the Senate would approve. Because the House and Senate have to pass bills with the exact same language, the two chambers must negotiate over the final version of any bill.

In the Senate, there was considerably more doubt about securing enough support among Republican senators to vote for the House bill to repeal and replace Obamacare. Unlike House members who represent very narrow districts, senators represent entire states, and the impact of repealing Obamacare on an entire state was considerable in terms of lost opportunity for health insurance coverage for constituents. Consequently, Republican senators had to choose between party loyalty to the campaign promise of repealing Obamacare and leaving their own voters without health insurance. Up until the time that Senator McConnell brought up the bill for consideration, there was still doubt that he had enough votes to pass it but they were hoping to get fifty of fifty-two Republicans to vote or it, and then Vice President Pence could break the tie as president of the Senate. But McConnell fell one vote short when Senator John McCain (R-AZ), who had just been diagnosed with brain cancer and had flown back to Washington to participate in the ACA repeal and replace debate, joined Senator Susan Collins (R-ME) and Senator Lisa Murkowski (R-AK) in voting against the bill, which failed on a 49–51 vote margin. McCain had been a vocal critic of Trump but was also known as a social and fiscal conservative and opponent of Obamacare, so his vote came as a major surprise. McCain and Murkowski had just been reelected in 2016, and Collins in 2014; none of them was facing reelection in 2018 and thus they did not feel overly pressured to toe the Republican Party line.

Despite his victory in the House on the second try, the failure to repeal and replace the ACA in the Senate constituted a first lesson for Trump, in that presidents can hope to exercise no more than partial and temporary influence over legislative actions and outcomes in Congress. Presidents such as Franklin

Roosevelt, Lyndon Johnson, and Ronald Reagan won great victories, but all suffered serious setbacks. Others, like Dwight Eisenhower, sought to exercise influence largely in private ways. Nonetheless, even the weakest post–World War II president, Republican Gerald Ford, who rose from serving as an unelected vice president to face a hostile, activist Democratic Congress in the wake of Nixon's resignation in 1974, wielded considerable power. In his 1974–1977 tenure, Ford set much of the legislative agenda through his budget-writing authority, and he regularly employed his constitutional weapon of the veto, thereby affecting legislative consideration of controversial matters.

At various times in their presidencies, Bill Clinton, George W. Bush, and Barack Obama proved formidable at shaping the congressional agenda and placing their own stamp on the implementation of laws passed by previous Congresses. In his first term, President Bush turned back much of Clinton's environmental policy by reversing various Clinton directives and reinterpreting legislation. Later in his presidency, however, Bush implemented new environmental regulations on fuel economy (CAFE) standards. He did so partly in response to pressure from the Democrats when they took control of Congress in 2007. Obama continued and expanded upon this use of presidential power during his administration by issuing regulations for even tougher fuel-economy standards and limits of carbon emissions. President Trump has taken a page from George Bush's playbook by issuing executive orders to reverse environmental protections put in place by President Obama, including those very same fuel-economy standards that Bush and Obama both supported.

Presidents can also keep in place bureaucratic infrastructure and policies from prior administrations. Obama used the two congressional authorizations for use of military force—provided to President Bush in 2001 and 2002 after the 9/11 attacks to wage war in Afghanistan and Iraq—to do two things. First, he used them to oversee the conflicts in those countries when he first came into office and later to wind down the U.S. military combat role there. Second, he used them to launch attacks on terrorist groups such as Al-Qaeda and ISIL in Iraq, Yemen, Syria, and Pakistan. Thus, as president, he expanded the military authorization granted by Congress to his predecessor. The same can be said for his use of the Department of Homeland Security, a cabinet-level department established under Bush, to try to prevent terrorist activity in the United States.

President Trump is also using military power under the same longstanding authorization granted to President George W. Bush by Congress to launch strikes in Afghanistan. In Syria, President Obama did not ask for or receive the same authorization from Congress, and Trump, early in his term, did not ask for that authorization either. Trump has also tried to use executive power to expand border security by imposing a temporary travel ban against individuals seeking visas to come to the United States from seven foreign countries that were *alleged* to support terrorism: Iran, Iraq, Libya, Somalia, Sudan, Syria, and Yemen. In addition, the Trump executive order suspended the refugee program from these countries as well. Individuals and civil liberties organizations such as the ACLU filed suit to challenge the ban; they argued that the ban targeted individuals from predominantly Muslim countries and thus violated the U.S. Constitution, which prohibits action by the government that disproportionately

SPOTLIGHT

Representative Justin Amash: A Republican Opposing Trump in a Partisan Era

First elected to the House of Representatives in the 2010 midterm elections, Rep. Justin Amash (R-MI) has built a unique congressional profile that often cuts against his fellow partisans, including a willingness to oppose President Donald Trump.

Elected with support from the Tea Party, Amash is a member of the House Freedom Caucus, a conservative descendent of the Tea Party Caucus. But Amash is not just another Tea Party conservative; he has a libertarian streak as well. He serves as the chair of the House Liberty Caucus—which is conservative but with a more libertarian emphasis on limited government and economic deregulation than the Freedom Caucus. He also endorsed libertarian Ron Paul for president in 2012 and has been an outspoken opponent of domestic government surveillance. Amash's ideological positioning has sometimes served to confound Republicans. As his congressional career progressed, Michigan business leaders expressed disdain for his unwillingness to work with party leadership. In 2014, local businessman Brian Ellis launched a primary challenge against Amash, but rather than positioning himself as a more moderate Republican willing to work with leadership, Ellis attacked Amash from the right, accusing Amash of "turning his back on our conservative principles." Representative Amash was able to hold off Ellis in the primary 57 to 43 percent, which is a relatively narrow victory for an incumbent in a primary election, but Ellis's challenge likely suffered from a lack of available ideological space to the right of Amash.

Representative Amash has also emphasized forging a good relationship with his constituents since taking office. After every vote, he takes to Facebook to explain and justify to his constituents why he voted the way he did. From January 2011 when he first took office until March 10, 2017, Amash did not miss a single roll call vote out of 4,289 votes during that period. His streak ended when he was outside of the chamber talking to reporters while the House went on voting without him. Upon learning of his missed vote, Amash was in tears and later tweeted an apology to his constituents.

Consistent with the Tea Party and House Freedom Caucus's unyielding opposition to government spending (see the spotlight feature in chapter 3), Amash has regularly voted against appropriations bills and continuing resolutions in the 115th Congress even when those measures passed the House by wide margins. While such votes would not be unexpected under a Democratic president, it is significant that Rep. Amash continues to vote in ways that cut against the wishes of a Republican president. Perhaps, for example, the fact that the short-term appropriations bills passed in April and May of 2017 that avoided government shutdowns, each passed with hundreds of votes to spare, allowed Amash the luxury of opposing the measure in order to maintain his credibility as a strict fiscal conservative. Indeed, in the case of the American Health Care Act (AHCA), a bill which passed the House with only one vote to spare on May 4, 2017, Amash did side with the Trump administration's position and voted for the measure. He posted on Facebook that he decided to support the bill after it became "increasingly clear that a bill to repeal Obamacare will not come to the floor in this Congress or in the foreseeable future."

But Rep. Amash has opposed Trump more decisively in ways that do not appear in his voting record. During the presidential campaign Amash declined to formally endorse Trump, stating that he would vote for neither Trump nor Hillary Clinton. When President Trump issued an executive order banning refugees, noncitizens, and lawful permanent residents from certain Muslim-majority countries from entering the United States, Amash attacked the action as an unconstitutional overreach. And perhaps his most visible critiques of Trump have come on social media: in response to a Trump tweet attacking congressman and civil rights icon John Lewis, Amash replied, "Dude, just stop." On another occasion, Amash posted a criticism of President Trump's "constant fear-mongering" about terrorism as "irresponsible and dangerous." And in response to Trump's tweets decrying federal court decisions against his immigration ban, Amash tweeted that Trump needs to "stop attacking the

legitimacy of the judiciary." While there is certainly a heightened pressure in the contemporary Congress to support both party leadership and same-party presidents, Justin Amash shows that there is still room for individual members to oppose their party's leaders in various ways.

The information in this section is taken from multiple sources as follows: Philip Rucker, "Some Tea Party Congressmen Find Signs of Political Backlash at Home," *The Washington Post*, October 6, 2013, https://www.washingtonpost.com/politics/some-tea-party-congressmen-find-signs-of-political-backlash-at-home/2013/10/06/d13d698a-2d27-11e3-b139-029811dbb57f_story.html?utm_term=.479d06ce5c56; Philip Rucker, "Tea Party Favorite Amash Draws GOP Primary Opponent," *The Washington Post*, October 8, 2013, https://www.washingtonpost.com/news/post-politics/wp/2013/10/08/tea-party-favorite-amash-draws-gop-primary-opponent/?utm_term=.398e5bec9a20; Rachael Bade and Jennifer Haberkorn, "Amash Cries After Missing First Vote in Congress," *Politico*, March 10, 2017, http://www.politico.com/story/2017/03/justin-amash-cries-after-missing-vote-235928; Natalie Andrews, "Justin Amash Emerges as Leading Critic of Fellow Republican Donald Trump," *The Wall Street Journal*, February 20, 2017, https://www.wsj.com/articles/justin-amash-emerges-as-leading-critic-of-fellow-republican-donald-trump-1487599201; Rep. Justin Amash, Facebook post, May 6, 2017, https://www.facebook.com/justinamash/posts/1411436255562443.

favors or discriminates against one religion. Although many members of Congress (most Democrats and some Republicans) opposed the travel ban, they did not have the power to suspend or stop the travel ban.

One of those members was a self-described conservative Tea Party Republican named Justin Amash (R-MI), who was vocal in his opposition to President Trump in some arenas like the travel ban, but supported him in others areas.

Ultimately, multiple federal courts considered constitutional basis of the travel ban, and it was struck down by multiple federal district court judges. The Trump administration subsequently suspended it and then issued a second version of the ban, which removed Iraq from the list of specified countries and modified other elements so that it would pass constitutional tests.[6] But again, two federal judges struck down the ban for the same reasons as the first set of judges had done—that it was discriminatory based on religion.[7]

One of the key elements of the controversy over the travel ban was President Trump's own words from the campaign trail during the 2016 election. He was quoted on numerous occasions as saying he supported a ban on Muslims coming into the United States and the federal judges who struck down the travel ban referenced these remarks in their rulings saying that they reflected the essence of the intent of the ban was to discriminate against Muslims.[8] The federal court rulings also determined that the administration had not presented sufficient evidence to suggest that individuals from these countries posed a sufficient national security threat to warrant such action. As we noted in chapter 2, the administration appealed these lower court decisions to the Supreme Court, which ruled that some parts of the Trump travel ban could go into effect for the time being until the Court reviewed the constitutionality of the entire travel ban during its 2017–2018 term.

The federal court limitations on the travel ban and the difficulty getting a repeal and replace Obamacare bill through Congress represented early instances when President Trump experienced the limits of the presidency within a separation of powers system of government. Coming from the private sector, he had plenty of experience with the courts as private citizen, but he underestimated the extent to which both the Congress and the judiciary can check the presidency. It was one thing to cut a deal with one or two people across a table, but Congress contains 535 potential deal makers and substantial opportunities to oppose presidential initiatives.

For all the early missteps for President Trump's administration, there is plenty of time for him and his staff to recover, as well as his fellow Republicans in Congress. Presidents before him, notably Bill Clinton, also had very rocky starts to their administration, both within the executive branch and with his own party in Congress. Despite losing control of Congress in 1994 to the opposite party, Bill Clinton adapted and worked with the Republicans to produce several major pieces of legislation, and he easily won reelection in 1996. For a president who is willing to change course and adapt, there is always the potential to forge a successful relationship with Congress, although the increasingly partisan nature of American politics may limit these opportunities.

This chapter emphasizes the core elements of the presidency in a separation of powers system, with an emphasis on presidential-congressional relations, ranging from constitutional roles to the centralization of policymaking that derives from the power to tax and spend, which is constitutionally based in Congress. In addition, the chapter explores the differences in presidential-congressional relations under divided government (when the presidency and the Congress are controlled by opposing parties) in comparison to unified government under one party's control. Related to—but different from—divided government is the notion of gridlock, or the extent to which presidential-congressional relations encourage deadlock, regardless of whether or not one party controls both branches of government.[9] Finally, we consider the temporary nature of any president's capacity to provide focus and direction to the necessarily messy business of writing laws. The president may win numerous legislative victories and suffer his share of defeats, but many bills pass with little presidential expression of interest. In short, the modern presidency, no matter its size and reach, cannot dominate either the policy debates or the outcomes of all policy initiatives.

THE PRESIDENT AS CHIEF LEGISLATOR

The Congress, with its potential for fragmentation and individualism, can ordinarily benefit from focus and direction. Although in 1995 the speakership of Newt Gingrich offered a historic alternative to strong presidential leadership, none of the speakers who followed him, Hastert, Pelosi, Boehner, and Ryan, wielded the same power over the national agenda. In contemporary U.S. politics, it has been the president who has had the best chance of generating a coherent vision of where the nation should be headed. Convincing the Congress to act on this vision is quite another matter, however.

As a rule, no member of Congress is as important a legislator as is the chief executive, but the strong partisanship of the postreform era has certainly increased the power of party leaders, especially those in the majority. Whether in setting the congressional agenda, twisting a lawmaker's arm to support a favored measure, or threatening to veto an unsatisfactory bill, the president can affect the legislative process more forcefully, and in more ways, than the most influential senator or representative. But does this mean that presidents get what they want? Hardly. The separate institutions of the Congress and the presidency must both share and compete for power.[10]

The Constitution offers only modest guidance in defining presidential-congressional relations. For example, Article I gives the Congress the power to declare war, but since 1950 presidents have committed U.S. troops to wars (in Korea, Vietnam, Iraq, and Afghanistan) without any formal declaration of war. Congress did agree to the actions in both legislation and appropriations, but its attempt, through the 1973 War Powers Act, to wrest effective control from the president of most decisions to commit troops has not proved to be successful.[11] Likewise, the presidential power to veto legislation is a potent formal weapon, especially in times of divided party government, but one that is often most effective when used sparingly. Recent presidents Clinton, Bush, and Obama used the veto thirty-seven, twelve, and twelve times, respectively.[12] Clinton's higher number of vetoes makes perfect sense because he spent six out of eight years working with a Congress controlled by the opposing party, whereas Bush spent only two years under divided government.[13] Obama had the most complicated governing configuration: unified party government for two years, quasi-divided government (Republicans controlled the House, but not the Senate) for four years, and fully divided government for the last two years of his term. But presidents do not have to actually veto legislation to make full use of their veto powers. By merely threatening to veto legislation before it passes Congress, presidents try to persuade Congress to shape legislation to avoid being vetoed, thus turning a negative power into a positive tool to influence policymaking on Capitol Hill.[14]

Agenda-Setting and the Prospects for Presidential Influence: It's All in the Timing

The core of presidents' legislative strength lies in their ability to influence national policy agenda issues in both ordinary and extraordinary ways. The most consistent and predictable impact of the presidency comes through the centralization of the annual budget and the executive's capacity to filter and coordinate disparate proposals that bubble up within dozens of separate bureaucratic units. Indeed, the federal government's agenda is always full; that is, there are always many issues, initiatives, and problems for presidents and legislators to consider. As Charles Jones observed,

> Since it is not possible to treat all issues at once, members of Congress and others anxiously await the designation of priorities. These presidential choices are typically from a list that is familiar to other policy actors. Nonetheless, a designator is important. . . . As in any organization, there is a need for someone in authority to say: "Let's start here."[15]

Aside from designating certain issues as priorities in the course of normal policymaking, almost all presidents offer up some major initiatives that depart markedly from past policies. Such proposals—Carter's energy plans, Reagan's tax cuts, Clinton's welfare proposals, George W. Bush's education package, Obama's health-care bill, and Trumps' tax reform initiative—required large-scale changes in existing policies and have the potential to disrupt established policy subsystems made up of congressional committees, interest groups, and bureaucratic units.[16] The president can move only a limited number of major items on to the legislative agenda—all presidents must therefore be careful in what they choose to push as they approach the Congress.

The annual State of the Union message and upcoming year's budget are the earliest and most visible statements of a president's policy agenda. They are intertwined because the policy changes that the president proposes in the State of the Union message always either cost more money (more typically) or reduce government spending (less typically). So when the fiscal-year budget is sent to Congress by the president in February (the federal fiscal year starts on October 1), it anticipates the changes associated with the president's proposed policies. Through these public pronouncements, presidents have the opportunity to try to direct the policy agenda within the Congress and with the public at large.[17] Presidents have more opportunity to use these instruments in shaping the agenda with unified party government than divided government, but under both conditions, presidents benefit from being a single national actor who focuses the attention of the press and the public on a few key issues. On occasion, as with Franklin Roosevelt and Lyndon Johnson, the context permits a broad agenda of large-scale changes. But even for these energetic, forceful leaders, who enjoyed the favorable circumstances of large congressional majorities of their own party, the windows of opportunity for focusing legislative attention were relatively brief.[18]

Regardless of political circumstances, presidents are well-advised to set the agenda on major issues in the first and second years of their term—either "move it or lose it."[19] Presidents begin their terms of office with election victories that provide them with substantial amounts of political capital, and rarely do they increase this store of assets; rather, the longer they wait to introduce key pieces of legislation, the lower the chance of passage.[20] Bill Clinton won a balanced budget and the North American Free Trade Agreement (NAFTA) in his first year; President George W. Bush got education reform and tax cuts in his first year in office; and President Obama enacted three major economic reform bills to address the recession, as well as making progress on health-care reform, ultimately passed early in his second year. President Trump had ambitious goals in his first year to repeal the ACA, enact major tax reform, and enact a large infrastructure spending bill. He did not succeed in accomplishing that agenda, in large part due to a failure to build successful partnerships with Republican members of Congress.

Beyond the initial year, presidential agendas face increased skepticism in the halls of Congress. Delay is the enemy of change and defines the very nature of the policy process in Congress—one that requires a succession of majorities in the House and Senate, in committees, on the floor, and in conferences or other negotiations between the two chambers. Leading 535 legislative horses to the trough does not mean that a president can make them drink, but it is typically easier when Congress is controlled by the president's party.

President Obama faced especially strong opposition to his major policy initiatives from the Republicans in Congress, both when they were in the minority and in the majority. Although he managed to pass health-care reform, his other major policy proposals, such as long-term deficit reduction and immigration reform, were met with staunch resistance. In the summer of 2011, for example, President Obama proposed a deal with Speaker Boehner known as the "grand bargain," which would have reduced the federal deficit by billions over a ten-year period through a combination of spending cuts and tax increases. After agreeing in principle to the details of the deal, Speaker Boehner returned to his House Republican caucus and encountered immediate and fierce opposition, in large part led by his second in command, House Majority Leader Eric Cantor (R-VA). Within a few days, the deal fell apart, ultimately to be replaced with a shorter-term compromise that imposed automatic across-the-board cuts in federal spending, known as the sequester. Rather than putting a long-term deficit reduction plan in place based on careful cuts in spending in specific areas, the sequester cut many federal programs equally, which is generally considered a less effective policy tool.

More than two years later, President Obama had been reelected to a second term, and the economy was getting better, but more slowly than expected, in part because of the reductions in government spending. The Republicans in the House refused to pass a continuing resolution to fund the government in the fall of 2013, and when the federal government partially shut down as a result, they took most of the immediate public blame. The combination of the negative public reaction to the partial government shutdown and the impact of the sequester budget cuts forced Republicans in Congress to negotiate with the president. They came to an agreement that, as then-House Budget Committee chairman Paul Ryan (R-WI) put it, "cuts spending in a smarter way. . . . In divided government you don't always get what you want."[21] In something of a grand irony, House Majority Leader Cantor ended up losing his 2014 GOP primary contest to Dave Brat, an economics professor and Tea Party candidate, who criticized Cantor for supporting a bloated federal government. Nevertheless, voters did not penalize Republicans for tying up the government in 2013, as they sailed to victory in the elections of 2014, holding the House and taking back the Senate.

On immigration reform, President Obama and members of both houses proposed a number of bills over his tenure, but the main sticking points—pathways to citizenship for undocumented residents and border security—remained major obstacles to compromise. Article II, Section 3 of the U.S. Constitution grants the president the authority to ensure that laws are "faithfully executed," which allows the president to issue presidential directives, including executive orders and presidential memoranda, regarding how laws are implemented by the federal bureaucracy. With Congress failing to act on immigration, President Obama twice used his executive powers in the area of immigration enforcement to suspend deportations against undocumented residents who meet specific criteria, such as age of arrival, educational and working history, and no criminal record. At the same time, Obama used his executive power to deport over 2.7 million undocumented residents in the years 2009–2015.[22] President Trump continued the Obama policy of deporting undocumented residents with a criminal record, and in September 2017 he went further by terminating the DACA (Deferred Action for Childhood Arrivals) residents program, which had allowed undocumented residents who were brought to the United States as children to remain in the country and secure work permits. At the same time he left the door open to Congress to send him immigration legislation that would provide a legal pathway for DACA residents to stay in the United States.

Congressional investigations can also haunt presidential administrations. With Clinton, it was an investigation into a land deal known as Whitewater that lead to the revelations about his affair with Monica Lewinsky and impeachment proceedings against him (which did not succeed). Under Obama, Rep. Darrell Issa spent many of his years as chairman of the House Oversight and Government Reform Committee (2011–2015) launching investigations on issues such as the embassy attack in Benghazi, the Internal Revenue Service's alleged targeting of conservative political groups, and the "Fast and Furious" failed gun sting. For President Trump, both the House and Senate intelligence committees investigated whether there was collusion between the Russian government and the Trump campaign during the 2016 election (discussed below). While these investigations can go very far, as in the case of Clinton, or amount to nothing, as in the case of Obama, they serve as a continuous distraction to the president and can negatively affect his working relationship with Congress.

It remains to be seen how President Trump works with Congressional Republicans moving forward in his first two years, and what may happen if the Democrats regain control of Congress after the 2018 midterm elections. But, in reality, every president faces resistance from Congress to the exercise of strong executive power, because it ultimately diminishes legislative power. As a presidential term progresses, members of Congress and the public continually

SPOTLIGHT

Representative Darrell Issa: Opposing Obama and Supporting Trump in an Increasingly Blue District

Representative Darrell Issa (R-CA) is an example of how unwavering support for same-party presidents can endure even when a member of Congress is electorally vulnerable. Issa has served in Congress since 2001 and is perhaps

best known for his tenure as chairman of the House Oversight and Government Reform Committee from 2011 to 2015, when he relentlessly pursued the Obama administration but these investigations often failed to implicate the administration in ways commensurate with the amount of media coverage the investigations received. Moreover, as of the 114th Congress, Darrell Issa is the wealthiest member of Congress with a net worth north of $250 million.

Issa first entered electoral politics in 1998 when he sought to challenge incumbent Democratic U.S. Senator Barbara Boxer. A successful businessman and frequent donor to local Republican campaigns and conservative ballot initiatives during the 1990s, Issa raised millions for his campaign and became a serious contender for the Republican nomination. But Issa lost the Republican primary by five percentage points despite outspending his top primary opponent, Matt Fong, by nearly nine million dollars. Issa's primary campaign fell short in part because of the negative coverage generated by his opponents' opposition research into his past; for example, it came to light during the campaign that at various points throughout Issa's life he had been arrested for carrying a concealed

weapon, indicted for stealing a car, had a troubled stint in the U.S. Army, and was suspected of committing arson. Issa recovered quickly from his loss in the Senate race, successfully running for Congress in the 2000 election cycle in what is now California's 49th congressional district.

The 49th district, located in southern California and encompassing much of northern San Diego County along with portions of Orange County, has seen an influx of Latinos and younger voters over the past decade, trends that favor the Democratic Party's electoral prospects. Indeed, when Issa won reelection in 2002, he received 77 percent of the votes, compared with his 58 percent vote share in 2012. In the 2016 election, Issa was reelected for his ninth term with only 50.3 percent of the vote and his Democratic opponent reaching 49.7 percent; a margin of fewer than 1,700 votes out of about 310,000 votes cast in the district. Moreover, Hillary Clinton carried Issa's district at the presidential level by a margin of 7.5 percentage points.

Representative Issa was a steadfast supporter of President Trump despite Trump's unpopularity in his district and the increasing ascendancy of Democratic electoral prospects against him. Early on in the Republican presidential primaries, Issa supported Marco Rubio and criticized Trump. But when candidate Trump started piling up victories into the spring, Issa became one of the first Republican elected officials to offer Trump a formal endorsement and he even penned an Op-ed rebuking fellow Republicans for not joining him in his support. Even as many Republicans distanced themselves from Trump when the "Access Hollywood" recording was released in October, Issa remained firm in his support. That support during the campaign has translated into congressional support. In the early months of the Trump administration, Issa voted 100 percent in line with the president's positions. On May 4, 2017, Issa voted for the American Health Care Act (AHCA), an immensely consequential bill that has failed to receive support from either major health care interest groups or stakeholders or close to a majority of the public. The bill passed the House by one vote, including crucial votes from fourteen Republicans who, like Issa, represent districts carried by Clinton in 2016.

After the Republicans' immense electoral success in the 2010 midterms, which political scientists have suggested was largely attributable to voters' reactions to individual members' roll call votes on the ACA; one would think that electorally vulnerable members of Congress would be particularly risk-averse when it comes to consequential roll call votes. Perhaps Rep. Issa is aware of the ramifications of

his health care vote as well as the consequences of his unwavering support for a president who is unpopular in his district, and plans on retiring in anticipation of an uphill battle for reelection. If Issa does not retire before his term ends, he will be a prime target for a Democratic challenge to him in 2018 and his AHCA vote may come back to haunt him.

_____

The information in this section is taken from multiple sources as follows: Noah Bierman, "California's Darrell Issa Loses Power Along with House Oversight Committee Post," *The Los Angeles Times*, March 20, 2015, http://www.latimes.com/nation/politics/la-na-darrell-issa-20150321-story.html; Roll Call, "Wealth of Congress Index," November 2, 2015, http://media.cq.com/50Richest/; Ryan Lizza, "Don't Look Back," *The New Yorker*, January 24, 2011, http://www.newyorker.com/magazine/2011/01/24/dont-look-back-ryan-lizza; Ryan Lizza, "The Trumping of Darrell Issa," *The New Yorker,* August 31, 2016, http://www.newyorker.com/news/news-desk/the-trumping-of-darrell-issa; David Nir, "Daily Kos Elections' Presidential Results by Congressional District for the 2016 and 2012 Elections," *The Daily Kos*, November 19, 2016. http://www.dailykos.com/story/2012/11/19/1163009/-Daily-Kos-Elections-presidential-results-by-congressional-district-for-the-2012-2008-elections; FiveThirtyEight.com, "Congress Tracker: Darrell E. Issa," https://projects.fivethirtyeight.com/congress-trump-score/darrell-e-issa/; Nyhan, Brendan, Eric McGhee, John Sides, Seth Masket, and Steven Greene. 2012. "One vote out of step? The effects of salient roll call votes in the 2010 election." *American Politics Research*, 40(5): 844–79.

update their evaluation of the president's performance, and these evaluations factor heavily in producing either cooperation or conflict between the branches. If voter confidence in the president increases, his clout with Congress can increase; if voters lose confidence, he will find it more difficult to be a persuasive force both with Congress and in U.S. politics more generally.

The Contexts of Presidential Influence

In the wake of extended scholarly debates over the nature of presidential influence on Congress, a rough consensus has emerged that paints presidential power within the legislative process as an important force but subject to many limitations. At a minimum, some restrictions include those of the "pure context" of a separation-of-powers system—each bill must pass two different chambers with a majority before it can reach the president's desk. Moreover, the internal rules of the Senate, even in the age of unified party government, generate continuing obstacles to the adoption of radical or fundamental policy changes. Informal Senate practices, such as the reliance on unanimous-consent agreements (described in chapter 7) to conduct much of its business, are beyond the president's control.

More troubling for the president is the filibuster (extended debate), which is used to delay and frequently prevent legislation from being voted on, much less passing. Over the past thirty years, the filibuster has also obstructed presidential nominations and judicial appointments, from U.S. district courts all the way up to the U.S. Supreme Court. However, as we noted earlier in chapter 5, in November 2013, the Senate Democratic majority changed the rules to prohibit the use of the filibuster on judicial nominations, except for the U.S. Supreme Court. The Supreme Court was exempted given its overwhelming power, and Democrats wanted to be able to block a Republican president's appointment of a very conservative Supreme Court justice.

Democratic fears came to pass in 2017 when President Trump nominated Neil Gorsuch to fill a vacancy left by the death of Antonin Scalia in February of 2016. The 2017 battle was especially fierce because the Senate GOP had blocked consideration of President Barack Obama's nominee, Merrick Garland, nominated in February 2016. The GOP's rationale was that it was too late in Obama's presidency to grant him the power to make a Supreme Court appointment—an argument that had never been successful before in the history of the Senate. Reasonable or not, GOP leadership used its power of agenda control to prevent the Senate from conducting a hearing on Merrick Garland, much less holding an up or down vote on his nomination. Had Hillary Clinton won the presidency, the GOP Senate leader claimed that he would have given her nominee a fair hearing, but Trump's victory spared him that test. Instead, Trump nominated Neil Gorsuch, a conservative Court of Appeals justice, with experience similar to Garland's but a different ideological perspective. In sum, when Democrats attempted to filibuster the Gorsuch nomination, Senate Majority Leader McConnell employed a procedural maneuver using the so-called nuclear option that required just fifty-one votes to confirm Supreme Court justices. In doing so, the GOP majority effectively eliminated the power to filibuster all Supreme Court nominations some point in the future.

For now, the Senate still has a legislative filibuster, which can only be overcome by targeting policies toward senators who sit at what political scientist Keith Krehbiel has identified as "pivot points."[23] In reality, if any president wishes to see his agenda enacted, he needs 60, rather than 51, votes in the Senate to overcome filibusters; the 60th senator thus becomes the filibuster pivot. Beyond this, other important elements of the policymaking context further restrain executive success. These include a president's margin of victory in the previous election, the partisan balance of congressional seats, and the president's standing with the public, all of which contribute to his ability to pressure Congress into passing his proposals.[24] Regardless of the executive's formal, constitutional powers, much of the president's ability to affect legislation results from the policymaking context, which comes principally from the president's electoral base, his popularity in the country, and the partisan balance within the Congress.[25] Although these elements do not determine legislative outcomes, they do shape the content and scope of executive initiatives and the strategies that the president constructs for winning congressional majorities. The president's task grows more difficult in a second term because he cannot run for reelection, and this limitation diminishes his role as a political power broker between members of Congress and voters.

Consider, for example, the range of different circumstances faced by newly elected presidents from the 1960s to 2017 as they worked with their first Congresses; table 6.1 sets the stage for the presidents who served during this time period. In 1965, Democratic Lyndon Johnson began his first full term as president with an overwhelming margin of victory, large Democratic majorities

Table 6.1 Electoral, Partisan, and Popularity Context for Newly Elected Presidents, 1960–2016

President	Year Elected, Percentage of Vote	Initial Party Balance		Approval after First Year (percent)
		House	Senate	
Kennedy	1960, 49	262D–175R[a]	64D–36R	79
Johnson	1964, 61	295D–140R	68D–32R	69
Nixon	1968, 43	243D–192R	58D–42R	67
Carter	1976, 50	292D–143R	61D–39R	59
Reagan	1980, 51	243D–192R	46D–54R	49
Bush	1988, 54	260D–175R	55D–45R	75
Clinton	1992, 43	258D–176R[b]	57D–43R	49
Bush, G. W.	2000, 48	212D–221R[c]	50D–50R[d]	62
Obama	2008, 53	257D–178R	59D–41R[e]	54
Trump	2016, 46	194D–241R	48D–52R[f]	—

Source: Harold W. Stanley and Richard G. Niemi, *Vital Statistics on American Politics* (Washington, DC: CQ Press, various years); Thomas E. Mann, Norman J. Ornstein, and Michael J. Malbin, *Vital Statistics on Congress* (Washington, DC: American Enterprise Institute, various years), http://www.senate.gov; http://www.house,gov; http://www.polling.com.

[a] Includes one extra member for Alaska and Hawaii.
[b] Rep. Bernard Sanders (Vermont) elected as Independent.
[c] Two Independents elected.
[d] In June 2001, Senator James Jeffords (R-VT) changed to Independent and caucused with the Democrats.
[e] Bernard Sanders (VT) and Joseph Lieberman (CT) were Independents who caucused with the Democrats.
[f] Bernard Sanders (VT) and Angus King (ME) were Independents who caucused with the Democrats.

in each house, and a backlog of social programs on the congressional agenda, many of which had received full committee hearings in the previous session. With that momentum, Johnson could seek passage of dozens of significant pieces of legislation in the 89th Congress (1965–1967), profoundly changing the role of government in society with Medicare, civil rights legislation, federal aid to education, and environmental initiatives, along with other elements that made up his Great Society vision.[26]

In contrast, Republican George H. W. Bush entered 1989, his first year as president, with a modest margin of victory, Democratic control of the House and Senate, and a deficit of roughly $200 billion (a very large sum at the time). As president, Bush operated more as a partner to an assertive opposite-party Congress than a leader commanding his troops. Bush needed to work with Congress on environmental legislation (the Clean Air Act); he threatened to veto the first version of the bill that Congress passed, but when the conferees produced the final product, he signed it into law. Much more politically damaging to President Bush was the deficit-reduction legislation that Congress passed because it led Bush to accept a modest tax increase, which broke his "no new taxes" election pledge, split the Republican Party, and may well have cost him reelection in 1992, even though this policy set the stage for dramatic reductions in the deficit during the Clinton administration.[27]

His son George W. Bush encountered more friendly circumstances when he assumed office in 2001 with unified party control, a budget surplus, and a Republican-controlled Congress. President Obama had a unified party government, but he faced much larger deficits than George H. W. Bush did, and a deeper recession. Even though both presidents won reelection, they found the last two years of their second terms to be quite difficult in facing a Congress controlled by the opposite party.

With his unexpected, narrow victory in the Electoral College, while losing the popular vote, President Trump began his tenure at some disadvantage. The presidential campaign was bitter and divisive, and the lingering resentments on all sides did not diminish after inauguration day. Additionally, the Trump administration faced a Federal Bureau of Investigation (FBI) inquiry into its ties with the Russian government during the presidential campaign, with several of Trump's campaign aides at the center. Several senior Republicans in the Senate, including Lindsey Graham (R-SC), who is featured in chapter 2, and John McCain (R-SC), expressed their strong concerns about Russian interference in the campaign generally, but stopped short of directly accusing the Trump campaign of wrongdoing. The House and Senate Intelligence Committees each launched their own bipartisan investigations into these ties as well. The situation was further complicated when President Trump fired James Comey, the Director of the FBI on May 9, 2017; it was Comey's fourth year in office in what is typically a ten-year term. In response to the Comey firing, the Department of Justice appointed a special prosecutor named Robert Mueller, who was a former FBI director under George W. Bush and Obama, to oversee the FBI investigation. Essentially there were two parallel investigations going at the same time by the executive branch and the Congress. New FBI director Christopher Wray was confirmed by the Senate in August 2017, and he pledged not to interfere with any ongoing investigations into Russian activity in the 2016 election.

More generally, Congress's partisan balance and the president's overall political strength shape the chief executive's capacity to focus legislative attention, both in setting the agenda and in helping to move legislation through the labyrinth of Capitol Hill. Even in difficult circumstances, the president remains a powerful centralizing force in that, first, his agenda items require congressional attention (if not agreement). Second, the president alone commands the position to conduct authoritative negotiations with lawmakers. Legislating in the fragmented context of the U.S. Congress, even in times of intense partisanship, necessarily includes focusing attention and deal-making, which puts enormous pressure on the president to consistently try to work out compromises with Congress. Given the extent of congressional partisanship and polarization, it proved more difficult for President Obama than for most of his predecessors, so he frequently turned to using his executive orders to get around Congress to pursue his policy objectives. President Trump also used executive orders to implement his policy preferences early in his first year in office, but with mixed success.

Legislating: Presidential Tools in a Retail Politics Era

My vote cannot be bought, but it can be rented.

—Rep. John Breaux (D-LA), 1981

The last time someone ordered me to something, I was 18 years old. And it was my daddy. And I didn't listen to him, either.

—Unnamed member of Congress, 2017[28]

Even though more than thirty years separate those quotes, they are timeless in reflecting the traditional nature of Congress and its relationship with the president. Until recently, members of Congress were open to cutting deals in order to accomplish their policy goals and to serve their districts and states effectively. That also meant they were willing to work with the president when he was willing to give them something in return. Today, the political landscape has changed considerably, with members of the opposition party very fearful of crossing the partisan aisle. Under President Obama, Republicans perceived the antipathy to Obama as so intense among their constituents that they opposed him on nearly everything he wanted to do, and would not even be seen in a photograph with him. Democrats are fast becoming as wary of working with President Trump in any way, as their partisan base has become highly energized in the wake of Hillary Clinton's defeat. This environment makes it almost impossible to engage in the kind of deal-making that has historically been the hallmark of congressional lawmaking.[29]

Nevertheless, most major legislative initiatives require "cross-partisan" majorities.[30] In times of narrow majorities in the House and Senate, major legislative victories ordinarily require constructing majorities across party lines, especially in the Senate, with the potential for filibuster. Although there is little bipartisan cooperation today, congressional history has witnessed extended periods where cross-party cooperation was essential. For example, moderate northern Republicans would sometimes join liberal Democrats in the 1950s and 1960s to provide the margin of victory for urban initiatives. And in 1961, a handful of Republicans gave the Kennedy administration and Speaker Rayburn their crucial victory in expanding the House Rules Committee, thus wresting control from the conservative coalition of southern Democrats and many Republicans.

Twenty years later, in 1981, it was crucial for Ronald Reagan to negotiate with moderate Democratic Representative John Breaux about Louisiana's oil and gas interests as he sought to push through spending cuts. It was not essential that Breaux buy into the entire Reagan program, but the president could "rent" the congressman for a few important votes in return for protecting a handful of key Louisiana interests. More than a decade later, President Clinton worked closely with the opposition Republican Speaker Gingrich and the Republican Party to enact NAFTA over the objections of many members of his own party. Likewise, in 2001, when President George W. Bush sought to regain "fast-track" negotiation authority on free-trade issues, he struck numerous bargains—but in this instance, he addressed broad concerns of interest groups rather than a specific legislator's concerns. Thus,

> the Administration turned to protectionism to realize both its political and policy aims, [as President] Bush curried favor with steel-state lawmakers— and voters—by imposing tariffs on imported steel. He secured support among Western senators by slapping tariffs on Canadian lumber. And he caved in to farm-state legislators on massive subsidies for agriculture.[31]

As one observer noted of President Bush's single-vote, fast-track victory in the House, "What's happening on Capitol Hill is not pretty," in that the Congress demanded "restrictions on Vietnamese catfish, Caribbean and African clothing, and shoes from Bolivia and Peru—precisely the countries that might benefit most from open markets."[32] President Obama faced similar challenges in seeking fast-track authority for the Trans-Pacific Partnership trade agreement in 2015 (see chapter 3) that ultimately failed as Trump raised objections to trade agreements on the campaign trail in 2016, leading Republicans who had previously supported the deal to back away from it. Once he became president in 2017, Trump signed a presidential memorandum withdrawing the United States from negotiations on the TPP, and he sought to renegotiate the terms of NAFTA as well as other international trade treaties.

In short, the president can usually win the close votes, but the policy costs are often substantial. Presidents possess their greatest advantages on such close votes when they can pressure, bargain with, and cajole fence-sitting lawmakers. Even so, presidents may have to give up a lot to achieve a victory. As a rule, presidents can neither dictate the final content of legislation nor cut an infinite number of deals with members of Congress to produce majorities on the floor. Presidents have a small window of opportunity at the beginning of their first terms (and second terms if they win reelection) to force Congress to address presidential priorities. But addressing an issue is a far cry from creating a new program or cutting an old one. To enact legislation according to their preferences, presidents must carefully negotiate with party leaders, committee chairs, individual senators, and powerful interest groups, using all the tools at their disposal. Moreover, there are hundreds of other policy obligations that presidents address during their years in office that require congressional approval or attract congressional interest and oversight. Many of these items are put on the legislative agenda by members of Congress, and only when passage is within shouting distance can presidents actually affect the outcome.

The Presidential Record

Political scientists and pundits have long attempted to measure rates of presidential success in winning congressional support for their proposals. On occasion, as with the outpouring of legislation in 1964–1966 under Lyndon Johnson, the evidence of presidential impact is overwhelming. Most of the time, however, the results are mixed and often depend on how success is measured. Until 1975, *Congressional Quarterly* generated a so-called box score of presidential success, but this measure was flawed and ultimately discontinued.[33] Subsequently, scholars have relied both on other broad measures, such as overall success rates, and on more specific indicators, such as the key votes for a given Congress. In addition, many scholars have either constructed their own sets of important votes and attempts at presidential influence or relied on historical evidence that indicates those issues on which presidents sought to influence outcomes.[34] As recent scholarship on the core idea of presidential influence illustrates, all-encompassing measures of success rates rarely provide much insight into overall presidential influence.[35] This is illustrated by two examples of *Congressional Quarterly*'s scoring of presidential success rates. In 1981, Ronald Reagan achieved 82 percent support on issues on which he took a position; in 1994, Bill Clinton obtained an 86 percent rating.[36] No sensible analysis of these presidents and these years would have found Clinton's record better than Reagan's. Indeed, Clinton not only lost his major initiative, health-care reform, but he found himself stymied by Senate Republicans for much of 1994 in that many major bills never even came to a vote. Moreover, in his sixth year as president (1998), with a Congress controlled by the opposing party, Bill Clinton achieved a 51 percent success rate on legislation on which he took a position. Ronald Reagan and Richard Nixon, in similar circumstances, won 56 percent and 60 percent of the time, respectively.[37]

It is more useful to view congressional contexts as offering presidents varying options as they pursue their legislative agendas. Should their lists be long or should they be short—emphasizing only a few key issues? Peterson notes, "large agendas invite problems," yet "as LBJ powerfully demonstrated, extremely ambitious, diverse, and sizable programmatic agendas can be guided through the legislative labyrinth."[38] In the end, a skillful president can offer centralized guidance for a coherent set of proposals, but the congressional context of committees, individual legislative entrepreneurs, and wavering support by some party leaders renders questionable any consistent attempts to exert strong executive leadership.

Perhaps the greatest problem in pinning down presidential influence is the task of disentangling context from presidential impact. Republican presidents who faced Democratic congressional majorities—Nixon, Ford, Reagan, and George H. W. Bush—won 61.5 percent of the votes on which they took a position; Democrats from Kennedy to Clinton won 81.5 percent, a margin of 20 percent over the Republicans. President George W. Bush reversed the trend for Republican presidents—in his first four years in office (2001–2005), he won 81 percent of the votes on which he took a position, and whenever he used the presidential veto.[39] A large part of this success came from having Republican majorities in the House and Senate for most of that time, but it also reflected a style of leadership that set legislative priorities. Bush successfully pushed for only a few major pieces of legislation and, of course, for the authority to wage war in Iraq, but in his first term, he did not establish a broad and sweeping set of initiatives that would have fractured his strong party backing among members of Congress. In his second term, however, George W. Bush faced greater resistance from his own party when he tried to privatize part of the Social Security retirement program, and as the Iraq War became less popular, voters gave Democrats control of the Congress for his last two years.

President Obama's success rate in Congress also varied with party control of the House and Senate. In 2009, he had a success score of 93 percent in the House and 98 percent in the Senate, followed by a 2010 score of 86 percent in the House and 75 percent in the Senate. Moreover, Democratic Party loyalty voting was nearly 90 percent in both years, so there was strong congressional party unity among Democrats working with Obama.[40] Predictably, however, Obama's success rate in Congress decreased once the Republicans took control of the House in the 2010 midterm elections. In the years 2011–2013, with a Republican House and a Democratic Senate, Obama averaged about an 85 percent success rate in the Senate but only a 27 percent success rate in the House.[41] In the first year of the 114th Congress (2015–2017), with Republicans controlling both chambers of Congress, President Obama's success rate declined dramatically to 45.7 percent.[42] The intense polarization that pervades congressional policymaking is reflected in the difference in party support for policies that Obama expressly supported. In the House, Republicans backed him on only 11 percent of such votes versus Democrats who voted with him 86 percent of the time. In the somewhat less partisan Senate, Republicans supported him on 53 percent of such votes, while Democrats backed him 87 percent of the time.[43]

BUDGETARY POLITICS: CENTRALIZATION THROUGH CONSTRAINT

When Congress consents to the Executive making the budget it will have surrendered the most important part of a representative government.

—Former Speaker of the House Joseph Cannon, 1919[44]

One of the president's most significant powers in setting the national policy agenda is the capacity to propose an annual budget.[45] The Congress, of course, retains the power of the purse—the appropriations authority—but the president and executive budgetary staff provide both the overarching thrust of proposed spending (e.g., by proposing new programs) and the myriad details of where federal monies will be spent. As federal responsibilities and spending increased from the 1930s through the early 1970s, executive budget officials came to play an important role in shaping policy initiatives, large and small, old and new.[46] The president and Congress generally agreed on the expansion of executive authority as the scope and complexity of public policy grew steadily. Budget scholar Howard Shuman concludes that "in almost every case the delegation [of congressional authority] resulted in the aggrandizement of the executive at the expense of the Congress, but this was done willingly, even joyously, and had few narrow or partisan or siege-mentality overtones."[47]

By the late 1960s, however, the Congress and the president had begun to engage in budget wars, as spending levels and priorities began to be vigorously contested. Party leaders and increasing numbers of backbench legislators wanted to exercise some control over spending, and Republican president Nixon had sought to gain more control over spending levels and priorities through the use of the veto and his willingness to impound funds (refuse to spend them) that the Congress had appropriated.

The president's ability to dominate the agenda results in part from his control over the budget through the Office of Management and Budget (OMB).[48] OMB was created by President Nixon to coordinate all federal policy and expenditures in one central location; prior to the OMB, there was only the Bureau of the Budget, which did not have nearly as much power. With its capacity to review all executive-branch regulations and thus ensure their compliance with presidential priorities, the OMB can thwart the legislative intent of laws, directing executive agencies to carry out specific policies that differ in substantial ways from what the Congress apparently meant. In going about its business, Congress must regularly peer over its collective shoulder, back down Capitol Hill and all the way to the White House. No matter who occupies 1600 Pennsylvania Avenue or which party organizes the congressional proceedings, legislative outcomes are shaped by the chief executive's preferences and the authority for program and budget review held by the OMB.[49]

With the creation of the OMB under Nixon, the Democratic-controlled Congress grew frustrated with both an aggressive Republican president and its own incapacity to control overall levels of spending, and so the stage was set for major reform of the budget process. In the spring of 1974, Congress enacted the Congressional Budget and Impoundment Control Act; President Nixon was in the midst of the Watergate scandal and was politically very weak by this point, resigning less than two months later. Although originally meant as an attack on executive power over the budget, the 1974 legislation also sought to rationalize budgetary policymaking (to control overall expenditures and increase capacities to set priorities) and to strengthen the budget-related capacities of the Congress. By both accident and design, the reforms have paradoxically led to members' greater participation in budgetary politics and, simultaneously, to increased party centralization of the ultimate budget decisions.

By setting a supposedly firm timetable for action and by requiring the Congress to address total levels of spending early in the process, the 1974 budget act sought to give Congress greater control over the levels and composition of federal spending. To do this, the Congress needed more resources and some organizational changes—both houses created budget committees and the non-partisan Congressional Budget Office (CBO) was established. The CBO provides the legislative branch with an independent capacity to analyze the mountains of budget-related data and to make the projections for future revenue and spending patterns that are the heart of contemporary fiscal politics. The new committees increased the number of legislators who played a major role in budgetary politics; the well-respected CBO offered leaders, committees, and even individual members the opportunity to pose alternative budget scenarios to those put forward by the executive branch's OMB. In a sense, budgetary politics became more open in the aftermath of the 1974 reforms. Various factions, ranging from conservative Republicans to the Democratic-dominated and liberal Congressional Black Caucus could propose their own budgetary priorities, even if they had little chance of winning congressional approval.[50]

In fact, the adoption of the budget reforms, especially when combined with the major tax cuts of 1981, conspired to "fiscalize" congressional politics during the 1980s.[51] With annual deficits escalating, budgetary restraints required that key legislators—budget committee members and party leaders, in particular—consider overall patterns of spending. Political scientist Ken Shepsle concludes:

> The most significant consequence of the Budget Act has been that Congress has had little time to consider anything else. . . . The fiscalization of politics has diminished the stature of standing committees, encouraged members to become generalists rather than specialists, ceded political advantage to those in party leadership positions, and put a premium on coordination among policy areas.[52]

Ronald Reagan's performance as president demonstrates the potential for central coordination of the policymaking process. Immediately after entering the presidency in 1981, President Reagan placed a large tax cut on the legislative agenda and lobbied consistently for its passage. The Congress had little choice but to act on this initiative, but there was still much politicking and posturing on the exact nature of the reductions. In the end, President Reagan won much of what he desired, even though most legislators did not agree with his "supply-side" economic assumptions, and they avoided making any major changes to the overall tax code. However, five years later, in 1986, Reagan worked with the GOP Senate and the Democratic House to pass a sweeping overhaul of the U.S. tax code that retained the initial Reagan tax cuts, but extended them to lower levels of income, and closed many loopholes.

Still, over the next two decades, the federal deficit swelled under the pressure of those tax cuts, which reduced the amount of revenue to the U.S. government. Other presidents, notably George H. W. Bush (R) and Bill Clinton (D), dealt with that fallout by raising taxes, until the federal budget was balanced and even went into surplus by the late 1990s. When President George W. Bush took office in early 2001, he followed in Reagan's footsteps, and working with a Republican-controlled Congress, he enacted a sweeping tax-cut package. President Obama signed an extension of those tax cuts into law in 2012, so the Bush tax legacy persists to this day. It may be that President Trump succeeds in working with Congress to change the tax code and revamp the Bush/Obama tax structure. But as Bush and Obama each learned, revising the tax system takes presidents on a tortuous path through the halls of Congress.

From Nixon to Reagan's tax cuts to George W. Bush's deficits to Obama's economic responses to the Great Recession, the budget-deficit pendulum has swung back and forth between periods of large deficits, budget surplus, and back to large deficits. The cumulative effect of the budget deficits has been two-fold. First, it has produced a very large national debt (more than $19 trillion in 2017), which is the sum of all deficit spending year after year, plus the interest on the money the U.S. government borrows to meet its financial obligations. Second, it has concentrated the budget process by increasing the power of party leaders and committee chairs over rank-and-file members, and, combined with party polarization, it has created a very unstable fiscal environment. In other words, fights over spending within and between the political parties bring more uncertainty into whether budgets will pass, programs will be cut, or bills will be paid in any consistent way. At a time when the United States is facing very real policy problems, from crumbling infrastructure to education to threats from terrorism, uncertainty in the budget process makes it difficult to address such major issues in a coherent way.

Moreover, as we noted in discussing the failed "grand bargain," rank-and-file members of the party can disrupt the centralized power of party leaders, committee chairs, and the president by rejecting the deals these leaders strike with each other. Indeed, as top legislators and presidential envoys meet to nego-tiate, both sides have to bear in mind their constituents. Congressional lead-ers know they have to convince majorities of their followers to approve their actions, whereas the president's constituents are the voters whom he faces when he runs for reelection. During the years 2011 through 2015, Speaker Boehner had a particularly difficult time managing the Tea Party wing of his party in the House on budget bills—whose members revolted against the deals he forged with President Obama. As a result, he repeatedly had to rely on House Democrats to pass the legislation necessary to keep the government running. Democrats voted with the Speaker on budget matters not because they wanted to cooperate with the Republican majority but because they wanted to avert a governmental shutdown and ensure that President Obama could continue to use his executive-branch powers (including executive orders) to their fullest during his last term of office.

Under a unified GOP Congress and a Trump presidency, it should be much easier to come to budget agreements. However, President Trump, Speaker Paul Ryan, and Senate Majority Leader McConnell each face challenges in this arena from the conservative wing of their parties notably the Freedom Caucus in the House, and Senators Rand Paul, Mike Lee, Ted Cruz, and Jim Inhofe to name a few in the Senate. This dilemma came front and center to American politics in September 2017, when President Trump chose to cut a budget/debt ceiling/disas-ter aid deal with Democratic congressional leaders in both chambers. Although the long-term implications of this maneuver are unclear, President Trump demonstrated no patience with the struggles of Republican leaders Ryan and McConnell to effectively control their respective party majorities. In addition, the Trump-Democratic bargain served to further alienate the most conservative wing of the Republican Party which, in turn, may damage the potential for party unity on other issues in the future.

As Trump concluded, if the government is just partially shut down, even the most powerful president can do little to advance his policy agenda. Overall, then, for chief executives and congressional leaders alike, there remain real limits to the exercise of centralized power, limits currently produced by the intensity of partisan politics, as opposed to the decentralized nature of Congress in an earlier era.

POLICY AND POWER UNDER DIVIDED AND UNIFIED PARTY GOVERNMENT

Between 1969 and 2018, divided partisan control of the national government has served as the rule not the exception, with unified control existing for just fifteen of fifty years. Only Jimmy Carter (1977–1981), Bill Clinton (1993–1995), George W. Bush (part of 2001–2002, 2003–2007), Barack Obama (2009–2011), and Donald Trump (2017–) served as presidents while their fellow partisans controlled the Congress. Politicians and journalists have often assumed that divided government produced legislative gridlock, a pejorative term linked to the apparent inefficiencies and incoherence of Congress. To be sure, divided government can lead to deadlock, as the 2011–2015 battles between a Republican House, a Democratic Senate, and a Democratic president demonstrated. This standoff intensified during the last two years of the Obama presidency, when Republicans captured the Senate. Divided government requires congressional negotiation with the White House, whether on budget issues, climate change, national security, or immigration reform. Such negotiation encourages centralization in that only a handful of leaders can effectively represent the legislature, especially as they confront the White House and the executive branch.

Whether the federal government is under divided or unified party control, the separation of powers forces Congress and the president to negotiate continually over legislation. In surveying presidential and congressional relations, Charles Jones concluded that the "system is now, and always has been, one of 'separated institutions sharing powers,' as [Richard] Neustadt puts it [originally in 1960]."[53] Indeed, within the context of an extended period of split-party control of government, Jones reformulated Neustadt's observation as "separated institutions competing for shares of power."[54] But a bicameral system, with its separation of powers, denies the likelihood of congressional dominance, save through overwhelming majorities. Rather, as John Bader states, congressional leaders must ordinarily strive to maintain "a balance . . . between heavy-handed leadership and fragmenting anarchy"[55] as they struggle against a branch of government—the executive—that typically tries to speak with one voice, not 535 separate voices.

Political scientist David Mayhew has argued that there is no significant difference in federal legislative productivity in times of divided versus unified government. He has demonstrated that divided government has not prevented the federal government from enacting major legislation on important public policy topics.[56] Digging deeper shows that divided control may hamper the ability of the federal government to take new initiatives or anticipate future problems—and recent congressional history supports this assertion. This reflects the so-called denominator argument, which emphasizes not only the number of major issues decided (the numerator), but also the number of potential major issues (the denominator).[57] Sarah Binder has noted that gridlock may stem from divisions between the congressional chambers as much as between Capitol Hill and the White House.[58] Thus, one major problem facing congressional Republicans in "repealing and replacing" Obamacare was that legislation that passed the GOP-controlled House was unlikely to make it through the Senate, despite its Republican majority in its original form. Indeed, in 2017, it did fail to pass the Senate.

Leon Panetta, a former member of Congress, who also served as White House chief of staff (Clinton), CIA director (Obama), and secretary of defense (Obama), argues that given the partisan dominance of congressional organization in the modern era, we should not expect bipartisanship across a wide range of concerns. He observes that

> institutional power in both House and Senate resides with the parties [that] rely on activists and interest groups that tend to bunch on the left and right. . . . [Moreover,] the legislative process allows centrist coalitions little power or time to coalesce for action. . . . Once party discipline descends on an issue, it leaves little room for representatives to gather at the center without the risk of angering the party leadership.[59]

The reverse is also true, whereby the party leadership shies away from working across the aisle for fear of a backlash from the partisan rank-and-file membership in the House and Senate, as well as direct backlash from voters across districts and states.

The reality is that the structure of Congress prevents the president from enjoying "easy" legislative successes. Whether in terms of representation (e.g., the different apportionment of the House and Senate) or rules (the Senate filibuster) or the constitutional requirement to reconcile House and Senate legislation into a single bill, Congress remains a body that is resistant to single-minded unity. For better or worse, presidential and congressional relations continue to evolve as part of the continuing experiment in self-government that defines U.S. politics.

Recommended Readings

Edwards, George C., III. *The Strategic President: Persuasion & Opportunity in Presidential Leadership*. Princeton, NJ: Princeton University Press, 2009.

Genovese, Michael A., Todd. L. Belt, and William W. Lammers. *The Presidency and Domestic Policy: Comparing Leadership Styles. FDR to Obama*. 2nd ed. Boulder, CO: Paradigm, 2014.

Jones, Charles. *The Presidency in a Separated System*. Washington, DC: Brookings Institution Press, 2005.

Krehbiel, Keith. *Pivotal Politics*. Chicago: University of Chicago Press, 1998.

Mann, Thomas E., and Norman J. Ornstein, *It's Even Worse Than It Was: How the American Constitution Collided with the New Politics of Extremism* (New York: Basic Books, 2016).

Useful Resources

Congressional Budget Office: http://www.cbo.gov
Office of Management and Budget: http://www.omb.gov
The White House: http://www.whitehouse.gov

Notes

[1] George C. Edwards, III, *At the Margins* (New Haven, CT: Yale University Press, 1989), 234.

[2] Mark Peterson, *Legislating Together* (Cambridge, MA: Harvard University Press, 1990), 295 (emphasis added).

[3] Ibid., 295.

[4] Robert Pear, "Obamacare took months to craft: repeal may be much swifter," *New York Times*, March 9, 2017, https://www.nytimes.com/2017/03/07/us/politics/obamacare-repeal-of-health-law-republicans.html.

[5] Thomas Kaplan, Robert Pear, and Emmarie Huetteman, "Lacking the Votes for passage, House Calls off Obamacare Repeal Vote," *New York Times*, March 23, 2017, https://www.nytimes.com/2017/03/23/us/politics/health-care-trump-vote.html.

[6] Nicholas Kulish, Caitlin Dickerson, and Charlie Savage. "Court Temporarily Blocks Trump's Travel Ban, and Airlines Are Told to Allow Passengers," February 3, 2017. *The New York Times*, https://www.nytimes.com/2017/02/03/us/visa-ban-legal-challenge.html.

[7] Alexander Burns, "2 Federal Judges Rule Against Trump's Latest Travel Ban," March 15, 2017, *New York Times*, https://www.nytimes.com/2017/03/15/us/politics/trump-travel-ban.html.

[8] Michael D. Shear "Who Undercut President Trump's Travel Ban? Candidate Trump," March 16, 2017, *New York Times*, https://www.nytimes.com/2017/03/16/us/politics/trump-travel-ban-campaign.html.

[9] The literature here includes, most notably, Keith Krehbiel's *Pivotal Politics* (Chicago: University of Chicago Press, 1998), and Sarah Binder's *Stalemate* (Washington, DC: Brookings Institution Press, 2003).

[10] Richard Neustadt, *Presidential Power* (New York: Wiley, 1960); Charles O. Jones, *The Presidency in a Separated System* (Washington, DC: Brookings Institution, 1994).

[11] Pfiffner, "President and the Post-Reform Congress," 233. More generally, see Louis Fisher, *Presidential War Power* (Lawrence: University Press of Kansas, 1995).

[12] John Woolley and Gerhard Peters, "The American Presidency Project," http://www.presidency.ucsb.edu/data/vetoes.php (accessed April 15, 2017).

[13] Bush entered the presidency with a tied Senate, but Senator James Jeffords (R-VT) switched his party affiliation to Independent in June 2001, and he caucused with the Democrats, which gave them majority control until Republicans won it back in the 2002 midterm elections.

[14] See Charles Cameron, *Veto Bargaining: Presidents and the Use of Negative Power* (New York: Cambridge University Press, 2000).

[15] Jones, *Presidency in a Separated System*, 181.

[16] See Frank R. Baumgartner and Bryan D. Jones, *Agendas and Instability in American Politics* (Chicago: University of Chicago Press, 1993) and Paul R. Schulman, *Large-Side Policy Making* (New York: Elsevier, 1980).

[17] See Jeffrey Cohen, "Presidential Rhetoric and the Public Agenda," *American Journal of Political Science* 39 (February 1995): 87–107.

[18] See James L. Sundquist, *Politics and Policy* (Washington, DC: Brookings Institution, 1968) and Arthur Schlesinger, Jr., *The Cycles of American History* (Boston: Houghton Mifflin, 1986).

[19] Light, *President's Agenda*, 218.

[20] Paul C. Light, "Passing Nonincremental Policy: Presidential Influence in Congress, Kennedy to Carter," *Congress and the Presidency* 9 (Winter 1981–1982): 78.

[21] Susan Davis, "Leaders in Congress Unveil Two-Year Budget Deal," *USA Today*, December 10, 2013. Comments included in embedded video from AP, http://www.usatoday.com/story/news/politics/2013/12/10/congress-budget-deal/3966641 (accessed February 19, 2015).

[22] Department of Homeland Security. "Table 39: Aliens Removed or Returned: Fiscal Years 1892-2015," https://www.dhs.gov/immigration-statistics/yearbook/2015/table39 (accessed April 15, 2017).

[23] Krehbiel, *Pivotal Politics*, 47.

[24] Somewhat strangely, Peterson labels these elements as "malleable" context (Mark Peterson, *Legislating Together* [Cambridge, MA: Harvard University Press, 1990], 118ff), but of the three, only the president's popularity can change between elections, and ordinarily not as a direct result of his actions.

[25] Jon R. Bond, Richard Fleisher, and B. Dan Wood, "The Marginal and Time-Varying Effect of Public Approval on Presidential Success in Congress," *Journal of Politics* 65 (2003): 92–110.

[26] For a recent perspective by a Johnson loyalist, see Joseph Califano, *The Triumph and Tragedy of Lyndon Johnson* (New York: Simon & Schuster, 1991).

[27] See Jones, *Presidency in a Separated System*, 266–68 and Barbara Sinclair, "Governing Unheroically (and Sometimes Unappetizingly): Bush and the 101st Congress," in *The Bush Presidency: First Appraisals*, ed. Colin Campbell and Bert Rockman (Chatham, NJ: Chatham House, 1991), 175.

[28] Daniel Polti, "Bannon Pushed Trump to Use Health Care Vote to Write Up "Enemies List,'" March 25, 2017 wwwslate.com http://www.slate.com/blogs/the_slatest/2017/03/25/bannon_pushed_trump_to_use_health_care_vote_to_write_up_enemies_list.html (accessed April 15, 2017).

[29] Thomas E. Mann and Norman J. Ornstein, *It's Even Worse Than It Looks: How the American Constitution Collided with the New Politics of Extremism* (New York: Basic Books, 2016).

[30] See Jones, *Presidency in a Separated System*.

[31] Paul Magnusson, "Bush: What Price Fast-Track?" *Business Week*, June 3, 2002, 38.

[32] Ibid.

[33] For a discussion of this measure and others, see Edwards, *At the Margins*, 16ff.

[34] See Edwards, *At the Margins*; Jones, *Presidency in a Separated System*, chap. 7, and Peterson, *Legislating Together*, especially appendix B, which offers an excellent review of quantitative research.

[35] See, in particular, Jon R. Bond, Richard Fleischer, and Glen A. Krutz, "An Overview of the Empirical Findings on Presidential-Congressional Relations," in *Rivals for Power*, ed. James A. Thurber (Boulder, CO: Westview, 1996), 103–39 and Nathan Dietz, "Presidential Influence on Congress," in *Rivals for Power: Congressional-Presidential Relations*, 2nd ed., ed. James Thurber (Washington, DC: CQ Press, 2002), 105–39.

[36] *Congressional Quarterly Weekly Report*, December 31, 1994, 3654.

[37] David Hosansky, "Clinton's Biggest Prize Was a Frustrated GOP," *Congressional Quarterly Weekly Report*, January 9, 1999, 76.

[38] Peterson, *Legislating Together*, 220–21.

[39] Joseph J. Schatz. "Presidential Support Vote Study: With a Deft and Light Touch, Bush Finds Ways to Win," *CQ Weekly*, December 11, 2004.

[40] Jeffrey E. Cohen, Jon R. Bon, and Richard Fleisher, "Placing Presidential-Congressional Relations in Context: A Comparison of Barack Obama and His Predecessors," *Polity* 45, no. 1. (2013): 105–26.

[41] Meredith Shiner, "Senate Democrats Backed Obama on Overwhelming Number of 2013 Votes, CQ Roll Call Vote Studies Show," *Roll Call*, February 3, 2014, http://atr.rollcall.com/senate-democrats-supported-obama-on-overwhelming-number-of-votes-in-2013/ (accessed February 19, 2015).

[42] CQ Press Vote Studies. "Obama and Republicans Got Some Things Done," 2015 CQ Almanac, B-2, https://library.cqpress.com/cqalmanac/file.php?path=Presidential%20Support%20Tables/2015_Presidential_Support.pdf (accessed April 15, 2017).

[43] Ibid., B-3.

[44] Honorable Joseph Cannon. *The National Budget*. House of Representatives, 66th Congress 1st Session, Document No. 264. (Washington, DC: Government Printing Office, 1919), 28.

[45] Allen Schick, *Congress and Money* (Washington, DC: Urban Institute Press, 1980), chap. 2.

[46] Lance T. LeLoup, *Budgetary Politics*, 3rd ed. (Brunswick, OH: Kings' Court, 1986), 6ff.

[47] Howard E. Shuman, *Politics and the Budget*, 3rd ed. (Englewood Cliffs, NJ: Prentice-Hall, 1992), 213 (emphasis added).

[48] See Richard E. Neustadt, "Presidency and Legislation: The Growth of Central Clearance," *American Political Science Review* 48 (1954): 641ff and John Hart, *The Presidential Branch*, 2nd ed. (Chatham, NJ: Chatham House, 1995).

[49] James P. Pfiffner, "The President and the Post-Reform Congress," in *The Postreform Congress*, ed. Roger H. Davidson (New York: St. Martin's, 1992), 216–17.

[50] Schick, *Congress and Money*, chap. 2.

[51] Barbara Sinclair, *Legislators, Leaders, and Lawmaking: The U.S. House of Representatives in the Postreform Era* (Baltimore: Johns Hopkins University Press, 1995), 143.

[52] Kenneth Shepsle uses this term in "The Changing Textbook Congress," in *Can the Government Govern?* ed. John E. Chubb and Paul E. Peterson (Washington, DC: Brookings Institution, 1989), 259ff.

[53] Jones, *Presidency in a Separated System*, 207 (emphasis added).

[54] Ibid.

[55] John Bader, *Taking the Initiative: Leadership Agendas in Congress and the Contract with America* (Washington, DC: Georgetown University Press, 1996), 222–23.

[56] David Mayhew, *Divided We Govern* (New Haven, CT: Yale University Press, 1991).

[57] George C. Edwards, III, Andrew Barnett, and Jeffrey Peake, "The Legislative Impact of Divided Government," *American Journal of Political Science* 41 (April 1997): 545–63; Sarah Binder, "The Dynamics of Legislative Gridlock, 1947–96," *American Political Science Review* 93 (September 1999): 519–33. See also the articles by James Pfiffner ("The President and Congress at the Turn of the Century") and Nathan Deitz ("Presidential Influence on Congress") in Thurber, *Rivals for Power*.

[58] Sarah Binder, *Stalemate* (Washington, DC: Brookings Institute Press, 2003).

[59] Leon E. Panetta, "Politics of the Federal Budget Process," in Thurber, *Rivals for Power*, 205.

CHAPTER 7

Policymaking in the House and Senate

When U.S. presidents want to celebrate the passage of a law, they hold a public signing ceremony with members of Congress and policy advocates. Here, President Franklin Delano Roosevelt signs the Servicemen's Readjustment Act, commonly known as the GI Bill, in 1944. It provided benefits to veterans, from housing assistance, to stipends, to funding for college tuition.

We want to see the bill.

—Senator Rand Paul (R-KY) March 2, 2017

The 115th Congress marked the first time that the Republican Party controlled both chambers of Congress—the House of Representatives and the U.S. Senate—as well as the White House, since 2006. In preceding chapters, we have discussed how Congress operates under unified government and divided government. But even under unified party government, the two chambers of Congress do not always see eye to eye, and they do not always cooperate with each other in the policymaking process.

Take this one day in March 2017 for example. As noted in chapter 6, one of President Trump's campaign promises was to repeal and replace the Affordable Care Act (ACA; Obamacare). The Republicans in Congress had been advocating for this since its 2010 enactment. The problem was that they had not produced an alternative that both chambers could agree on. In 2017, when Speaker Paul Ryan (R-WI) asked the Chair of the House Energy and Commerce Committee and the Chair of the House Ways and Means Committee to produce a repeal and replace bill, the deliberations on that bill were kept top secret to the point that most rank-and-file Republican House members had little idea of what the bill contained. And House Democrats were kept completely in the dark because, given House rules, the majority party can usually pass what it needs on the floor without the opposition party's votes.

The smaller Senate, however, operates quite differently. Each individual senator has the power to object to consideration of a bill or an amendment and delay it indefinitely; this is commonly known as the power to filibuster. Because that power to object is available to both majority and minority senators, the Senate majority party, in this case the Republicans, does not have the same kind of power to control the content and agenda of legislation that the House majority typically has.

This brings us back to Senator Rand Paul, who wanted to know the content of the House repeal and replace bill to determine whether he would support or oppose it in the Senate. He knew he had the power to filibuster. Thus, when Senator Paul physically walked across the Capitol Grounds to get a copy of the bill, making sure reporters were covering his efforts, he was quoted as saying "We're here asking for a written copy of this because this should be an open and transparent process."[1] But Senator Paul was refused entry into the committee chambers and told he could not see the bill. When the ranking Democrat on the House Energy and Commerce Committee also asked to see the bill, he too was turned down.

This brief episode in the ACA repeal and replace saga reflects the contemporary differences between the House and Senate when it comes to policymaking. Power and information about legislation is tightly controlled in the House by the Speaker and Committee chairs, whom he appoints with caucus approval, and even many members of the majority party do not know what is in a bill until just before it is brought to the House Rules Committee and

SPOTLIGHT

Senator Rand Paul: Policy Proponent and Policy Critic

Senator Rand Paul (R-KY) is the junior senator from Kentucky and was a Republican candidate for president in 2016. Though his first venture into electoral politics came in 2010 when he successfully ran for Kentucky's open U.S. Senate seat, the libertarian- and Tea-Party-backed Paul had long shown an interest in politics. He ran the Baylor University chapter of the Young Conservatives of Texas in the 1980s before working on his father's 1988 Libertarian Party presidential campaign. His father, the consummate libertarian Rep. Ron Paul (R-TX), served eleven terms in Congress between 1976 and 2013 and was a three-time presidential candidate. Rand Paul's political involvement deepened in 1991 when he formed the anti-tax North Carolina Taxpayers Union in response to President George H.W. Bush's failure to follow through on his "read my lips" promise not to raise taxes. During Ron Paul's 2008 presidential campaign, Rand, an ophthalmologist by training, was a prominent surrogate and in 2010 sought to parlay access to his father's staffing connections and his loyal grassroots following into a successful political campaign of his own.

Paul's opponent in the Republican primary for the open U.S. Senate seat was the more mainstream Republican Trey Grayson, who had the backing of Kentucky senator and Republican Senate leader Mitch McConnell. While Paul's more unconventional ideology prompted major pro-Israel and neoconservative groups to back Grayson, Paul's hard stances on cutting spending, eliminating the Federal Reserve, and his criticisms of the Patriot Act and the wars in Afghanistan and Iraq helped him consolidate enough Tea Party support to win the primary by 23 percentage points. He went on to easily win the general election in deep-red Kentucky.

As senator, Paul serves on the Foreign Relations Committee, the Committee on Health, Education, Labor, and Pensions, the Homeland Security Committee, and the Committee on Small Business. Consistent with his libertarian-leaning ideology, Paul has emerged as a prominent player in the Senate on range of different issues: he has proposed legislation to legalize medical marijuana on the federal level and prevent recreational users from being federally prosecuted, he has vocally opposed foreign military intervention, he advocates significant spending (and tax) cuts, and he is a prominent opponent of government surveillance programs. During a Senate debate on whether to confirm John Brennan as CIA Director on March 6, 2013, Paul spoke on the floor through the night, continuing for nearly thirteen hours in opposition to the Obama administration's use of drone strikes. Paul staged another talk-a-thon (which lasted about ten hours this time) in May 2015 to oppose the reauthorization of the Patriot Act, starting the use of the hashtag "#StandWithRand," which would later become his presidential campaign slogan. Needless to say, Paul's style and policy positions do not align perfectly with the Republican Party's, and he has criticized traditional Republican positions and, as we have seen in this chapter, the party's handling of the policymaking process.

The information in this section is taken from multiple sources as follows: Sam Tanenhaus and

Jim Rutenberg, "Rand Paul's Mixed Inheritance," *The New York* Times, January 25, 2014, https://www.nytimes.com/2014/01/26/us/politics/rand-pauls-mixed-inheritance.html?hpw&r-ref=us&_r=1; Ashley Parker, "Taking Stand Against Spying, Rand Paul Stages Senate 'Filibuster,'" *The New York Times*, May 20, 2015, https://www.nytimes.com/politics/first-draft/2015/05/20/taking-stand-against-spying-rand-paul-stages-senate-filibuster/.

then the House floor. In the Senate, because any senator can obstruct a bill, the party leadership and committee chairs must reveal its content well before it comes to the floor in order to build enough support to overcome individual obstruction. The distinct rules and structures of the House and Senate produce different policymaking environments, and these greatly influence negotiations between the two chambers on any final version of legislation that is sent to the President.

From universities to corporations to legislative bodies, changing the rules or rewriting laws happens under parallel sets of expectations, one established by formal rules and structures, the other resulting from informal arrangements that have grown over an extended period of time. As the key lawmaking institution in our constitutional system of separation of powers, Congress is the wellspring of policy actions. Consequently, studying the impact of rules and norms on individual and collective behavior in Congress is essential to understanding national policymaking.

The House and the Senate operate under separate sets of formal rules, and each chamber fosters its own so-called folkways[2]—expectations about behaviors that influence actions on Capitol Hill. Folkways are especially important in Congress because members are technically equal, in that they each can cast a single vote and because members must interact with each other in some way, shape, or form on a daily basis. In such an organization, power relationships are often delicate and unstated, expressed through agreed-upon norms rather than explicit procedures.

Neither chamber can function effectively without a blend of formal and informal limits, but the mixes of procedures and norms differ greatly on the two sides of the Capitol. Formal rules play a more important role in the House, whereas norms are more significant in the Senate. This makes sense because the larger House must rely on procedures in order to reach decisions in a timely, less-than-chaotic manner. Members of the smaller Senate depend much more on informal agreements reached among all senators.[3]

In this chapter, we trace the development of the evolution of these rules and norms over time and explain why it appears that more recent changes in rules and behavior in both the House and the Senate have made Congress a less productive policymaking institution.

RULES, PROCEDURES, AND THE LEGISLATIVE PROCESS

If you let me write procedure and I let you write substance,

I'll screw you every time.

—Rep. John Dingell (D-MI), the longest-serving member in the history of the House of Representatives. He retired in 2014 after serving for fifty-nine years.[4]

Looking back to the 1950s, the "textbook Congress" era seems positively quaint. Speaker Sam Rayburn could sincerely counsel incoming House members to "get along, go along." In the Rayburn-era House (late 1930s–1961), apprenticeships were long, specialization was expected, and virtually all members assumed that courtesy and reciprocity would govern their relations. In the Senate, Majority Leader Lyndon Johnson would give each new senator a copy of journalist William S. White's *Citadel*, with its glorification of the chamber's *Inner Club*, where "Senate types" of legislators informally dominated the institution. To be sure, Rayburn's advice was generally sound, and White's description roughly accurate. For all their formal rules, leadership organizations, and committee structures, both bodies harbored well-accepted sets of norms—informal rules of the game—that governed the behavior of most, if not all, members.

In contrast, the Congress of the twenty-first century has become a thoroughly contentious and intensely partisan place. The turning point came in 1995, when there was a large influx of new House and Senate members; that stream of largely Republican new members prompted a reevaluation of legislative folkways[5] and caused some to observe a substantial "decline in comity" in the House.[6] More than twenty years later, the situation has worsened. No contemporary Speaker could—or would—deliver Rayburn's fatherly advice, and there is no club of insider senators who can dominate their chamber. Social ties in both the House and Senate have weakened substantially since the 1950s, in part because more and more congressional actions are conducted in public by legislators whose workloads have grown steadily and who have spent increasing amounts of time fund-raising in Washington, DC, and traveling back to their districts to meet with constituents. Although the data are sketchy, the trend is clear: fewer than half the junior members completely accept the bedrock norms of courtesy and reciprocity. In addition, almost all of these legislators reject the notions of apprenticeship and institutional loyalty. More generally, members of Congress may well reflect the declining levels of trust and civility within the public at large, so it should be no surprise that in 2017, only 16 percent of the public approves of Congress's job performance.[7]

The decline in respect for the opposition scarcely means that the symbolic trappings of politeness have disappeared.[8] Viewers of the House and Senate proceedings can still observe the elaborate formalities and courtesies of the legislative process. But these niceties are often more perfunctory and forced than they were a generation or two ago. The social fabric that holds together congressional life has been frayed, sometimes beyond repair. Although the partisan, often acidic, nature of debate has greatly reduced civility in the House, this chamber has never relied completely on informal ties to maintain order. The Senate, however, is a different story, with the lack of cooperation and the growth of partisanship combining to increase individual rancor and reduce the institution's capacity for deliberation to the point that majority leaders have had to use their procedural power in new and more forceful ways.

CONGRESSIONAL LAWMAKING

Congress is a thoroughly rule-oriented institution, but only a few of its procedures are mandated by the Constitution; these include the requirement that each chamber maintain a journal, that half the membership constitutes a quorum, that tax bills must originate in the House of Representatives, and that the two chambers can override a presidential veto by a two-thirds vote in each body.[9] Notably, the Constitution includes a Speaker of the House but makes no mention of a majority leader of the Senate. Beyond these basics and the more expansive constitutional limitations on the entire federal government, the House and Senate have been free to establish their own distinct sets of rules. The point of origin for a public law begins with bill sponsorship. House members and senators each introduce a number of bills throughout the two-year congressional session. From the vantage point of individual legislators, introducing bills can allow them to claim credit for addressing an issue that is important to their constituents or perhaps enables them to become a key player on a legislative issue, even if the bill fails to win approval.[10]

Over the past decade, from the 109th through the 113th Congresses, there was an average of 6,593 bills introduced per session in the House and 3,731 bills introduced per session in the Senate, with a slight overall decline in both chambers in recent years. Over the same period, an average of 268 House bills and 114 Senate bills became law, with fewer laws passed overall in recent years. In fact, the 112th and 113th Congresses saw the fewest laws passed in forty years.[11] In the 114th Congress, there were 6,239 bills introduced in the House and 3,382 bills introduced in the Senate; 151 House bills became law and 75 Senate bills became law.[12] The hurdles to enacting legislation are substantial. First, the bill has to get out of subcommittee and full committee and then garner a majority of votes on the House and Senate floors. On many major issues, a compromise version must be worked out between the two chambers in a conference committee, which consists of members of the House and Senate appointed by the leadership to lead interchamber negotiations. Only when the House and Senate can agree on identical language is the bill sent to the president for signature or veto. In more recent years, the conference committee role has diminished sharply as party leaders have taken a more direct role in negotiating between the chambers; in some cases bills are simply sent back and forth between the House and Senate until one chamber agrees to approve the other chamber's bill verbatim.

Because the House floor is so tightly controlled by party leaders and firm rules, representatives have far fewer opportunities to push their own legislation than do senators, who can offer their bills as amendments on the Senate floor. In both chambers, laws most frequently flow from bills sponsored by members who hold a committee or subcommittee chair and can thus influence their progress in the legislative process. For a more extensive overview of congressional activity, see table 7.1.

Committees

After their introduction by individual legislators, bills are referred to committees by the Speaker or the Senate's presiding officer, who consults when necessary with the parliamentarians of the respective chambers. As appointees of the majority party, the parliamentarians work closely with the leadership. In the Democratic House of the 1980s and 1990s, a steadily growing number of bills were referred to multiple committees.[13] Starting with the 104th Congress in 1995, majority Republicans refashioned House committee jurisdictions, which reduced the need for such referrals and enhanced Speaker Gingrich's role in determining where a bill would be sent after it was introduced.[14] From then on, subsequent Speakers Hastert, Pelosi, Boehner, and Ryan each maintained tight control over bill referrals to committees in order to maximize the party's control over legislative content.

From the first days of the Republic, both the House and the Senate have used committees to process and draft legislation. Early on, most of these were ad hoc bodies that reported back to their chambers on specific bills. By 1810, however, the 142-member House had organized ten standing committees, including familiar panels, such as Interstate and Foreign Commerce and Ways and Means. Increasingly, legislation began its journey toward passage within committees, rather than following from an initial floor discussion in which the House would constitute itself into the Committee of the Whole and conduct less formal consideration of the issue at hand.[15] The Senate did likewise, and by 1820, it too had established a system of standing committees.[16] The existence of standing committees produced greater continuity from one Congress to the next, both in terms of organizational stability and members' ability to gain expertise on particular subject matters over time. Between the early 1800s and the onset of the Civil War, committees slowly became integral to the legislative process, even though most key decisions were made on the floor. The number of standing committees grew steadily (see figure 7.1), but their memberships changed substantially from Congress to Congress.

From 1862 to 1919, committees most often served the purposes of both chambers' party leaders, who controlled appointments and the capacity to move legislation on the floor. Nonetheless, committees became increasingly important elements of the legislative process, and their memberships grew more stable as lawmakers constructed careers inside the Congress—careers that were often based on expertise accumulated in specialized committees and subcommittees. In large part, such stability grew from the reliance on committee-based seniority in determining which veteran legislators would serve on given committees in each new Congress, to the extent that "by the turn of the century, [seniority] had become such an 'iron-clad formula' that in both House and Senate, party leaders' real discretion in committee assignments was limited primarily to new members."[17]

Table 7.1 Congress by the Numbers, 1993–2016

	103rd Congress		104th Congress[a]		107th Congress[b]		110th Congress[c]		111th Congress[d]		113th Congress[e]		114th Congress[f]	
	1993	1994	1995	1996	2001	2002	2007	2008	2009	2010	2013	2014	2015	2016
Days in Session														
House	142	123	168	122	142	123	164	119	159	127	160	135	157	131
Senate	153	138	211	132	173	149	190	184	191	158	156	136	168	165
Time in Session (Hours)														
House	982	905	1,525	919	922	772	1,478	890	1,247	879	768	705	805	633
Senate	1,270	1,244	1,839	1,037	1,236	1,043	1,376	988	1,421	1,075	1,095	908	1,074	781
Average Hours/Day														
House	6.9	7.4	9.1	7.5	6.5	6.3	9.0	7.5	7.8	6.9	4.8	5.2	5.1	4.8
Senate	8.3	9.0	8.7	7.9	7.1	7.0	7.2	5.4	7.4	6.8	7.0	6.7	6.4	4.7
Bills/Resolutions Introduced														
House	4,543	2,104	3,430	1,899	4,318	2,711	4,930	2,410	5,699	3,098	4,434	2,505	5,060	2,714
Senate	2,178	999	1,801	860	2,203	1,563	2,524	1,217	3,380	1,506	2,280	1,432	2,823	1,466

Recorded Yea/Nay Votes

House	615	507	885	455	512	483	648	472	535	450	299	248	300	275
Senate	395	329	613	306	380	253	442	215	397	299	291	366	339	163

Public Laws

Enacted	210	255	88	245	136	195	165	282	125	258	73	224	115	214
Vetoes	0	0	9	6	0	0	7	4	1	1	0	0	5	5

Source: U.S. Senate, Statistics and Lists, *Resume of Congressional Activity*, various years, 1993–2016, https://www.senate.gov/pagelayout/reference/two_column_table/Resumes.htm.

[a]Republicans take control of House and Senate.
[b]First two years of George W. Bush presidency.
[c]Democrats take control of House and Senate.
[d]First two years of Barack Obama presidency.
[e]Republicans take control of House beginning in 2011 (112th Congress).
[f]Republicans take control of Senate.

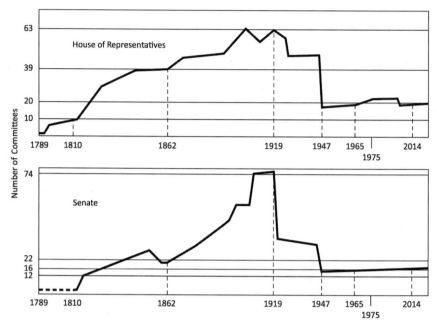

Figure 7.1 Number of Congressional Standing Committees, 1789–2014.

Source: Adapted from Steven S. Smith and Christopher Deering, *Committees in Congress*, 2nd ed. (Washington, DC: Congressional Quarterly Press, 1990), 25 and Norman J. Ornstein, Thomas E. Mann, and Michael J. Malbin, eds., *Vital Statistics on Congress: 1997–1998* (Washington, DC: American Enterprise Institute/Congressional Quarterly Press, 1997), 120–21. Data gathered from http://www.house.gov and http://www.senate.gov.

Although Rep. Joseph Cannon (R-IL) would challenge the seniority basis for appointment during his speakership (1903–1911), the House's 1910 revolt against him and its decision to reduce the Speaker's powers dictated that seniority would prevail on committee assignments; in turn, this meant that both committees and their chairs would become increasingly powerful over the next fifty years. Not only did the chambers accept the seniority system, but they also steadily consolidated committee jurisdictions during the 1915–1965 period. The Legislative Reorganization Act of 1946 sharply reduced the number of committees in both House and Senate to nineteen and fifteen, respectively (see figure 7.1). By reducing the number of committees, the act created more work for the remaining committees. As a result, most committee jurisdictions expanded tremendously, and the chairmen became even more powerful, which led the Congress into a relatively brief, but important, period of committee government (roughly 1947–1970).[18]

The generally conservative nature of the Congress and the modest goals of the Eisenhower administration (1953–1961) coexisted smoothly under the decentralized nature of committee government. Committee chairpersons, drawn disproportionately from the states of the old Confederacy, generally represented the sentiments of the southern Democrat–Republican Conservative Coalition that dominated the Congress. Eventually, large numbers of new members, most notably the herd of young activist Democrats who arrived after the 1958 elections, would begin to restrict the power of committee chairs. But through the 1950s, congressional decision-making was dominated by an informal oligarchy of senior party and committee leaders, along with a few other key legislators.

From 1959 through 1975, committees and their chairs faced a dual threat to their independent influence—the simultaneous effort by party leaders to centralize their own authority and by junior members to win power by having more responsibilities delegated to subcommittees. The most active period of reform occurred between 1971 and 1975, when the House acted consistently to reduce the authority and discretion of its full-committee chairs.[19] Some significant House changes came from reforms passed by the entire chamber, but the most profound developments emerged from the Democratic caucus, which effectively controlled the organization of the body. The two most important elements of reform focused on subcommittee rights and responsibilities and on the selection of committee chairs (and those of Appropriations Committee subcommittees). By 1974, the following limitations had been imposed on full committees and their chairs:

Subcommittee Reforms

* Democrats could hold only one legislative subcommittee chair.
* Subcommittee chairs could select one professional staff member for their panel.
* A "Subcommittee Bill of Rights" guaranteed referral of legislation to subcommittees; bidding for subcommittee seats, which protects junior members; and fixed jurisdictions for subcommittees.

Democratic Caucus/Leadership Reforms

* Automatic secret-ballot caucus votes would be held on the appointment of all committee chairs and Appropriations Committee subcommittee chairs at the beginning of each new Congress.
* The Steering and Policy Committee was created and given committee-appointment powers (stripped from Democratic membership of Ways and Means).
* The Speaker would nominate Democratic members of the Rules Committee and also had the right to remove these members.

Although the powers of full committees and their chairs were limited in the 1970s, subcommittees did not become dominant. Rather, particularly in the House, they emerged as important units, whose decisions often set the agenda for subsequent full-committee and floor actions. Subcommittees have proved most significant on relatively routine, low-profile issues, where their specialized knowledge often helps to define problems and prospective legislative solutions. More controversial policies and more highly visible actions, such as health-care reform or gun control proposals, move the locus of decision-making to the full committee or to the House and Senate floors. In addition, chairs of

House subcommittees are responsible to the party caucuses of their respective full committees, much as committee chairs must win approval of the party caucus as a whole, so individual chairs remain beholden to their party peers. To an extent, they must follow their colleagues' preferences in order to lead them.[20]

The Senate has been far more resistant than the House to forces of decentralization in committee structure, largely because the Senate is a very individualistic institution. Because senators can go to the floor and offer amendments at any time, chairs must negotiate with their committee members, whether from the majority or minority party. Individual senators have more power in committees relative to their House counterparts, so their desire to overthrow or circumvent their chairs has been less intense; thus, no real changes were made in their party caucuses.

Few Senate subcommittees, save for those in the Appropriations Committee, acquired the power to "mark up" draft bills, vote on them, and then send them to the full committee. In general, the full committee constitutes the Senate venue for markup activity. Absent that key agenda-setting power, subcommittees mostly provided forums for hearings and policy discussion, rather than policy action. Senate subcommittee chairs often make reputations for themselves in certain policy areas, even when they cannot dominate the crafting of policy outcomes. In general, conflict has occurred less frequently between chairs of subcommittees and full committees in the Senate than in the House. Senators also hold multiple committee assignments, so that if they disagree with a chair of one of their committees, they can turn their attention to another, or to the Senate floor, in attempting to influence policy.

Although committees in the Senate are less central to policymaking than those in the House, they continue to dictate action on the floor. In other words, when a committee reports a bill to the full Senate, its members can be relatively certain that their bill will remain intact. Senators certainly realize that if committee proposals were continually overturned on the Senate floor, their own committee-based power would diminish.

Committees and subcommittees remain important and powerful because their existence makes such good sense, both for individual legislators and the Congress as a whole. Acting on their own, 435 House members or 100 senators cannot reasonably be expected to hammer out coherent legislation across the entire spectrum of issues on each year's congressional agenda. Like most large organizations, the Congress has profited from a division of labor among smaller work groups. Committees specialize in particular policy areas, ranging from the myriad issues taken up by the broadly inclusive Commerce Committee to the relatively narrow focus of the Small Business Committee. Committees are designed to serve their parent chambers, and as such, they have changed over the years in the number, membership levels, and jurisdictions of the units. Viewing committees as efficient sharers of information allows one to see how decentralization can benefit the Congress as a whole.[21] For a list of the standing committees in the House of Representatives and the U.S. Senate, respectively, see tables 7.2 and 7.3.

Given an annual budget and a federal government that regulates everything from trucking to tuna, congressional decentralization through the committee system allows lawmakers to specialize and make informed decisions on a wide range of complex, often conflicting proposals. In fact, by sharing information across committees, Congress as a whole may produce a relatively coherent, consistent set of policies. In short, committees and subcommittees can and do serve the Congress as a whole by providing specialized information to the chamber at large. At the same time, though, the very decentralization of the committee system allows for particular interests to be well represented on very specific subjects where the stakes are high and the visibility of committee actions is low.

Even as party leaders have assumed more power over committee chairs and the content of bills reported to the floor, the committee system can still serve more individualistic ends. Members often seek committee seats to advocate for their constituents' interests. For example, in the House, most members who sit on the House Natural Resources Subcommittee on Water, Power, and Oceans traditionally come from coastal areas or areas that are heavily dependent on water supply, such as Arizona, whereas the House Agriculture Subcommittee on Conservation and Forestry has members who are from rural constituencies. In the Senate, members can sit on more than one major committee, so the membership tends to be more dispersed. However, most of the U.S. senators who sit on the Agriculture Committee have major farm constituencies in their states; likewise, senators on the Energy Committee come disproportionately from the West, where the federal government controls a great portion of the lands.

Richard Fenno's simple observation that congressional committees differ one from another still holds true.[22] Their environments (including the range of their interests and the scope of their policies) differ, as do the motivations of their members. Members construct the kind of committee system they want, and they seek positions on these committees based on their districts' interests (such as agriculture), their own policy aims (such as those concerning science and technology), or a desire for power within the institution (such as a seat on the House Appropriations Committee, which oversees all government spending, or the Senate Finance Committee, which deals with entitlement programs and taxes).

There is no doubt that veteran legislators who have seniority and hold key committee positions can exercise more internal power and affect a wider range of policies than their less senior colleagues. Nevertheless, all representatives and senators use their committee service to pursue multiple goals. Comparing three cohorts of new House members, Steven Smith and Christopher Deering found a mix of motivations for seeking committee seats, especially on panels that offer power and prestige. The jurisdictional fragmentation of the committees allows lawmakers, especially representatives, to find assignments that serve their particular mix of goals.[23]

Historically, junior members have waited a term or two before moving to "power" committees of Appropriations or Ways and Means in the House, and Appropriations or Finance in the Senate. However, when there is a large influx of new members, as occurred in 1995 and 2011 for Republicans in the House, and 1995 and 2015 in the Senate, more slots open up on prestigious committees than is typical. In those cases, members with relatively little seniority can

Table 7.2 Standing Committees, 103rd, 104th, 109th, and 115th Congresses

House of Representatives

103rd Congress (1993–1994) (22 Committees)	104th Congress (1995–1996) (19 Committees)	109th Congress (2005–2006) (20 Committees)	115th Congress (2017–2018) (20 Committees)
Agriculture	Agriculture	Agriculture	Agriculture
Appropriations	Appropriations	Appropriations	Appropriations
Armed Services	National Security	Armed Services	Armed Services
Banking, Finance, and Urban Affairs	Banking and Financial Services	Financial Services	Financial Services
Budget	Budget	Budget	Budget
District of Columbia	—	—	—
Education and Labor	Education and the Workforce	Education and the Workforce	Education and the Workforce
Energy and Commerce	Commerce	Energy and Commerce	Energy and Commerce
Foreign Affairs	International Relations	International Relations	Foreign Affairs
—	—	Homeland Security	Homeland Security
Government Operations	Government Reform and Oversight	Government Reform	Oversight and Government Reform
House Administration	Oversight	House Administration	House Administration
Judiciary	Judiciary	Judiciary	Judiciary

Merchant Marine and Fisheries	—	—	—
Natural Resources	Resources	Resources	Natural Resources
Post Office and Civil Service	—	—	—
Public Works and Transportation	Transportation and Infrastructure	Transportation and Infrastructure	Transportation and Infrastructure
Rules	Rules	Rules	Rules
Science, Space, and Technology	Science	Science	Science, Space, and Technology
Small Business	Small Business	Small Business	Small Business
Standards of Official Conduct	Standards of Official Conduct	Standards of Official Conduct	Ethics
Veterans' Affairs	Veterans' Affairs	Veterans' Affairs	Veterans' Affairs
Ways and Means	Ways and Means	Ways and Means	Ways and Means

Source: Politics in America, 1994 and 1996; *Congressional Quarterly Weekly Report*, February 1, 1997, 310–16; the U.S. House of Representatives and Senate websites: http://www.house.gov and http://www.senate.gov; see the committee membership lists.

Table 7.3 Partisan Membership on Sixteen Standing Senate Committees

	103rd Congress	104th Congress	Jan.–June 2001	July 2001–Dec. 2002	109th Congress	115th Congress
Agriculture, Nutrition, and Forestry	10D/8R	9R/8D	10R/10D	11D/10R	11R/9D	11R/10D
Appropriations	16D/13R	15R/13D	14R/14D	15D/14R	15R/13D	16R/15D
Armed Services	12D/10R	11R/10D	12R/12D	13D/12R	13R/11D	14R/13D
Banking, Housing, and Urban Affairs	11D/8R	9R/7D	10R/10D	11D/10R	11R/9D	12R/11D
Budget	12D/9R	12R/10D	11R/11D	12D/11R	12R/10D	12R/11D
Commerce, Science, and Transportation	11D/9R	10R/9D	11R/11D	12D/11R	12R/10D	14R/13D
Energy and Natural Resources	11D/9R	11R/7D	11R/11D	12D/11R	12R/10D	12R/11D

obtain key committee positions. At the other end of the career ladder, seniority is still an important element in securing a powerful committee chair; a list of the seniority of House and Senate committee chairs is presented in table 7.4.

In addition to issue-based committees, the House also has an Ethics Committee, which is authorized to investigate any House member who is accused of violating House codes of conduct, use of office resources, rules about accepting campaign gifts and donations, or, at worst, engaging in criminal behavior. In the cases of suspected criminal behavior, the Ethics Committee turns over evidence to federal or state legal authorities. Any member of the House can lodge a formal complaint against a member and ask the Ethics Committee to look into it, but the committee can decide not to pursue an investigation if they determine there is not enough evidence to do so. After gaining seats in the 2004 elections, Speaker Hastert (R-IL) and majority House leader Tom DeLay (R-TX) proposed several major changes to weaken the enforcement of ethics rules in the House, and a majority of the party caucus tentatively approved these changes, which were to go into effect at the start of the 109th Congress. In a surprise turn of events, by May 2005, the party leadership reversed itself on these changes because Republican members of the House had received an outpouring of negative press about the new rules, and when scrutiny

Table 7.4 Seniority of House and Senate Committee Chairs, 115th Congress

House Committee	Chair (Years)	Senate Committee	Chair (Years)
Agriculture	Conaway (12)	Agriculture, Nutrition, and Forestry	Roberts (20)
Appropriations	Frelinghuysen (22)	Appropriations	Cochran (38)
Armed Services	Thornberry (22)	Armed Services	McCain (30)
Financial Services	Hensarling (14)	Banking, Housing, and Urban Affairs	Crapo (18)
Budget	Black (6)	Budget	Enzi (20)
Education and the Workforce	Foxx (12)	Health, Education, Labor, and Pensions	Alexander (14)
Energy and Commerce	Walden (18)	Commerce, Science, and Transportation	Thune (12)
		Energy and Natural Resources	Murkowski (14)
		Environment and Public Works	Barrasso (9)
Foreign Affairs	Royce (22)	Foreign Relations	Corker (10)
Homeland Security	McCaul (12)	Homeland Security and Governmental Affairs	Johnson (6)

intensified on the allegations of unethical behavior by Rep. DeLay, he was subsequently forced to resign his leadership position and House seat. He was later
convicted of state campaign law violations, but his conviction was overturned
on appeal.[24] In large part, the leadership was forced to backtrack because the
Democratic minority-party members of the Ethics Committee refused to attend
any meeting at all, thereby denying a quorum and preventing the committee
from doing any business at all. Rarely does the party leadership reverse itself so
publicly, and this case illustrates the limits of party leaders' powers when they
are not fully supported by their rank and file. House Republicans were not willing to adopt rules that would tarnish the reputation of the entire majority party
to protect a single party leader.

   In 2008, after the Democrats gained control of the House the previous year,
the Office of Congressional Ethics (OCE) was established to allow a request for
an ethics investigation against a House member to be filed by the general public. Such complaints are processed by the OCE, and then, it can make a recommendation to the House Ethics Committee to proceed with an investigation.[25]
At the start of the 115th Congress, the Republican majority in the House met
and agreed to roll back the scope and powers of the Ethics Committee, but once
the news went public, the reaction was so negative, including from President
Trump, that they reversed their decision the very next day. [26]

   In the Senate, ethics complaints are handled by the Select Committee on
Ethics, which has the same general responsibilities and powers as its House
counterpart; initiation of an ethics complaint in the Senate can come from both
inside and outside the chamber. Overall, the House and Senate ethics committees serve as relatively weak vehicles by which Congress monitors its own
behavior. A number of powerful members have been forced to resign, including
DeLay, House Majority Leader Coelho (D-CA), and Speaker Wright (D-TX);
other members, such as former House member Charles Rangel (D-NY), came
under continuous investigation but was not found guilty of violations serious
enough to warrant resignation. Rep. Aaron Schock (R-IL) came under scrutiny
for possible ethics violations in how he spent campaign funds on an automobile,
decorating his Washington, DC, office, and accepting trips abroad paid for by
foreign organizations that were not formally approved by the Ethics Committee.
Ultimately, he resigned from his House seat in March 2015; in November 2016,
he was indicted on twenty-four counts of illegally using government funds as
well as campaign contributions to pay for personal expenses.[27]

   Over the past two decades, leaders from both the Republican and
Democratic parties have tightened their grip on all committees. When the
Republicans won control of the White House and the Congress in the 2000
elections, unified party government created an even greater incentive to consolidate the party leadership hold over committees—in terms of chairs, members,
and policy content of legislation. When Democrats took hold of the House in
2007, and then the White House in 2009, party leaders maintained much of
the powers over committees, except that the Democrats revoked term limits on
committee chairs. After the pendulum swung back to the GOP after the 2010
election, Republican Speakers have maintained tight control over committees in
keeping with the trend of the prior decades.

DIFFERENCES IN THE LEGISLATIVE PROCESS IN THE HOUSE AND SENATE

All bills are not created equal, nor do they move along the same path toward the final passage in the House and Senate. In this section, we briefly describe the ways that bills are considered in each chamber, and using the ACA, we show how these procedures can affect the final content of bills that become law. Box 7.1 presents a timeline for the legislative pathway of the ACA including the attempt to repeal and replace it.

The House

Minor bills appear on the House Consent Calendar and are considered on the first and third Mondays of each month; other legislation can take the shortcut of being considered under a suspension-of-the-rules procedure, which requires a two-thirds affirmative House vote and cannot routinely exceed $100 million in expenditures.[28] Major legislation moves to the floor from House committees in two ways. Budget and appropriations measures are entitled to a privileged status that allows them to be brought to the floor at almost any time; most other important legislation must go before the Rules Committee to receive a rule that will govern debate and amendments. Given the sheer size of the House, the Rules Committee is necessary to maintain an orderly flow of legislation. Otherwise, the politics of delay could dominate, and chaos might well reign on the House floor. Important legislation, such as budget resolutions and large-scale, or omnibus, spending packages almost always obtain rules that set out strict constraints on deliberation and waive procedural points of order.[29] Thus, the amount of time for debate and the number and sequence of amendments will often be clearly defined within a rule.

Under Republican control of the House since 1995, the basic legislative process did not change that much in that the Speaker still retains the right of referral, and major legislation is frequently sent to more than one committee. For example, H.R. 1, the Medicare Prescription Drug and Modernization Act of 2003, constituted a major addition to the Medicare program, and as such, it was referred to both the Energy and Commerce Committee and the Ways and Means Committee. Ultimately, the leaders of these committees worked out a compromise version with the party leaders, who brought that bill to the House floor. In rare instances, a bill is so broad that it is referred to a majority of the standing committees of the House. This occurred with the Homeland Security Act of 2002 (H.R. 5005), which affected almost every department in the federal government. In that case, the White House acted as the major policy negotiator, and the party leaders acted more as coordinators of all of the involved committees and, later, as advocates for the bill among the party's rank and file.

The ACA highlights the ways in which bills cross multi-committee jurisdictions. When it was first introduced in the House by Rep. John Dingell (D-MI) in 2009, the bill potentially covered a number of areas falling under several committees. The bill was referred to two major House committees: Energy and Commerce and Ways and Means. Senior House member Henry Waxman (D-CA) was chair of Energy and Commerce, and he took charge of bringing the

Box 7.1: Pathway of the Affordable Care Act

- **February 24, 2009:** In a joint session of Congress, President Obama says: "Health care reform cannot wait . . . and it will not wait another year."
- **March 5, 2009:** White House holds its first health care summit.
- **April 21, 2009:** Senate Finance Committee Chairman Max Baucus and ranking member Chuck Grassley hold the first of three roundtables of health policy and industry experts to discuss developing health care legislation.
- **July 15, 2009:** The Senate's Health, Education, Labor and Pensions Committee passes the Affordable Health Choices Act, including more than 160 Republican amendments accepted during the month-long mark-up.
- **July 31, 2009:** The bill is reported by the House Committee on Energy and Commerce by a 31–28 vote.
- **August 2009:** Obama travels in support of the bill. Tea Party members and conservatives attack the bill at town halls. Obama battles a false rumor that the legislation includes "death panels" that could make life or death decisions.
- **August 26, 2009:** Health care advocate Senator Edward "Ted" Kennedy dies, jeopardizing Senate Democrats' sixty-seat filibuster-proof supermajority.
- **September 29, 2009:** The Senate Finance Committee rejects two amendments for a government-run public health insurance option.
- **October 13, 2009:** The Senate Finance Committee approves Baucus's landmark bill, the America's Healthy Future Act.
- **November 7, 2009:** The House of Representatives passes a version of the health care bill by a 220–215 vote.
- **December 19, 2009:** Senator Ben Nelson, a conservative Democrat, becomes the sixtieth vote needed to pass the Senate health care bill.
- **December 24, 2009:** The Senate passes its health care bill 60–39.
- **January 17, 2010:** Obama stumps for Martha Coakley in her Massachusetts Senate race to replace Kennedy against Republican Scott Brown, who pledged to vote against Democratic health care efforts.
- **January 19, 2010:** Brown wins the special election, jeopardizing the health care legislation.
- **February 25, 2010:** Obama holds a televised heath care summit with congressional party leaders to explain the health care bill.
- **March 11, 2010:** In a letter to Senate Minority Leader Mitch McConnell, Majority Leader Harry Reid says Democrats will use "reconciliation," needing only fifty-one votes, to pass the health care bill.
- **March 21, 2010:** The Senate passes the bill, sending the legislation to Obama for his signature. A separate package of changes expanding the reach of the measure also passes the House over unanimous GOP opposition, to be taken up by the Senate.
- **March 23, 2010:** Obama signs the health care bill into law.
- **August 12, 2011:** The 11th Circuit Court of Appeals rules that parts of the law are unconstitutional.

- **November 8, 2011:** The DC Court of Appeals rules the law is constitutional.
- **November 14, 2011:** The Supreme Court agrees to hear a challenge to the law after twenty-six states, led by Florida, petitioned it.
- **March 26, 2012:** The Supreme Court begins three days of oral arguments over the law's constitutionality.
- **June 28, 2012:** The Supreme Court rules the individual mandate portion of the health care law may be upheld within Congress's taxing power.
- **June 25, 2015:** The Supreme Court rules 6–3 that federal subsidies provided to individuals who purchase health insurance in state exchanges are constitutional.
- **March 24, 2017:** The House approves the Rule on a bill designed

to repeal and replace the ACA but later that day, Speaker Ryan subsequently pulls the bill from the House floor due to a lack of sufficient votes among House Republicans to support final passage.
- **May 4, 2017:** The House approves a bill designed to repeal and replace the ACA by a vote of 217–213.
- **July 28, 2017:** The Senate rejects a bill designed to repeal and replace the ACA by a vote of 49–51 with three Republicans senators, Susan Collins, John McCain, and Lisa Murkowski, voting against it.

Source: Based on Emily Smith, "Timeline of the Health Care Law," CNN, June 28, 2012, http://www.cnn.com/2012/06/28/politics/supreme-court-health-timeline, and compilations and updates by authors.

two committees together to write one bill and of reaching out to other committees with jurisdiction over specific provisions of the larger bill. The bill brought to the House floor, H.R. 3200, was actually the product of five committees; it passed 220–215, with no Republican votes.[30] The Senate's version of the ACA came under the jurisdiction of two committees: the Finance Committee and the Health, Education, Labor, and Pensions (HELP) Committee. Each committee reported its portion of the bill to the Senate floor separately, so committee chairs and party leaders had to work to combine the bills into one. The Senate did finally pass one version of the bill in late December 2009 by a 60–39 vote, also without any Republican support. Although both chambers were under Democratic control, their versions of the bill differed and needed to be exactly the same in order to be passed and sent to President Obama for his signature. Ultimately, a final version of the bill was passed by the House and signed into law in March 2010.

Once a bill makes it through the committee process, as the ACA did, the typical procedure is for it to go to the House Rules Committee, which determines how the bill will be debated. The Rules Committee can determine the length of time that will be devoted to the bill, whether any amendments can be offered to it, and who can offer them (majority or minority members). These guidelines are commonly known as the "rule" on a bill, which can range from open (any amendments) to restrictive (few amendments) or closed (no amendments). In times of intense partisanship in the House, the majority party is likely to use its majority control of the Rules Committee to limit amending opportunities by the minority party.

In sum, within a majoritarian institution, the majority party invested in their leadership (the Rules Committee included) the power to structure legislation so that it would have the best chance of winning, often in a highly partisan vote. The only recourse available to opponents of the bill is to defeat the rule on the House floor; on occasion this occurs, but ordinarily, the majority-party leadership can hold its troops together on the procedural vote to approve the rule.

The use of the Rules Committee and more generally the power to restrict debate and amendments on the House floor, combined with majority-party power in committees, has increased the sense among minority-party members that they have little incentive to cooperate to pass legislation that they have not affected. When party control of the House switches, leaders typically promise to make the House more open both to rank-and-file majority and to minority members. In reality, however, they rarely deliver on that promise because they do not want the minority party (a) to succeed in amending a bill or (b) to force the majority to take politically difficult votes that might hurt them in subsequent elections.

In addition to the rule, there are also other formal procedures that typically accompany legislation being considered by the House and Senate. Among them is what is known as "scoring" by the Congressional Budget Office, which tells members of Congress what the impact of a bill will be in terms of spending and revenue. If a bill is not self-financed through taxes, it will likely increase expenditures which can raise the overall federal budget deficit if other programs are not cut to pay for it. To some members who are very fiscally conservative, the CBO score is a key piece of information about a bill and without it, they may refuse to support it. One such member of Congress is Barbara Comstock (R-VA), who voted against the bill to repeal Obamacare, who argued it did not have a CBO score that would allow her to assess its impact on the federal budget.

When Gingrich and the GOP took the reins of the House in 1995, Democrats complained that although rules might have been more open, the Republican leadership enforced tight time restrictions on legislation that served the same old purpose—to restrict debate and amending activity. One study concluded that the Republicans did follow through on their promise of greater openness in that, compared to the 103rd Congress, there was more debate, more amendments offered, and more amendments passed in the first, highly partisan session of the 104th Congress (1995–1997).[31] Nonetheless, as the 104th Congress wore on, and conflict erupted within the party and with President Clinton, the Republicans, as the Democrats had done before them, relied on a substantial number of restrictive rules.

The partisan differences between the Democrats and Republicans in the 1990s were compounded by the continued Republican opposition to President Clinton. And when George W. Bush won election to the White House in 2000, Democratic opposition to him was equally intense, except in the cases of national security and the response to the attacks of September 11, 2001. The

SPOTLIGHT

Representative Barbara Comstock: The Struggle for Policy Consensus

With the contemporary Republican majority in Congress containing members of varying degrees of ideological intensity and with the possibility of producing notable legislation that will garner a significant number of Democratic votes an unlikely prospect in our ultra-polarized environment, the difficulty of crafting policies that are palatable to opposing ideological wings within the party becomes apparent. Though virtually all congressional Republicans are accurately described as conservative these days, Rep. Barbara Comstock (R-VA) stands out as a relative moderate when compared to her fellow partisans.

Though Rep. Comstock was first elected to Congress in 2014, her history in politics is that of a Washington insider rather than a Washington new-comer. After working as a lawyer and congressional staffer in the early 1990s, Comstock served on Rep. Dan Burton's (R-IN) staff. Burton was the chair of the House Oversight and Government Reform Committee from 1997 to 2003, and Comstock was tasked with digging into alleged wrongdoings of the Clinton administration during Clinton's second term, including the investigation into the Clintons' real estate investments in the Whitewater Development Corporation, an investigation into Democratic Party fund-raising, and a controversy surrounding improper administration access to FBI security clearance documents. After working for Burton, Comstock ran the Republican National Committee team charged with conducting opposition research against then-Governor

George W. Bush's opponent in the 2000 presidential election, Vice President Al Gore. When Bush was elected, Comstock served in the Justice Department.

Comstock entered electoral politics in 2009, when she was elected to a seat in the Virginia House of Delegates, narrowly defeating a Democratic incumbent. She gained a reputation for working across the aisle when her signature piece of legislation that increased penalties for human trafficking passed the Virginia General Assembly with bipartisan support. She set her sights on Congress in 2014 when the seventeen-term Republican incumbent in Virginia's tenth congressional district, Frank Wolf, announced his retirement. Virginia's tenth district, located in the Washington, D.C. suburbs in northern Virginia, has the nation's highest median income and more than half of its residents have a college degree. Voters in the district consistently reelected Wolf with a ten to twenty percentage point margin, but recent presidential margins in the district have been increasingly close: Bush carried the district in 2004 by 11 points, Obama won the district in 2008 by 2.8 points, Romney prevailed in 2012 by 1.1 points, and Clinton carried the district in 2016 by 10 percentage points. Considering Clinton's margin and Comstock's own narrow five-point victory in 2016, her electoral vulnerability in 2018 combined with her relatively moderate legislative record suggest that her vote may be difficult for party leadership to court in the 115th Congress.

Like many Republicans elected since 2010, Comstock was elected while promising during her campaign to "repeal and replace" the ACA. In March 2017, the House considered legislation, the American Health Care Act (AHCA) that would overhaul the health care system and significantly change parts of how the ACA worked. After a Congressional Budget Office report that suggested as many as 24 million people could lose health insurance coverage in the coming years if the AHCA were to be passed, Comstock publicly came out in opposition to the bill, citing "the uncertainties in the current version," but she was sure to reiterate her opposition to the ACA in the same statement by characterizing it as "in a death spiral." Though the House Freedom Caucus was largely credited with being the bloc that caused Speaker Ryan to cancel a scheduled vote on the AHCA, moderates like Comstock also helped ruin the bill's prospects. When the AHCA was revived in early May, this time with the support of the House Freedom Caucus and no Congressional Budget Office analysis, Comstock again opposed the bill because of its "uncertainties." In the end, the AHCA, the bill to repeal the ACA, narrowly passed the House by winning over enough Freedom Caucus members and moderates. This episode shows the struggles that party leadership can have in crafting policies that are acceptable to both ideological hard-liners in the party and moderates like Rep. Comstock.

The information in this section is taken from multiple sources as follows: Joshua Green, "Playing Dirty," *The Atlantic*, June 2004 Issue, https://www.theatlantic.com/magazine/archive/2004/06/playing-dirty/302960/?single_page=true; Kyle Kondik and Geoffrey Skelly, "House 2016: How a Democratic Wave Could Happen," *Sabato's Crystal Ball*, April 14, 2016, http://www.centerforpolitics.org/crystalball/articles/house-2016-how-a-democratic-wave-could-happen/; David Nir, "Daily Kos Elections' Presidential Results by Congressional District for the 2016 and 2012 Elections," *The Daily Kos*, November 19, 2016, http://www.dailykos.com/story/2012/11/19/1163009/-Daily-Kos-Elections-presidential-results-by-congressional-district-for-the-2012-2008-elections; The Editors, "Barbara Comstock for Congress," *National Review*, September 29, 2014, http://www.nationalreview.com/article/389045/barbara-comstock-congress-editors; Barbara Comstock (@RepComstock) on Twitter, March 24, 2017, https://twitter.com/RepComstock/status/845388825706795008; Barbara Comstock (@RepComstock) on Twitter, May 4, 2017, https://twitter.com/RepComstock/status/860227724606140416.

rhetoric and rancor of differences in policy positions spilled over to personal interactions: the days when Democrat and Republican members could play basketball together or dine together in the House dining room were largely over. After the November 2004 elections ensured continued Republican control of the House in the 109th Congress and a second term for George W. Bush, the Republican Party leadership in the House adopted new operating procedures designed to strengthen majority control over the legislative process. Speaker Hastert, who had taken over after Gingrich resigned in 1998 (see chapter 4), announced that he would not bring any measure to the House floor (through the Rules Committee) unless a majority of the Republican Party membership indicated support for the bill—this principle became known as the Hastert Rule.[32] By declaring that principle, Speaker Hastert was essentially saying that he did not want to have to forge bipartisan coalitions to pass legislation—if a bill could not pass with Republican votes alone, it simply would not be brought to the House floor. By definition, such a policy reduced the number of possible bills brought to the House floor; moreover, it caused substantial problems for former Speaker Boehner's speakership in the 112th to 114th Congresses because it was a significant obstacle to bringing legislation to the floor in the absence of party agreement. On several different occasions, Speaker Boehner was forced to violate the Hastert Rule to bring essential legislation to the floor, and he relied on minority party members to pass it (see chapter 5). As noted in chapter 6, Speaker Ryan faced his own internal party divisions on issues such as the ACA repeal, and hewing to the Hastert Rule makes bringing legislation to the House floor all the more challenging.

When the Democrats won control of the House back in the 2006 midterm elections, they maintained their former procedural rules for the most part, while promising to open up the process to the minority party. From 2007 to 2009, that made sense for the Democrats because they were working with a Republican president, who could veto legislation that did not reflect Republican policy views. But in 2009, when Democratic president Obama came into office in the midst of the great recession, House Democrats faced more intense pressure to pass his legislative agenda. That partisan pressure, combined with intense Republican opposition to Obama's plans, led the Democrats to limit the opportunities for minority-party members to offer amendments in committee or on the House floor.[33] Table 7.5 provides a summary of restrictions placed on amendments offered on the House floor from 1977 to 2016.

Then, in 2010, Republicans regained control of the House and, in contrast to past practice, did not readily promise to allow more minority-party access to the legislative process. Instead, during the years 2011–2015, Speaker Boehner encouraged his party to stay unified in opposition to President Obama and Democratic Party policies. When Paul Ryan became Speaker in fall 2015, he maintained opposition to President Obama all the way through to the 2016 presidential election.

In sum, within a majoritarian institution, the majority-party members invested in their leadership the power to structure legislation to reflect party policy and have the best chance of winning. The only recourse available to the minority party is to defeat the rule on the House floor; on occasion this occurs, but ordinarily the majority-party leadership can hold its troops together on the procedural vote to approve the rule. However, running the House in such a purely partisan fashion is risky no matter which party is in control because party unity can prove fragile. When the majority party starts to fight within itself, it becomes very difficult for the House to produce any legislation at all.[34] And when the House ceases to function at all effectively, the entire federal government can be brought to a standstill. Ironically, while the Senate (see below) has often been fingered as the culprit in congressional gridlock, the post-2010 House has proven to be equally problematic.

Table 7.5 Restrictions on Amendments

Congress	Open Rules	Restrictive Rules	Percent Restrictive
Democratic House, 1977–1994, 2007–2010			
95th (1977–1978)	179	32	15
96th (1979–1980)	161	53	25
97th (1981–1982)	90	30	25
98th (1983–1984)	105	50	32
99th (1985–1986)	65	50	43
100th (1987–1988)	66	57	46
101st (1989–1990)	47	57	55
102nd (1991–1992)	37	72	66
103rd (1993–1994)	31	73	70
110th (2007–2008)	23	140	86
111th (2009–2010)	0	111	100
Republican House, 1995–2006, 2011–2016			
104th (1995–1996)	83	59	42
105th (1997–1998)	74	66	47
106th (1999–2000)	91	88	49
107th (2001–2002)	40	67	63
108th (2003–2004)	34	99	75
109th (2005–2006)	24	101	81
112th (2011–2012)	25	115	82
113th (2013–2014)	12	137	92
114th (2015–2016)	8	147	95

Source: *Congressional Quarterly Weekly Report*, November 19, 1994, 3321; data for 1995–2016 compiled by Donald Wolfensberger, Resident Scholar, Bipartisan Policy Center, see http://bipartisanpolicy.org/library/114th-congress-house-rules-data/; see also his papers, "The House Rules Committee under Republican Majorities: Continuity and Change," presented at the Northeastern Political Science Meeting, November 2002; and "A Reality Check on the Republican House Reform Revolution at the Decade Mark," presented at the Woodrow Wilson International Center for Scholars, January 24, 2005. Michael Thorning "Final Analysis: 114th Congress Improves, but Gridlock Overshadows," January 19, 2017, Bipartisanpolicy.org https://bipartisanpolicy.org/blog/114th-congress-improves-but-gridlock-overshadows/ (accessed April 18, 2017).

The Senate

Unlike the House, the Senate has far fewer formal rules, largely attributable to its smaller size (one hundred members). Senators have a formal right to speak on the Senate floor, and this power confers their right to object to consideration of any bill brought to the floor.[35] Moreover, a senator may use his or her right of speech to extend debate on a bill or an amendment indefinitely, the filibuster (see chapter 5). Therefore, the Senate must essentially operate on a unanimous consent basis, which gives tremendous leverage to a single senator in negotiating the conditions of debate. Overall, individual U.S. senators are more powerful than their individual House counterparts because of their right to filibuster, but also because in a smaller chamber, one or two votes can make the difference between a bill's passage or failure more frequently than in the House.

Unanimous consent means precisely that: all senators must acquiesce to the provisions of the agreement. In many ways, unanimous consent agreements resemble House rules, but they are hatched in very different ways. As opposed to the domination of the House process by partisan majorities in the chamber and the Rules Committee, Senate leaders must satisfy all of their interested colleagues from both parties in crafting a set of conditions for debating and amending legislation. In the absence of formal rules that structure debate, limit amendments, and impose time limits, the Senate is more governed by informal interactions and negotiation than the House. Although the filibuster was limited (see below) in 2013 for the first time in almost forty years, and again in 2017, the fundamental power to block legislation still remains in the hands of individual senators. Despite the rise in intense partisanship in the Senate in the past two decades, most individual rank-and-file members still see little reason to give their leaders the kinds of procedural powers to accomplish majority party goals as we have seen happen in the House. Although that could change, depending on the pressure that builds on Senate Republicans, who are in the majority, to pass components of President Trump's agenda, more than sixty senators have expressed the strong desire to maintain the legislative filibuster that requires sixty votes to move bills forward.

The Senate Then and Now

In his classic study of the 1950s Senate, political scientist Donald Matthews approvingly quoted a senator who noted that each member "of the Senate has as much power as he has the sense to use. For this very reason he has to be careful to use it properly or else he will incur the wrath of his colleagues."[36] Such restraint typified the unspoken limits imposed by the "folkways" that Matthews discovered in his research.

Six important norms governed Senate behavior, according to Matthews:[37]

1. Apprenticeship, which included performing menial tasks (such as presiding over floor debate on routine matters), speaking only occasionally on the floor, and generally deferring to senior senators.
2. Legislative work, which emphasized doing the unglamorous tasks that fill up most days, as opposed to seeking publicity for one's actions and statements.
3. Specialization, which meant focusing virtually all of one's efforts on work within two or three of the ten-plus subcommittees and committees that a member was assigned to.
4. Courtesy, which "permitted competitors to cooperate"[38] by discouraging public personal attacks, especially in floor debate, and encouraging

elaborate compliments between senators of all political stripes (e.g., "My good friend, the most distinguished senator from _____, has made an excellent point, but I must offer an alternative perspective").

5. Institutional patriotism, which translated into a willingness to defend the Senate with a strong emotional commitment to the body and its members.

6. Reciprocity, which was perhaps the single most important folkway, because the bargaining among senators depended on the unstated premise that no individual would take advantage of the practice of performing mutual favors on a host of issues and procedures.

One effect of general adherence to the Senate's folkways was to reinforce the decentralized power of the committee system, where the norm of seniority, a well-established element of reciprocity, had been elevated to a governing principle for both parties in advancing members toward committee chairmanships. Relying on seniority meant that consecutive service on a committee was virtually the sole criterion for selecting a chair. This encouraged senators to build careers on given panels and defend the related programs and jurisdictions (the turf) against all challenges. This was a tidy state of affairs for a relatively conservative, southern-dominated Senate that had a limited policy agenda.

Although the large, liberal Democratic "class of 1958" increased pressure on some of the norms, such as apprenticeship, it was Lyndon Johnson who initiated the slide toward individualism. In a bid to strengthen his own position as Senate minority leader in 1953, Johnson instituted a committee-assignment rule that guaranteed every Democratic senator a seat on at least one major committee. He continued this practice as majority leader (1955–1960), and Republican leaders did it too. The "Johnson Rule" thus enhanced the individual standing of all incoming senators while simultaneously placing each in the debt of the party leadership. Although this practice did not demolish the apprenticeship norm, it did increase the expectations that every senator had something to contribute, even during their initial months of service.

In two distinct but related ways, power within the Senate changed dramatically between the late 1950s and the 1980s. First, liberal and mostly non-southern Democrats rose to occupy key committee positions.[39] Second, the Senate became more thoroughly individualistic as various institutional norms evolved or, in the case of apprenticeship, simply disappeared. As the public role of the media and interest groups in the legislative process intensified throughout the 1970s, senators faced more pressure to appear attentive and active on a wider range of issues than ever before.[40] This external force eroded the incentives for senators to stay quiet in their early years in the Senate because they simply did not have the time to wait in the background. All one hundred senators were expected to participate in the process, and there was little time for learning the ropes through years of committee experience.

By 1984, David Rohde and his colleagues concluded that "the egalitarian trend that opened up the Senate and shared power more widely among its members still holds sway."[41] Moreover, they observed a decline in the other general benefit norms, as an increasing workload and greater ideological divisions had begun to undermine some of the traditional Senate comity. The Senate that

John McCain (R-AZ) entered thirty years ago was much more hospitable to the cultivation of a reputation as a maverick than was the Senate of 1958, when the iconoclastic William Proxmire (D-WI) was first elected. Senator McCain shared many of Proxmire's traits; he went his own way and did not seem to care whom he offended in the process. This was on clear display in the early morning hours of July 28, 2017, when McCain became the third and decisive Republican senator to vote against the ACA repeal and replace bill, thereby dooming Republican efforts to undo Obamacare.

The juxtaposition of behavior and norms is, of course, one of the problems in assessing the importance of informal rules of the game. Sooner or later, if there are many violations of norms, we are justified in asking if the folkways have any effect in restraining behavior. Still, the fact remains that the procedures that govern the Senate have reinforced some degree of cooperation and comity among senators because each senator can retaliate against any other at any time by blocking legislation.

Obstructionism and the Partisan Impulse in the Contemporary Senate

Given its informality and reliance on cordial, respectful relations among its members, the functioning of the Senate is threatened by declining reciprocity and courtesy. The Senate has always provided great leeway to its members, and its processes have emphasized lengthy deliberation rather than speedy action. Indeed, the filibuster is probably the best-known single element of Senate procedure, as much a result of Jimmy Stewart's performance in *Mr. Smith Goes to Washington* as of the long speeches of Senator Robert La Follette (R-WI), or the record-setting effort of Senator Strom Thurmond (R-SC)—more than twenty-four hours straight—or the well-organized southern opposition to civil rights legislation in the 1950s and early 1960s.

Filibusters have become much more common in the contemporary chamber, as both individual members and organized factions have used the tactic to bring the chamber's business to a halt over minor issues, and even for matters of convenience (such as a scheduling dispute). Despite the procedural importance of filibusters, their frequent use and even more frequent threatened use demonstrate a pernicious side of the increasingly individualistic Senate. Congressional scholar Barbara Sinclair concluded that the Senate has created this situation "not by changing its rules, but by being unwilling and unable to prevent senators from fully exploiting the power those rules grant to each of them."[42]

Majority leaders have had an increasingly difficult job managing senatorial behavior and forcing senators to conduct filibusters according to the strictest definition. Typically, a filibuster requires senators to be on their feet the entire time that they are talking in opposition to the pending business on the floor. But in today's busy political world, most senators no longer have the time to do that, so they merely threaten a filibuster and speak for a few hours on the floor. Leaders are forced to accommodate these senators. As a consequence, in the absence of real costs to mounting a filibuster, senators have come to view this tactic as just one more tool to get what they want. A majority leader who tried to penalize a senator for engaging in a filibuster might very well face the wrath of all the other senators in his or her party, and such opposition might threaten the majority leader's position.

In the past decade, however, the filibuster has gone from an occasional tool used by individual senators for bargaining purposes on specific bills to the minority party's near-constant strategy to block the majority party's legislation. The Democrats used it against the Republican majority from 2002 to 2006, mostly to block President Bush's appointments, and the Republicans returned the favor when they fell into the minority in 2007. When Barack Obama won the presidency in 2008, Mitch McConnell, then the Republican Senate minority leader, said it was their goal to make sure that he would be a one-term president. In fact, the Democrats were forced to package the ACA as a measure under the Reconciliation procedure, which is designed to be a budget measure that reconciles revenues with outlays, and by Senate rule cannot be filibustered, in order to pass it. In addition to using this type of protected legislative vehicle, former Democratic majority leader Harry Reid (D-NV) also used his right of recognition to fill the legislative amendment tree, which has seven branches through which senators can offer amendments to an underlying bill. Reid filled all these branches with his own amendments and blocked all other amendments from majority and minority senators alike. His rationale was that if Republicans were going to object to even considering a bill, and/or filibuster every bill, he would only bring bills to the floor if he could protect Democratic Party policies within them, and that meant drastically limiting the opportunities to try to change those bills on the Senate floor. Reid used this tool so much that he holds the record as a majority leader for doing so.

The less opportunity that Republicans had to influence legislation through typical Senate channels, the more they filibustered both legislation and presidential appointments. The obstruction reached a breaking point in November 2013, when majority Democrats decided to use their power over procedural rulings to bar a filibuster against presidential appointments and judicial nominees lower than the Supreme Court. In 2015, when McConnell took over as majority leader of the Senate after Republicans picked up eight seats in the 2014 midterm elections, he expressed hopes that the obstruction would lessen, but Democrats mirrored the delaying tactics of the GOP from the very start of the 114th Congress.[43]

That obstruction only continued more intensely when the Republicans refused to grant a hearing for President Obama's Supreme Court nominee, Judge Merrick Garland, a judge on the D.C. Circuit Court of Appeals. President Obama nominated him in March, 2016, after the death of sitting Supreme Court Justice Antonin Scalia. Majority Leader Mitch McConnell refused to refer the nomination to the Judiciary Committee for consideration, much less allow it to come to the floor for an up or down vote. It was the first time that a majority party in the Senate had outright refused to even consider a Supreme

Court nomination from an opposite party president. The Garland nomination sat longer than any other in the entire twentieth century except for Justice Louis Brandeis, whose nomination took 125 days to complete but unlike Garland, who never even received a Senate hearing, Brandeis was eventually confirmed to the Supreme Court. [44]

As discussed in chapter 6, the Republicans were successful in stalling so long that a new President—a Republican—was elected. With the end of the 114th Congress, Garland's nomination automatically died, and President Trump was free to make a new nomination to fill the Scalia vacancy. He chose Neil Gorsuch, who was also a judge on the 10th Circuit Court of Appeals, but much more conservative than Garland. The Republican-controlled Senate quickly acted to send the nomination to the Judiciary Committee, which held hearings and reported the nomination to the full Senate by a party line vote of 11–9.

When Majority leader McConnell tried to bring up the Judiciary Committee's recommendation on Judge Gorsuch on the Senate floor, Democrats objected and promised to filibuster it. Given the choice between allowing the Democrats to defeat a conservative Supreme Court nominee under a Republican President and preserving the right to filibuster all Supreme Court nominees, McConnell chose party over procedural rights. On April 6, 2016, using a similar parliamentary move to that of his predecessor, Harry Reid, McConnell made a motion that filibustering Supreme Court nominees was out of order. McConnell's motion was upheld by a vote of 52–48, and cloture was invoked by the same vote margin. Gorsuch was confirmed the next day by a vote of 54–45 with 3 Democrats voting for Gorsuch.

The frequent use of the filibuster over the last decade and the responses by party leaders to limit the ability to filibuster, along with limitations on offering amendments to bills on the Senate floor, have all taken their toll on the Senate as an institution; it has become less fundamentally different than the House of Representatives, which has traditionally been more partisan and majoritarian than the Senate.[45] In past years, when a bill was introduced in the Senate, or an idea for legislation was proposed informally, members on both sides of the aisle would try to work together to see if they could pass legislation and all Senators worked hard to preserve their own individual powers. Today, the starting point for negotiation has actually become the end point, because one or the other party often stakes out the position of "no" under all circumstances. Just as the House becomes paralyzed when there is infighting within the majority party, the Senate comes to a halt when all bipartisan cooperation ceases. With the failure to repeal ACA in 2017, there were some attempts by Republican and Democratic senators to work on fixes for the program in terms of stabilizing insurance markets, but the odds were stacked against bipartisan success. At the same time, other bipartisan pairs of senators sought to work together to find a legislative solution for DACA residents in terms of legal pathways to citizenship. At the very least, it may take another election cycle or two to sweep in new leadership for both parties to break the impasse.

RULES AND POLICYMAKING IN
THE MODERN CONGRESS

Structurally, the legislative process has become more complex over the past forty years in that it has moved from generally closed and informal sets of interactions between legislators to a more public and more formal environment. The parties have asserted strong control over committees and legislators in the House, discouraging individual influence and requiring absolute party loyalty. The Senate has always been more individually focused, but it too has become infused with highly partisan policy positions. These developments have affected the possibilities for congressional integration and coherence in distinct ways, with the majoritarian House often facing a Senate that is hard-pressed to act quickly and effectively. Conversely, a conflicted House will find it very difficult to pass a compromise bill that has made it through the Senate. In a political environment that discourages cooperation across party lines and rewards the promotion of individualism, generating the succession of majorities necessary to pass important legislation has grown more and more difficult. Given both new and continuing legislative challenges, one might predict that at least one chamber, more likely the Senate, will ultimately adopt a different set of standards and practices for the legislative process.

The broader implications for—and costs to—the policymaking process also clearly relate to partisanship and the breakdown of negotiations in the House and Senate. For major policies enacted at the federal level to attract widespread public support, multiple views have to find their way into the deliberation process before bills are passed. When the parties shut each other out of that process and only pass bills that reflect their own party's policy preferences, they risk alienating much of the public. This may well be what has happened with Obamacare. Republicans argue that they opposed it so strongly precisely because they did not have a chance to amend it before its passage. Without bipartisan cooperation, any federal legislation is harder to implement and faces more resistance especially in states governed by the minority party in Congress. Typically, Congress has reviewed and improved large federal programs on an incremental basis, which is good from a policymaking standpoint and an appropriate exercise of congressional oversight over the executive branch's implementation of the law. When the capacity to negotiate across party lines disappears, both the policymaking process and our separation of powers system suffer as a result.[46]

Recommended Readings

Adler, E. Scott, and John D. Wilkerson. *Congress and the Politics of Problem Solving.* New York: Cambridge University Press, 2013.

Arenberg, Richard A., and Robert B. Dove. *Defending the Filibuster: The Soul of the Senate,* Revised and Updated Edition. Bloomington, IN: Indiana University Press, 2015.

Smith, Steven S. *The Senate Syndrome: The Evolution of Procedural Warfare in the Modern U.S. Senate.* Norman: University of Oklahoma Press, 2014.

Volden, Craig, and Alan E. Wiseman, *Legislative Effectiveness in the United States Congress: The Lawmakers.* New York: Cambridge University Press, 2014.

Useful Resources

Office of the Clerk, U.S. House of Representatives: http://www.clerk.house.gov

U.S. Senate Committee on Rules and Administration: http://www.rules.senate.gov

Library of Congress: Congress.gov

Notes

[1] Jessie Hellmann and Peter Sullivan "Rand Paul Creates Storm Over Access to ObamaCare Draft Bill," *The Hill.com*, March 2, 2017, http://thehill.com/policy/healthcare/322016-rand-paul-creates-storm-over-obamacare-access (accessed April 18, 2017).

[2] Donald Matthews first employed the "folkways" notion in his groundbreaking *U. S. Senators and Their World* (New York: Vintage, 1960).

[3] See Ross K. Baker, *House and Senate*, 2nd ed. (New York: Norton, 1995), 71–73.

[4] Timothy R. Homan. "Borrowing Authority Hinges on Senate Rule Shortcuts," *Bloomberg.com*, October 16, 2013, https://www.bloomberg.com/news/articles/2013-10-15/legislative-process-matters-in-ending-government-shutdown (accessed May 10, 2017).

[5] Eric Uslaner, *The Decline of Comity in Congress* (Ann Arbor: University of Michigan Press, 2002), chap. 2.

[6] Ibid., chap. 5.

[7] Gallup.com "Congressional Job Approval," September 2017 http://www.gallup.com/poll/1600/congress-public.aspx (accessed October 15, 2017).

[8] See, for example, Judd Choate, "Changing Perspectives on Congressional Norms," paper presented at the American Political Science Association Meeting, San Francisco, August 29–September 1, 1996.

[9] The Constitution of the United States, http://www.archives.gov/exhibits/charters/constitution_transcript.html.

[10] Wendy J. Schiller, "Senators as Political Entrepreneurs: Using Bill Sponsorship to Shape Legislative Agendas," *American Journal of Political Science* 39 (1995): 186–203.

[11] Congress.gov (data computed from the Library of Congress).

[12] Ibid.

[13] Gary Young and Joseph Cooper, "Multiple Referral and the Transformation of House Decision Making," in *Congress Reconsidered*, 5th ed., ed. Lawrence Dodd and Bruce I. Oppenheimer (Washington, DC: CQ Press, 1993), 214.

[14] The Speaker can refer a bill to multiple committees, but he or she designates a lead committee and sets deadlines.

[15] Steven S. Smith and Christopher Deering, *Committees in Congress*, 2nd ed. (Washington DC: CQ Press, 1990). The House ordinarily dissolves into the Committee of the Whole to conduct its legislative business under lenient rules that allow for the more efficient conduct of business. Decisions made in the Committee of the Whole are formalized in subsequent passage through the House.

[16] Elaine K. Swift, *The Making of an American Senate* (Ann Arbor: University of Michigan Press, 1996).

[17] Smith and Deering, *Committees in Congress*, 35.

18. Ibid., 38ff. Why, one might ask, did many committee chairs allow their positions to be eliminated, especially in the House? Many chaired panels with modest jurisdictions, and the 1946 act provided benefits to those who were displaced and to those who had anticipated becoming chairs. Consolidation of the number of committees worked hand in hand with the rise in resources to empower the chairs as individuals and as a group.

19. Norman Ornstein, "Causes and Consequences of Congressional Change: Subcommittee Reforms in the House of Representatives, 1970–1973," in *Congress in Change*, ed. Norman Ornstein (New York: Praeger, 1975), 88–114.

20. The classic study here is John Manley's analysis of Ways and Means Committee chairman Wilbur Mills (D-AK): "Wilbur Mills: A Study of Congressional Influence," *American Political Science Review* 63 (1969): 442–64.

21. Keith Krehbiel, *Information and Legislative Organization* (Ann Arbor: University of Michigan Press, 1990).

22. Richard F. Fenno, Jr., *Congressmen in Committees* (Boston: Little, Brown, 1973).

23. Smith and Deering, *Committees in Congress*, 110.

24. Editorial Staff, "Ethics Retreat," *Roll Call*, January 10, 2005; Catalina Camia and Susan Davis, "Texas Court Overturns Tom DeLay Conviction," *USA Today*, September 13, 2013, http://www.usatoday.com/story/news/politics/2013/09/19/tom-delay-conviction-overturned-money-laundering/2837053.

25. House Ethics Committee, "Committee History," http://ethics.house.gov/about/committee-history (accessed February 23, 2015). Also see U.S. Senate Select Committee on Ethics, "Jurisdiction," http://www.ethics.senate.gov/public/index.cfm/jurisdiction (accessed February 23, 2015).

26. Eric Lipton and Matt Flegenheimer, "House Republicans, Under Fire, Back Down on Gutting Ethics Office," *New York Times*, January 3, 2017, https://www.nytimes.com/2017/01/03/us/politics/trump-house-ethics-office.html?_r=0 (accessed April 16, 2017).

27. Anna Palmer, John Bresnahan, and Jake Sherman, "Schock Lawyers Up," *Politico.com*, February 24, 2015, http://www.politico.com/story/2015/02/schock-lawyers-up-115476.html; Katherine Skiba and Todd Lighty "Former U.S. Rep. Aaron Schock Indicted on 24 Criminal Counts." *Chicago Tribune*, November 10, 2016, http://www.chicagotribune.com/news/local/breaking/ct-aaron-schock-indicted-20161110-story.html.

28. Roger Davidson and Walter Oleszek, *Congress and Its Members*, 4th ed. (Washington, DC: CQ Press, 1994), 330–31.

29. Allen Schick, *The Federal Budget* (Washington, DC: Brookings Institution, 1995), 79.

30. The five committees were Budget, Education and Labor, Energy and Commerce, Oversight and Government Reform, and Ways and Means; Congress.gov, https://www.congress.gov/bill/111th-congress/house-bill/3200 (accessed February 24, 2015).

31. Kristen Kanthak and Elizabeth M. Martin, "House Republicans and Restrictive Rules: A New Regime?" Paper presented at the American Political Science Association meeting, San Francisco, August 29–September 1, 1996, 4–7.

32. Charles Babington, "Hastert Launches a Partisan Policy," *Washington Post*, November 27, 2004, A1.

33. Walter Oleszek, "The Evolving Congress: Overview and Analysis of the Modern Era," in *The Evolving Congress* (Committee on Rules and Administration, S. PRT 113–30, December 2014, 32–33).

34. For an excellent overview of how Republican factionalism has grown over the past twenty years, see Tim Alberta, "The Cabal That Quietly Took Over the House," *National Journal*, http://www.nationaljournal.com/magazine/the-cabal-that-quietly-took-over-the-house-20130523.

35. Floyd M. Riddick and Alan S. Frumin, *Riddick's Senate Procedure* (Washington, DC: Government Printing Office, 1992), 1092–97.

36. Matthews, *U.S. Senators and Their World*, 101. The Senate of the 1950s was a white male institution and Senator Margaret Chase Smith (R-ME) was the single exception. Today, there are twenty female U.S. senators.

37. Ibid., 92ff.

38. Ibid., 99.

[39] See Randall B. Ripley, *Power in the Senate* (New York: St. Martin's Press, 1969); David W. Rohde, Norman J. Ornstein, and Robert L. Peabody, "Political Change and the U.S. Senate, 1957–1974," in *Studies of Congress*, ed. Glenn Parker (Washington, DC: CQ Press, 1985), 147–88, and Barbara Sinclair, *The Transformation of the U.S. Senate* (Baltimore: Johns Hopkins University Press, 1989).

[40] Sinclair, *Transformation of the U.S. Senate.*

[41] Rohde, Ornstein, and Peabody, "Political Change and the Senate," 183.

[42] Sinclair, *Transformation of the U.S. Senate*, 125.

[43] Burgess Everett and Manu Raju, "Senate Nears DHS Deal," *Politico.com*, February 25, 2015, http://www.politico.com/story/2015/02/senate-democrats-mitch-mcconnell-homeland-security-funding-115490.html.

[44] Christian Farias "Obama's Supreme Court Nominee Makes History for Waiting the Longest for Confirmation," *The Huffington Post*, July 19, 2016, http://www.huffingtonpost.com/entry/merrick-garland-senate-louis-brandeis_us_57892bfbe4b08608d334728f (accessed April 18, 2017).

[45] Steven S. Smith, *The Senate Syndrome: The Evolution of Procedural Warfare in the Modern U.S. Senate* (Norman: University of Oklahoma Press, 2014).

[46] For an excellent discussion of presidential/congressional gridlock over time, see Sarah A. Binder, *Stalemate: Causes and Consequences of Legislative Gridlock* (Washington, DC: Brookings Institution Press, 2003).

CHAPTER 8

The Individual Enterprise

Members of Congress who are in the minority party will sometimes take extreme measures to draw attention to their policy causes. Here, Congressional Democrats, led by Representative John Lewis (D-GA), a prominent activist in the Civil Rights movement, engage in a sit-in on the House floor to call for action to reduce gun violence.

In January 2015, Rep. John Dingell (D-MI) retired from the U.S. House of Representatives after a record-setting fifty-nine-year career. Over the course of almost six decades, Dingell's congressional enterprise—the resources and personnel that he controlled—waxed and waned, depending on the stage of his career, his committee position, and whether he was serving in the majority or minority. For the first forty years, which corresponded with extended Democratic control of the House, his enterprise grew unabated. Succeeding his father, who died in office, Dingell had just a handful of personal staff members in 1955; even senators in those days would only command ten to fifteen staffers. Over the years, mostly through his service on, and chairmanship of, the House Energy and Commerce Committee,[1] Dingell's enterprise grew to more than 120 staffers by the mid-1980s, in part because of his continual push to expand the jurisdiction of his panel.

After the GOP capture of the House in 1994, Dingell served as the ranking minority member of Energy and Commerce, but his enterprise shrank considerably to about forty-five personal and committee staffers. In 2007, with Democrats back in control, he regained his chairmanship, but with the decline in committee power, his enterprise didn't approach that of the 1980s high-water mark. Finally, in 2009, Rep. Henry Waxman (D-CA) successfully challenged Dingell for the committee chair position, and Dingell spent his last few years of congressional service as a subcommittee chair or, after 2010, a ranking member. His enterprise declined to almost where it had begun sixty years before. After announcing his retirement, the congressman's wife, Debbie Dingell, won his Detroit-area seat, keeping the family tradition alive. As of 2017, in her second term, Rep. Dingell commands a basic personal office enterprise of about sixteen staffers.[2]

Many junior members of the House can work effectively with personal staff, their communications operations, and electorally based resources of campaigns or personal leadership PACs (see below for more details). In addition, congressional caucuses offer robust opportunities for less senior lawmakers to affect House politics and policies. Take Republican Rep. Mark Meadows (NC-11), for example. He won his congressional seat in 2012, took office in 2013, sought to defund the Affordable Care Act in his first term, and put forward a motion declaring the Office of Speaker vacant in 2015. In conventional terms, such an action would have been political suicide; in fact, the party leadership did retaliate by removing Meadows from his subcommittee chair position. Still, he did win the admiration and support from members of the far-right House Freedom Caucus (HFC), whose members helped push Speaker Boehner toward resigning later that year.

SPOTLIGHT

Representative Mark Meadows: Making His Mark

Representative Mark Meadows (R-NC) entered North Carolina politics in the 1990s, where he served as chairman of the Macon County Republican Party. Prior to his political career, he owned and operated a restaurant in Florida. He also owned a real estate company called Highland Properties. After the Republican-controlled North Carolina state legislature redrew the state's congressional district lines following the 2010 census, Meadows saw an opportunity to enter electoral politics in his own right. Meadows' home district, North Carolina's eleventh, was redrawn to exclude a large portion of a Democratic stronghold in the city of Asheville.

The eleventh district incumbent was moderate Blue Dog Democrat Heath Shuler, who represented the district since 2007. Shuler, just 40 years old at the time, decided to retire from Congress prior to the 2012 elections rather than trying to win reelection in a district that had been redrawn to advantage the Republicans. Meadows, with the support of the Tea Party movement, easily won the Republican primary to fill the open seat. During the general election, Meadows made national headlines when he made a comment falsely insinuating that President Obama was not born in the United States, stating, "We'll send him back home to Kenya or wherever it is." Meadows won the general election with 57 percent of the vote and has since been reelected twice.

After frequently appearing on television as a spokesperson for far-right House members, Meadows won election as head of the HFC in December 2016. He also could put his money where his mouth was, in that his leadership PAC was the fifth largest in the House and distributed almost $700,000 to his congressional allies. By March 2017, after barely more than four years on Capitol Hill, he led opposition to the Republicans' attempt to repeal and replace Obama's Affordable Care Act, because he did not believe it should be replaced at all, and in doing so, took on both Speaker Paul Ryan and President Trump.

Even with an enterprise of fewer than twenty staffers, Rep. Meadows demonstrates how an ambitious individual legislator can make his mark in the House.

The information in this section is taken from multiple sources as follows: wsj.com, "Mark Meadows (R)," *The Wall Street Journal*, http://projects.wsj.com/campaign2012/candidates/view/mark-meadows--NC-H; Jennifer Haberkorn and Alex Isenstadt, "Shuler Won't Seek Reelection in 2012," *Politico*, February 2, 2012, http://www.politico.com/story/2012/02/shuler-wont-seek-reelection-in-2012–072388; Mark Barrett, "Mark Meadows Has Taken Chances in Rapid Rise to Power," *Asheville Citizen Times*, April 1, 2017, http://www.citizen-times.com/story/news/local/2017/04/01/mark-meadows-has-taken-chances-rapid-rise-power/99865648/ (accessed April 3, 2017).

THE LEGISLATOR AS ENTERPRISE

Nothing captures the fragmentation of congressional politics better or contributes to it more than the husbanding of resources in 535 separate congressional enterprises.[3] The enterprise notion is extremely useful in understanding the actions of individual legislators within the context of the Congress as a whole. Simply put, House members and, even more so, senators must allow others to act for them; there is so much to do and so little time. Thus, staffers negotiate agreements, answer letters, feel out allies, return constituents' calls, and perform a thousand other tasks. On occasion, staffers may act on their own, but ordinarily, their actions follow the dictates—however general—of their bosses, who historically have had the absolute power to hire and fire their congressional employees.[4]

The idea of an enterprise *purposefully* blurs the distinction between members of Congress and those who work on their behalf. In the end, the legislators earn the accolades for the actions of the staffers, whose careers rise or fall with their bosses' fortunes. Using this idea, we can examine a legislature filled with enterprises—a hallmark of the post-1960 Congress. As Robert Salisbury and Kenneth Shepsle concluded in 1981, "The result of the actions and interactions of one hundred senatorial enterprises generates a quite different institution than the one of a century ago, or even a few decades ago, consisting of individual senators acting more or less alone."[5] If enterprises provide more structure to Senate individualism, they exert even more influence in the larger House, where 435 separate legislators have come to possess enough resources to insert themselves into policymaking and constituency affairs in dozens of ways, each crafted to serve the individual representative's preferences.

Since World War II, congressional resources have grown in multiple dimensions (table 8.1). Personal office and committee staff numbers have risen sharply, as have the number of special-interest caucuses, the budgets of legislative-support agencies,[6] and campaign expenditures. Despite some modest cutbacks in official funds, most legislators benefit from increasing amounts of resources, as campaign fund-raising has soared. In short, senators and representatives control adequate resources to pursue multiple, individually defined goals, which range from winning reelection to influencing policy decisions to running for higher office.

Congressional enterprises for veteran legislators often become multimillion-dollar small businesses that must maintain themselves as they seek to promote their members' interests. Despite some variation, most enterprises look roughly like the one depicted in figure 8.1. At the heart of the mini-conglomerate is the legislator, often in tandem with his or her top aide—usually the chief of staff. Around this essential nucleus, each legislator builds a unique combination of contributing components. Although some senior members may construct their organizations from all the building blocks, most emphasize a few key elements, always including the personal office.

Table 8.1 Growth in Congressional Staff by Number of Employees, 1930–2015 (Selected Years)

	1930	1947	1960	1980	2000	2015
House						
Members' Staff	870	1,440	—	7,371	7,226	6,030
Committee Staff	112	167	440	1,917	1,176	1,110
Senate						
Members' Staff	280	590	—	3,746	4,087	3,917
Committee Staff	163	232	470	1,191	762	888

Source: Data from Norman J. Ornstein, Thomas E. Mann, Michael J. Malbin, Andrew Rugg, and Raffaela Wakeman, eds., *Vital Statistics on Congress, 2017 Edition* (Washington, DC: Brookings Institution), tables 5.2 and 5.5. https://www.brookings.edu/wp-content/uploads/2017/01/vitalstats_ch5_full.pdf.

Note: 1960 members' staff data unavailable.

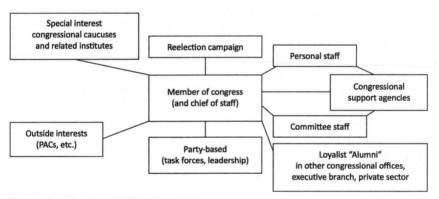

Figure 8.1 The Congressional Enterprise.

The Personal Office

Except for a handful of lawmakers, such as top party leaders or committee chairs, the personal office lies at the heart of each legislator's congressional enterprise. In the House, even the most junior minority-party representative is entitled to the same personal office allowances as the most senior majority-party member: up to eighteen staffers and an overall budget of approximately $1,268,520 million. Thus, Rep. Mike Gallagher (R-WI), elected to his first term in 2016, can command the same basic personal office resources (staff, travel, communications, computers, etc.) as those purchased by his fellow member from Wisconsin, Speaker Paul Ryan, who has served in the House since 1999.

In the Senate, office budgets are determined by state population size; therefore, senators from more populous states typically have much larger enterprises than their colleagues from small states.

Although there is some variation in structure and work assignments, the cast of characters in most congressional offices is roughly the same. It includes a chief of staff responsible for overseeing the entire operation; several legislative aides, with one usually designated as a legislative director; a personal secretary; an office manager; a communications director; caseworkers (in Washington and in the home district); a top district aide; and other district staff. Senate offices are larger and more likely to encourage specialization, but the basic configuration is similar. For an example of job titles and salaries for a single office, see table 8.2.

Variation also occurs in *what* legislators do with their office staff and other resources, and *where* they do it. Two major generalizations hold true here. First, there are some tasks that virtually all legislators must attend to: answering constituent mail (and email), pursuing "cases" (often regarding bureaucratic glitches) that constituents bring to their attention, seeking new benefits and protecting existing ones for local interests, and maintaining at least minimal knowledge about major legislation under consideration. Much of this work reflects the service and allocation responsiveness that make up a good part of representation (see chapter 1).

Beyond these essential tasks and routine office maintenance, such as person-nel and scheduling, the personal office can be constructed to serve the specific

Table 8.2 Rep. Justin Amash (R-MI) Staff Salaries, 114th Congress

Position	Salary ($)
Chief of Staff	145,000
District Director	105,000
Senior Advisor	105,000
Senior District Representative	71,000
Legislative Assistant	55,000
District Representative	50,000
Legislative Aide	50,000
District Representative	47,000
Scheduler	45,000
Staff Assistant	35,000
District Representative	32,000
District Assistant	25,000
Shared Employee	19,000

Source: Rep. Justin Amash (R-MI), http://amash.house.gov/about-me/financial-disclosures.

interests of a particular legislator. Thus, the second generalization: members of Congress have tremendous discretion over how they use their basic resources. A marginal-seat representative may establish several district offices to deliver the best possible constituency service; she may use substantial amounts of franked mail and send out the maximum number of newsletters each year, all the while making do with a couple of legislative assistants. Conversely, a member who considers herself relatively safe, having consistently won 65 percent of the vote in reelection contests, might hire six or seven legislative aides to assist in achieving her own policy goals.

All House offices receive almost identical resources,[8] but because of the great differences in state populations, Senate operations vary considerably. For example, senators from large-population states may hire several press aides and open five district offices around the state. Because it is unlikely that large-state senators will meet most of their constituents face-to-face, they need more staff who are devoted to meeting with constituents directly and getting publicity. In contrast, a small-state senator has less need for press aides in a less extensive media market and needs fewer staff in the district. An alternative enterprise structure for the small-state senator might include more legislative aides on the personal staff in Washington.

The congressional enterprise, though stable in many ways since the 1970s, has changed substantially when it comes to communication; indeed, staffers for personal offices, committees, and party leaders all must become adept at handling a huge volume of communications. As Glassman notes, "In 2011, over 243 million emails were received by the House of Representatives, more than 20 times the amount of postal mail."[9] (See figure 8.2.) It may well be, however, that faxes represent the best way to make sure that legislators or relevant

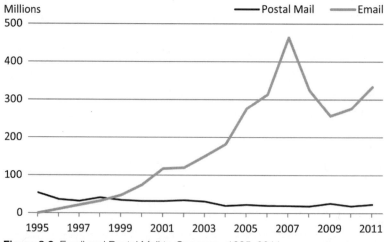

Figure 8.2 Email and Postal Mail to Congress, 1995–2011.

Source: Figure 1 from Matthew Glassman, "Tweet Your Congressman: The Rise of Electronic Communications in Congress," from the Congressional Research Service, *The Evolving Congress*, December 2014. Data provided by the House CAO and Office of the Senate Sergeant-at-Arms.

staffers receive a message in a timely way, in that emails are impersonal and regular U.S. Postal Service mail is scrutinized for possible problematic contents (e.g., anthrax or other dangerous substances).

Representatives and senators have become extremely active in initiating social media contacts, building up large followings. Almost all lawmakers have both Twitter and Facebook accounts, which allow for extensive direct communication with constituents and other interested parties. Leaders can certainly get their messages out widely, but the real advantage accrues to backbenchers, who can send targeted messages at virtually zero cost to large numbers of individuals who agree with them on given policy issues. Thus Rep. Meadows, as a HFC leader, or Rep. Steve King (R-IA), as a fierce opponent of illegal immigration, can communicate directly with national constituencies, and using social media they can bypass committee as well as party leadership structures. Moreover, their frequent appearances on cable TV news shows further advance their ability to develop a wide advocacy constituency.[10] In essence, marketing often overwhelms any impulse toward legislating.

In 1995, the Congress placed itself under the Fair Labor Standards Act and adopted the Congressional Accountability Act, both of which imposed some modest limitations on staff hiring and working conditions. Nevertheless, personal staff still serve at the pleasure of each legislator, who retains primary control over running their offices. Over the years, members have modestly cut expenses for personal staffs, but given the rise of technology and the expansion of campaign resources, overall enterprises have become larger and more expansive.

In sum, personal office resources represent a key source of individual power for any legislator. Legislators can use such resources, along with the control of their votes in committee and on the floor, to pursue their specific goals. These resources can also be used to build coalitions and seek consensus—even the most isolated and iconoclastic members need cooperation from their legislative peers if they are to act effectively in passing legislation. If offices tend to look roughly the same, this is largely because of a general similarity in members' goals—to win reelection (and perhaps advance to higher office), to produce good public policy, and to exercise power within the Congress. Their considerable resources allow members a base from which to act effectively as individuals; in particular, they can establish strong constituency ties that make it very difficult for challengers to mount effective challenges. Given the resources that allow 535 legislators to play to their constituencies and to operate with such flexibility, the personal office contributes greatly to the centrifugal tendencies of the Congress.

Committees and Subcommittees

There are strict budgetary limits on personal office resources, particularly on the numbers and salaries of staff. Whatever the member's goals may be, if a congressional enterprise is to grow, it must lay claim to other assets. Since the 1970s, the Congress has been generous in complementing the resources available to all its members, especially for those in the majority party, who, by dint of their status, chair all committees and subcommittees. Holding a committee or subcommittee chair in the House or Senate gives members a separate but connected source of public visibility and exposure. Members can use these positions to advance policy goals through hearings and bill markups; they can also use the investigative arm of committees to conduct oversight of the executive branch. Either way, members incorporate their committee power into their larger personal enterprise.

As table 8.1 illustrates, committee-based staff in the House tripled in the 1970s, and committee budgets grew even faster. If the committee system of the 1950s and early 1960s had remained intact, this change would simply have meant more resources under the control of a handful of powerful full committee chairs. But subcommittees proliferated in the 1970s, and their chairs came to control substantial resources and power. Not only did the total committee staff in the House grow between 1970 and 1990, the subcommittee allocation of staff also grew, from 23.2 percent of total committee staff in 1970 to 45.2 percent twenty years later.[11] In 1970, only one in four subcommittee chairs controlled their own staff, an average of four aides. By 1989, almost half the subcommittee chairs had such control, and the average staff was ten. These figures understate the actual control of staff by subcommittee chairs in the pre-1995 era, however. Although various full committee chairs may have formally controlled hiring, their subcommittee chairs often chose their own aides. In short, the committee structure greatly bolstered the centrifugal tendencies in Congress, even as Democratic House leaders were becoming more powerful.

In the 104th Congress (1995–1997), the majority Republicans moved immediately to enhance the power of full committees by placing the responsibility for hiring staff with committee chairs and limiting the number of subcommittees permitted for most committees to five. In addition, committee staff numbers were cut by one-third, as Republicans made good on their promise to trim staffing levels (see table 8.1). Overall, the individual enterprises of many members—most notably Democrats and subcommittee chairs—were substantially reduced, while Republican committee chairs came to control a much greater proportion of available resources. In an admittedly extreme example, as noted, former Energy and Commerce Committee chair, Rep. John Dingell, went from having hundred aides as committee chair to twenty aides as a ranking member.[12] According to the Congressional Research Service, House committee staff decreased by 44 percent during the years 1993–1996, and in the post-2011 period, after Republicans regained control of the House from the Democrats, staff levels for both chambers have stabilized at considerably lower levels (around 1200 in the House, 900 in the Senate) than existed between the late 1970s and the early 1990s.[13]

On the Senate side, committee and subcommittee aides are not as important to individual enterprises, given the much larger personal staffs that most senators command. In addition, about a third of majority-party senators chair full committees and thus control these considerable resources. Even so, with the relatively small number of senators, committee staff play major roles in developing policies, and Senate staff are ordinarily much more aggressive in their efforts on behalf of their bosses.[14] Given senators' larger numbers of committee assignments and attendant responsibilities, it makes sense that staff members take on great responsibilities in the Senate. Indeed, many top Senate aides function as entrepreneurs who operate to further the influence of their own bosses.[15] Such reliance serves to extend the reach of individual senators as they designate knowledgeable, skilled, and unelected staffers to act in their stead.

Still, many close observers of the Congress have concluded that the legislative branch has reduced its staffing too much, so that representatives and even senators rely too much on lobbyists and the executive branch for information. Exacerbating this problem are reductions in salaries for many staff positions, which makes leaving the Congress for lobbying positions (the so-called revolving door, see chapter 3) all the more enticing.

Enterprise and Influence: Two Illustrations

It is one thing to generalize that legislative enterprises allow representatives and senators to exert independent influence and quite another to demonstrate how such influence is exerted. Both Senator John McCain (R-AZ) and former representative Henry Waxman (D-CA) proved themselves masters at using their enterprises to affect policies beyond their obvious and immediate interests. McCain, of course, is a familiar figure from his POW days in Vietnam, his 2008 presidential campaign, and his high-profile success at passing campaign finance reform. Waxman, too, is well known, but more so among congressional junkies and policy wonks. Still, his policy impact over his forty-year tenure in Congress (1975–2015) may be viewed by historians to outweigh even that of the highly visible McCain. Below we provide in-depth profiles of the careers of each of these two congressional powerhouses.

John McCain: The Modern Maverick Given his 2008 presidential campaign (he ran for the nomination in 2000 but lost to George W. Bush), the 2002 passage of the McCain–Feingold campaign reform legislation, and his efforts to influence U.S. defense and foreign policies, John McCain has become perhaps the best-known U.S. senator. Such notoriety allowed him to gain attention for his policy ideas; for his often quirky, nonpartisan critiques of U.S. politics; and for his frequent attacks on pork-barrel spending.

McCain has benefited from having a fair number of personal office staff members, which he was able to supplement with those he received as chair of the Senate Commerce Committee from 1999 to 2004. Thus, when the space shuttle *Columbia* exploded, McCain used his committee-based enterprise to hold hearings on the space program and address an important issue in a timely way. In the 114th Congress (2015–2017), McCain became chair of the Armed Services Committee, which provides him with a platform to address a wide range of military issues. In the era of the Trump presidency, Senator McCain's role grew, simultaneously as the chair of a major committee within a unified Republican government *and* as a powerful, accessible source of questions and criticism toward the president, especially on international affairs, and of course his No vote on the bill to repeal Obamacare.

These committee and personal staff resources merely complement McCain's highly visible, media-friendly approach to politics and policymaking, in which he used the press to air his criticisms and ideas. In addition, McCain's enterprise directly assisted a wide range of Republican candidates, both before and after his 2008 presidential election loss to Barack Obama. Between 2009 and 2014, McCain, whose own Senate seat was never in danger, spent more than $26 million through his campaign committee and his leadership PAC.[16] These funds, which far outstrip his Senate resources, allowed him to travel, make contributions to other candidates, and appear at various candidates' fund-raisers.

To be sure, Senator McCain would have received a good deal of media attention simply because of his prominent positions and charismatic style, but his DC-based enterprise has helped him extend his reach throughout the Republican Party and beyond on a systematic basis. Over the years, McCain waxed and waned as a self-proclaimed "maverick," whose somewhat unpredictable policy stances and cross-party alliances have often provided him with political leverage. Although the increasingly partisan nature of the Senate constrained McCain somewhat, over the course of both Republican and Democratic administrations, he has retained substantial individual power, given his committee position, his status as a former presidential candidate, and his history as an independent voice.

Henry Waxman: Politics, Policy, and Persistence For sixteen years (1979–1995), Rep. Henry Waxman (D-CA; first elected in 1974) chaired a key House Energy and Commerce subcommittee, from which he had a platform to engage in extensive "policy entrepreneurship" activities on health and the environment. Waxman, who cultivated a highly expert and loyal staff, both in committee and in his personal office, developed a range of expertise across a host of health issues and helped rewrite the extension of clean air standards. Combining a powerful subcommittee chairmanship with substantial staff and his own energetic, persistent efforts to expand health and environmental coverage, Waxman personified the aggressive, tough-minded liberal who sought results rather than stardom. Not only did he involve himself in political campaigns through his well-oiled, Hollywood-based organization, but he also fought his own committee chairman (John Dingell) in a lengthy battle over clean air standards.

As interesting and important as Waxman's activism was in his first twenty years of service, it became all the more important in his last twenty years in the House leading up to his retirement in 2014. As a member of the minority between 1995 and early 2007, Waxman demonstrated how important a single member's enterprise could be. It was especially true after 1997, when he became the ranking minority member on the Government Reform Committee. Ironically, Waxman benefited mightily from the committee's well-staffed and thorough investigation into Bill Clinton. Chairman Dan Burton (R-IN) bulked up his committee with dozens of new hires, and in the process, Waxman obtained substantial new staff resources, given the two-to-one allocation ratio that the Republicans had agreed to. As ranking member, Waxman found himself with thirty to forty staffers, whom he could direct as he chose. Both Burton and Waxman used their committee position to bolster their individual powers, albeit in distinct ways.

Waxman did little to counter Burton's prosecution of Clinton; after all, the White House had plenty of resources to address his complaints. Rather, he created a minority staff operation that could provide research to fellow House members (and potential challengers) and establish a policy organization that could challenge both majority House Republicans and (later) President Bush over myriad issues, such as nuclear weapons in Iraq, irregularities in the 2004 elections, flu vaccines, House ethics rules changes, and food safety.

Subsequently, when Democrats gained control of the House after the 2006 elections, Waxman became, first, chair of Governmental Reform and then, in 2009, after successfully challenging John Dingell, chair of the Energy and Commerce Committee, which would provide him with a two-year stint with a Democratic Congress and president. Given the administration's emphasis on health care and economic stimulus, his impact as chair was not so much as a writer of legislation but as a coordinator within the House of the administration's bills (see chapter 7). After he returned to the minority in 2011, Waxman's ability to act effectively was reduced by budget cuts and the even more partisan nature of the House. At age seventy-five, he declined to run for reelection in 2014; he stated that neither the minority status nor the partisanship provoked his decision. In this age of intense polarization between parties and tighter party leadership control of committees and subcommittees, it is doubtful whether a newly elected member of the House can achieve the level of individual influence that Waxman did over his long career.

Congressional Caucuses

As much as the House members have taken advantage of expanding subcommittee resources, so too have they enlarged their enterprises by advancing to leadership positions in a host of special-interest caucuses, formally labeled Congressional Member Organizations (CMOs). These caucuses are subgroups of legislators who share common interests. By the mid-1980s, almost 150 such groups had formed, with House organizations outnumbering those in the Senate by a three-to-one ratio (91 in the House to 31 in the Senate; 25 more were bicameral groups).[17] For members, especially junior ones, caucuses have provided an opportunity to participate in the policymaking process in various ways, from constituency service, as with the Auto Task Force, to building a policy-based coalition, such as the Military Reform Caucus. Resources vary greatly across caucuses, but the strongest groups often command budgets into hundreds of thousands of dollars and substantial numbers of staff, but the largest, such as the Congressional Black Caucus (CBC) or the Congressional Hispanic Caucus (CHC), are usually connected to outside institutes.

Writing in the 1990s, Susan Webb Hammond argued that caucuses are significant precisely because the Congress requires "centralization to build majorities from disparate points of view" and to reflect the decentralizing pressures of representation.[18] As congressional centralization has increased, the role of caucuses has grown in importance, as witnessed by the number of CMOs that now exist—an incredible eight hundred as of 2016, according to the Congressional Research Service.[19] They represent a wide swath of interests, from American Kurds (the Kurdish American Caucus) to Republican physicians (GOP Doctors Caucus) to particular medical issues (the Lyme Disease Caucus). These groups can not only build bridges across members, parties, and committees, but they can also further decentralization by emphasizing differences in the interests of members' constituents.

The range of Congressional Member Organizations is great, and they allow individual members the opportunity to express their interests, at a very modest cost. Ringe and Victor note, "Lawmakers can decide for themselves how much time and effort they are willing to expend on their involvement in LMOs . . ., meaning that the transaction costs . . . are only as high as individual members want them to be."[20]

Indeed, joining most caucuses can be a cost-free task, often requiring little more than agreeing to place one's name on the membership roster—mere membership in a caucus does have its benefits. Former representative Bill Richardson (D-NM) observed, "If someone writes me on an arts issue, I can write back and say, 'I'm a member of the Congressional Arts Caucus.'"[21]

In addition, depending on the caucus, members can obtain different kinds of useful information. For example, *party-based* caucuses, such as the moderate-to-conservative Democratic "Blue Dogs," frame issues from their own perspective. *Personal-interest* caucuses offer information on subjects that unite members with similar interests, such as bourbon (!) or motorsports, and various *constituency-based* caucuses provide members who represent national (the CBC), regional (the Sunbelt Council), state/district (the Suburban Caucus), and industry (the Textile Caucus) interests with organized means to share information and help set the legislative agenda.[22]

Moreover, junior members have often found opportunities for action within caucuses that committees or party structures would not have allowed for years. Although many caucuses provide no resources to their leaders, some well-established groups have staffs that complement their leaders' regular enterprises. The access to such resources makes the leaders of such important caucuses as the CBC or CHC important forces within the House, all the more so as the numbers of African American and Hispanic members have grown sharply since the 1980s.

Finally, there can be some tangible benefits for holding a caucus leadership position, as individual donors and PACs seek out those with apparent influence on their specific issue, for example, the congressional drone caucus, whose formal name is the House Unmanned Systems Caucus (USC). In 2014, the USC was co-chaired by Rep. Buck McKeon (R-CA), who also chaired the House Armed Services Committee. His co-chair was veteran Democratic legislator Henry Cuellar (D-TX). Aerospace businesses have been eager to contribute to McKeon and Cuellar, along with the other fifty-six members of the caucus. From 2011 to mid-2013, the USC members received, in total, more than $2.3 million from drone-related businesses, as unmanned aircraft expenditures soared into the billions of dollars.[23] Moreover, the drone market is expected to double in coming years, which means drone manufacturers will likely look to the caucus to protect their industry.

With more than fifty members, and now led by Representatives Frank LoBiondo (R-NJ) and Daniel Lipinski (D-IL), the drone caucus is drawn largely from western and border states, where the manufacture and use of drones are concentrated. The USC does not go out of its way to publicize itself, but key lobbyists, some from universities and PACs, know who they are. Multiply this kind of arrangement many times over, and it becomes clear that caucuses provide a host of ways for organized interests to build close ties with lawmakers.

As Ringe and Victor demonstrate, LMOs do offer members a host of informational benefits at a very low cost.[24] Thus, both from an informational perspective and an influence-based point of view, the proliferation of congressional caucuses serves as a significant centrifugal force within an increasingly partisan, centralized institution.

Congressional Offices and Political Expenditures

On top of staff and office resources are piled hundreds of thousands of dollars of political expenditures, which the Congress has defined exceptionally broadly. For example, former representative and later convicted felon Carroll Hubbard (D-KY) once paid $3,000 in campaign funds for a portrait of his father. Although the exact political purpose of the painting remains unclear, the congressman enjoyed great freedom in defining political expenditures.[25] A wide range of so-called political expenditures systematically contributes to the overall congressional enterprise of many, though not all, incumbents. These include

- a professional campaign staff;
- substantial entertainment budgets;
- travel expenses (such as auto leases);
- political consultants;
- lawyers and accountants;
- civic and political donations;
- a fund-raising apparatus (parties and direct mail);
- investments, such as certificates of deposit[26] and a building that housed former representative Steve Neal's (D-NC) campaign organization; and
- contributions to civic groups and establishment of college scholarships.

Beyond using their own campaign funds, senators and representatives have made it a standard practice to set up their own PACs, called leadership PACs. These organizations have raised an average of about $46 million in each of the last four two-year election cycles.[27] There were almost six hundred such PACs in 2016, and their fund-raising and distributing capacities vary greatly. For example, in 2016, House Majority Leader Kevin McCarthy made contributions of more than $3.5 million, while Rep. Paul Gosar (R-AZ) gave not quite $3,000. Regardless, following an outside strategy of distributing leadership PAC funds to fellow partisans plays a major role in helping legislators gain powerful committee and party leadership positions *inside* the chamber.

With the continuing growth in campaign and PAC fund-raising by safe incumbents, their enterprises have amassed large political slush funds that they can use to build their political careers at home, through gifts, entertainment, and scholarships—and in the Capitol, through large contributions to other members' campaigns or to national party organizations. Moreover, with few limitations on spending, leadership PACs can bring on staff, fund dinners, and subsidize further fund-raising. Thus, lobbyists, who are barred from buying legislators anything of value, including meals, are invited to a fund-raising dinner, often hosted by a lobbying firm or a set of the firm's clients. The candidate attends and pays for the dinner from his or her own PAC account, while receiving tens of thousands of dollars in contributions at the event. Some lawmakers go so far as to hire their own relatives to staff their personal PACs, often at substantial salaries. How far these limits extend was dramatically demonstrated in 2003, when former representative Gary Condit (D-CA), whose career was cut short by an affair with a DC intern who was later murdered, distributed most of his $200,000 in excess campaign funds to his two children.[28] He labeled them as consultants on a documentary film but provided no clear records of any work.

Although congressional rules formally require expenditures to have a direct political purpose, almost no enforcement has taken place. Indeed, when contemplating a run against an entrenched incumbent, challengers not only face the Herculean task of raising funds to match those of sitting legislators, but they also confront established enterprises that have often been constructed over the years by substantial spending of both federal funds and privately raised political monies. Crucial here is the fact that many of these funds were expended to perpetuate strong, continuing enterprises—organizations that allow incumbents maximum flexibility in pursuing their individual goals. Both the necessity of raising money (for competitive races) and the benefits of raising money (for relatively safe legislators who can distribute it to others) lead to the establishment of permanent, highly professional campaign finance operations for most sitting legislators. Fund-raising to provide for a large campaign establishment has become a constant preoccupation. Although it is theoretically and legally separate from a House or Senate member's office enterprise, the advantages that come with incumbency in building a personal enterprise directly affect his or her reelection chances and increasingly relate to advancement within the Congress, as prospective leaders offer financial assistance to candidates in competitive races.

Additional Enterprise Resources

Legislators' enterprises extend far beyond the structures of personal offices, committees, caucuses, and reelection operations. Many additional resources are available to all, and access to others resides formally or informally with key committee and party leaders.

Congressional Support Agencies One key resource on Capitol Hill is the Congressional Research Service (CRS), whose six hundred researchers respond to requests from all members —no matter their party or majority/minority status—in a reasonably equitable manner. In terms of providing basic information on a wide range of questions (from setting up an office to an economic analysis of the North American Free Trade Agreement [NAFTA]), CRS is an invaluable source of timely insights. On more complex questions, which can require extensive staff time, CRS is more likely to act quickly and comprehensively on requests from formal leaders within the committee or party hierarchy.

Likewise, the Governmental Accountability Office (GAO), with 3,350 employees and a $557 million budget, and the Congressional Budget Office (CBO) provide only modest assistance to legislative backbenchers, even though any member can request studies or information.[29] On the other hand, all members of Congress benefit from the independent information generated by these support agencies through reports and testimony. More than any other legislative body in the world, the Congress has sources of information and analysis that are intentionally separate from the executive branch and the federal bureaucracy. All members can use the volumes of information to help form their own policy positions, explain these positions and related votes to their constituents, and resist the entreaties of party leaders and presidents alike.[30]

Leadership Resources During the Democratic postreform era in the House (1981–1994), the joke went that any time one wanted to get the attention of a House Democrat and couldn't remember his name, all one had to do was call out "Mr. Chairman," and the legislator would respond; approximately half the 258 Democrats in the 103rd Congress chaired a committee or subcommittee, and almost all Democratic senators were chairs of some committee or subcommittee. This inclusive leadership structure helped define the Democratic postreform House, but relatively few resources accompanied most of these positions.

Only at the top of the ladder do leadership roles confer many resources, for either political party in either chamber. For these few representatives and senators, though, the benefits are substantial. Serving as a majority or minority leader in the House or Senate typically adds twenty or so staffers to a leader's individual enterprise. In addition, the four chairs of the respective parties' House and Senate campaign committees enjoy increased staffing and travel budgets as they raise funds, recruit candidates, and provide campaign assistance in each election cycle. Also, as congressional parties organize more legislative activities, leadership staffs have steadily increased (table 8.3), almost doubling over the past thirty years, while staffing for personal offices and committees has declined.[31]

Table 8.3 Congressional Party Leadership Staff Levels, 1981–2015

Year	1981	1991	2001	2011	2015
House	127	149	166	201	201
Senate	106	125	221	214	173

Source: Data from Norman J. Ornstein, Thomas E. Mann, Michael J. Malbin, Andrew Rugg, and Raffaela Wakeman, eds., *Vital Statistics on Congress, 2017 Edition* (Washington, DC: Brookings Institution), table 5.1. https://www.brookings.edu/wp-content/uploads/2017/01/vitalstats_ch5_tbl1.pdf.

SPOTLIGHT

Senator Charles Schumer: An Enterprising Leader

Senate Minority Leader Charles "Chuck" Schumer (D-NY) has been a fixture in New York politics for over four decades and his ambition, self-promotion skills, and a heavy reliance on a small network of trusted staffers have propelled him and his enterprise to the height of party leadership in the Senate. Schumer entered electoral politics in 1974 when his friend and mentor Steve Solarz (D-NY) was elected to Congress, leaving vacant his seat representing Brooklyn in the New York State Assembly. With Solarz's endorsement, Schumer won the Assembly seat. Six years later, Schumer successfully ran for the open U.S. House seat adjacent to Solarz's district in Brooklyn. During his House tenure, Schumer developed a reputation for self-promotion. During a disagreement with Senator Bob Dole (R-KS) over the 1995 Major League Baseball strike, Dole famously remarked about Schumer, "The most dangerous place in Washington is between him and a camera."

Schumer was elected to the U.S. Senate in 1998, defeating the former vice-presidential candidate Geraldine Ferraro in the primary and unseating three-term incumbent Republican Al D'Amato in what remains the widest margin of defeat (ten percentage points) since 1982 for an incumbent senator when that senator's party did not control the White House. Senator Schumer did not get along well with Majority Leader Tom Daschle (D-SD) and seriously considered entering the 2006 New York governor's race to face off against the then state Attorney General Eliot Spitzer in the Democratic primary. But the new Senate Majority Leader Harry Reid (D-NV) respected and admired Schumer, offering him both the chairmanship of the Democratic Senatorial Campaign Committee (DSCC) and a seat on the powerful Finance Committee to entice him to remain in the Senate. Schumer agreed, and the Democrats' success in the 2006 midterm elections prompted Reid to create and appoint Schumer to a new leadership position: Vice Chairman of the Democratic conference. When Senator Reid announced that he would retire at the end of the 114th Congress, he endorsed Schumer to be the next party leader. Senate Democrats elected Senator Schumer as Minority Leader on November 16, 2016, making him the first Jewish party leader in Senate history.

During his time in the House and the Senate, Schumer became known for relying on a tight network of trusted staff that specialized in facilitating different aspects of his job. As former staffer Jim Kessler put it, "His staffers are his inner circle. He uses his staff as his counsel to a great idea." Schumer demands long hours and a high quality of output from his staffers, which led Hillary Clinton to once call his office "the boot camp of politics." Mike Lynch, Schumer's chief of staff since his 1998 Senate campaign, focuses on the bigger picture for Schumer and suggests ideas for action based on the senator's preferences. Another staffer is charged with keeping Schumer attuned to local issues and coordinating local travel for the senator, as he makes a point to visit all sixty-two New York counties every year, something one of his Senate predecessors from New York, Daniel Patrick Moynihan, also did. Other staff roles include acting as the main point of contact for other Senate members, translating Schumer's policy ideas into concrete legislation, serving as the major communication link to the media, and crafting party caucus floor strategy.

In short, Senator Schumer's rise to power was not only a function of his own personal style and ambition; it reflected his ability to effectively utilize the resources and personnel at his disposal.

The information in this section is taken from multiple sources as follows: Seung Min Kim, "Inside Schumer's Inner Circle," *Politico*, January 3, 2017, http://www.politico.com/story/2017/01/senate-schumer-233047; Alexander Bolton, "Schumer Grabs New Power," *The Hill*, March 28, 2015, http://thehill.com/homenews/senate/237269-schumer-grabs-new-power; Emily Heil, "Chuck Schumer and that 'Most Dangerous Place' Joke," *The Washington Post*, April 1, 2015, https://www.washingtonpost.com/news/reliable-source/wp/2015/04/01/chuck-schumer-and-that-most-dangerous-place-joke/?utm_term=.c35c230dd572; Richard L. Berke, "Washington at Work: Side by Side by Solarz and Schumer: A Rivalry," *The New York Times*, April 7, 1991, http://www.nytimes.com/1991/04/07/nyregion/washington-at-work-side-by-side-by-solarz-and-schumer-a-rivalry.html?pagewanted=1.

For the most part, party-based resources assist in centralizing the power of leaders, but this is not always the case. In 1993, House Democratic whip David Bonior (D-MI) emerged as the leading critic of NAFTA, a pact that Speaker Foley and President Bill Clinton strongly supported. Bonior pledged not to use the resources of his office to oppose the treaty, but given the integrated nature of the congressional enterprise, it was difficult for him not to use— directly or indirectly—his party resources as he fought the policy position of his legislative party and his president.[32] Overall, however, larger staffs have meant that party leaders in both chambers have the organizational, policy, and—increasingly—communications resources to hold their caucuses together throughout the legislative process. Moreover, since both chambers have remained electorally competitive since 1994, leadership staffs increasingly work more at political messaging than communications designed to help pass legislation. In short, winning or maintaining power has become the central goal for congressional leaders.[33] It does not mean that party leaders always get what they want. Republican Speaker John Boehner had a very testy relationship with GOP House members who were affiliated with the Tea Party in the 112th–114th Congresses. And these problems did not disappear when Paul Ryan took over for Boehner as Speaker. For example, in the early months of the 115th Congress in 2017, he was opposed by vocal GOP members of the HFC. If there is a serious disagreement over policy or tactics, whether among Democrats in the 1990s or Republicans in recent years, no amount of staff work or other leadership incentives can overcome the intraparty fragmentation. Charles Schumer (D-NY), who became Senate Minority Leader in January 2017, works to corral the Senate Democrats and faces constant challenges to hold the party together as an effective opposition to Republican policies when necessary.

THE CONGRESSIONAL ENTERPRISE:
BLESSING AND CURSE

Of all the changes that have affected the U.S. Congress in the post–World War II era, none has been more striking than the expansion of the individual lawmaker's enterprise. From the moment new members take the oath of office, they each control $1.25 million worth of staff, communications, travel, and research capacities that allow them to commit substantial resources to running for reelection, drafting legislation, overseeing the bureaucracy, or seeking higher office. Moreover, most of them raise campaign funds that underwrite an almost limitless array of political purposes. The congressional enterprise helps all lawmakers to claim credit for governmental programs, take positions on the issues of the day, and relentlessly advertise their accomplishments. But this is just the minimum enterprise, the stripped-down model that every first-term member gets upon arriving on Capitol Hill (along with the smallest, most distant office from the floor of the House or Senate).

Virtually all senators and many House members enjoy the services of committee staffers, many of them benefit from caucus positions, and most create their own PACs to reward their fellow legislators and advance their own careers. At the heart of every congressional enterprise stands the individual senator or representative, to whom each of their respective staff members, campaign consultants, and fundraisers owes his or her job. And their collective task is to promote the career and interests of their principal—the representative or senator. Party leaders and committee chairs regularly seek their support, but legislators know that they *can* defy their leaders and retain their seats. When it comes to reelection, party leaders and committee chairs enjoy no control over the average legislator's enterprise. All House members understand that if re-elected, they will retain the core personal staff of their enterprise, to say nothing of the other campaign, committee, and caucus resources they may have accumulated. In short, party leaders must negotiate with 435 representatives and 100 senators, who control their own electoral destinies and have enough resources to affect the policy process when they so desire. For all the decentralizing forces of subcommittees, committees, and incumbency, the heart of congressional fragmentation lies in the strength and flexibility of the legislator as enterprise, and this is especially so for the smaller Senate, whose members enjoy procedural advantages that provide extensive individual leverage.

Even so, most legislators, especially in the House, have chosen more and more to operate as part of a party team. As the legislative process, again more so in the House, has become increasingly centralized and party dominated, the individual entrepreneur, with his or her own enterprise, has become less significant. Within the House, at least, the highly partisan context of postreform congressional politics has reduced the benefits, and increased the costs, of independent action.

Recommended Readings

Caro, Robert. *The Path to Power*. New York: Knopf, 1982.

Frank, Barney. *Frank: A Life in Politics from the Great Society to Same-Sex Marriage*. New York: Farrar, Straus and Giroux, 2015.

Grimmer, Justin, Sean J. Westwood, and Solomon Messing. *The Impression of Influence: Legislator Communication, Representation, and Democratic Accountability*. Princeton, NJ: Princeton University Press, 2015.

Loomis, Burdett. *The New American Politician*. New York: Basic Books, 1988.

Ringe, Nils, and Jennifer Victor. *Bridging the Information Gap*. Ann Arbor: University of Michigan Press, 2013.

Useful Resources

Congressional Management Foundation: http://www.congressfoundation.org

Congressional Research Service: http://www.crs.gov

Congressman Justin Amash: http://amash.house.gov

Notes

[1] Called the Commerce Committee until 1981.

[2] For details on congressional offices, see various useful publications from the Congressional Management Foundation, including *Setting Course: A Congressional Management Guide* (Washington, DC: Congressional Management Foundation). There are various editions.

[3] See Robert Salisbury and Kenneth Shepsle, "U.S. Congressman as Enterprise," *Legislative Studies Quarterly* 6 (November 1981): 559–76; Burdett A. Loomis, "The Congressional Office as a 'Small (?) Business,'" *Publius* 9 (Summer 1979); and Loomis, *The New American Politician* (New York: Basic Books, 1988).

[4] An excellent example here is Eric Redman's description of his work on behalf of former Washington senator Warren Magnuson, who gave Redman and other staff members broad latitude to formulate legislation that encouraged doctors to serve in needy areas. See Redman, *The Dance of Legislation* (New York: Touchstone, 1974). In 1995, the Congress adopted the Congressional Accountability Act, which requires it to adhere to almost all federal laws, including those on conditions of employment. This may have a modest effect on the relations between legislators and their staffers, but the essentially personal and political nature of these ties remains.

[5] Salisbury and Shepsle, "U.S. Congressman as Enterprise," 563.

[6] These include the General Accounting Office, the Congressional Research Service, and the Congressional Budget Office.

[7] This is an approximate figure, which includes all salaries, benefits, and other expenses. Travel allowances vary considerably depending on distance from Washington; see Ida A. Brudnick, *Congressional Salaries and Allowances: In Brief* (Washington, DC: Congressional Research Service), http://www.senate.gov/CRSReports/crs-publish.cfm?pid=%270E%2C*PL%5B%3D%23P% 20%20%0A.

[8] See Brad Fitch, *Setting Course: A Congressional Management Guide* (108th Congress ed.) (Washington, DC: Congressional Management Foundation, 2003).

[9] Matthew Glassman, "Tweet Your Congressman: The Rise of Electronic Communications in Congress," from the Congressional Research Service, *The Evolving Congress*, December 2014, 95–106, http://www.gpo.gov/fdsys/pkg/CPRT-113SPRT89394/pdf/CPRT-113SPRT89394.pdf.

[10] Jane Mansbridge, "Rethinking Representation," *American Political Science Review* 97 (November 2003): 515–28.

[11] Data from Steven S. Smith and Christopher J. Deering, *Committees in Congress,* 2nd ed. (Washington, DC: CQ Press, 1990), 152.

[12] Allen Freedman, "A Survivor Steps into Minority Role," *Congressional Quarterly Weekly Report,* April 8, 1995, 989.

[13] Thomas Mann, Norman Ornstein, and Michael Malbin, *Vital Statistics on Congress,* 2016, Washington, DC: Brookings, "Staffs of House and Senate Committees, 1891–2015." https://www.brookings.edu/wp-content/uploads/2017/01/vitalstats_ch5_full.pdf.

[14] See Michael J. Malbin, *Unelected Representatives* (New York: Basic Books, 1980).

[15] See David Price, "Professionals and 'Entrepreneurs': Staff Orientations and Policy Making on Three Senate Committees," *Journal of Politics* 33 (May 1971): 316–36.

[16] "Senator John McCain, *Opensecrets.org,* https://www.opensecrets.org/politicians/summary.php?type=C&cid=N00006424&newMem=N&cycle=2014 (accessed February 26, 2015).

[17] Susan Webb Hammond, "Congressional Caucuses in the Policy Process," in *Congress Reconsidered,* 4th ed., ed. Lawrence C. Dodd and Bruce I. Oppenheimer (Washington, DC: CQ Press, 1989), 355. See also Susan W Hammond, *Congressional Caucuses in National Policy Making* (Baltimore: Johns Hopkins University Press, 1998).

[18] Susan Webb Hammond, "Congressional Caucuses in the 104th Congress," in *Congress Reconsidered,* 6th ed., ed. Lawrence J. Dodd and Bruce I. Oppenheimer (Washington, DC: CQ Press, 1997), 276. See also Hammond, *Congressional Caucuses in National Policy Making.*

[19] Matthew E. Glassman, "Congressional Member Organizations: Their Purpose and Activities, History, and Formation," *Congressional Research Service* report, January 26, 2017; Sarah Mimms, "Got a Hobby or a General Interest? There's a Congressional Caucus for That," *National Journal,* April 18, 2014, http://www.nationaljournal.com/congress/got-a-hobby-or-general-interest-there-s-a-congressional-caucus-for-that-20140418 (accessed February 27, 2015).

[20] Nils Ringe and Jennifer Victor, *Bridging the Information Gap* (Ann Arbor: University of Michigan Press, 2013), 6.

[21] Loomis, *New American Politician,* 150.

[22] Hammond, "Congressional Caucuses in the 104th Congress," 278ff.

[23] Jill Replogle, "Dronemakers and Their Friends in Washington," KPBS, April 11, 2013, http://www.kpbs.org/news/2012/jul/05/drone-makers-friends-washington (accessed February 27, 2015).

[24] Ringe and Victor, *Bridging the Information Gap,* 49.

[25] Sarah Fritz and Dwight Morris, *Gold-Plated Politics* (Washington, DC: CQ Press, 1992), 29–30.

[26] Investment income in the 1980s was often truly substantial in that bank CDs paid handsomely. With lower rates of return in the 1990s, some members invested their excess cash in the stock market.

[27] "Leadership PACs," *Opensecrets.org,* https://www.opensecrets.org/pacs/industry.php?txt=Q03&cycle=2014 (accessed February 27, 2015). The remainder of this paragraph also relies on this source.

[28] Michael Doyle, "Condit Paid His Children $210k from Political Fund," *Fresno Bee,* February 4, 2003.

[29] Another support agency, the Office of Technology Assessment, was defunded and dismantled by the Republican-controlled 104th Congress.

[30] At the same time, party and committee leaders can commission studies that will serve to support their own positions. Information can serve both centrifugal and centripetal purposes.

[31] See Frances Lee, *Insecure Majorities* (Chicago: University of Chicago Press, 2016) for an extended discussion of the growth of leaders' messaging staffs, pp. 113–17.

[32] Majority Leader Richard Gephardt (D-MO) also opposed the pact but took a less publicly aggressive stance. He announced that any actions against NAFTA taken by him would emanate from his personal office, but again the relationships among various parts of the enterprise make such a commitment difficult to monitor.

[33] Lee, *Insecure Majorities.*

CHAPTER 9

The Competitive Congress

Centrifugal Forces in a Partisan Era

Conflict and competition between the two major political parties, Republicans and Democrats, is more than 150 years old. When conflict grows too intense, gridlock results and Congress comes to a virtual standstill. However, when pressing public policy needs to be addressed, the two parties can sometimes come together to produce a solution.

In both the House and the Senate, the combining of individualism/fragmentation with enhanced partisanship has made for a Congress that encourages—simultaneously—both centrifugal (decentralizing) and centripetal (centralizing) forces. Do we have a Congress in which a majority party sets out a coherent agenda that it can act on? Or do we have a new phase of governing where presidents become increasingly powerful in an era of congressional dysfunction, regardless of which party nominally controls the legislative branch?

The week of May 1–5, 2017, offered a perfect illustration of the two conflicting tendencies that we have emphasized throughout this book. The week started out with Congress under enormous pressure to reach a compromise on a spending bill for the remainder of Fiscal Year 2017, which ran through September 30 of that year. This bill reflects the sort of measure that Congress must pass in order to keep the government functioning. President Trump had demanded that Congress include $1.5 billion to continue building a wall along the nation's southern border to enhance security, but conservatives in the GOP were skeptical of both the wall's cost and its effectiveness. At the same time, many of these conservatives demanded that the bill delete all federal funding for health care services provided by Planned Parenthood. President Trump supported this, but more moderate GOP members of the House and Senate objected. In the end, neither funding the border wall nor defunding Planned Parenthood was included in the omnibus spending bill, which passed both houses by the end of the week with bipartisan support, thus avoiding the pitfalls of some previous budget battles that lead to government shutdowns.

This relatively smooth funding process stands in stark contrast to previous years with GOP majority control in the House (and the Senate as of 2015) and a sitting Democratic president. In their opposition to President Obama, enough House Republicans were so intent on their small-government agenda that they prevented their majority from acting as a unified party to pass these types of bills.[1] These conflicts have created greater uncertainty in the legislative process and more frequent partial government shutdowns than has been typical of Republican- or Democratic-controlled Congresses in the past. The ability of both parties to avoid a shutdown in May 2017 may signal a change under a unified Republican government, although budget and debt ceiling issues continued to test the legislative process for the remainder of the year.

That same May 2017 week, the House of Representatives passed the American Health Care Act (ACHA), which was designed to repeal and replace the Affordable Care Act (Obamacare); the vote was 217–213, a margin of victory much smaller than the 24-vote GOP House majority. Republicans had tried earlier in the year to pass a similar bill but could not muster enough support in their own party to do so (see chapter 6). This second vote was considered a "nail-biter" by most observers because earlier in the week conservatives and moderates were lined up against it. However, after some personal lobbying by President Trump, and some changes to the bill removing protections for pre-existing conditions but adding extra funding to help individuals in high risk categories pay for coverage, conservatives supported it bill. Still, twenty Republican House members voted against the legislation over concerns ranging from a lack of cost estimate for it to specific provisions that would roll back protections for pre-existing conditions.[2] Despite a victory for the majority party, it was a very slim one that did not resolve some of the decentralizing constituency-based conflicts within the House GOP. Indeed, an even weaker repeal effort did not pass the Senate in August, leaving Republican promises to overturn Obamacare unfulfilled.

These two examples tell us a lot about the state of the contemporary Congress. It is polarized between the two parties, and even the GOP majority in the House has a difficult time in agreeing to the most basic legislation. The Senate, under both Democratic and Republican control, while remaining slow, unwieldy, and obstructionist, has proved somewhat more capable of governing. In addition, tensions and showdowns between the legislative and executive branches have increasingly shaped the politics of Capitol Hill.

THE OXYMORONIC CONGRESS: INDIVIDUALISTIC PARTISANSHIP

If, as John Aldrich and David Rohde contend, the "condition" of party (as measured by the size and unity of the majority, especially in the House) defines congressional politics,[3] why doesn't Congress function more efficiently under majority-party control, both in times of unified and divided government? In part, the answer is self-evident; that is, we live in a system of checks and balances, where the president and the courts, to say nothing of the bureaucracy, have their say. In this book, we have provided examples of how the courts and Congress can check presidential powers, as well as the president's ability to use bargaining and the veto power to accomplish his policy goals. Still, some of the limits on parties derive from the nature of congressional politics, both in permanent and transitory ways. Among the permanent limitations is the strength of individual lawmakers, both to win reelection and to use the resources of their enterprises (see chapter 8) to affect the policy process.

In the past twenty years, however, the greatest limitation on even well-disciplined legislative parties has been the relatively small size of the majorities. The elections of 1994 through 2002 produced an average majority of 228 for the Republicans in the House, against 206 Democrats (and one Democratic-leaning Independent). The election of 2004 expanded the Republicans' House majority by three seats (232–202–1), returning the Republicans to their largest margin since the 1994 elections. In 2007, the Democrats took control with an almost identical majority of 233–202, which they increased two years later to 258–181, before losing control of the House in the 2010 midterm elections. Since then the Republicans have held control of the House by an average of 239–196; in the 115th Congress it was 241–194. Although it is an accomplishment to retain control of Congress for multiple years, Republicans have done so by depending on a core group of very conservative members. When those members, many of whom constitute the House Freedom Caucus, do not support the party leadership, it becomes very difficult to guarantee victory for the party's policies on the House floor.

SPOTLIGHT

Representative Charlie Dent: The Tuesday Group and the Price of a Narrow House Majority

In the era of the competitive Congress, winning over as many party votes as possible, including moderates like Rep. Charles "Charlie" Dent (R-PA), became crucial as to whether the majority party can govern effectively. Representative Dent, first elected to Congress in 2004, was a center-right member who represents a center-right congressional district. Prior to entering electoral politics, Dent worked as a development officer for Lehigh University, as an electronics salesman, and as an aide to Rep. Don Ritter (R), who, like Dent would more than a decade later, represented Pennsylvania's 15th congressional district. Dent served for eight years in the Pennsylvania House of Representatives, and six years in the State Senate. During his time in the state legislature, Dent developed a penchant for crafting legislation that could garner bipartisan support, such as creating a program designed to expand health insurance coverage for low-income, working adults. In the House, Dent sponsored legislation that advances the use of clean energy technology in public transportation, increases funding for medical research through the National Institutes of Health, and ensures fair compensation for injured medical patients. Dent served on the House Appropriations Committee, and until 2016, he was the chair of the House Committee on Ethics.

In the 114th and 115th Congresses, Rep. Dent served as co-chair of the Tuesday Group, an informal caucus of moderate House Republicans originally formed after the 1994 Republican wave to counterbalance the newfound conservatism in the Republican membership. Though not as organized and difficult to persuade as the far-right House Freedom Caucus (HFC), Tuesday Group members can still make party leadership think twice about acceding to the demands of the HFC. While the group has occasionally proposed moderate legislation, especially in its earlier days, members admit that its greatest impact has been behind the scenes, preventing many potentially divisive measures from seeing the light of day.

But even the most devoted and experienced politicians have their limit, and in late 2017, Charlie Dent reached that limit and announced that he would not seek reelection. Dent gave a number of reasons for his departure from the House, and one of them was that "even the most simple basic tasks of government have become excruciatingly difficult."[4] As discussed in this chapter, narrow House majorities of either party are frequently beholden to a myriad of internal factions, whether ideological, economic, or geographic. Moreover, constant and repeated infighting takes its toll, especially on members of Congress who value legislative productivity.

Democrats greeted Dent's announcement with cautious optimism because Pennsylvania's 15th district can be described as somewhat competitive. In 2008, for example, Barack Obama won the district by five percentage points. But in 2016, the district swung back to the GOP at the presidential level when Donald Trump won by seven points. In such a competitive district, whoever holds the seat will sometimes have to oppose their party to appeal to the majority of their constituents, as Dent did when he twice voted against the Obamacare repeal bill. When a party holds a narrow House majority, as the Republicans do in the 115th Congress, Tuesday Group-type moderates in relatively competitive districts like Charlie Dent can make governing in a polarized environment more challenging. It remains to be seen who will succeed him, but that person will no doubt face the same pressures, inside and out of the halls of Congress.

The information in this section is taken from multiple sources as follows: Jesse Zwick, "Tuesday Mourning," *The New Republic*, January 29, 2011, https://newrepublic.com/article/82420/tuesday-group-gop; David Nir, "Daily Kos Elections' Presidential Results by Congressional District for the 2016 and 2012 Elections," *The Daily Kos*, November 19, 2016, http://www.dailykos.com/story/2012/11/19/1163009/-Daily-Kos-Elections-presidential-results-by-congressional-district-for-the-2012-2008-elections; Ballotpedia, "Pennsylvania's 15th Congressional District," https://ballotpedia.org/Pennsylvania%27s_15th_Congressional_District; United States Congressman Charlie Dent, " Biography," https://dent.house.gov/biography.

At the same time, the Republican Party has a smaller group of moderate members who can also exert their political will on the party's agenda and its subsequent success on the House floor. One such member is Charlie Dent (R-PA) who has proven that he will buck the party when he believes its policies do not serve his constituents well.

Two well-established trends indicate that a rough partisan balance is likely to remain for some time. First, the capacity of incumbent House members to win reelection remains a cornerstone of Congress in the modern era. After the relatively high turnovers of 1992 and 1994 (see chapter 4), incumbent survival rates averaged about 95 percent over the next ten elections, through 2016. The price of entry to mount a competitive congressional House campaign stands at about $1.5 million; for a Senate seat, that number rises to $11 million.[5] Second, and directly related to the first trend, most House members come from relatively homogeneous districts that are not ordinarily competitive. Two decades ago, the number of truly competitive House seats stood at fewer than fifty, and in recent years, that number has approached twenty. One look at the geography of representation in the House demonstrates the implications of this development (see figure 9.1). Districts in much of the South, substantial parts of the Midwest, and much of the Mountain West are disproportionately represented by Republicans, often of a very conservative stripe. Conversely, Democrats clearly dominate in the East, on the West Coast, and some of the upper Midwest. Overall, the congressional map favors Republicans, whose strength is more widely distributed than that of Democrats.

Ironically, the small number of competitive races—the remainder of the "vanishing marginals" (see chapter 5)—has not meant that less money is spent on congressional campaigning. Rather, the national parties have focused their attention and funding on a relatively small number of hotly contested seats; in 2014 and 2016, there were about thirty "toss-up" races, and that was probably a generous estimate.[6] In addition, both parties' congressional leaders in Congress have encouraged their colleagues to send excess campaign funds to the closest races. In short, the campaigns for a small number of competitive House seats have become nationally important. Indeed, the 2017 Georgia 6th district special election race to succeed Tom Price, who became HHS Secretary, exceeded $50 million. Still, no matter how much party and party-related funding funnels into a handful of close races, narrow House majorities of either party will remain beholden to a myriad of internal factions, whether ideological, economic, or geographic.

At the same time, since 2006 there have been several "wave" elections in which national forces favor one party or the other. Despite the relative safety of most incumbents, such waves can change partisan control of Congress in any given election.

In the Senate, a higher percentage of the seats are competitive, and a higher percentage of members turn over each Congress than in the House. Since 1981, this has meant that the pendulum has swung back and forth more frequently in determining majority status. A single election can bring majority control of the Senate to a party, but the very next election can take it away. Recent history shows this pattern starkly: Republicans controlled the Senate from 2002 to 2006, Democrats controlled it from 2007 to 2014, and control returned to

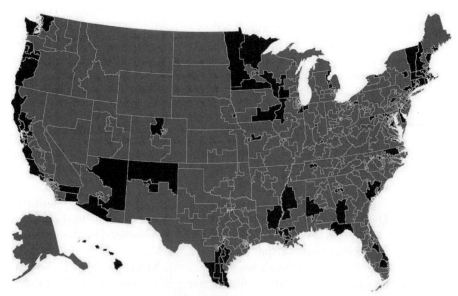

Figure 9.1 The 114th House of Representatives.

Source: RealClearPolitics, http://www.realclearpolitics.com/epolls/2014/house/2014_elections_house_map.html (accessed March 5, 2015).

Note: Republican seats are represented in medium gray, Democratic seats in black.

the Republicans in 2015. The major difference in terms of numerical majorities in the House and Senate is the relative weight of each additional member. In the House, a simple majority with a margin of one or two votes can win a floor vote; thus, even a bare partisan majority in the House offers the potential for complete control of floor proceedings. In the Senate, the key majority size for legislative victories is sixty senators, nine more than a simple majority, because that is what is required to invoke cloture and shut down a filibuster. Although the Democrats had a majority of sixty seats in 2009, it only lasted for one year; Republican Scott Brown won a special election in 2010 for the vacant seat of the late Senator Ted Kennedy (D-MA); thus the Democratic majority fell back down to fifty-nine. The loss of that one seat meant that Democrats no longer had the sixty votes necessary to break a filibuster; to do so after Scott Brown came to the Senate would require that they pull votes from the Republican minority. Beyond that, the individualistic nature of the Senate means that getting to fifty votes can prove difficult for a Senate majority, as has been the case in the first year of the Trump administration.

Congressional parties consistently act, through agenda control, messaging, and the distribution of campaign funds, to create the best chance possible to retain (or gain) majority status.[7] To do that requires coordination and strong leadership, even in the Senate, where leaders have limited powers.

Even though party unity has intensified in the Senate since the 1990s, a senator's individual power ultimately does not derive from the party. Rather, the nature of the Senate is such that even if one party gains seats, each individual senator remains a political entity all his or her own. As both Democratic and Republican Senate leaders fully understand, any senator can be obstructionist, even to his own party, but minority-party senators are far more likely to do so than their majority-party peers. Therefore, even complete majority-party discipline does not guarantee victory on the Senate floor, where, on most issues, sixty votes are required to overcome a filibuster or its threat.

Ironically, the contemporary Senate continues to fulfill its traditional role of being the slower, more obstructionist chamber while simultaneously becoming more responsive—at least in terms of election results—than the House. This is especially true in the wake of three House redistricting cycles—1992, 2002, and 2012—where the ordinary safety of incumbents has been supplemented by the drawing of districts—both through sorting and gerrymandering—that clearly favor one party or the other.

A parallel irony is that as incumbents have grown safer in the House, and majority control has shifted more frequently, the chamber's decentralizing forces have reasserted themselves to encourage obstruction in the House. As we have detailed, the House is fundamentally a majoritarian institution that relies on majority-party unity to function. Members of the majority party must see it in their interest to act cohesively to pass party-preferred policies in order to maintain their power over the policymaking agenda.

From the Contract with America in 1994 to their electoral gains twenty years later, Republicans have demonstrated the potential for issue-based, even ideological, accomplishment by a unified congressional party, much as the Democrats did in 2009–2010. But party unity and ideological zeal count for

SPOTLIGHT

Representative Cathy McMorris Rodgers: The View from Party Leadership

If Charlie Dent represents the rank-and-file's perspective in the House majority's difficulty in governing when it holds a narrow majority of seats, then Rep. Cathy McMorris Rodgers (R-WA), the Chair of the House Republican Conference, brings this point home from the point of view of party leadership.

Representative McMorris Rodgers entered Washington state politics in 1994 when she was appointed to fill an open state representative seat. She retained her seat in a special election later that year and subsequently won reelection four more times in her eastern Washington district. During her state legislative tenure, McMorris Rodgers gained a reputation for being a staunch social conservative, and she worked her way up in party leadership to become the House Minority Leader in 2002. She ran for Congress in 2004 in Washington's fifth congressional district after the Republican incumbent decided to mount an eventually unsuccessful Senate bid. The district is safely Republican, encompassing many small towns in eastern Washington and parts of the cities of Spokane and Walla Walla. McMorris Rodgers won her first congressional election by 19 percentage points and has been comfortably reelected ever since. During her time in Congress, she has been a vocal critic of Democratic policies like the Affordable Care Act (ACA), and she was instrumental in gathering the necessary House votes for the passage of the House Republicans' answer to the ACA, the American Health Care Act, in May 2017.

Since 2013 Rep. McMorris Rodgers has served as the Chair of the House Republican Conference, thus presiding over conference meetings of all House Republicans. The Conference meets most weeks to discuss pending legislation, set the party's agenda, and agree on messaging strategies. Conference chairs, such as former Speakers John Boehner and Joseph Cannon, have often used this position to move up the leadership ladder. But for now in the GOP-controlled House, she and other party leaders must contend with the difficult task of unifying enough rank-and-file caucus members to move forward the party's agenda and work effectively with President Trump.

The information in this section is taken from multiple sources as follows: Ballotpedia, "Washington's 5th Congressional District," https://ballotpedia.org/Washington%27s_5th_Congressional_District; Biographical Directory of the United States Congress, "McMorris Rodgers, Cathy, (1969–)," http://bioguide.congress.gov/scripts/biodisplay.pl?index=m001159; US House of Representatives History, Art, and Archives, "Republican Conference Chairmen," http://history.house.gov/People/Office/Republican-Conference-Chairmen/.

only so much in a political system that historically has encouraged fragmentation and delay but needs congressional functionality now more than ever. The federal budget is approximately $4 trillion, and most Americans are connected to federal programs in some way or another. Congress has the constitutional responsibility to oversee federal taxation and spending; it must provide legal authority to the executive branch to spend money and make clear its intent as to how to implement federal law. When the Congress ceases to provide these basic functions, the federal government can either come to a screeching halt or ramble on, with presidents accruing more and more power. Even when Congress avoids a government shutdown, its failure to address issues through legislation can leave programs outdated and less than effective in addressing the most fundamental concerns of voters.

These concerns are aired through the voices of constituents, organized interests, and public opinion, all traditional sources of centrifugal politics. With the growth in the size and scope of the federal government, the rise of social media, and the increased role of money in campaigns, these outside forces have amplified their voices in recent years. In a time when conventional wisdom laments the rigid polarization between parties, it is also important to recognize that elected officials in the same party can still have serious differences that undermine majority-party power in both the House and Senate. The overarching conflicts of partisanship and ideology, sometimes exacerbated by personality, have defined the politics of Capitol Hill and its relationship with the president since 1994. Between 1995 and 2018, we have had numerous examples of congressional majorities governing with same- and opposite-party presidents. A review of that history follows, and if the past is any prediction of the future, there is little evidence that the difficulties in governing will change soon.

CONGRESS AND THE PRESIDENT: WHAT HISTORY CAN TELL US

Bill Clinton

The Clinton years, after 1995, were marked by periods of legislative cooperation, for example, NAFTA, welfare reform, and health insurance reform, along with economic growth and budget surpluses. But they witnessed intense partisan conflict, culminating in the impeachment proceedings launched by the Republican House against Clinton in 1998. Although the Senate ultimately refused to convict Clinton on charges of obstruction of justice emanating from testimony he gave regarding his affair with Monica Lewinsky, the damage done to both branches of the government was significant. Impeachment proceedings, although ultimately unsuccessful, dominated the congressional/presidential relationship for the majority of the last two years of Clinton's second term.

George W. Bush

When George W. Bush won the presidency he did not necessarily believe that he had any obligation to GOP leaders in Congress. Moreover, at the start of his term, Republicans held only a slim majority in the House and were tied in the Senate (with Vice President Cheney casting the deciding vote) until June 2001, when Republican senator Jim Jeffords became an Independent and caucused with the Democrats, giving them a two-vote majority. Consequently, Bush had to reach out to some Democrats if he wanted to get his agenda passed in his first two years. He did so with the passage of tax cuts and his No Child Left Behind educational program. When the attacks of September 11, 2001, occurred, Republicans and Democrats joined together to support the president's military and foreign policy, agreeing to authorize the use of military force in Afghanistan and Iraq and to create of a new cabinet department, Homeland Security. After the Republicans won back control of the Senate in the midterm elections of 2002, Bush also managed to secure a bipartisan domestic policy victory in expanding Medicare to include a prescription drug benefit.

On the face of it, President Bush's reelection and gains in the House and Senate boded well for presidential success in 2005, because Republicans maintained control of both houses of Congress. However, President Bush proposed major changes in the Social Security program, which generated consternation among his fellow Republicans in both the House and the Senate. Additionally, deficit spending for Fiscal Year 2005 was increasing, exceeding $300 billion, with a substantial portion going to the wars in Iraq and Afghanistan. By 2006, opposition to the war in Iraq began to solidify, and, since the president could not seek reelection, voters took their frustrations out on the Republicans by giving control of the House and Senate to the Democrats. The Republican losses in the 2006 midterm elections were in part the mirror image of their prior success: the nationalization of House elections and the insistence on party unity. As the pressure to stay united with the party and the Republican president intensified, individual members found it more difficult to separate themselves from the negative sentiment about the war.

The last years of George W. Bush's administration were marked by conflict with the Democratic majority, and even though the president proposed taking on key issues, such as immigration, the party divide prevented any substantial action on the issue. Then, in 2008, the economy took a sharp turn for the worse when the housing and auto sectors suffered significant losses, creating the worst economic downturn since the Great Depression. In addressing these crises with legislation to bail out these economic sectors, Bush relied on the Democrats more than his own Republicans, who were now in the minority. In the elections of 2008, the public laid the blame for the looming recession and a ballooning deficit squarely at the feet of the Republicans, helping Barack Obama win the White House and increasing the Democratic Party's majorities in both the House and Senate.

Barack Obama

By all measures, Barack Obama worked very well with the Democratic Congress in 2009–2010, passing legislation designed to spur the economy, such as a nearly $800 billion stimulus package, a second phase of the auto industry bailout, student loan reform, and the Affordable Care Act. However, the backlash against both Obama personally from Republicans and concerns about the health-care legislation gave rise to the active Tea Party movement within the GOP, which manifested more general concerns among some voters over the growth of government. Republicans remained unified in their opposition to nearly everything Obama proposed and used that opposition as the foundation for their campaigns in the 2010 midterm elections, when they succeeded in taking back the House (but not the Senate). This situation remained in place after the 2012 election, with Obama winning reelection but continuing with a GOP majority in the House and a Democratic one in the Senate. Thus, from 2011 through 2014, Obama governed with a quasi-divided Congress and an energized, if not totally unified, opposition party.

The years 2013–2014 proved to be especially contentious for Obama because the Tea Party wing of the House Republicans, joined by vocal members in the Senate, such as Ted Cruz (R-TX) and Rand Paul (R-KY), became more entrenched in their opposition tactics, going so far as to block spending bills to partially shut down the government in 2013. At the time, Republicans took the blame for the costs of that shutdown, which by some estimates reached $2 billion. Historically high rates of partisan polarization so dominated congressional-presidential relations that the two Congresses of the 2011–2015 period stand as arguably the least productive in post–World War II history.

In spite of such chaotic governance (or maybe because of it), Republicans did extremely well in the 2014 midterm elections, picking up twelve additional House seats and winning eight seats in the Senate, which earned them control of both chambers of Congress for the first time in eight years. Faced with a unified Republican Congress, President Obama responded by taking unilateral action in two important areas—immigration and foreign policy. On November 21, 2014, just three weeks after the elections, Obama issued a presidential memorandum essentially stopping deportation of undocumented residents who met specific criteria, such as length of residence, work or educational history, and lack of criminal record.[8] By various estimates, his order covered between 3 and 5 million people. The second action he took, in December 2014, reinstated diplomatic relations with Cuba. This reversed a policy established in 1961 when the United States cut ties to Cuba after Fidel Castro took power and established a Communist regime.[9] Republicans in Congress were understandably angry about both actions because they occurred before the beginning of the 114th Congress in January 2015, when they could exert majority control.

Speaker Boehner and Senate Majority Leader McConnell made it clear that they viewed these steps by the president as too aggressive, and in the case of immigration, vowed to use their powers to force a reversal of what were, in their view, unconstitutional actions. As discussed previously, congressional leverage is most forceful when it comes to spending bills, and the Republicans knew that the funding for the Department of Homeland Security (DHS) was going to run out by March 1, 2015. The immigration program that Obama put forth was administered by the United States Citizenship and Immigration Services agency, which is self-funded through user fees. Thus, Congress could not cut off funding for the program. Instead, they proposed holding up or limiting funding for the DHS until Obama relented; the problem was that the DHS enforces border security, so Republicans were in the awkward position of undermining the very agency that deals with undocumented immigration.

As the deadline of March 1 loomed, the Republican majority in the House passed a funding bill with language reversing Obama's presidential order, but the Democrats in the Senate used their power to filibuster legislation to stop the bill from being considered. Faced with the prospect of shutting down the entire DHS, Senate Majority Leader McConnell put a "clean" bill to fund the DHS for the rest of the fiscal year (until September 30) on the Senate floor, and it passed. President Obama's immigration order had already been blocked by a temporary injunction issued by a federal district court judge so the actual policy that Republicans opposed was suspended, which gave them less firm ground to stand on in shutting the DHS down over the issue. In June 2016, the Supreme Court refused to lift the injunction in a tie vote (4–4), which essentially blocked President Obama's action.[10]

Still, when the Senate sent its version of the funding bill back to the House, enough members of the conservative wing of the GOP rejected this bill that Speaker Boehner was forced to settle for a week-long stopgap funding measure, passed just two hours before the funding ran out. Boehner recognized that the Republicans would once again take the political blame for shutting down part of the government. This would be especially damaging, in that it involved the department charged with protecting national security. Boehner decided to violate the Hastert Rule (again), and with the help of Democratic votes, he brought the "clean" funding bill to the House floor, where it passed by a vote of 257–167; only 75 of 245 Republicans voted for it, while 182 Democrats did so. In short, despite holding a sizable majority in the House, Speaker Boehner was forced to rely on Democratic votes to govern.

The conflicts over immigration and funding the DHS is just one example of not only the partisan struggle between the president and Congress in divided government but also of the continuing power struggle between the two branches. It also exemplifies the Tea Party/House Freedom Caucus era difficulty of sustaining a cohesive Republican majority in the House of Representatives, where party unity is essential to governance. Unlike the Senate, in which individual power remains the most potent obstacle to party government, the House is structured to empower the majority party at the expense of the minority. Yet that power is conditional on majority-party unity; without it, the majority cannot guarantee passage of bills on the floor. If the majority is constantly forced to rely on the minority party to pass legislation, it loses much of its capacity to accomplish its partisan policy goals.

Things did not get much better for John Boehner (see chapter 5), and he resigned as Speaker, and from the House, in the fall of 2015; Paul Ryan (R-WI) was subsequently elected Speaker. In the remaining months of 2015, Ryan and McConnell managed to get the House and Senate to work with President Obama to approve spending bills and increase in the debt limit, effective through March 2017, and reauthorize education and infrastructure programs which President Obama signed into law. Those months would turn out to be the most productive in the entire 114th Congress, the rest of which was overshadowed by the presidential election of 2016, with Donald Trump as the anti-establishment candidate in the Republican Party, and Bernie Sanders challenging Hillary Clinton's seeming inevitability as the Democratic Party nominee. Both Republicans and Democrats in Congress were forced to choose a candidate to support, and in doing so, they ran the risk of alienating a portion of their own base for either being too much a part of the establishment or not sufficiently anti-establishment. In this environment, it was nearly impossible for President Obama and the GOP Congress to accomplish much of anything except keeping the federal government open for business.

Donald Trump

As noted earlier, Donald Trump's election to the presidency took the country by surprise as he had been consistently trailing Hillary Clinton in the weeks immediately preceding the election. Republican members of Congress had been bracing for a Clinton victory and the possible loss of control of the Senate, complemented by a loss of seats but not majority control in the House. Although the Republicans lost a few seats in the House, they held on to the Senate and won the White House.

Even Donald Trump was admittedly surprised that he won the election, and while the Clinton campaign had been preparing to transition to run the executive branch, the Trump team found itself scrambling to fill the fifteen Cabinet Secretary positions as well as other key advisory positions, not to mention the thousands of political appointee jobs in the federal bureaucracy. Because President Trump came from the business world and did not have a lot of elective office experience, his network was entrenched in the private sector, which largely constituted the basis for cabinet selection. Some of his choices were greeted with intense opposition before the Senate even considered them formally for approval; some were withdrawn, but overall he got the cabinet he wanted.

However, a cloud hovered over the Trump presidency because of suspicions that the Russian government led by Vladimir Putin had actively interfered with the U.S. election with charges ranging from financing the hacking of the Democratic National Committee and the Clinton campaign to actively colluding with and financing the Trump campaign. Both the House and Senate Intelligence Committees started separate investigations into these charges, and it was revealed in early 2017 that the FBI was investigating several individuals who were paid advisors to the Trump campaign. On May 9, 2017, President Trump fired James Comey, the Director of the FBI, but the reasons were not entirely clear for the dismissal. Days earlier, Comey had requested additional resources for the investigation into the Russian interference in the 2016 election. Subsequently, the deputy director of the Justice Department (in the wake of Attorney General Jeff Sessions' recusal from the Russia election-meddling investigation) appointed former FBI chief Robert Mueller as an independent counsel to carry out a thorough investigation, which remained ongoing as of late 2017.

Beyond the Mueller investigation, the Trump White House was riddled with factions and in-fighting, largely among individuals with little experience in administering a large enterprise, although the president's reliance on retired generals for major roles (chief of staff, Secretary of Defense, and National Security Advisor) provided some sense of order. Still, within the first eight months of his tenure, Trump had fired or was forced to resign his initial National Security Advisor, two press secretaries/communications directors, his initial chief of staff, and an influential senior staff member, Steve Bannon, formerly (and subsequently) head of Breitbart News. Party leaders found it extraordinarily difficult to communicate clearly with the White House, in large part because they could never be sure who, if anyone, was speaking for the president. Indeed, President Trump frequently conveyed very different messages on important topics such as health care reform, overturning Obama's immigration policies, and tax reform.

With the appointment of retired general and Homeland Security secretary John Kelley as White House chief of staff in mid-2017, a semblance of normal order was attained. Still, President Trump remained unpredictable, as with his willingness to reach a hasty disaster aid/debt ceiling/government funding package with Democratic congressional leaders in September 2017, rather than working with Speaker Ryan and Majority Leader McConnell.[11]

More generally, several months into his administration, Trump appeared to be settling into the job of the presidency and making progress toward filling the many positions in the bureaucracy that come with a new presidential administration. For most presidents, it typically takes nearly the entire year to completely staff the political appointee positions in the executive branch. But in the twenty-first century, the pressure on the president to deliver on his campaign promises starts on day one and voters have little patience for "learning on the job." The public wants more immediate solutions, especially when the White House has changed partisan hands. Congress can either make that process easier or harder for the president, under either divided or unified government.

As Trump's term progressed, his capacity to work effectively with the Congress as a whole, and the Republican Party leadership in particular, came under serious doubt, as was illustrated by the debt/hurricane relief package deal with congressional Democrats. Indeed, the president regularly questioned the tactics and skills of Majority Leader McConnell. Well into his term, the president could count only the confirmation of Supreme Court justice Neal Gorsuch as a clear victory. Though the Republican Party seemed deeply committed to accomplishing significant tax reform, that seemed to be an ambitious goal in late 2017. The promise of a unified Republican government was fading in the face of the institutional centrifugal forces of the U.S. Congress.

PROSPECTS FOR ONE-PARTY DOMINATION AND GOVERNING IN CONGRESS OVER THE LONG TERM

Although parties have grown stronger inside the Congress and as organizing forces within the electoral system, they will not be able to dominate congressional policymaking unless one of them produces enough of a majority to survive the influences of small groupings of majority-party members who have their own policy preferences. In fact, the region-based homogeneity of the parties, which could conventionally be seen as strengthening them, may serve to reduce their capacity to act effectively in an era of narrow partisan margins. Even if leaders want to compromise and deliberate in good faith, their members' constituencies may make such reconciliation difficult, if not impossible. When there is a president of the same party as the majority in Congress, who wants to accomplish his own agenda, Congress faces additional challenges in reconciling their own ideas and pushing forward their president's agenda.

In the end, a Congress of strong, closely divided parties may be able to act only when they can produce large majorities in both chambers, regardless of whether the government is formally divided. As with the Congress circa 1900, the contemporary Congress, for all its centralization of power in the House, retains much of its fragmentation. The very nature of representation demands that tensions among individual legislators eat away at strong, centralized party (or presidential) leadership. In the end, presidents and legislative leaders can do little to affect the fates of the lawmakers they seek to lead. On occasion, members provide the votes and cede the authority that makes for strong leadership. But party leaders and presidents must constantly compete with constituents for legislators' loyalty, because legislators from Rhode Island to Kansas to California are always returning home to renew their personal contracts with the electorate. In and out of Washington, interest groups are also feeding information and opinions to individual members. The very nature of representation, in Hannah Pitkin's words—"acting in the interest of the represented, in a manner responsive to them"[12]—means that the tensions between action and delay, and between centralization and decentralization, will continue to define the contemporary Congress, even in a partisan age.

Recommended Readings

Dahl, Robert A. *How Democratic Is the American Constitution?* New Haven, CT: Yale University Press, 2001.

Jenkins, Jeffrey A., and Eric M. Patashnik, eds. *Congress and Policy Making in the 21st Century*. New York: Cambridge University Press, 2016.

Pitkin, Hannah F. *The Concept of Representation*. Berkeley: University of California Press, 1967.

Useful Resources

The American Presidency Project, John Woolley and Gerhard Peters: http://www.presidency.ucsb.edu

Center for the Study of the Presidency and Congress: http://www.thepresidency.org

Miller Center, University of Virginia: http://www.millercenter.org

Notes

1. Robert Draper, *When the Tea Party Came to Town* (New York: Simon & Schuster, 2013).

2. Thomas Kaplan and Robert Pear, "House Passes Measure to Repeal and Replace the Affordable Care Act," *The New York Times*, May 4, 2017, https://www.nytimes.com/2017/05/04/us/politics/health-care-bill-vote.html?_r=0 (accessed May 5, 2017).

3. John H. Aldrich and David W. Rohde, "Measuring Conditional Party Government," paper presented at Midwest Political Science Association meeting, Chicago, April 23–25, 1998.

4. Laura Olson, "Congressman Charlie Dent will not seek re-election in 2018," *The Morning Call*, September 7, 2017, http://www.mcall.com/news/nationworld/pennsylvania/capitol-ideas/mc-nws-charlie-dent-will-not-seek-reelection-in-2018-story.html (accessed September 10, 2017).

5. Soo Rin Kim, "The Price of Winning Just Got Higher, Especially in the Senate," *Open Secrets*, https://www.opensecrets.org/news/2016/11/the-price-of-winning-just-got-higher-especially-in-the-senate/ (accessed April 27, 2017).

6. Staff, *Battle for the House*, http://www.realclearpolitics.com/epolls/2014/house/2014_elections_house_map.html (accessed March 5, 2015).

7. Frances Lee, *Insecure Majorities* (Chicago: University of Chicago Press, 2016).

8. The White House, "Presidential Memorandum—Modernizing and Streamlining the U.S. Immigrant Visa System for the 21st Century," November 21, 2014, http://www.whitehouse.gov/the-press-office/2014/11/21/presidential-memorandum-modernizing-and-streamlining-us-immigrant-visa-s.

9. The White House, "Fact Sheet: Charting a New Course on Cuba," December 17, 2014, http://www.whitehouse.gov/the-press-office/2014/12/17/fact-sheet-charting-new-course-cuba.

10. Rachel Brody, "Views You Can Use: Immigration Action, Delayed," *US News & World Report*, February 17, 2015, http://www.usnews.com/opinion/articles/2015/02/17/texas-judge-temporarily-stalls-obamas-executive-actions-on-immigration; Jonathan Masters, "The U.S. Supreme Court and Obama's Immigration Actions," Council on Foreign Relations *CFR Backgrounders*, June 23, 2016, http://www.cfr.org/immigration/us-supreme-court-obamas-immigration-actions/p37630 (accessed May 7, 2017).

11. Thomas Kaplan and Michael Shear, "House Passes Hurricane Aid and Raises Debt Ceiling," *The New York Times*, September 8, 2017, A1.

12. Hannah F. Pitkin, *The Concept of Representation* (Berkeley: University of California Press, 1967).

Photo Credits

Index

Note: Page numbers with *f* refer to *figures*, page numbers with *t* refer to tables, and page numbers with *b* refer to boxes.

AARP, 47
access
  Committees, 45
  lobbyists, 48–50
Adams, John Quincy, 40n24
advocacy explosion, 47–48
Affordable Care Act (ACA)
  committees and, 179–180
  Cornhusker Kickback, 8–9
  democratic control, 34
  GOP controls, 115
  Lance, Leonard, 43
  pathway of, 178*b*–179*b*
  policymaking process, 160
Afghanistan War, 130
African Americans, 76–78
agenda setting and prospects
  budget and NAFTA, 140
  Congress, 65
  congressional investigations, 141, 143
  economy, 140
  Jones, Charles, 139
  immigration reform, 141
  presidential influence, 99, 139–141
  sequester, 140
Agriculture Committees, 45, 171
Albert, Carl, 103
Aldrich, John, 108, 217
Aldrich, Nelson, 26–28
Allison, William, 26–28
allocation responsiveness, 9
Amash, Justin, 135–136, 199*t*
amendment rules
  democratic majority, 188–189
  Hastert Rule, 183–184
  restrictions, 184*t*
  Senate majority, 116–18
American Farm Bureau Federation (AFBF), 44
American Health Care Act (ACHA), 133, 135, 143, 216
  Amash, Justin, 135
  Comstock, Barbara, 181–182
  Issa, Darrell, 142–143
Americans for Prosperity, 47

apprenticeship, 163, 185
Appropriations
  Committee, 169
Armed Services
  Committee, 203
Armey, Richard, 111, 126n21
auto industry bailout, 129, 225

Bader, John, 65, 154
Baker, Howard, 120
Banks, Nathaniel, 24
Barone, Michael, 53, 68n39
Baucus, Max, 54, 178*b*
Benton, Thomas Hart, 23
bicameral structure, 20–21
bills of tax
  Congress, 164, 166*t*
  legislative process, 165, 166*t*, 183
  sponsorship of, 164
Binder, Sarah, 155
Bipartisan Campaign Finance Reform Act, 90–92
Bishop, Tom, 43
Boehner, John, 33
  essential budget votes, 59, 153
  GOP control, 12, 34, 183
  Obama issues, 225
Bonior, David, 51, 211
Boxer, Barbara, 142
Boyda, Nancy, 80, 81*t*
Brat, Dave, 141
Breaux, John, 147–148
Brown, Scott, 95n4, 178*b*, 221
Brownback, Sam, 81*t*, 99
Brown v. Board of Education, 29
Buckley v. Valeo, 90
budget, 54, 56–57
  Gingrich, Newt, 86
  partisanship votes, 59
  President Obama, 99–100, 140, 150–152
  See also federal spending
Budget Reform Act, 57
Burton, Dan, 204
Bush, George H. W.
  congressional environment, 46

democratic majorities, 145, 145*f*
  party-based initiatives, 121
Bush, George W., 33, 71, 224
  accomplishments, 146
  Congress, 224
  congressional environment, 145*f*, 146
  Democrats' control of Congress, 150
  tax cuts, 140
  trade policy, 51
  unified government, 129
Butterworth, Benjamin, 25
Byrd, Robert, 30, 69n57, 120–121
Byrd Rule, 69n57

cable television, 63–64
Calhoun, John, 23
California redistricting fight, 79
campaign techniques
  centrifugal Congress, 6
  centralization and decentralization, 94
  congressional politics, 87–93
  finance reform, 90–92, 203
  gain substantial recognition, 84
  Senate and House expenditures, 88*t*, 209
Campbell, Ben Nighthorse, 95n2
Cannon, Joseph
  committee assignments, 168
  electoral results, 100
  formidable weapons, 25–26
Cantor, Eric, 82, 140–141
Capitol Hill, 6, 38, 48, 65, 100, 208
Carter, Jimmy, 30
  congressional environment, 145*f*
  unified government, 139–140
centrifugal forces, 6–10, 13, 43
  benefits, 45–46
centripetal forces, 13, 21
  environment, 42–65
  future, 216

history of, 21–38
partisanship, 215–229
centripetal forces, 13
and centrifugal forces, 13, 21
future of, 216
increase, 13
parties, 6
chairs
assignment, 117
demographics of, 41n42
resources of, 209–210
seniority, 174, 175*t*
term limits, 33, 111, 113
Cheney, Dick, 72, 109, 224
Citizens United v. Federal Election Commission, 20, 90, 92, 97n54
civil rights movement, 28
Clay, Henry, 22–24, 38
Clean Air Act, 146
Clinton, Bill, 109, 134, 223
accomplishments, 146
Congress and, 140, 223
congressional makeup, 145*f*
deficit reduction, 4
impeachment and acquittal of, 20, 33, 141, 223
Margolies, 4
success with Congress, 149–150
taxes, 46
trade policy, 51, 52
unified government, 139
Clinton, Hillary, 31, 99
cloture, 27, 116
Coakley, Martha, 178*b*
Coelho, Tony, 68n48, 86, 176
Collins, Susan, 133, 179*b*
committees
access, 45
Affordable Care Act, 179–180
development of, 22–23, 28
enterprises, 201–203
functions of, 170
House, 10
legislation, 164–176
motivations for seeking seats, 171
pace of change, 29
party leadership, 8–9, 168, 180
reforms, 169–172
See also chairs
communications, 200, 200*f*
competition, 215
Comstock, Barbara, 181–182

Condit, Gary, 208
Congress, 1–15
Constitution, 19–21
demographics of, 41n42, 81*t*, 192n36
environment of, 42–65
functions of, 7–12
future of, 228–229
history of, 21–38, 60
inherent problems of, 60–64
popularity of, 11, 60–61, 61*f*
statistics, 166*t*
Congressional Accountability Act, 201, 213n4
Congressional Budget and Impoundment Control Act, 151
Congressional Budget Office (CBO), 152, 209
Congressional Research Service (CRS), 202, 208
Conservative Opportunity Society, 109
constituencies
caucuses, 206–207
types of, 76–80, 81*t*
constituents
access, 43
O'Neill on, 30
Constitution
Congress, 19–21
presidential-congressional relations, 138, 141
procedures, 163–164
Seventeenth Amendment, 21, 27
Consumer Financial Protection Bureau (CFPB), 31
Continuing Resolutions, 59, 110, 114
Contracts (America)
legislative agenda, 11, 75, 86, 221–222
Cooper, Joseph
power and politics, 40n29
Progressives, 25
standing committee system, 39n11
corporate interests, 47, 66n16
courtesies
permitted competitors, 185–186
textbook Congress era, 163
Crisp, Charles, 25
Cruz, Ted, 153, 225
Cuba, 225
Cuellar, Henry, 206

dark money, 92, 93*f*
Daschle, Tom, 52, 82, 122
Davidson, Roger, 7, 25, 40n25
Davis, Earl, 78
debt limit, 34, 59, 226
decision making, 11–12
Deering, Christopher, 171
defense spending, 46, 53
deficits, 34, 46, 130
approaches, 4, 140, 146
DeLay, Tom, 33, 79, 111, 175
deliberation, 10–11
DeMint, Jim, 49
democracy
campaign financing and, 90
deliberative, 10
Democratic Congressional Campaign Committee, 107
Democratic Party
deficit reduction, 4
demographics of, 103, 121
ethics investigations, 176
majority, 32–35, 101–108
reforms, 169
Democratic Study Group, 29
denominator argument, 155
Dent, Charlie, 218–219
Department of Homeland Security, 56, 134, 225
Dingell, Debbie, 177
Dingell, John, 177, 195, 202, 204, 205
discharge petition, 63
divided government
congressional unpopularity, 62
effects of, 154
president, 130, 138, 139, 154–155
Ryan, 140
Dole, Robert, 3, 30, 120–121
drone caucus, 206–207
Drutman, Lee, 47

Edwards, George, 131
Eisenhower, Dwight D., 29
elections, 70–94
campaign spending, 87–94
careerism and, 82–83
local issues, 75–82
margins, 83–84
post-1994 era, 74–75
elections of 1958, 29–30
elections of 1994, 4
and Congressional unpopularity, 64
and decision making, 11
factors affecting, 85–87

Gingrich and, 32–33, 85–87
legacy of, 172–174, 91
and lobbying, 64
nationalization of, 86
and partisanship, 6
and party leadership, 109–115
elections of 2006, 111
elections of 2008, 75
elections of 2010, 12, 84
elections of 2014, 225
elections of 2016, 13, 34, 35,
  61, 72, 88–89, 92, 115
congressional campaign
  finance, 87–88
Graham, Lindsey, 36–37
intelligence committees, 141
Issa, Darrell, 142
Russian activities, 146–147
Trump, Donald, 137, 227
email to Congress, 199, 200f
Energy and Commerce
  Committee, 80, 132, 177,
  195, 202, 205
enterprises, congressional,
  194–212
influence of, 203–205
nature of, 197, 198f
political expenditures and,
  207–208
resources for, 198
entitlement programs, 46
environment
factors in, 42–65
and presidential influence,
  146–149
environmental lobby, 45
Erickson, Robert, 74, 95n6
Ethics Committee, 175–176
Eulau, Heinz, 9
executive branch
access to, 44
and Congress, 7
partisan wave elections
  and, 7, 75
See also presidential-
  congressional relations
executive powers, 134, 141

Fair Labor Standards Act, 201
farm lobby, 44
fast-track authority, 52, 148
Federal Election Campaign
  Act, 90
Federal Register, 55, 55t
federal spending
increase in, 53–54, 54t
Obama and, 140
See also budget

Feingold, Russ, 90–91
Fenno, Richard E., Jr., 100
on committees, 171
on constituencies,
  75–76, 79–80
on nature of Congress, 12
on parties, 100
filibuster, 7, 27, 35, 160, 187
effects of, 189
president and, 144
reforms of, 35, 188
Finance Committee, 171, 179
Fiorina, Morris, 83,
  96n31–n32
fiscalization, 46, 57
527s, 92
Foley, Tom, 82, 107
folkways, 14, 162–163,
  185–186
Ford, Gerald, 134
foreign policy, Obama and, 225
Fox, Jon, 5
Framers, 19–21
Freedom Caucus, 21, 132, 133
Frist, Bill, 35, 122–123
Frost, Martin, 79

General Accounting Office,
  48, 213n6
General Agreement on Tariffs
  and Trade (GATT), 51–52
geographic constituencies,
  76–79, 81t
term, 76
geographic regions
and caucuses, 206
demographics of, 121
and partisanship, 34
representation of, 219, 220f
and structure of Congress, 20
Georgia, 85
Gephardt, Richard,
  51, 214n32
gerrymandering, 76–77,
  77f, 78–79
Gingrich, Newt
and decision making, 11
and 1994 election, 4, 32–33,
  85–87, 148, 165
and party leadership,
  109–110
Goldwater, Barry, 29
government shutdown, 34, 59,
  113–114, 140, 153, 223
Graham, Lindsey, 36–37
gang of, 36
procedural and substantive
  pressure, 36–37

Grand Old Party (GOP), 2
Great Society, 11, 44, 146
Gulf War, 11

Hagan, Kay, 87
Hammond, Susan Webb, 205
Handel, Karen, 85
Hart Benton, Thomas, 23
Hastert, Dennis, 33, 111, 138,
  165, 175, 182
Hastert Rule, 33, 182
Health, Education, Labor, and
  Pensions Committee, 161
health-care reform, 51, 130,
  140, 149
See also Affordable Care Act
Heck, Joe, 119
Helms, Jesse, 32
Hibbing, John, 60–61
Hilliard, Earl, 78
Hollings, Ernest, 52, 89,
  97n47
Homeland Security Act, 177
House Appropriations
  Committee, 112–113, 171
House Freedom Caucus, 3,
  124, 195, 217, 218, 226
House of Representatives
campaign costs in,
  87–90, 88t
committee system and, 7
history of, 21–38
incumbents in, 71–72
and legislation, 177–184
norms of, 163–164
organization of, 22–23
and PACs, 47
partisanship in, 216
party leadership in, 99
reforms in, 30–32, 103, 169
standing committees in,
  172–173t
Hubbard, Carroll, 207
Huelskamp, Tim, 2–3

ideology
1994 election and, 32,
  117, 87
and party division, 115
and party
  leadership,107–108
and policy, 65
in Senate, 116–123
immigration, 140–141, 224,
  225–226
incumbents
careerism and, 82–83
financial pressure and, 89

funding constituencies
 and, 80
House, 82–84
1994 election and, 71
popularity of, 62
and stability, 71
individualism
 committee system and, 170
 and partisanship, 121,
  217–220
 and Senate, 7, 23–24
individual mandate, 130
influence
 enterprises and, 203–205
 lobbyists and, 48–50
 presidential, environment
  and, 146–149
information
 caucuses and, 207
 committees and, 170–171
 lobbyists and, 48–50
 support agencies and,
  208–209
 types of, 48
Inhofe, James, 63, 69n69, 153
interests, 7, 43
 and structure of Congress, 20
Iraq War, 33, 111, 150
Issa, Darrell, 142

Jackson, Andrew, 20
Jacobson, Gary, 74, 87
Jefferies, Jim, 81t
Jeffords, James, 33,
 72, 156n13
Jenkins, Jeffrey, 24
Jenkins, Lynn, 80, 81t, 82
Johnson, Lyndon B., 11,
 28–29, 45, 120, 134, 163
 and agenda setting, 146
 Congressional makeup,
  145, 145f
 and norms, 186
Johnson Rule, 186
Jones, Charles, 126n28, 139
judicial branch
 access to, 43
 and Congress, 19

Kansas redistricting, 229, 81t
Karps, Paul, 9
Kasten, Bob, 99
Kennedy, Edward (Ted), 31,
 178b, 221
Kennedy, John F., 45, 53
 Congressional makeup,
  145f, 148
Kennelly, Barbara, 4

Keys, Martha, 81t
King, Steve, 201
Koch brothers, 47
Krehbiel, Keith, 126n31, 144

labor unions, 47, 90
La Follette, Robert, 187
Lance, Leonard, 43
Latinos, and representation,
 76, 115
leadership. See party
 leadership
leadership PACs,
 207–208, 214n27
Lee, Frances, 35
Lee, Mike, 153
legislation
 House and, 177–184
 president and, 138–150
 process, 143–144
 scheduling, as power, 26,
  101–102, 110
 Senate and, 184–187
 volume, 27, 114, 152
Legislative Reorganization Act,
 28, 168
Lewinsky, Monica, 33
Lipinski, Daniel, 207
lobbying
 elements of, 48–50
 explosion of, 47–48
 history of, 47
 and trade policy, 50–53
LoBiondo, Frank, 207
local issues, and
 elections, 75–82
Lott, Trent, 121–122
Lowi, Theodore, 55
loyalty, 150
Luntz, Frank, 86

Madigan, Edward, 109
Madison, James, 21, 39n7
Magnuson, Warren, 213n4
mail to Congress, 199, 200f
Majette, Denise, 78
majorities, size of, 217
Mansfield, Mike, 120
Margolies(-Mezvinsky),
 Marjorie, 4–5, 6, 57
Masto, Catherine Cortez,
 119–120
Matthews, Donald, 185
Mayhew, David, 154
McCain, John, 90–91,
 133, 146, 179, 187,
 203–204, 214n16
McCain-Feingold bill, 90

McConnell, Mitch, 31, 35,
 37, 91, 99, 118, 131,
 133, 178b, 188–189,
 225–226, 228
 115th Congress, 31–32
 and GOP control, 153
 and leadership, 118, 123
 and Obama, 225
McConnell v. Federal Election
 Commission, 91
McCormack, John, 103
McKeon, Buck, 206
McKinley, William, 27
McKinney, Cynthia, 78
Meadows, Mark, 196
media
 and Congressional
  unpopularity, 63–64
 party leadership and, 123
Medicaid, 46, 53, 131–132
Medicare, 53–54, 146,
 177, 224
Medicare Prescription Drug
 and Modernization Act,
 54, 177
members of Congress
 and nature of Congress, 15
 popularity of, 62, 62t
Metzenbaum, Howard, 32
Michel, Robert, 109
minorities, 7
 caucuses, 205
 committee chairs, 41n42
 Congress, 102t
 representation, 76–78
minority-majority
 districts, 76–77
Mitchell, George, 32, 121
money
 and competitive races,
  219–220
 and elections, 80, 84, 86–92
 and lobbying, 47
Moran, Jerry, 2–3
Mulvaney, Mick, 58–59
Murkowski, Lisa, 133, 179b

Nader, Ralph, 51
NAFTA, 51–53, 140, 208
National Association of Wool
 Manufacturers, 44
National Republican
 Congressional Committee
 (NRCC), 86
Neal, Steve, 207
Nelson, Ben, 8–9, 178b
Neustadt, Richard, 154,
 156n10, 158n48

Nixon, Richard M., 20, 45, 108
  and budget, 151
  Congressional makeup, 145*f*
nomination process, 100
norms
  changes in, 162–163
  in Senate, 185–186
North American Free Trade
  Agreement (NAFTA),
  51–53, 140, 208
North Carolina
  campaign costs in, 87, 92
  districts, 77–78, 77*f*

Obama, Barack, 8, 33,
  224–227
  accomplishments, 146
  and Affordable Care Act,
  178*b*–179*b*
  and Congress, 19, 134–137,
  139, 224–27
  Congressional makeup,
  145*f*, 146
  opposition to, 140, 142,
  147–148, 183
  success with Congress,
  150–151
  and trade policy, 51
  and unified government, 139
Obamacare. *See* Affordable
  Care Act
obstructionism, 33, 99,
  187–189, 223
  effects of, 114
  and norms, 187
  and Obama, 99, 140, 142,
  147–148, 183, 224–226
Office of Congressional
  Ethics, 176
Office of Management and
  Budget, 57, 126n35, 151
Oleszek, Walter, 7, 25, 40n24
O'Neill, Thomas P. (Tip), 30,
  93, 104
open process, 63, 183

PACs. *See* political action
  committees
Palazzalo, Dan, 111, 126n33
Panetta, Leon, 155
parliamentary systems,
  7, 16n20
parties
  and caucuses, 206
  as centripetal force, 6
  condition of, 217
  and congressional
  elections, 86

development of, 24–25
functions of, 99–80
limits on, 217
polarization within, 223
partisanship, 215*f*, 216–229
  and budgets, 59
  changes in, 7, 104–105,
  106*t*, 187–188
  and individualism, 121,
  217–220
  and lobbying, 50–52
  and norms, 163
  in post-1994 era, 74–75
  rise of, 34–35
  in Senate, 121–122
party leadership
  challenges in, 99–100
  and committee system, 8–9,
  168, 180
  and congressional
  elections, 86
  Democratic majority and,
  101–108
  development of,
  23–24, 25, 30
  functions of, 104–105
  history of, 99–108, 102*t*
  legacy of, 120–123
  and legislation, 164
  powers of, 27, 32, 99–101,
  103, 116–118
  Republican majority and,
  109–115
  resources of, 209–211, 209*t*
  in Senate, 116–123
party unity, 111
  changes in, 104–105, 105*t*,
  122*t*, 221
  leadership and, 111
  and majority power, 113
Paul, Rand, 32, 153, 160,
  161–162
PAYGO, 46
Pelosi, Nancy, 6, 33, 112–113
Pennington, William, 24
Pennsylvania, 129
Perot, Ross, 51
personal constituencies,
  79–82, 81*t*
  term, 76
personal-interest caucuses, 206
personal office, 198–201
  allowances for, 198
Peterson, Mark, 131, 149
Pitkin, Hannah, 9, 229
polarization
  changes in, 6, 87, 225
  development of, 100–101

1994 election and, 87
  within parties, 223
policy making, 11–12,
  159–190
  explosion of, 53–56
  information for, 50
  president and, 137
policy responsiveness, 9
political action committees
  (PACs), 3, 47, 80, 207–208
  contributions by, 86
political expenditures,
  207–208
  types of, 207
political intelligence, 48
political representation, 9–10
presidential-congressional
  relations, 22,
  128–55, 223–28
  early in first terms, 141,
  143–145, 145*f*
  and legislation, 138–150
  party leadership and, 123
  powers of president, 137
  success in, measuring,
  149–150
  tools for, 147–149
press relations, 48
primary constituencies, 79, 81*t*
  term, 76
primary elections, 100
professionalism
  and Congressional
  unpopularity, 61
  and elections, 82–83
Proxmire, William, 187

quorum, 25, 40n24, 164

Rangel, Charles, 176
Rayburn, Sam, 28, 101,
  103, 163
Reagan, Ronald, 30, 108
  Congressional makeup,
  145*f*, 148
  success with Congress,
  149–150
reciprocity, 163, 186, 187
reconciliation process, 130,
  178*b*, 188
redistricting, 64, 76–79, 221
  and margins, 84
Redman, Eric, 213n4
Reed, Thomas Brackett,
  25, 40n26
reelection constituencies,
  79, 81*t*
  term, 74

regulations, increase in, 54–55, 55f
Reid, Harry, 35, 117, 119, 178b, 188
Reno v. Shaw, 77
representation, 9–15
drama of, 1–17
geography of, 219, 220f
as responsiveness, 9–10
Republican Party
and deficit reduction, 4
demographics of, 121
and ethics investigations, 176
and federal spending, 53–54
Fox and, 5
as majority, 32–34, 109–115
and Obama, 65, 140, 142–143, 147–148, 183, 224–226
and organization of Senate, 26–27
systematic advantage of, 64, 79, 84
responsiveness, 9–10, 221
types of, 9–10, 12
Richardson, Bill, 206
Ringe, Nils, 206
Roberts, Pat, 92
Rodgers, Cathy McMorris, 222
Rohde, David, 108, 186, 217
roll call votes, 104, 106t, 126n19
Roosevelt, Theodore, 27
Rothman, David, 26, 40n30
Roy, Bill, 81t
rules, 163–164
development of, 25
on filibuster, 35
Rules Committee, 103, 107–108, 177, 180, 185
powers of, 101
Ryan, Paul, 70, 99, 160
Ryun, Jim, 80, 81t

Salisbury, Robert, 56, 68n47, 197
Schiller, Wendy J., 191n10
Schlozman, K. L., 66n16
Schock, Aaron, 176
Schumer, Charles, 210–211
secret hold, 118
Senate
campaign costs in, 87–90, 88t
competitive seats in, 220–221
demographics of, 192n36
history of, 21–38

individualism and, 23
legacy of party leadership in, 120–123
and legislation, 184–187
norms of, 163–164
organization of, 22–23, 26–27
and PACs, 47
partisanship in, 34–37, 187–188, 216
party leadership in, 99, 116–123
reforms in, 30–32, 169
Seventeenth Amendment and, 21, 27
staff tasks in, 200
standing committees in, 166t–167t
Senate majority leader
functions of, 116
powers of, 116–17
seniority, 101, 118, 165
and chairs, 174, 175t
reforms and, 103
in Senate, 186
separation of powers, 20–21, 38
September 11, 2001, 44, 180, 224
sequestration, 46, 140
service responsiveness, 9
and margins, 84
Seventeenth Amendment, 21, 27
Shelby, Richard, 86, 95n2
Shepsle, Kenneth A., 28–29, 41n40, 152, 158n52, 197
Shuman, Howard, 151
Simpson, Alan, 121
Sinclair, Barbara, 30, 41n52–n53, 107, 187
Slattery, Jim, 80, 81t
slavery, 23
Smith, Margaret Chase, 192n36
Smith, Steven S., 191n15, 193n45, 214n11
social media
and Congressional unpopularity, 63
interests and, 48
and staff tasks, 201
soft money, 91–92
Speaker of the House, 71
Constitution on, 164
powers of, 27, 33, 71, 82, 99
specialization, in Senate, 185
Specter, Arlen, 8

sponsorship, 164
staff, 194–212
committee-based, 201–203
increases in, 195, 198f
of party leadership, 209–211, 209t
salaries of, 199t
tasks of, 199–200
standing committees, 166t–167t
development of, 22
functions of, 165
number of, 165, 168f
Steering and Policy Committee, 103, 125n10, 169
Stefanik, Elise, 71, 73f
American Health Care Act, 73
fresh energy, 73–74
Stewart, Charles, 24
Stewart, Jimmy, 187
subcommittees, 29, 169–170
enterprises and, 201–203
reforms and, 169
subsidies, ACA, 130
sugar lobby, 45, 66n4
Sullivan, Leonore, 41n42
supermajority, 110
support agencies, 208–209
Supreme Court, 29, 144, 179b, 226
symbolic responsiveness, 9

tax policy, 103, 111
Constitution on, 157
Tea Party, 12, 34, 65, 82, 113, 130, 225
Tea Party legislators, 58–59
Texas redistricting, 78–79
textbook Congress, 28–29
and access, 45–46
norms in, 163
term, 28
Theriault, Sean, 35
Thurber, James, 47, 57
Thurmond, Storm, 31, 36, 187
Tierney, John T., 66n16
Tillis, Thom, 87
Tocqueville, Alexis de, 23
Trade Adjustment Assistance Program, 52
trade interests, 66n16
trade policy
lobbying and, 50–53
presidents and, 115
Trans-Pacific Partnership, 51–53, 148

triangular relationships, 45
Trump, Donald, 14, 52, 128,
    154, 227–228

unanimous consent, 116, 185
unified government, 86
    president and, 99, 115,
    139–140
United States Department of
    Agriculture, 45
Unmanned Systems
    Caucus, 206

Van Buren, Martin, 23
veto override, 164

veto power, 131
Victor, Jennifer, 206
Voting Rights Act, 76, 77

Waldman, Sidney, 10
war powers, 138
War Powers Act, 138
Warren, Elizabeth, 31–32
Washington, George, 19, 21
Waxman, Henry, 177, 195,
    203, 204–205
Ways and Means Committee,
    101, 125n10, 132, 160,
    165, 171, 177
    powers of, 171

Webster, Daniel, 23
whip system, 4, 107, 124
White, William S., 163
Whitewater, 141
Williams, Pat, 4–5
Wilson, Woodrow, 7,
    16n15, 25–26
Wright, Gerald, 74
Wright, Jim, 104, 107

Yellow Dog Democrats, 104
    term, 126n18